Contesting Citizenship in Urban China

Contesting Citizenship in Urban China

Peasant Migrants, the State, and the Logic of the Market

DOROTHY J. SOLINGER

University of California Press

BERKELEY   LOS ANGELES   LONDON

This book is a print-on-demand volume. It is manufactured using toner in place of ink. Type and images may be less sharp than the same material seen in traditionally printed University of California Press editions.

STUDIES OF THE EAST ASIAN INSTITUTE, COLUMBIA UNIVERSITY

The East Asian Institute is Columbia University's center for research, publication, and teaching on modern East Asia. The Studies of the East Asian Institute were inaugurated in 1962 to bring to a wider public the results of significant new research on modern and contemporary East Asia.

University of California Press
Berkeley and Los Angeles, California

University of California Press, Ltd.
London, England

Library of Congress Cataloging-in-Publication Data

Solinger, Dorothy J., 1945–.
    Contesting citizenship in urban China : peasant migrants, the state, and the logic of the market / Dorothy J. Solinger.
        p.   cm.
    Includes bibliographical references and index
        ISBN 0-520-21347-5 (alk. paper). — ISBN 0-520-21796-9 (pbk.: alk. paper)
        1. Rural-urban migration—China.   2. Urban poor—China.
3. Citizenship—China.   4. Peasantry—Legal status, laws, etc.—China.   5. Labor market—China.   6. Communism—China.
7. China—Economic conditions—1976– I. Title.
HB2114.A3S65   1999
307.2'4'0951—dc21   98-8337
                                                                                CIP

Printed in the United States of America

The paper used in this publication meets the minimum requirements of ANSI/NISO Z39.48-1992 (R 1997) (Permanence of paper)

To my husband, Thomas P. Bernstein,
whose sympathy for the peasants has rubbed off on me

Contents

Illustrations

Preface

In the wake of the wrenching occasioned by the events of spring 1989, I was searching for a new project about people and their struggles—one that would engage my emotions and involve the consideration of moral issues, as those events did. For suddenly it seemed to me then that most of the scholarship I had done before had been too abstract, too theoretical. Fortunately, as a participant in the First International Urban Anthropology/Ethnology Conference in China, organized by Gregory Guldin and Aidan Southall and held in Beijing at the end of that year, I became aware of that so fascinating and then burgeoning category, the "floating population." It promised me an opportunity to meet all these needs, one that, indeed, has been perfectly fulfilled. Perhaps I, then living at my tenth address in a decade, identified with the migrants a bit, as well.

At first the topic seemed simply to humanize the generally much more academic and formalistic researches about the transition from plan to market that were much in vogue at the time. But soon I began to fashion my inquiry around questions of citizenship in the city, about the modes of incorporation of outsiders in daily life in town once markets had let them in, and of their inclusion or noninclusion in the urban community by residents and bureaucrats, as well as the discrimination that attended these processes.

Markets were supplanting commands in the workings of the economy, certainly. But what, I wanted to know, did markets do to peasants' membership in the city? How, in short, did the economic changes that ushered farmers into the metropolises translate into incipient political changes, at least, for a start, by permitting the farmers to be viewed by the settled folk as deserving urbanites? And in just what ways, with what effects on the outcome, did the older institutions of state socialism linger behind—

institutions that were then very much in the midst of becoming dislodged by economic transformation?

In the end I concluded that the interaction between incipient markets and migrants is quite a complicated one in the twilight of state socialism, one in which each party—markets, migrants, and the state—has a profound effect on the others. It became very clear, despite clichés in the literature, that there is no simple or linear path along which the coming of markets can readily convert outsiders into citizens. The volume that follows spells all this out.

Over the past eight years, as my acquaintance with the subject of the floaters steadily deepened, I accumulated many debts. The first to finance my endeavor was the Center for East Asian Studies at Stanford University, which granted me the funds for a short trip to Wuhan, where I began my study in 1990. The next year I received a research award from the Committee on Scholarly Communication with the People's Republic of China that enabled me to visit Harbin in 1991 and Guangzhou, Nanjing, Wuhan, and Tianjin in 1992. And in 1993 a postdoctoral fellowship from the Chiang Ching-kuo Foundation paid for my leave as I began to write. I wish to acknowledge with many thanks the financial support of all of these institutions.

Other institutions helped in various ways. Most crucially, the East Asian Institute at Columbia University generously housed me, duty-free, as an adjunct senior research scholar in the winter and autumn of 1992, and in the autumns of 1993, 1995, 1996, and 1997. The time, space, stimulation, and resources that I got there were absolutely invaluable to this project. Of course none of that would have been realized had it not been for the magnanimity of my dean, Willie Schonfeld, who agreed in 1991 to allow me to spend one academic quarter a year on leave at Columbia after I got married.

I also owe a heavy debt of gratitude to several institutions in China: the Tianjin Academy of Social Sciences, especially its director, Wang Hui, and Zhou Lu and Han Maishou; the Wuhan Foreign Affairs Office, especially Ding Hua and Yin Guilan; the Wuhan Policy Research Office; the Johns Hopkins-Nanjing University Center for Chinese and American Studies, especially Anthony Kane; and the Social Science Academies of Heilongjiang, Guangdong (especially Li Xiaolin), and Wuhan (especially Huang Hongyun). Thanks also to Danching Ruan for introducing me to her friends at the Tianjin Academy.

Portions of some of the chapters in this book were presented at the following conferences or during invited talks at the following institutions:

the Association for Asian Studies (1991, 1994); the Universities Service Centre, the Chinese University of Hong Kong (1991); the East Asian Institute, Columbia University (1991); Nanjing University-the Johns Hopkins University Center for Chinese and American Studies (1992); the Tianjin Academy of Social Sciences (1992); the conference City Living, City Lives, convened by the Asia Program of the Woodrow Wilson International Center for Scholars (1992); Yale University's Council on East Asian Studies (1992); the National Science Foundation Conference on the Politics of Economic Reform in the Former Communist-Bloc States, held at the University of Southern California (1993); the Asia Program of the Woodrow Wilson International Center for Scholars (1993); the Workshop on East Asia, University of Chicago (1993); the workshop The Chinese Work Unit in Historical and Comparative Perspective, at the Center for Chinese Studies, University of California, Berkeley (1994); the Modern China Seminar at Columbia University (1995); the conference Rural China: Emerging Issues in Development, at the East Asian Institute, Columbia University (1995); the Council on Foreign Relations, Study Group on China and the Environment (1995); the Workshop on the Development of Labour Resources and Economic Development in South China, at Shantou University, Shantou, China (1995); the Carnegie Council on Ethics and International Affairs (1995); the conference China and World Affairs in 2010, at Stanford University's Institute for International Studies (1996); the International Conference on Migration and Floating, Cologne, Germany (1996); the conference The Non-Economic Impact of China's Economic Reforms, at the Fairbank Center for East Asian Research at Harvard University (1996); the Carnegie Council on Ethics and International Affairs' Third International Workshop on the Growth of East Asia and Its Impact on Human Rights: New Issues in East Asian Human Rights, at Seoul National University (1996); the Division of Social Science of the Hong Kong University of Science and Technology (1996); and the workshop Rural Labor and Migration in 1990s China, at the University of California, Irvine (1997). While obviously I cannot thank each of them one by one here, I am deeply grateful to the participants at them all for the opportunities they offered me to present my ideas and receive attentive listening and stimulating feedback. Often I was prodded by comments at these meetings to rethink some of my findings or to conduct further research.

Many friends and colleagues have also read chapters or parts thereof or discussed my ideas with me. Rick Baum, Francesca Cancian, Anita Chan, Fred Deyo, David Easton, Thu-huong Nguyen-Vo, Tim Oakes,

and security with its inability to dominate.[12] At the same time there was a reciprocal effect: because of the peasants' presence, the former rules and norms about community and inclusion, and about the official allocation of public goods in the city, came under assault.

In many ways this so-called floating population joined an ancient saga. Leaving home and becoming "other" is an experience known to multitudes of millions around the globe and over the centuries who stepped across the borders that defined their identities to brave a life in a realm unknown. Like migrants elsewhere, China's mobile peasants appeared to be cut loose and drifting, seemingly pouring out in waves, sometimes in torrents, into regions whose citizens and their governors—though usually well cognizant of the economic contributions of these sojourners—often reacted to them with distaste and repulsion at worst, with profound ambivalence at best.

For migration throws up a specter of an overwhelmed state, of assaulted citizenry, and of rampant social turmoil: the vision of the optimists—that it can simply deposit docile toilers who will become assimilated settlers, acquiescent and conforming to the mode, enriching the nation—seems to many to be just a mirage. Put starkly, the immigration of "foreigners," whether internal farmers or truly "other" folks from afar, frequently entails confrontation. That confrontation, while not without its benign dimensions, is often fraught, surely at first, with dangers and hostility for both parties. The broadest themes (and even many of the details) are everywhere the same: these people are viewed as an incursion on locals' perceived deserts; they quite typically carry the brunt of discriminatory treatment.

I present this encounter in the urban areas of China at the end of the century as a contest over citizenship (and its changing content) waged primarily between the state—with its socialist system disappearing—and an enormous set of seemingly interloping peasant migrants who jostled uneasily with it, in a context of accelerating market transition.

Citizenship

Why citizenship? In late twentieth-century urban China, markets and the migrants they bore together challenged the city *hukou*, a most fundamental political institution, one that really amounted to an emblem of (urban) citizenship. The very presence of this pair of newcomers in town precipitated a crucial systemic alteration. As one Chinese writer phrased it,

The floating population is summoning the household registration system, which is based on stable management, to transform into [one of]
dynamic management.[13]

After migration took off in the early 1980s, Chinese journalists explicitly compared outsiders making their lives in the city to inferior citizens.
One, discussing a governmental decision of 1984 that permitted peasants
to acquire a new special *hukou* (household registration) for residing in
towns, wrote of "the third kind of citizen, who had left the ranks of the
peasantry and become an urbanite, but whose *hukou* is not the same as a
real urban *hukou*." Another sympathized with "peasants in the city"
who, "because they still have the rural *hukou* while living in the city,
have a very low social position, no house, no grain and oil supply, no
labor guarantee, and who, therefore, become second-class citizens."[14]
Indeed, the exclusion of peasants from state-sponsored benefits in
cities[15] entailed their rejection from what Harry Eckstein terms "civic
inclusion," or "access to institutions that provide capacities and resources."[16] For, as a Chinese scholar remarked, the *hukou*—very much
as a badge of citizenship in a Western society would do—determined a
person's entire life chances, including social rank, wage, welfare, food
rations (when these were in use), and housing.[17]
Any individuals living in a Chinese city without urban registration
there were denied free compulsory education, deprived of many of the
perquisites that went with permanent employment in state-owned factories, could normally not receive free health care, and could not even be
conscripted into the army from their urban home.[18] Without the *hukou*,
transients were virtual foreigners within the cities of their own country
because this elemental fact of urban life guaranteed citizenship there and
the "goods and opportunities that shape life chances."[19] Indeed, at the
March 1995 session of the National People's Congress, then minister of
labor Li Boyong actually proposed establishing a "system similar to international passport and visa requirements," with the purpose of curbing
transprovincial migration![20] Thus, even as there were similarities between, on the one hand, the reactions and behavior of Chinese urbanites
toward incoming peasants in China and, on the other, those of national
citizens toward aliens in other "host" environments around the world, in
this case the "strangers" who were despised were China's own people;
peasants from China's own countryside were put outside the pale.[21]
Perhaps most centrally, as with residence requirements aimed at ex-
cluding foreign immigrants from political participation in liberal states,

the Chinese *hukou* even served as a means of preventing floating farmers from exercising the franchise in a city (for whatever it was worth in socialist China), no matter how long they lived there, and thus from being genuine members of the municipality.[22] In other contemporary states, as Rogers Brubaker surveys them, a grant of the perquisites of "citizenry excludes only foreigners, that is, persons who belong to other states."[23]

By contrast, in many regards the level of discrimination experienced by China's ruralites residing in its metropolises exceeds that visited upon urbanizing peasants in Latin American, Southeast Asian, or African cities. In the first place, the various perquisites of urbanhood in China formally marked city folk off from ruralites much more decisively than is generally the case in other societies. Indeed, ordinary urbanites at all levels of income in China were recipients of benefits that made for a much wider gap than we see elsewhere.[24]

But in addition in those other places, it is obstacles that might theoretically be overcome—such as poverty, class, low skills and lack of education, or inadequate social connections—that stand in the way of incorporation.[25] Certainly these same factors isolated farmers in Chinese municipalities, but they were not at the core of the problem. Instead the Chinese peasants' lot in the city was much more akin to that of black people in South Africa before the 1990s or of blacks and Asians in the United States throughout the first half of the twentieth century.[26]

In these similar cases, native residents were not just thrust to the bottom of a ladder of social mobility, as are ordinary rural transients upon arrival in third-world towns; instead—as in China—they were denied basic civil and even human rights as well.[27] What all such outcasts have in common is that they all bore the brunt of a form of institutionalized discrimination so stringent that it barred them from becoming full citizens in their own home countries.[28]

So sojourners from China's rural areas entered the cities (unless ushered in with a post arranged for them in a Chinese work unit) not just temporarily bereft of state-granted wherewithal for their daily existence in town. In addition, they arrived altogether and categorically ineligible for this sustenance as well; this was so since their lack of association with the city *hukou* barred the great lot of them from enjoying any of the welfare benefits and social services that urbanites received as their natural birthright. For these reasons, to view Chinese peasants in the metropolises as foreign immigrants there—as noncitizens—is fully in line with the general literature on citizenship.

Citizenship has been variously defined. Most fundamentally, as Bryan S. Turner frames it, "the modern question of citizenship is structured by two issues," which are much the same as those that pertain to possession of the urban register in China. The first of these has to do with social *membership*, or, one might say, with belonging to a community; the second concerns the right to an *allocation of resources*.[29] From another angle, the hallmark of citizenship (and of the urban *hukou*) is exclusivity, as it "confers rights and privileges" just to those legally living within specifically designated borders.[30] The boundaries that define members are usually drawn around the geographical community. But they may also delineate only some of the groups within it.

Various scholars term citizenship primarily a legal-cum-social status; a source of political identity; a claim for fulfilling duties and civic responsibilities; or a guarantee of social or welfare services, and of political rights. For some, the triad of citizenship rights attained by British citizens by the mid-twentieth century—civil, political, and social (in that order, historically)—identified in T. H. Marshall's seminal essay on citizenship must all be present and reciprocally reinforcing for the status to become truly operational.[31] Others underscore the access to goods that its ownership affords, its entitlements or privileges, and the expectations that accompany these.[32]

Whatever the disagreements among analysts on the content of citizenship, up to now the literature on this topic has been dominated by Westerners and, for the most part, evinces a Western perspective. That is, writers have anchored their definitions in a European/American understanding, one that connects the practice of citizenship primarily with participation in the political life of the community, whether in decision making or in taking part in the electoral process, and roots it in a civil and legal status.[33]

But there is also sometimes a recognition that the meaning of the concept and the nature of its content may vary from one place to the next;[34] and also that the phenomenon itself is part of or subject to a changing process.[35] Across societies, such differences may be a function of how the status is acquired—whether it is attained through struggle or bestowed as a gift from above; over time, the push of new peoples for entry, alterations in the supposed "global political culture" and attendant worldwide ideas about rights, and economic crisis all may result in contractions or expansions of the eligible population or of the treatment its possession accords.[36]

These insights help in generalizing about the specific substance of citizenship in any given context. It will vary in accord with the nature and with the prevailing conception of the political community in which it appears.[37] Correspondingly, and most critically, the values and behaviors that citizenship endorses in a society will reflect the norms of whatever might be the dominant participatory and allocatory institutions in the community with which the citizen is affiliated. And the society's receptivity to international influence is a function of the nature of the institutions already in place. Accordingly, the alleged shift in the "discursive order of rights at the global level"—a shift that Yasemin Soysal heralds as reshaping the practice of and eligibility for citizenship in Western Europe[38]—is one that by no means necessarily takes root in all national soils, at least not with dispatch.

Turning to China, we find that the latest version of the state constitution, adopted in 1982, leaves the specific content of the country's citizenship vague. For this document simply announces in Article 33 that "All persons holding the nationality of the People's Republic of China" are citizens, equal before the law, and enjoying the rights while performing the duties prescribed in the constitution and the law.[39]

For our purposes—since the chance for meaningful political participation in law making or in the electoral process was yet negligible to nonexistent for the urban resident in late 1990s China; and since gross disparities in social status and benefits exist between members of urban and rural communities—I follow the characterization offered by Turner and emphasize, as he does, not the political but just the identity/membership and distributive components of citizenship.

Accordingly, I consider as full, official, state-endorsed urban citizens those who had a form of valid, official membership or affiliation in the city, and who consequently were the recipients of state-disbursed goods. We will see that at century's end, though some peasant transients (those working, temporarily, in state-owned institutions) obtained a portion of these privileges and so could be viewed as half- or second-class citizens, officially ruralites in big cities were still denied genuine membership, the right to belong officially. Nonetheless, with the progression of marketization and economic "reform," socialist distribution steadily declined for *all* residents of the nation's municipalities. As this occurred, unentitled farmers subsisting on the fringes experimented with a new style of urban living, an untried model of city citizenship, in post-1949 China.

The Logic of the Market

Much social science theorizing centers on the indeterminate relation between economic and political institutions; this study contributes to that inquiry. My focus is the linkage between two great forces: the incursion of capitalism and challenges to established citizenship. As a form of capitalism—with its privileging of prices, profits, and market principles—resurged in China after decades of state planning; and as aliens entered where they were in the main shut out before, Chinese urban areas in the 1980s and 1990s became a field for studying this interaction at its inception.

Granted, both migrants and markets existed in China—if always in positions of ambivalence—in brief periods in the pre-1980 days domineered by the thought of Mao Zedong.[40] But during most of the time between the mid-1950s and the early 1980s the Chinese economy operated largely in the absence of markets. Moreover, the government treated the people of the cities and those in the rural areas as members of two separate worlds apart. What is novel about the experience of migrants and markets after 1980 is the freedom they each started to experience with accelerating vigor after that point. For these two reasons—the sudden license for capital, markets, and movement, and the vast differences between two populations rather abruptly thrust amongst each other—the introduction of two new and powerful forces, markets and migration, into Chinese cities after 1980 constitutes an excellent vantage point for observing the interaction of some very fundamental institutions and shifts, and for exploring the interactions among them.

My largest finding is a paradoxical one: as of the late 1990s both the extant state and the reemergent markets were blocking the achievement of normal urban citizenship, as once conceived in China. But at the same time those same markets set up a novel mold of urban citizenship, one whose content was quite different from what the state once forged. As for the state, a prior institution, the *hukou*, derived its stickiness and its suppleness long after the economic transition was well under way from the range of social and official groups that supported it, namely, most urbanites, along with the powerful bureaucracies of public security and labor, and the wealthier, magnet regions of the country. Because of this weighty, if latent, coalition disposed to conserve this one institution, the influences of market incentives had by no means changed the model of official urban citizenship as the century drew to a close.

For the foreseeable future—and this is the crux of my argument—the outcomes of marketization (a transition from bureaucratic modes of allocating, distributing, and exchanging factors of production and economic goods to market-based modes) must be understood in conjunction with institutional legacies left from the former socialist system.

Not just the Communist state, through its officials, its rules, and its set of bureaucracies, obstructed peasants from becoming regular, state-endorsed citizens in cities. In addition, markets here as elsewhere engendered among the original urbanites a competitive mentality that counted costs and whose rationality was geared to revenue-generation. This state of mind enhanced discrimination and xenophobia against outsiders who threatened city people's own accustomed shares of goods, especially as free markets knocked up against still-standing political institutions that had enshrined principles of distributive justice, principles expressly geared to block the market's untrammeled allocations. For Chinese urbanites had become accustomed to a range of benefits and entitlements I call the "urban public goods regime."[41]

Moreover, the modalities of these markets also encouraged bureaucrats to commodify underclass outsiders, that is, to gain financially from their presence. This they achieved by employing against them a constantly improvised, nontransparent, and slippery schedule of fees and charges. And even when outsiders managed to get the means to buy a *hukou*, it could turn out to be a piece of paper without much worth.[42] So both of these forces, the state and the market, stymied peasants' acquisition of actual, normal citizenship in the cities, at least as this institution had been constituted in Chinese municipalities since the 1950s.

Yet the presence of markets—plus the use that peasant migrants made of them—did not just undercut peasants' participation in the old community. Markets also made possible new forms of association, new rules, and unprecedented modes of city life—in short, a space for agency—that transgressed the state's definitions of urban citizenship as long enunciated and enacted.

Alternatively, we could term the association between the state, markets, and migrants (or, also, that between capitalism and citizenship) a dialectical, recursive one.[43] For, under assault from the complex effects of markets and migrants, the state itself underwent some change, even as it excluded, discriminated against, and commodified peasant sojourners in the cities, and even as it prevented migrants from being full members of the metropolises. It was forced to accommodate the lifestyles of actors beyond its reach.

Thus, this study highlights the point that economic change (in this case the shift back to markets from a planned economy) does not occur in a political vacuum. To evaluate a given polity's chances for concomitant political transformation while it is experiencing an economic transition, we must be attentive to the social offshoots of the markets themselves and to the lingering fallout from the institutions of the previous regime that enabled prior modes of economic behavior.

This attention to the impact from previous arrangements has implications beyond China and other once-socialist societies. The switch from a planned to a market economy involves an institutional dislocation that has much in common with the decline of the welfare state in the West. Both transformations were departures from systems that had protected their recipients from the force of the free market.[44] Just as the neoliberal "conservative project" in the West, with its dictate of social spending cuts—a consequence of the 1970s global economic crisis—introduced rampant uncertainty and shocks to the expectations of old beneficiaries,[45] triggering accusations and exclusionary initiatives against foreigners, so in China we find urbanites blaming peasants in their midst for the social ills induced by the market.[46] In both environments, the resentments and scapegoating against newcomers, as state-sponsored distribution diminished, were very similar. And in both milieus, immigrants suffered as a result.[47]

All this implies that a market transition from socialism cannot easily breed the beneficent effects for newcomers (such as assimilation, conventional citizenship, perhaps democracy) that liberal ideology often predicts.[48] The point is that marketization by itself cannot promote inclusion and citizenship for outsiders while prior institutions retain some power. And indeed, marketization does not necessarily readily dismantle such institutions, even if it may alter them.

Thus, another set of findings concerns the interactive nature of the meeting of markets, the socialist state, and uprooted ruralites. As for the state, the farmers' settling in the cities set up endless predicaments for its agencies. These were dilemmas whose resolution threatened to change the shape of the urban community, and of the state itself since an uncommonly large proportion of urban life had been entitled, exclusive, and tightly patrolled under the Chinese city's earlier socialist system.

There were manifold effects on the migrants as well. They were undertaking their mobility while this core institution, the *hukou* (along with its informal legacies in behavior, expectations, and status markings), kept much of its original potency (even as many of the benefits it once bestowed became available on open markets). Therefore, in order to survive with even a modicum of decency, the migrants entering the city had to attempt to garner an array of disparate resources—but without any hope of using these to gain higher status or upward social mobility—resources commensurate with the range of institutions shaping their existence: cash, the currency in markets, and connections to city offices and cadres, the medium in the state bureaucracy.

Migrants also had to learn to contend with a medley of rules that pertained to one or the other of these contending institutions, even as their own daily praxis was undercutting these rules. Perhaps the most stable refuge in this shifting milieu, for those with access to it, was bits of community—their own social networks—that they had brought from home. In the chapters that follow, I explore the multifold ways in which the state's ongoing presence differentially conditioned the coming of different groups of peasants, as well as variably mediating their lot once in town. For instance, those recruited by or contracted to state agencies fared very differently from those who were not. I also examine the ways that peasants coped, some of them by creating their own separate societies whose existence mocked the state or their own largely discrete labor markets that disturbed official monopolies.

Organization of the Study

This book explores the manner in which peasant migration into the cities of China at the end of socialism distinguished it (sometimes subtly so, sometimes more blatantly) from seemingly similar cityward movement elsewhere in the developing world. In short, the differences were the result of remnant socialist institutions—both positive and negative—and their impact on the process.

Thus I organize the study by beginning from this point: China's style of socialism-supporting statism encompassed three powerful institutions relevant to our story: (1) a form of exclusive and state-managed migration, bolstered by the (hereditary) household register (the *hukou*); (2) a set of mighty urban bureaucracies; and (3) a regime of planning and rationing that privileged an ascriptively composed group, the officially registered urbanites. This was a regime underwritten for over two decades in part by the combined action of these institutions: they excluded the peasantry from the cities and bureaucratically decreed and enforced their mandatory delivery of grain, all in order to keep the city-based, industrializing population fed and, in the main, quiescent.

The book is arranged to show how these three institutions from the days of socialism that privileged the cities affected the movement of migrants and their new, yet ultimately transient city lives; channeled officials' responses; and prejudiced urbanites' perceptions. But they did so even as the transition toward markets and the arrival in town of peasants reshaped these institutions in turn. In each chapter we will find that, in the midst of socioeconomic transition, state institutions, markets, and migrants continually determined and redetermined one another.

The study begins with three chapters about *structure*, though this was a structure undergoing transformation. Each of them, respectively, presents one of the three institutional features of the old system noted above—state-managed migration policies, state bureaucracies in the cities, and the urban planning regime, respectively. And at the same time each chapter demonstrates how markets and migrants affected these institutions.

Chapter 2 outlines the stance of the Chinese state toward the geographical mobility of its subjects, from imperial times to the present, contrasting the position—and the behavior—of earlier regimes with that of the People's Republic. It indicates how in the first decade of the P.R.C. the leadership managed—for its own developmental purposes—to make of the peasantry an ascribed underclass. Chapter 2 also reviews the changes introduced by the post-Mao state, which, despite its economic reforms that began in 1980, modified—but only somewhat—the post-1949 political elite's essential inclination to keep peasants' physical persons outside the urban system even as their labor shored it up.

Chapter 3 lays out the second structural feature, the set of bureaucracies that managed migrants; it also inquires about the ways in which transients in the municipalities helped, along with markets, bring about institutional change. I investigate the lineup—among urban bureaucracies and among various cities and regions—for and against mobile peasants. I then survey the changes that those most hostile to the outsiders underwent as these "hosts" found ways to profit from the peasants' presence. Here it is as if migrants, in their pairing with markets, appeared in the guise of siren (unwittingly enticing their antagonists with the lure of lucre) more than of specter.

Chapter 4 focuses upon the third institutional, structural feature of the old regime, the planning system and its perquisites for urbanites. It considers the effect that the evisceration of this system under economic reform had on the permanent, original urban residents, those people whose own entitlements were being winnowed away as markets and migrants impinged on their world. In particular, it examines migrants' specific imprint upon the public goods Chinese cities offered in the days of socialism—employment, public order, urban services, and low, steady prices. Here we see how migrants served as a metaphor for the market in urbanites' perceptions about the impact of these intruders on the cities. This process, of course, stymied the assimilation of these outsiders into urban society.

The second section of the book brings *migrants' agency* more to the fore. Each chapter here corresponds to one of those in the first section. Chapter 5 takes up peasants' departure from the countryside, the factors that shaped their choices, the recruitment channels that charted their pathways out of the villages, and the impact of migrants on their native places. But, it shows, theirs was an agency that was somewhat hobbled or bounded. For this chapter documents the ways movement was mediated both by state policies and practices and also by the specific ecosystems formed by native-place geography, resource endowments, and locational situations, in short, by economic and market forces that vary across the countryside. This chapter fleshes out chapter 2's overview of state stances and policies toward peasants.

The sixth and seventh chapters situate the sojourners in cities and consider their differential fates once there, as well as highlighting the interactive connections into which they were thrust with both markets and the state. They demonstrate that, despite marketization (which greatly assisted the transients in their efforts to subsist materially in cities), the existing political institutions did nearly nothing to permit outsiders to begin to belong. Instead, they forced most of the peasants to construct excluded worlds of their own.

Chapter 6, on the migrants' entry into urban labor markets, relates to chapter 3 (on state bureaucracies), as it describes how the arrangements of the labor bureaucracy in particular, in conjunction with the *hukou*, and the ways in which the old labor market was organized—with its dominant and exclusive state-owned enterprises—forced peasants in the cities to create their own labor markets. But depending upon the nature of the occupation chosen and the native place specializing in it, some of these markets were more benign than others; and a job in a state firm generally promised more benevolence than one outside.

Chapter 7 then asks how the outsiders coped with dailiness without official services and benefits, that is, as noncitizens in the city in the eyes of the state. It is paired with chapter 4 in examining how the migrants created a new lifestyle entirely outside the urban public goods regime. Certainly the marketization of the wherewithal for subsistence allowed them to exist in town; also, markets helped generate new, unofficial intermediary groups outside the state. Equally important, the networks of native place and/or job helped them set up a wide variety of lifestyles that, taken together, did away with the monotony that used to characterize the socialist city in China. The chapter shows how three gross sets of transients surfaced: those who were state-protected, those who were community-connected, and the anomic isolates.

Chapters 6 and 7 together show how urban peasants, excluded by the state institution of the *hukou* and working within incipient markets, participated in writing new rules of urban life. They focus on the peasants' persistent occupation of urban spaces (made possible by markets) that called into question the exclusivity of official urban citizenship. For— to return to Turner's usage—both the highly limited belongingness and the customary patterns of distribution (i.e., the marks of citizenship) that had existed before economic reform were threatened when outsiders appeared on the premises. The conclusion draws out comparative insights inherent in the study and spells out the implications of the analysis for the future forms of peasant citizenship in urban China. It also formulates conclusions about the larger relationship between incipient capitalism and the bestowal or acquisition of citizenship.

The data for the study come from nearly 150 hours of interviews in China with city officials, with scholars, and with over fifty migrants in six major cities (Tianjin, Harbin, Wuhan, Nanjing, Guangzhou, and Beijing) during trips to China in 1990, 1991, 1992, and 1994. The study also draws on extensive documentary research in Chinese governmental reports and in scholarly Chinese journals—which in recent years contain a wealth of academic scholarship, statistical data, and results of surveys— and on the new genre of reportage and journalistic accounts. Its focus is the period 1983 to 1996. Before we launch into the story itself, a brief definitional, demographic appendix serves as orientation to the tale.

Appendix: What Is the Floating Population?

According to the Chinese conception, the "floating population" consists of people who have in fact *not* "migrated," officially speaking.[49] Instead, in Chinese parlance, their chief characteristic is that "they float and move," implying that they are not, and will not become, a permanently settled group.[50] This distinction is grounded in the fact that floaters have not been granted permanent, official household registration in the place where they are currently residing. Indeed, two separate official Chinese terms differentiate the two types of transfer: "floating" in Chinese is *liudong* (which could also be translated as "mobile"); "migration," however, is *qianyi*.[51]

Unlike the process known as migration elsewhere in the world, simply transferring one's place of residence to a new jurisdiction and remaining there for a specified time does not itself amount to "migration" in Chinese terminology.[52] To "migrate," one needs an official change of permanent registration. Thus, the floating population consists of persons who, because of this lack of official registration, are by official definition "engaged in partial temporary relocation." Further, they are characterized as people who "maintain their ties with their original place of abode, where their permanent residence registration stays."[53]

Those who qualify as floating have met three conditions: they have crossed over some territorial, administrative boundary; they have not altered their permanent registration (their *hukou*); and, at least in theory, they "flow in and out."[54] As a scholar at the Population Institute of the Guangdong Academy of Social Sciences explains, "If the household registration changes, the person has migrated, if not, the person is floating."[55] Although beginning with the 1982 census, all those who had been living in a location different from that of their place of permanent registration for a year or more were counted as migrants, that is, as residents of their new locations, in their actual daily lives they were still perceived and treated as outsiders.[56]

As these statements imply, the concept of floating is closely linked to the Chinese household registration system: it is the "strict permanent residence registration system [that] has prevented [floaters] from becoming legal migrants."[57] Until 1993 registration was inherited through the mother and administratively fixed; with only very rare exceptions, the urban registration (or urban *hukou*) adheres just for those born in cities.[58]

An alteration from rural to urban registration can by no means be made just by moving the place of habitation; rather, individuals migrate or, which is the same thing, change their residence registration only with the consent or at the order of government officials. Usually the move accompanies a transfer in work assignment; sometimes it occurs with permission to join family members. Peasants generally can become urbanites through serving in the army, rising within the party organization, or entering a college in the urban areas; also peasants whose land has been requisitioned for the use of urban work units may be compensated by attaining urban status (often on a one-status-change-per-family basis).[59]

Thus, the state's migration and registration policy forced transient Chinese people on the mainland to become floaters. Conveniently for the regime, this system limited at least to some degree an unplanned increase in the numbers of persons permanently resident in urban areas.[60] By enabling the regime to treat ruralites who had reached the cities as outsiders or noncitizens, the residence registration system thereby legitimated its policy of exclusive expenditure. This classification scheme for decades found its justification in the planned economy: as one scholar notes, "At all levels and in all localities, administrative management agencies plan their work and projects in accord with the size of the registered permanent population within their respective jurisdictions."[61]

Therefore, urban bureaucrats were especially concerned with the numbers of people present in and having an impact upon their resource systems at any time.[62] For this reason, the category of floaters encompasses everyone even temporarily present in a city, even for as little as three days. So in common usage, the term floating population includes those in town for public business, to see a doctor, to visit friends or relatives, for short-term study or meetings, or as tourists. This group, which always existed in the People's Republic, became a major issue when its numbers surged rapidly, even dramatically, after the state sanctioned the entry of peasants into the newly marketizing cities after 1983.[63]

Counting Floaters   Throughout the second half of the 1980s estimates of the numbers of peasants in cities and on the move mounted steadily.[64] Peasants allegedly represented between one-tenth and one-third of the numbers of the native population in the largest cities at the end of the 1980s.[65] Over the course of a decade, the inflow of these people exploded, such that they accounted for rapidly rising proportions of those of the permanent populations in major cities such as Beijing, Shanghai, Tianjin, Wuhan, Guangzhou, Shenyang, and Chengdu within just a few years' time. The increase was from 12.6 percent in 1984 to 22.5 percent in 1987 and to 25.4 percent in 1994, on the average.[66]

But inconsistencies abounded in counting this floating population, and the figures offered by scholars and governmental bureaucracies varied substantially, accordingly. By the mid-1990s, some researchers were willing to concede, there was no way to calculate the total accurately, indeed that it might range anywhere from 40 to 100 million.[67] Judith Banister even estimates that there were as few as 22 million net rural-to-urban migrants during 1990–1995.[68] But Hein Mallee asserts that "a consensus seems to have emerged that the number of rural labor migrants is probably between 50 and 60 million."[69]

The principal problem accounting for the indecision was the lack of comparability of the data.[70] For instance, among cities, in calculating its total numbers of floaters, Shanghai included those living in its suburbs, whereas Guangzhou did not.[71] Some researchers count those in transit, who were simply passing through a city; others begin their tally just with those who had been in the city for at least three days.

It is required to register for a temporary *hukou* after three months' stay; sometimes only those who had done so were added up. Some studies, such as the 1986 sample survey of migrants in seventy-four cities, investigate merely those living in city residents' homes;[72] others tabulate just those who had come to work or to do business. But most researchers attempt to include anyone who for any purpose was found in a specific city on the day of reckoning at the appointed time.

The other major source of discrepancies revolved around the difficulty of computing any itinerant group, particularly in cases where its members reside in a realm of uncertain legality. The numbers of such people are always inherently unstable, as they frequently move, shift back and forth between countryside and town, change occupations, and come and go with the seasons.[73] They tend intentionally to give interviewers false information. And perhaps the greatest source of their elusiveness was the failure of some large but indeterminate number of them to register their presence as temporary dwellers in the cities. Naturally there was wide variation in the estimates given of those who did not register, as there was obviously no concrete or firm foundation for judging their numbers.

All these caveats notwithstanding, from the late 1980s until the early 1990s a total figure of about 70 million floaters was the standard one.[74] Kam Wing Chan calculates in a piece of research done in 1995 that, as of 1994–95, their total numbers (including individuals present for any reason and however temporarily in a city where they were not permanently registered) were in the range of 100 million, a figure equivalent to about 30 percent of the total urban population size.

But probably only approximately 50 percent of these people were at that time remaining in the cities for more than half a year, he reports. And among them, he continues, 60 percent (or 30 million) were previously peasants. Thus he states that "this 30 million can be used to represent the size of additional 'permanent' rural-urban migrants in the floating population," a group mostly concentrated in the major cities and coastal provinces.[75] Government researchers participating in a major study in the late 1980s decided that 90 percent of the movement in the labor force involved workers leaving central and western China for the east.[76] And by 1990 observers were already lamenting a "serious" outflow of labor from remote areas having an undeveloped or single-product economy.[77] But, as table 1 documents, the estimates of researchers and reporters varied enormously, both over time and at the same time.

Demographic Data   Surely most of the itinerants are peasants. Reportedly, in the decade from 1978 when the reform period began until 1988, some 50 million farmers transferred to urban areas.[78] The movement of these staggering numbers is a reflection of the mammoth army of what has been controversially labeled "surplus" rural laborers—somewhere in the range of 100 to 220 million, in disparate accounts—who made their appearance with the disbanding after 1979 of the communes that had bound them to the land.[79]

A 1989 governmental study determined that in the eight large cities examined, only 59.34 percent of those called floaters had come from the rural areas. Similarly, a State Statistical Bureau survey report released six

Table 1. Descriptive Statistics on the Floating Population, 1993–1995
(in millions)

Category[a]	Number	Source, Date
Laborers to cities	20	*China Daily*, 6/28/93, 4
Peasants away from home all year	50–60	*Zhongguo nongcun jingji* 12 (1993): 33–36
Migrant workers	20	*Renmin ribao*, 1/7/94, 4
People who sought work in other areas, 1993	50	*Guanming ribao*, 1/11/94, 4
People who moved to cities	<10	Xinhua, 2/8/94
Floating population	88	*Ching Pao*, 2/14/94
Peasants who sought urban jobs/year	<50	*China Daily*, 3/3/94, 3
Peasants who left their villages	50–60	Xinhua, 3/15/94
Numbers on the move each year	20	Xinhua, 3/18/94
Peasants away from land and home to work	60	*Gaige* 4 (1994): 79
Peasants living in cities	20–30	*Wall Street Journal*, 4/26/94
Peasants who left land for cities	110	Xinhua, 4/29/94
and in transprovincial movement	20	
Peasants who left hometowns	50–60	*China Daily*, 5/17/94
and moved to cities	at least 25	
Migrants to other provinces or abroad	20	*China Daily*, 5/21/94, 4
Migrant population	80	Zhongguo xinwenshe, 6/2/94
Migrants in cities	80	Zhongguo xinwenshe, 6/2/94
from city to city	30	
from country to city	50	
country-city within own province	20	
Migrant workers	50–60	*Banyuetan*, 6/10/94, 8–10
within own province	30	

[a] Terms for categories come from the Chinese sources; [b] Ministry of Labor; [c] Ministry of Public Security.

continued

Table 1. *(continued)*

Category[a]	Number	Source, Date
Migrants in cities	50–60	*South China Morning Post,* 8/17/94, 1
Inland workers in enterprises in the east	<50	*China Daily,* 8/24/94, 2
Migrants to cities	20 per year	*Ching Pao,* 11/5/94, 38–40
Migrants to urban areas for work	<20	Xinhua, 11/22/94
Migrant workers	70–80	Xinhua, 12/1/94
Temporary residents	40	*Fazhi ribao,* 12/5/94, 3
Farmhands in cities along coast	<60	*South China Morning Post,* 12/14/94, 9
Migrant work force	25 (MOL)[b]	Zhongguo tongxunshe, 12/25/94
Transient laborers in large- and medium- size cities	71 (MPS)[c] 50	Xinhua, 1/24/95
Migrants off for odd jobs and in other provinces	<50 20	*Zhongguo gaige,* no. 2, 2/13/95
Migrating workers, 1993, 1994	20, 25 (MOL)	Xinhua, 3/7/95
Migrants traveling in search of work	30 (MOL)	Kyodo, 3/25/95
Peasants who migrated and migrated out of province	60 <20	*Nongmin ribao,* 3/30/95, 4
Flow of migrant workers to cities	80	*Eastern Express,* 4/8–9/95, 6
Floating surplus rural labor force across regions	50–60 (MOL) 20	Zhongguo xinwenshe, 4/26/95
Floaters in cities for job, no legal permit	<80 (MPS)	Li, "Tidal Wave," 4
Peasants away from home all year	50–60	*Shidian,* 6/8/94, 6–8

Table 1. *(continued)*

Category[a]	*Number*	*Source, Date*
Peasants away from the land	54 (MOL)	*South China Morning Post,* 6/18/95, 6
away and in other cities since 1979	about 50	
away and out of own province	13.5	
Migrants nationally	80 (Luo Gan)	Xinhua, 7/9/95

years later found that 58.4 percent of the floating population was made up of people who had moved from rural to urban areas over the years 1990 to 1995.[80]

According to the 1989 research, about 27 percent came from a given city's own distant suburbs and the counties it governed; another 32 percent from rural areas elsewhere; 40 percent from other urban areas; and just over 1 percent from abroad.[81] A half decade later, the findings were not too different: a study from early 1994 concluded that 31 percent moved within their own county, 33 percent stayed in their province, but left their county, and 36 percent left the province;[82] another found that 30 percent of all floaters were leaving their home provinces as of early 1995.[83]

As for their destinations, the 1994 researchers note that 28 percent went to large cities, 45 percent to medium and small cities, and 21 percent stayed within the rural areas;[84] the 1995 study reports that just 22 percent went to big cities, 49 percent to medium and small cities, and 23 percent remained in the countryside.[85] This second study claims that only 34 percent headed for the coast, while the first one alleges that just 10 percent of the total could be found in the major metropolises along the coast, as of mid-1994.[86]

The age structure of this social group in motion was just the same as that of migrant labor universally: young to middle-aged. Those between fifteen and forty-five accounted for 81 percent of the sojourners in Beijing in a November 1994 survey, for example.[87] In an October 1995 investigation of Shanghai's floaters, those between twenty and thirty years of age accounted for over 50 percent.[88] And in Dongguan City, in Guangdong's Pearl River Delta, those between sixteen and twenty-five in early 1994 amounted to 72 percent of the 800,000 migrants queried.[89]

More generally, the early 1995 national survey of leavers mentioned earlier (which is drawn from a rural population of 35,000) contained 76 percent under the age of thirty-five.[90]

As is the case for migrant labor around the world, this population was overwhelmingly male: by one account, the figure was 72 percent on the average in eight large cities in 1989.[91] This figure varied regionally, however; in areas of the Pearl River Delta, for instance, where young and impoverished peasant women were hired in droves to turn out toys, electronics products, and textiles in foreign-invested firms, as much as 80 percent of the floaters may have been female in the late 1980s.[92] But a study done under the auspices of the Ministry of Agriculture in 1995 reported an increase in the percentage of women nationwide, from 30 percent in 1987 up to 40 percent just eight years later.[93] A general statement that can be made about their educational background is that, like migrants anywhere, their level is lower than that of local residents in the receiving areas, but higher than that of the average dweller in their places of origin. Similarly, the proportion of illiteracy and semiliteracy among them is greater than that of the locals', but less than that of the total rural population.[94]

By early 1994, a study of leavers in 75 villages in 11 provinces had found that 10.3 percent of them had been to senior high and 45.4 percent to junior high, that is, that many of them (55.7 percent) had at least attended junior high; meanwhile, the comparable figures for the rural labor force as a whole were just 8.3 and 33 percent, respectively, at that time.[95] At the lower end, an early 1995 investigation discovered that, of the transients surveyed from the sample of over thirty-five thousand people in the rural areas noted above, 31.6 percent had been just to primary school and 3.8 percent were illiterate or semiliterate (as compared with the total population in the countryside, this was lower by 6.3 and 14 percent, respectively).[96]

Does the concept of "circulation" accurately characterize their movement? According to leading researchers who employ this term, it applies to short-term, repetitive, or cyclical movement by people who do not declare an intention to make a long-lasting change in residence. It does not, they explain, "alter the long-term distribution of people," a feature that distinguishes it from migration.[97]

In the case of Chinese floaters, perhaps many of the individuals were just circulating. But despite the bar of the *hukou*—and its official definition of their status as "peasants" or as just "temporary dwellers"—driven by state policies of economic reform and finding jobs or the hope of them in a variety of sectors, these people, at least in the aggregate, were becoming a definite and lasting structure within the large Chinese city in the 1990s. Their increasing permanence as a collective flew in the face of the inhospitality of the environment they faced, the unsavoriness of the lives they sustained, and the uncertainty of their individual futures. The rest of the book seeks to unravel this paradox.

PART ONE

Structure

2 State Policies I
Turning Peasants into Subjects

Why did the revolutionary Chinese state after 1949 convert country dwellers into members of an ascribed status group, altogether separate from their city kin?[1] This chapter explores how a new, much-heightened state-managed migration under Communist Party rule created a structural framework that turned peasants into subjects, noncitizens—people with no right to participate—should they venture into town.[2] This the Communist state did with its new priorities and its vastly bolstered power and resources that enlarged upon but did not eliminate the governing missions undertaken by previous regimes.

In the course of the 1950s, ironically enough in light of its Marxist pretensions,[3] the state drove a wedge between city and country that was novel in Chinese history.[4] Its chief purpose in doing so was to lock onto the land a potential underclass, ready to be exploited to fulfill the new state's cherished project of industrialization. In effect, the party used administrative orders and resource controls to isolate the peasantry, not just geographically but socially as well: to create what amounted to ethnic "boundary markers"[5] around them by the middle of the decade.[6]

This move enabled the state to draw upon this group as an industrial reserve army,[7] much as Marx had predicted only capitalist states would do.[8] Setting apart the cultivating class as what we could call victims of internal colonization, the state sequestered them from urbanites through a dualistic pattern of stratification.[9] This remaking of the Chinese farming class was crucial for the formation of what much later became the floating population.

MIGRATION BEFORE 1949

Under the Maoist state, from 1949 to 1978, the relative balance of migration shifted dramatically to governmental (coerced) from private (voluntary, even if at times induced by imperially mandated incentives and subsidies under the Qing). Another important distinction between the regime of the Communists and those of the previous two and a half centuries was that before but not after 1949, people of all classes were free to go on the move.

While permanent residents of Chinese cities may historically have been hostile to sojourners—at least to those of the lower, working classes—and governments suspicious of people on the move, the two regimes that preceded the Communist one either actively encouraged or at least permitted rather than restricted migration.[10] Indeed, privately organized geographical mobility predominated in both the late imperial (ca. 1700–1911) and Republican (1912–49) periods, despite their continuation of an ancient tradition of registering the population (both for land taxation and for local, mutual self-patrols through the *baojia* system).[11]

That the rulers did not discourage the people's voluntary geographical relocation had a lot to do with the guiding projects or missions of these regimes. The Qing state was concerned chiefly with empire building and consolidating, and, like earlier governments in China, with provisioning the population.[12] During the interregnum era from 1912 to 1949—the period of the Republican "state"—no potent central ruling power ever really held full sway; instead, warlordism, foreign intervention and invasion, and civil war dominated and often overwhelmed the business of government. So the most fundamental pursuits of these two regimes at their limiting edges—the fulfillment of imperial aspirations versus the stark survival of ruling parties, respectively—each meant that officials had other concerns and so tended to allow the populace to move where it would.

By contrast, under the People's Republic of China the state struggled to check urbanward population movement, beginning just after Communist takeover in the early 1950s, even if it did not achieve a significant measure of success until 1960. Not just politicians' purposes, but their resources as well inflated under the P.R.C. In the Communist period, with the regime's takeover of all land, industrial assets, and, in effect, every form of capital and property by 1956, the state became not just another new empire concerned with meeting the basic sustenance of its people; it also became an owner of assets and an employer, bent upon rapid industrial growth. Its substantial possessions thus bolstered its capability when it came to restraining its people's movement, as compared with previous regimes.

Dynastic Times

The traditional state was heavily involved in the movement of peoples. As James Lee shows, it was capable of using migration as its mechanism for meeting a number of diverse, but ultimately basically imperial, goals. These included expanding and guaranteeing control over new lands, especially along the borders; developing the country's resources; relieving the victims of natural disasters; relocating its own powerful domestic contenders; pacifying the unruly; and shifting people from denser to more open areas.

As the Han peoples moved outward, the net—and intended—effect was to assimilate the peoples along the borders into Chinese ways and to bring them within the scope of imperial rule. Lee judges that from the second century B.C. until approximately the seventeenth century A.D., the government was routinely involved in organized migration. He calculates that there were periods when this flow clearly outpaced that which was voluntary.[13]

But even in the absence of state involvement the Chinese people, left to their own devices, had a tendency to move, despite the ideals of the settled community and the duty to return to the ancestral home.[14] Private migrations predated those planned and guided by the state, and, Lee attests, were always sizable. In fact, from the time of the country's "medieval revolution," which began around the year 1000, the proliferation of handicrafts, markets, and new rural technologies and crops stimulated economic intercourse among regions.

By 1700, as long-distance markets grew in importance, previously prevalent causes of flight from home—such as poor person-to-land ratios, natural and human-sparked disasters, disease, and governmental harshness—were increasingly joined by entrepreneurial motives.[15] In the nineteenth century, commercial stimulation, in addition to dislocations resulting from the major uprisings of the late Qing, and finally by a post-Taiping revival of trade dating from the mid-1860s,[16] eventually prodded voluntary mobility to exceed that occurring under the aegis of the state.[17] And over time rulers became progressively disinclined to limit the relocation of people poised to better their lot on their own.[18]

In sum, ambitious as the imperial-style projects of the dynastic rulers might have been,[19] their objectives did not generally—and decreasingly so over time—encompass a strict regulation of the private movement of the subjects.[20] The government of the People's Republic drastically shifted this balance between statist and spontaneous migration, especially between 1960 and the early 1980s.

The class composition of those migrating was a second great difference between pre- and post-1949 migrations. Here three points can be made. First, the patterns of geographical mobility that various classes undertook historically in China differed significantly one from the next, both in style and purpose. The wealthy were more disposed to maintain homes in both town and country, while peasants were in normal times more apt to remain in the countryside.[21] Moreover, when indigent farmers did move into the city, they took up menial occupations, whereas those with means entering towns would retain their roles as landowners, if absent ones, while practicing business or becoming bureaucrats.[22]

And though the elite was eligible for a change in registration once in a new district, its members did not generally wish to make such a switch.[23] Intent on using their commercial skills in the city just on a temporary basis to further their careers and increase their fortunes, these sojourners were often wealthy or at any rate had talent and skills, unlike those from lesser backgrounds, who were more likely to come to town because they had lost their livelihood.[24] If not yet of means themselves— making the journey into town with financial support from their communities and clans, which had specially selected them to go—those with talent and skills could hope soon to become so.[25]

But despite this difference between classes in style and purpose of movement, a second class-related distinctive feature of pre-1949 migration was that at least in the late imperial period the relatively poor and even the very poor could move freely. Indeed, as early as the twelfth century in the southeast, and over larger areas in succeeding centuries, migration was not forbidden to any class. Lee finds it unusual by international standards that in China "long-distance migration was not confined to the rich."[26]

This feature of migration was facilitated by a third class-linked trait specific to Chinese migration before 1949 (as against the period that came later). Because of earlier regimes' tolerance of native-place associations (*tongxianghui*), at least some members of the less well-off survived in the cities through their connections with wealthier clanspeople, or with migrants from their native places who had preceded them there and been successful, with *tongxianghui* playing a role.[27]

The Republican Period

If it is possible to identify a project informing the actions of leaders of the Republican era, whether provincial-level warlord or contending party ruler, it was the desire to unify the country under their own command and then strengthen it, both economically and militarily. But none ever unequivocally mastered enough territory with sufficient authority to realize this objective. Instead, all became consumed with subduing and overcoming rivals, up until the time when the Communists finally achieved this end.

Except insofar as they could mobilize populations to assist in this cause, no leader before 1949 had the time or the power to direct the migratory behavior of the people. Thus, a great deal of the geographical movement that took place in these years was in the nature of a flight ordinary people made on their own from disaster of one sort or another. Both on the North China plain and in the region surrounding Shanghai, war and agrarian crisis in various guises propelled peasants off the land and into the big cities.

It was not just misery and dislocation that led farmers to desert the countryside in the Republican period, however. Industry and the heightened economic pulse in the foreign-dominated treaty ports drew many off the land, sometimes through the forceful intermediation of labor contractors and gangsters. Once in the city ruralites became craftspeople and machine hands, haulers and casual laborers. Especially in the 1930s and 1940s, when the rural economy had been ravaged by strife, natural hardships, and overpopulation and so offered little alternative, in some cases whole families, in others single young people, departed for the metropolises.[28]

Though the Republican authorities tried to use a variant of the old *baojia* system, which had used citizens to police their neighbors, their purpose in doing so was not so much to check mobility as it was to ferret out Communists.[29] In short, in these decades after 1912, the balance between statist and spontaneous forms of migration was thus heavily weighted toward the latter. And in contradistinction to later decades, the state did not assign an underclass status to the peasants, though the working and livelihood conditions of the great bulk of these transients were often deplorable once they settled in the cities.[30]

Class distinctions were considerable among migrants in the Republican era, just as they had been before the fall of the dynastic system. In the

Shanghai of the 1930s, for instance, illustrious capitalists and powerful gangsters originally from other places wielded significant clout.[31] But, as against what was more typically the case before the era of industrialization got under way, the bulk of the outsiders in the big cities tended to be lower-class refugees. Such people could only hope to achieve decent employment and a bearable existence if they hailed from homes higher up in the native-place hierarchy, and could draw upon bonds on this basis.[32] The *tongxianghui* of this era, at least in Shanghai, drew their members from middle- and upper-class businesspeople and usually closed their doors on the poor.[33]

For different reasons, then, privately organized geographical mobility was untrammeled in both late imperial and Republican periods. And in both eras, people of all classes might go on the move, though the style of migration of different classes as well as their fates after arriving (though free of state interference) varied considerably. In both eras movement was common, widespread, and frequent.[34]

By contrast, as we will see below, under the P.R.C. from the late 1950s until the reform era, statist choices about population location prevailed in all but a very few years. If people moved freely, it was just among rural areas and was strictly off the books.[35] Moreover, the government's abrogation of private property and assets after 1956 enabled it to eliminate classes and then to reconstitute a functional substitute on a locational basis, replacing the rich-poor distinction with an urban-rural one. Thus, even when people did make a voluntary move, there was no question of the poor forming linkages for survival in strange surroundings with rich people (for there were none), or of varying styles of geographical mobility according to wealth.

A TWOFOLD SOURCE OF CHANGE

Given that the post-1949 regime was able to reinvigorate the most statist, invasive traditions of regime involvement in its people's migration, and was quite committed to doing so, what tools did it utilize in this effort? And how did it construct an edifice of control for its purpose of pinning people into place? Two elements shaped its strategy: the Soviet experience and China's own special registration system. Both of the shifts from the Chinese past documented above—in the direction of more *dirigisme*, and toward restrictions on mobility by status—found their sources in these two factors.

The Soviet Experience

As China's new rulers after 1949 began to build their nation as a socialist one, they drew upon a range of practices pioneered by the Soviet Union. Surely the Soviet experiences in limiting the growth of major metropolises, in controlling movement through an exclusive permit (the *propiska*) for living in big cities, and in its creating internal passports after 1932 for urban people alone (a "privilege" not extended to ruralites until 1974) were practices that China aspired to copy, albeit with its own adaptations.[36]

The Soviet leaders were not always rigorous in checking movement, largely because of the persistent labor shortage in their country, which fed a special ambivalence toward rural-to-urban migration and indeed toward geographical mobility in general.[37] Consequently, a great deal of migration there followed universal, market-driven laws, according to which people moved simply in response to the promise of better living standards.[38] And in the late 1930s, in the wake of the country's brutal, extractive rural collectivization drive (which itself drove millions out, in flight from fear and famine), when the regime strove to recruit peasants for urban industry, as many as half the departures from the villages actually occurred voluntarily.[39]

The Soviets anchored their attitude toward migration in their understanding of Marxist-Leninist teachings. Since Marxism held capitalism to be the cause of urban overpopulation, a state aspiring to be socialist would ipso facto need to avoid allowing people to accumulate spontaneously in cities, even if it had to bring in labor on its own terms to develop the productive forces. Also, they concurred with Marx that the differences between town and country should be minimized, and that both people and industry must be spread as evenly as possible throughout different forms of residential concentration.[40]

A second set of Marxian tenets affected the treatment of workers. These dictated that the planned economy that socialist rulers took as the hallmark of a socialist system had to rely upon worker discipline and labor mobilization, which, in turn, demanded a registration system. Ideally, registration was to have stabilized the location of the individual worker as a means of facilitating production. Third, planning itself, with its manifold forms of arrangement, provision, and supply, was feasible only on the foundation of firm population figures; the registration of the population that furnished such data seemed more efficiently executed if movement were reduced to a minimum. If relocation was to occur, in the interest of the control that planning demanded, it would have to be deliberate.[41]

And fourth, the specific growth strategy that became associated with socialism—doubtlessly a result of Marx's dictum that the mission of the socialist, transitional stage was to increase the productive forces—was a strategy that enshrined what one scholar labels "direct industrialization."[42] This tenet, operative both in the Soviet Union and in all of its East European satellites as well, led to pouring the lion's share of investment into production for heavy industry.

The corollary was that allocations for consumption goods, services, and amenities in the cities, and, in particular, for urban housing, were drastically shortchanged.[43] Consequently, a kind of "underurbanization," marked by privileging just productive infrastructure, meant that the major urban centers simply could not accommodate an unlimited permanent resident population.[44] This outcome may have been only an unintended by-product of the pro–heavy industrialization growth strategy; nevertheless, it operated to achieve the same effect that related principles of Marxism directed.

The *propiska* system specified that all residents in capital cities, or in most ordinary cities having populations of more than five hundred thousand, were to have this residency permit stamped inside their passports. Moreover, only with official permission was it possible to work or reside legally in a number of specified, more desirable, larger cities, in short, to become an urban citizen in them.[45] Not only were members of the rural population not granted passports until 1974, they were also barred from obtaining a permanent residency permit for the cities.

Thus farmers, that is, the members of the *kolkhoz* population, could live in the cities only temporarily or illegally, although they were allowed, after 1961, to perform seasonal or permanent work there as long as they first received the permission of their *kolkhoz*.[46] The system, however, was far from airtight; those who have studied it closely conclude that "restrictions have impeded the growth of certain cities but not stopped or controlled it."[47]

Restraints on migration pioneered in the Soviet Union, along with the rationale that produced them, did a lot to shape the Chinese program of managing population mobility, thrusting it in a statist direction. But because of the overwhelming differences in the sizes of the labor forces available to each system—and the consequent huge divergences in the scale of potential urban populations—by the time the floating population surged into China's cities in the 1980s, its presence there undid a far more sturdily guarded urban fortress than the one on which it had been patterned.

The Hukou

By 1960 China's rulers had utilized their policy of household registration (for short, the *hukou*) to construct a residential system judged to be different from anything that had previously existed, either in China's own history or throughout the socialist world. For it was one that had succeeded in "fix[ing] people permanently on the basis of their birth place or their husband's residence."[48]

If the Marxist influence, filtered through the experience provided by the Soviet Union, was instrumental in reorienting the Chinese state's stance toward migration and away from the more laissez-faire mode of the late imperial and Republican periods, the *hukou* system could be said to have rewritten its class or status underpinnings. To say this is to twist reality a bit. In fact, once land reform had been largely accomplished by 1952 and the socialist transformation of industry and commerce in the cities achieved in 1956, to speak of classes rooted, in the Marxist sense, in people's relation to ownership of the means of production no longer made any sense. For only the state itself was truly an owner of assets from that time until legislation in the reform period sanctioned private enterprise in the late 1980s.

But if a class system in the customary sense was eliminated, one of status groups took its place and functioned similarly, for all intents and purposes.[49] These remarks of a Chinese writer bolster my claim:

> Just after liberation, peasant households did not feel lower rank [*diren yideng*] and urban ones did not feel higher. . . . Later, a great difference in interests came from the difference in where one lived. . . . A ranking structure was gradually established with the peasant household at the lowest level.[50]

And at least one group of Chinese scholars maintains that the *hukou* system actually set up a new class distinction between urbanites and ruralites:

> There are two social classes; [the difference between] the agricultural and nonagricultural *hukou* makes the rural population exert its utmost strength to squeeze onto the rolls of the urban *hukou*.[51]

This understanding of class draws upon Emily Honig's work on the ethnicity of native place in China, in which, while not fully conflating native-place identity and class, she offers the fruitful insight that native-place identity—and, by extension here, the urban-versus-rural-identity distinction—could serve as "a metaphor for class."[52]

The legal basis for what two anthropologists adjudge to be "the most important social distinction in modern China"—that between urbanites and peasants—was laid by a State Council directive of June 1955 establishing a system of household registration.[53] Accordingly, all persons were required to register their place of residence officially, with records maintained by the public security offices at the level of what was then the higher agricultural cooperative in the countryside and in the neighborhood in cities. Thenceforth, residence status became an ascribed, inherited one, determining an individual's entire livelihood and welfare simply on the basis of where the registration was located.

Not only the quality of the goods supplied, but the transportation conditions, the range of cultural entertainment, the nature of education offered, and the type of health care one received depended upon where one resided. And it was not just these more tangible goods that were allocated by the rank of the residents, but the wages people were paid, the prices they were charged, and the subsidies and welfare benefits they received were so fixed as well.[54] To illustrate the extremity of the lifestyle distinctions involved, a popular ditty had it that it is "better [to have] a bed in the city than a house in the suburbs" (*ning yao shiqu yizhang chuang, buyao jiaoqu yitao fang*).[55]

The *hukou* system also constructed a new set of categories, if not precisely a new class system, to supplant the dismantled class hierarchy of the past. For instance, one scholar lists six different levels of ranks, in ascending order: peasants, nonpeasants, city and town residents, urbanites, those in large cities, and those in cities directly administered by the central government.[56]

Through the *hukou*, regulations of the 1950s placed boundaries around the peasantry as a whole, remaking its members, in the eyes of urbanites, as "other," subaltern. The peasant of China thereby became a member of a separate, inferior class or status group, and the generic peasant was now specifically enjoined against migrating. Legal migration thus took on a totally state-determined and "class"-based dimension that it had not possessed in China before.

1949 TO 1978: FROM TAKEOVER TO REFORM
The Overall Policy

The Communist Party's new state after 1949 came to power with a vastly expanded project, though without jettisoning those pursued by its predecessors. This meant first of all that it persisted in affirming the imperial state's missions of empire building and consolidating,[57] and of popular provisioning; it also continued to pursue the party's own Republican-era objectives of unifying the nation and strengthening it economically and militarily.

But in the 1950s this new state was also prepared, as monopolist employer and owner, to amplify in particular one portion of previous rulers' programs: this was its passion to industrialize ruthlessly. Consequently, it was industrialization and its fiscal demands that dictated the pace of migration.[58] Other, related purposes included, as in the Soviet system, the facilitation of planning, the preservation of social order, the distribution of economic benefits, and the organization of production and urban services.[59]

The regime's leaders' vision of unimpeded modernizing economic development brooked no compromises; indeed, none were necessary. For they no longer had any competitors, whether political or economic. To accommodate this industrialization imperative, the new registration system's rationale became to ensure that peasants remained on the land,[60] producing the food that would enable the cities' residents to industrialize and modernize urban China.[61] This was an achievement increasingly possible as the state gathered more and more of the resources requisite to an urban existence into its own hands.[62]

The *hukou* system largely achieved its goal, even in the face of strong and at times acute pressure from peasants who yearned to enter, especially during chaotic political campaigns or intermittent natural disasters.[63] So, unlike other developing nations, in the four decades after coming to power the state managed to increase industrial employment by more than seven times, while urban population rose by only about three times.[64]

To reach its goal, the state needed to try to calibrate the number of legal urban residents with the amount of grain and the number of jobs available in cities.[65] Not only did the system economize on resources. By barricading the cities against the peasants, the state also made of the ruralites a labor reserve, available for the big spurts of industrial growth, and, it was hoped, disposable in tighter times.[66] Beneath this straightforward policy, though, lay a crucial contradiction: there would be times when the goal of growth—which called for bringing in peasants to the cities temporarily—would conflict with the priority of pacifying urban workers through provisioning them.

The specific policies that grappled with these issues fall into two categories: labor controls and registration and rationing. Policies in these two areas represent the regime's solutions to its two chief concerns about peasant in-migrants: checking the inflow of cheap rural labor that threatened the jobs of city workers and would have required more expenditures on urban infrastructure; and reserving grain supplies for the urban population.

Economic Policy and Labor Controls

State regulation of migration in the Mao years did not take the form of a blanket prohibition. Instead, denial of access alternated with a few periods when in-migration to cities was permitted, others when it was even actively encouraged. This control pulsated in accord with the regime's economic ends, though these ends were sometimes interrupted by the imperatives of political movements.[67]

The pattern of rural-to-urban migration between 1949 and 1978 was shaped by five distinct developmental periods: the early 1950s; the era of the first Five-Year Plan (1953–57); the Great Leap Forward (1958–60); the post-Leap recovery period (1961–62); and the Cultural Revolution (1966–76), along with the period leading up to it (1962–66). In each of these the peasantry, as a labor reserve, was made to serve the ends either of the national state or of its enterprises in the localities.

The early 1950s, just after takeover, was a time of free movement, characterized by a flow of people back and forth between town and country.[68] Some, on the losing side during the civil war, were retreating from the towns; some left because of the stagnation of the cities and the lack of employment opportunities there at first. But others scurried in, as a later account from Shanghai chronicled, in the hope of hiding out from the land reform, or in expectation of new chances for an urban job in the wake of peace and incipient economic recovery.[69] Even in this time of spontaneous migration, though, the state was not absent. In the interest of relieving burdens on the still fragile metropolises and reducing unemployment there, the government periodically dumped those without fixed occupations or jobs in town into the countryside.[70]

With full economic recovery at the end of 1952, the leadership began to launch the first Five-Year Plan, setting up a direct contradiction between the central state's wish for orderly metropolises, on the one hand, and its push for growth, on the other.[71] The heavy pressure the plan placed on enterprise managers to meet output quotas while keeping down costs led many of them to circumvent their local labor bureaus by recruiting in the countryside for low-paid, temporary peasant workers. Repeated injunctions over the next few years, beginning as early as August 1952, inveighed against employing peasants in urban firms, and also against the rural people's supposed "blind" movement into towns.[72] A directive dated March 1954 specifically noted that urban labor departments alone had the right to solicit workers.[73]

But Thomas Bernstein finds that, nonetheless, in 1954 nearly two and a half million people were hired in the cities, of whom as many as 70 percent were peasants.[74] All this suggests the constant push and pull that attended these efforts at control, as evidenced by the first major coercive repatriation a year later, which sent millions of peasants back to their villages.[75] On the North China plain, the curtailment of peasants' custom of leaving home to take seasonal employment began around this time.[76] But although even more emphatic statements on hiring only the workers assigned by local labor bureaus continued to appear, through early 1956 most firms were still privately owned and prone to hire independently.[77]

An uncharacteristically sympathetic State Council regulation of December 30, 1956, on halting the inflow of peasants, bearing the byline of Zhou Enlai, permitted peasants who were disaster victims, who had friends and relatives who could care for them in the cities, and who could find work there, to remain in and even transfer their work and household registration to the city. But within only two months, as the peasants poured in, the council had to issue supplementary, more restrictive provisions.[78]

Despite all the official efforts to check and regulate the flow of farmers into cities, the presence of technically illicit, pejoratively titled "black" labor markets, mediated by "black labor bosses," offered the migrants an informal opportunity. Such recruiters would round up gangs of peasants and insert them into the urban economy where need and private connections coalesced.[79] By the autumn of 1957, at least eight million peasant migrants were known to the authorities to have entered the cities.[80] Andrew Walder avers that as many as twenty million ruralites had poured into the towns between 1949 and 1957, and that the urban population had actually doubled; but the first Five-Year Plan (for 1953–57) was prepared to provide only one million new nonagricultural jobs per year.[81]

At the end of 1957 the State Council established a formal system for hiring rural labor, outlining it in Temporary Regulations concerning the Hiring by Units of Temporary Workers from the Countryside.[82] To engage temporary laborers from the rural areas, firms in the cities needed to acquire a letter of introduction from the rural labor department, and also obtain approval from the county and township governments in that locality. The hiring was to be done in the main by contracting for the workers in groups with the rural cooperatives that employed them. In addition, urban educational, labor, or public securities authorities had to issue a certificate approving the move.[83]

This was the birth of the "labor contract system," also known as the "worker-peasant system." It was to meet with vituperative criticism and protests by contract workers during the Cultural Revolution, and rightly so.[84] Its treatment of the peasants was blatantly exploitative: they were paid at a lower rate than the regular workers, got fewer, if any benefits, and had to hand over a part of their wages to the rural cooperative (and later the commune) to which they belonged.[85]

Displaying its disturbance over the unremitting influx, the central political leadership issued its harshest directive to date in yet another form in late 1957, complete with a threat of labor education and legal punishment for offenders, plus a firm warning to tighten controls over the urban grain supply. The document indicated that peasants were falsely reporting their household registration and purchasing grain ration coupons; those who did so were to be penalized. It called for immediately sending the interlopers home and set up special organs in the cities first to detain them briefly and then to escort them on their way.[86] And yet there was evidence that even then many peasants, once having made their way in, managed to stay on in town until the much more rigorous deportations of the early 1960s.[87]

Following this, in January 1958, a new set of rules on household registration appeared, further elaborating on the June 1955 State Council directive mentioned above.[88] In an accompanying explanatory note, then Minister of Public Security Luo Ruiqing focused on the implications of the new rules for labor. He charged that not only were the enterprises still finding their own workers; they were even illegally offering their peasant employees urban household registration and refusing to eject those illicitly in the city who lacked such registration.[89]

But a brand new calculus began to dominate policy in mid-1958, when Mao Zedong began his chiliastic advocacy of a program under which China would take a Great Leap Forward. This program temporarily voided the recent more stringent regulations and undid any success they might have had.[90] For over the next year and a half, massive investment in urban industrial growth took place, as extant urban firms were exhorted to produce at the most breakneck speed possible, even as new enterprises proliferated.[91] Statistical chaos and bureaucratic breakdown exacerbated the crisis atmosphere.

The enterprises reacted by hiring wildly. Jeffrey Taylor estimates that as many as 23 million peasants were recruited during this movement.[92] Michael Korzec claims that as much as 30 percent of the work force in state plants was made up of nonpermanent peasant workers at this point.[93] This era constituted the very clearest instance of the state and its local enterprises acting in unison to exploit that reserve army of peasants that the registration policies of the state had created.

It was not long before reality set in. During 1959, with food shortages threatening mass starvation even in the cities, the state made a drastic reversal.[94] This it did by reaffirming its earlier limits on urban capacity, and by turning its focus toward restoring normalcy to the shell-shocked urban sector and away from growth at any cost.[95] Meanwhile, the urban population had increased by 31.7 million, or 32 percent in just three years, with 90 percent of the increase the result of migration.[96]

Repatriation of peasants back to the countryside had occurred in 1955 and again in 1957. But the forced exodus after 1960 was totally unprecedented.[97] John P. Emerson cites figures of 20 million for 1961 and 30 million for the following year.[98] These deportations were not just more sizable than earlier ones; they were also far more successful.[99] Most important, they set down the model for migration control that lasted for the next two decades.[100]

In the years following, the stringency of prohibitions against inmigration came to match the formalization of a rigid stratification already implicit within the working class in the city: the inferior treatment accorded the peasant workers who remained (or were later recruited) produced what Andrew Walder calls "a pattern of dualism in employment."[101] This pattern stood as official evidence that the peasant migrants working in urban industry had arrived there as members of a separate, lower, class and would receive treatment as such relative to the permanent staff.

The urge to make use of temporary peasant labor continued unabated in the fifth developmental period, the era that followed the Leap. By 1962, peasants were once again being actively and even legally courted, if now on a much reduced scale, as a cheaper and more expendable labor force,[102] even as their own free movement into the cities was still discouraged.[103] In fact, in the spirit of "readjustment" reigning then, enterprises were actually urged to cut back on the numbers of permanent, urban employees they used and to replace them with temporaries.[104] Accordingly, some 13 to 14 million peasants were permitted to enter the cities under authorization from city labor bureaus in the decade between 1966 and 1976.[105]

Perhaps because peasant workers took the opportunity of the Cultural Revolution to complain loudly and thereby won the sympathy of Mao and his wife, Jiang Qing[106]—and also because Mao's attack on the worker-peasant system gave him one more charge against his enemy, Liu Shaoqi, its supposed author[107]—at the end of 1971 these peasants were granted the status of permanent employees.[108] Since the cities had recently been stripped of upward of 20 million educated Red Guard urban young people, who were languishing in the countryside and so were unable to fill the cities' needs for labor, peasants were presumably welcomed as a much cheaper substitute.[109]

In any event, by the eve of economic reform, in 1977, workers who had been recruited outside the state plan by state firms amounted to 13.5 percent of the work force within the plan; about 50 percent of these unplanned employees were ruralites.[110] By 1980, another 18 million had been brought in by the "back door."[111]

And yet injunctions against peasants' entering the cities on their own did not abate. At the end of the 1970s a number of rulings ordered that peasants who had been hired outside the plan be sent back home, so that their places could be taken by the urban unemployed (whom, presumably, city firms preferred not to hire, because of the welfare benefits that would have to be extended to them). Among these directives was one from 1977 ordering the removal of "black" labor teams and bosses from the cities, a regulation that had to be reenunciated two years later.[112]

This brief summary of the state's efforts to handle the inflow of job-seeking peasants to the municipalities in the first three decades of the People's Republic drives home the argument that cityward migration then was officially permitted only at the behest of the central state and its labor bureaucracy. Peasants also came semilicitly, through arrangements made by locally based state-owned firms, in the ardor of managers to fulfill state plan-driven tasks. But either way, they clearly came into the urban areas as members of a reserve employment army. So in post-1949 China migration was legally possible for the peasants, a lower "class," only at the state or its firms' invitation, and for the state's own purposes. Once in town, farmers labored as outsiders, generally without most of the most basic welfare rights enjoyed by the average urban-citizen worker.

Household Registration and Grain Rationing

Registration Because of the party's concern to industrialize with minimal externalities and maximal control, soon after its takeover in 1949 it embarked on an effort to obtain accurate statistics as to who was residing in the cities; later it went on to try to stabilize that population. The initial motive behind registering the population was simply to become clear about the numbers involved.[113] As Tiejun Cheng and Mark Selden note, the first, preliminary regulations on household registration of urbanites of July 1951 did not mention tying people in place and at least rhetorically included the protection of the people's freedom of residence and movement among their objectives.[114]

Over the next few years, however, the aim in keeping track of residence shifted. In 1953 registration was extended to the countryside, and household registration booklets were distributed in major cities as an adjunct to the execution of the first national population census, undertaken that year.[115] By 1955, if not before, the clear purpose of requiring households to record their domicile was to check geographical mobility and, more specifically, to make it difficult for outsiders—especially peasants—to subsist in the city.[116]

In that year, the state issued three pronouncements with profound implications for the peasantry: first, in June the State Council formalized its household registration system with the Directive on the Establishment of a Permanent System of Household Registration, encompassing all the households of the country, both urban and rural.[117] This law also included unwieldy and complex procedures to be used in applying for certificates to migrate.

Second, in August 1955, the same body promulgated Temporary Methods for Supplying Urban Grain Rations, which made it plain that only urban residents were eligible for the state's grain.[118] And third, in November the Criteria for the Demarcation of Urban and Rural Areas appeared.[119] They stipulated that "those living in the rural areas had different lifestyles and labored under economic conditions distinct from those of urban residents," so that "government work should vary as between the two kinds of areas." From this point on it became crystal clear that a boundary had been carved around the cities that peasants, unless explicitly invited, could traverse only at their own risk. And even when they ventured to move across it—under any auspices—they would still remain "peasants."

This third set of rulings was extended in early 1958 in definitive Regulations on Household Registration in the People's Republic of China, passed by the National People's Congress.[120] It was this 1958 law, in its Sections 15 and 16, that set forth the procedures required for legal temporary residence for stays longer than three days in the cities; these procedures are the same orders that are supposed to be followed by today's floating population.[121]

Unlike what had been claimed at the start of household registration in 1951, this 1958 set of directives no longer paid even lip service to any notion of freedom of movement; instead, a chief objective of registering the population was admitted to be serving the state's project of "socialist construction."[122] With the publication of this document, both food and grain were thenceforth to be denied anyone in the city not in the possession of proof of valid registration.[123] Thus, literally, unauthorized transience would have been dealt a lethal blow, had not the Great Leap Forward, with its hunger for hands, intervened. But in the wake of the famine this movement engineered, the directive's stipulations were finally executed quite rigorously after 1960.

Rationing   As the program of industrialization got under way by 1952, scarcities of grain made themselves felt in the cities, and the authorities judged that rationing was necessary.[124] Once they had begun the program in 1953 whereby peasants were made to sell a specified quota of their grain to the state, state leaders were in a position to begin rationing it out to urbanites, which they did in some cities as early as 1954.[125] The next year, when the State Council passed its measures on grain rationing, it still permitted peasants coming into the cities to bring their own grain with them.[126] But the state's monopoly and its watchfulness tightened considerably in the early 1960s, with the severe food shortages occasioned by the Leap.[127] Combined with the tighter control over urban employment and the termination of private home ownership after 1956 in the cities, these changes closed off cityward migration to the ordinary, law-abiding peasant.[128]

What had been constructed by the start of the sixties was largely locked into place for the two succeeding decades. This program of forcing farmers to remain in the fields, growing the foodstuffs to feed the workers and sustain the cities, had been achieved through a series of labor recruitment rulings, backed up by selective food allocation and a lack of residential space. It was not until the era of reform that the state offered the farmers a key to come in.

THE FLOATING POPULATION
IN THE ERA OF ECONOMIC REFORM

Seemingly, the advent of economic reform presaged a totally new stance of the state toward peasants and their labor power. After all, the communes that had dominated farmers' existence were disavowed and dissolved beginning in 1979; simultaneously, a series of economic policies facilitated and even encouraged many of these people's abandonment of the soil and their venturing into the metropolises. It appeared that the peasant, once beyond the grip of the rural cadre, would be self-activated, an agent in the resurrection of the spontaneous migration that had marked the pre-1949 years (and centuries). As one governmental report averred,

> Unlike the organized movement of population that characterized the first 30 years [of the People's Republic], now it is self-selected and motivated by the state's economic development strategy. . . . People go where there are employment opportunities and high wages.[129]

This mobility, granted, was voluntary. The movers were multitudinous and generally contravened any limiting procedures—lighter than in the past—with impunity.

And yet a closer look reveals that these migrants remained confined within the rubric of the state's persisting imperative: to ally urban growth and productivity with cost-saving, and, as a "socialist" state, to provide for the city dweller while reserving the ruralite as docile, disposable trespasser, and drudge. Statism and urban bias, though more masked than before, retained their wonted power to inform the relation between the Chinese migrant and the state.[130]

Even the increasingly permissive state policies enabling and authorizing peasants to enter the urban areas that I review below produced not potential citizens but, instead, made floaters out of farmers. For the pro-market mentality enshrined in the reforms elevated cost-consciousness as a value much higher than it had ever been placed before in post-1949 China; and the policy framework endorsing this mentality affirmed and legitimated the use of peasant subjects as low-wage labor.

The Implications of Reform-Era Policies for Migrant Labor

Certainly the state's explicit sanction for sojourning propelled many peasants to desert the soil. But their migrations were also a by-product of practically all of the other policies that made up the general program of economic reform. These policies either enticed or encouraged millions of peasants to move to cities after the early 1980s.

Labor migration really took off with the disassemblage of one of the central institutions of the planned economy, the rural commune. In the early 1980s when contracting land to the households replaced collective ownership, families regained the power they had had before 1949 to dispose of their labor wholly as they chose. As the surplus labor that had been hidden in the communes began to be revealed, millions of rural workers were freed from the redundancy under which they had been laboring.[131] As a result, no doubt often in line with family decisions, many set off for the towns.[132]

But not only did the termination of compulsory labor for all expose an immense waste of labor power. Where once people in the countryside could count on a basic, if meager, livelihood and (granted, often rudimentary) medical and educational services, the contracting of the land to individual households that followed this breakup, and the need for rural cadres to raise funds in the absence of a genuinely collective economy, led to privations and hardships for much of the peasantry, especially in the poorer, inland regions where rural industry was scarce.

For no longer were there joint funds allotted locally to finance common services; in their absence, publicly supplied amenities and benefits sometimes disappeared from the rural areas, especially where cadres squeezed the peasants and then used the exactions obtained to attempt to set up enterprises.[133] The floating population was not for the most part landless labor as it is in many third-world countries. It was instead surplus labor that in some cases struggled under burdens of extortion and often scrambled for social and economic security.[134]

Once these organizational rearrangements launched the floaters on their move, the state's investment decisions did much to influence the direction of their flow. Government researchers participating in a major study in the late 1980s conclude that 90 percent of the labor force movement as of that time involved workers leaving central and western China for the east, which chiefly meant the coast.[135] And this coastward surge derived directly from state policies that expressly privileged that region.

Politicians reasoned that the potential for rapid wealth generation was greatest along the coast and so offered preferential treatment to foreign (especially overseas Chinese) financiers after 1980 in that region alone.[136] This policy represented a significant switch from the previous state investment program, in which state planners had made a major effort to reallocate revenue receipts among provinces in a way that assisted the interior.[137] A scholar writing from Sichuan, from which more labor was drained than any other, resentfully decries this practice:

> In recent years the regional structure of investment has seriously lost balance. . . . This has sent false signals, which led a large amount of rural labor to flow blindly toward the coast and the large cities.[138]

Various market reforms in the cities each had at least one of two effects, both of which were crucial for enticing peasants to live and work in urban areas. First, in offering peasants ways to get the necessities of daily existence outside the state's monopoly, many reforms severely and directly undercut the bastions that had for decades barricaded the city. By legitimizing markets for these necessities, the new policies made feasible the livelihood of farmers in the cities.[139] And second, these measures engendered an urgent hunger for low-paid and flexible labor, which peasants were particularly well placed to provide.[140]

New financial arrangements after 1980 allowed local governments to retain a portion of the revenues from their tax receipts;[141] enterprises also received an increase in their freedoms, including the right to keep some of their own profits, along with less supervision over their hiring practices. These various incentives propelled a feverish construction drive that cried out for extra labor.[142] Judith Banister calculates that over the years between 1978 and 1988 nonagricultural employment increased at more than 6 percent a year.[143] Capital construction alone rose in Beijing, Tianjin, and Shanghai two- to threefold, while urban labor forces in those cities went up from 16.65 million to only 18.2 million, a growth of just 9 percent between 1981 and 1988. Moreover, the stringent one-child-per-family birth control policy beginning in the late 1970s, with its mounting decline in the urban birthrate, spelled a drop in the numbers of city people entering the work force.[144] Obviously, outside workers would have to make up the difference.[145]

It was not just that jobs increased in the cities; two other factors were also at work. After 1978, the Ministry of Labor relaxed the former recruitment system, whereby young people were forced to wait for job assignments from their local labor bureaus.[146] Already in 1979, with the termination of the policy of sending city youths to the countryside that had been a hallmark of the Cultural Revolution, rusticated young people started returning home. That summer, economic adviser Xue Muqiao proposed permitting young people to set up their own privately funded and operated enterprises, in order to remove the strain of creating jobs for them all from the shoulders of the state.[147] This assent to outside-the-plan, effectively private, employment, endorsed by the party Central Committee in summer 1980, laid a foundation that peasants soon built upon as well.[148]

And with the reforms inviting foreign investors into the country, city youths found new employment opportunities on their own in classy occupations such as tourism and foreign trade and therefore rejected

careers in the traditional trades, such as textiles, machinery, silk manufacture, and building materials.[149] As one source decried, "City people
would rather do nothing than this" (referring to such arduous jobs as
drilling waterways or repairing roads and bridges).[150] Their attitude, of
course, created openings for the peasant workers.

Furthermore, produce marketing and the service sector in general in
the cities had been decimated after twenty-five years of denigration and
banning.[151] Once legitimacy was lent the realm of circulation and competition after 1978, for the first time in decades big cities got a chance to
satisfy their gaping demands for fresh food as well as for services of all
sorts.[152] To give one example of the opening this afforded the peasantry,
as much as 69 percent of all the hired labor engaged by private enterprises
in industry and commerce in Beijing in the 1980s (over ten thousand
people) were outsiders.[153]

Besides these policies that called for drawing on a larger pool of workers beyond the cities, there was the impact of an increasing cost- and
profit-consciousness in the firms, an important product of the government's reforms. Factories that formerly had only to meet state-assigned
output targets and to care for the lives of their workers and staff now
found themselves developing a dependence upon more expendable workers who did not demand benefits. The use of temporary workers gradually
undermined the famous "iron rice bowl," as in the institution of the
labor contract system in 1986 and the decision in 1992 to require state
employees to contribute to their own pension funds.[154] And the floating
population, an often underentitled or unentitled group of laborers, became the limiting case of this trend.

The externalities created by all these policies that aimed at rapid
growth had a common effect. Finally the state had found a very cheap
way to make massive use of the labor reserve that peasants had long been
made to constitute, keeping them subjects—and urban noncitizens—as it
did so. They fostered economic growth even as, left to fend for themselves, they freed the state from its charge of provisioning all of the city's
residents.

Changing Policies toward Peasants' Movement

Besides all these other initiatives that stood at the core of the program of
economic reform, a separate series of decisions dealt directly with geographical mobility. But promigratory policies did not come immediately
with the birth of reform. In 1981, when some rural residents had just

begun to make their way into town,[155] a characteristically harsh State Council directive appeared. It ordered strict control over their flow and refused to grant them an urban *hukou*, even if they should become city dwellers.[156] This ruling was a product of the economic retrenchment then in force that was much akin to the one in the early 1960s, when economizing had predominated over growth.[157]

By 1983, however, more energetic reforming was afoot across the board, and in April a sufficient number of central politicians relented on migration accordingly, as evidenced in the State Council's Regulations concerning Cooperative Endeavors of City and Town Laborers. This was a document quite distinguished in spirit from what that council had decreed only sixteen months before. Now rural residents were permitted to move into market towns, albeit without shedding their rural registration and relying not on the state's grain rations but on food they had brought in themselves.[158] One major city, Wuhan, drew up its own local stipulations, in which, unlike in the 1950s, it was no longer necessary for a migrant to come in under a group contract signed between an urban firm and a collective or commune. Also, as against the national 1958 regulations on registration, this one let outsiders remain not just three but a full six months before having to renew their certificates.[159]

Following that, an even more lenient ruling appeared in the party Central Committee's Notice on Rural Work, the party's Document Number One for 1984.[160] By that time, at least some officials had discerned that peasants in cities could invigorate urban economies, provide much-needed services and fresh food, and serve as raw labor power there, even as their departure from the countryside simultaneously reduced problems of rural poverty and surplus agricultural population. This new document not only allowed any peasants who wished to work or do business to enter small towns, if equipped with funds and if eating their own grain; it even asked the localities to carry out experiments in which peasants would actually settle down in selected towns.

Later in the year the state offered peasants a chance to obtain a new kind of nonagricultural registration (titled the *zili kouliang chengzhen hukou*, the urban registration for those with self-supplied grain). According to the circular's preamble, this opportunity came as a result of "urgent demand" from the growing numbers of peasants streaming into the market towns. Thus it was probably more a recognition of a fait accompli than a license for a sudden change in reality. The decision, a State Council Notification on the Question of Peasants Entering Towns and Settling of

October 1984, was specifically aimed, like the two previous circulars, just at those who could raise their own funds, take care of their own grain, and find a place of abode in the market towns.[161]

But still, the document specifically excluded peasants from moving into county seats. Although this chance for switching *hukou* instantly enticed hundreds of thousands nationwide to surge into towns,[162] those who did so soon found that the treatment they received was clearly second-class.[163] Nonetheless, a number of researchers trace the first rush in numbers to this period, though this was also no doubt in part a result of a sudden reexpansion in the urban-rural income gap, which had been steadily closing in the early 1980s.[164]

In July 1985, the Ministry of Public Security issued Provisional Regulations on the Management of Population Living Temporarily in the Cities, an effort to ensure its control over the floating population and to increase its data on it. Perhaps the greatest significance of this new measure lay in its implicit recognition that the coming of peasants to towns was now a fact of life, thereby tacitly legitimizing the indefinite presence of peasants in cities of all sizes. It created a category of peasants whose work would keep them in town for more than three months and gave them their own special certificate, labeled the "card for residents living with others" (*jizhu zheng*).[165]

This document also specified that anyone staying in a town longer than three days (or the head of the unit providing domicile to them) needed to apply for temporary residence registration. But it made it possible for outsiders to rent dwelling places, or to live in hotels and inns in urban areas, and explained the procedures to use in doing so. A year later another document legalized the sale of grain at negotiated prices to peasants at work in the cities (regularizing what had already been taking place anyway); it did much to facilitate longer stays.[166]

Thus, by the middle of the decade the state had acquiesced in the right of ruralites to make at least a temporary home in the cities. But it took no responsibility for the material or physical well-being of peasants in the city, as this quotation makes clear:

> Large and medium-sized governments still strictly limit the transfer of the status of peasants, in order to control the extent and the burden of urban welfare, but [nonetheless] they have tacitly permitted and even welcomed peasants' entering towns.[167]

The unspoken message was that the peasants were embraced just so long as they remained "peasants" and did the work in the cities that only peasants would do, and so long as they refrained from expecting the treatment in the cities that "belonged" only to full-fledged urbanites.

Another big change was the citizen identification card, which the government introduced in the mid-1980s in addition to—and, supposedly, to strengthen—control over household registration.[168] The cards became mandatory for everyone over sixteen years of age on September 15, 1989.[169] But as one researcher points out, although not necessarily the intention, once the cards had been distributed they served as passes in their own right, enabling anyone to travel and take a job without first obtaining their local government's approval.[170]

In 1988 the State Council and the Ministry of Labor put still another stamp of approval on the outflow from the countryside, this time with a recommendation that provinces with impoverished populations "export" their labor.[171] As with all of the earlier "reform" announcements, this one too was very probably the legitimization of practices already under way.

And in both 1989 and again in 1991 the State Council issued rulings on the management of temporary labor in state enterprises, thereby formalizing this practice.[172] The two sets of rules, the first provisional, the second final, were both distinguished in an important way from similar measures of the 1950s. Along with the increases in enterprise autonomy in the reform years, firms could sign contracts directly with workers themselves, and only afterward report this to the local labor department for approval. Though the city labor department was to specify the numbers of such workers each enterprise could engage,[173] certainly the authorization to hire peasants one by one enhanced the likelihood that these rural workers would leave home. Indeed, over a period of less than a decade, more than 10 million rural residents got urban jobs following legal procedures.[174] The numbers who did so without reporting their employment is unquestionably far, far higher.[175]

The direction of policy evolution was obviously toward greater and greater permissiveness over the first decade after reforms began. This process was also one of simply accepting developments that were the product of other decisions. Despite the increasingly liberal policies, state leaders retained their urge to monitor and regulate the migration, and, by keeping peasants temporary residents, to ensure that this mobility would be cheap and fiscally advantageous, as this quotation indicates:

> Increases in city population mean increasing the burden on the nation [and the writer enumerates various strains already present in the city]. . . . If one wants to change this type of situation then the state has no

choice but to make large-scale investment in city construction. But we are at present involved in the very important task of the four modernizations, and if we are to put these magnificent undertakings into practice, then we will need huge amounts of capital. Therefore, if a city's rate of population increase outstrips the rate of economic development, it is bound to have a negative effect on the construction of the four modernizations.[176]

Leaders' Views

Although policies permitting peasants into the cities gradually emerged throughout the 1980s, a number of top leaders are on record as agreeing with this cautious and rather negative perspective. As the numbers in motion swelled by the late 1980s, many of the most important among them came down clearly on the side of keeping farmers at bay in the fields, far away. For instance, Yao Yilin, still a Politburo member and vice premier at the time, spoke purely from the perspective of an urban leader when he told a December 1988 national meeting of labor bureau managers that "labor departments ought to concentrate on reducing the numbers of people from the rural population coming into the cities," going on to explain the drain these intruders placed upon city budgets. "Each time we add one person in the city this increases the state's burden, from the point of view of subsidies," he instructed.[177]

Soon after, then-Premier Li Peng insisted at the second session of the seventh National People's Congress in March 1989 that

> Peasants entering the cities in large numbers isn't a way out; for the past few years we have specified a policy of "leaving the land but not the countryside"; I think this policy is still very feasible. In the rural areas, continue to develop agricultural production, engage in the tertiary industries and in town and village enterprises, absorb this labor power, create wealth, improve livelihood.[178]

Vice Premier Tian Jiyun's late 1992 advice to poor rural areas to encourage their workers to leave in search of income and to learn new skills was a rare exception to the chorus.[179]

By the mid-1990s, though new ideas had emerged among the leaders, the old emphasis remained for many of them. Vice Premier Zhu Rongji, then a member of the powerful Standing Committee of the party's Politburo, a man associated with economic reform who took a major role in the formation of national economic policy at the time of this remark, explained in a late 1994 interview that in order "to stop the influx, we are creating rural industries and liberalizing agricultural prices."[180] His rationale was that, if peasants received better compensation for their produce, they could be persuaded to stay put. Soon thereafter he fleshed out this concept more fully:

> We shouldn't talk lightly about "the mass relocation of the rural population" at this stage. Only when peasants' enthusiasm has been greatly raised and the output of agricultural produce has been greatly increased can we talk about their relocation to new towns and new large and small enterprises.
>
> If we talk about the mass relocation of the rural population now, peasants will all wish to go to the big cities to make lots of money. How can this be tolerated? Nowadays about 20 million peasants are migrating to the cities each year. This cannot be tolerated. . . . Today, we still need to . . . make peasants stay in the rural areas.[181]

Qiao Shi, then also a Politburo Standing Committee member, chairman of the National People's Congress (NPC), and formerly from the security network, similarly recommended putting the idle peasantry to work in the countryside at this point, building rural roads and water conservancy facilities. The other options he saw were to ensconce them in town and village enterprises (TVEs) or in small towns and cities, all plans that would keep them away from the metropolitan areas.[182]

State Councillor Chen Junsheng, who had responsibilities for public security affairs, referred in early 1995 to "some" who advocated shifting farm labor to large and medium cities or to economically developed regions. He, to the contrary, evincing distaste at the thought of farmers in cities, as well as confidence that the regime could control their mobility, proclaimed that

> This, however, will never become the principal way. The development of China's agriculture today requires the input of a large amount of human labor. The principal way to place the surplus rural labor still lies in the rural areas; they should be absorbed in the vast rural areas. It would be wrong to place our hopes solely on moving them to the large cities. China's level of urbanization is rather low, there are not too many cities, cities are inadequately developed, and the capacity of large and medium cities to accommodate labor is limited. Unemployment remains a rather acute problem in most of China's cities.
>
> If we adopt a hands-off policy, labor would rush to the cities in large numbers, aggravating the problem of urban employment. We should, rather, set our eyes on the rural areas, on absorbing the surplus labor force in the rural areas.[183]

Another high official, then Labor Minister Li Boyong, called for depending on the TVEs to solve the employment problem. Here once again was a major figure evincing a desire to keep farmers far from the urban centers, in his case in the interest of retaining city jobs for city folk.[184] Thus, as of the middle of the 1990s, more than a decade after the migration had begun, a number of prominent politicians with authority over general economic, employment, and security matters—as well as over the NPC, respectively—were united on the overarching goal of attempting to harness the farmers to the fields.

But some members of the top elite must have entertained different conceptions at that point. For a dichotomy of reactions and aims appeared in central-level proclamations at a summer convention of 1995 devoted to the administration of the floating population. While one leader announced that it was "necessary to absorb rural surplus laborers locally," another held that "firm and effective measures should be adopted to ensure a rational and orderly movement of rural surplus laborers."[185]

In general, then, over the years central-level politicians as a group modified their prereform exclusionary stance somewhat. This they did as they eventually decided—perhaps rather quixotically—that using officially engineered labor markets to bring in migrants could make for an all-around positive outcome. For such guidance could check any potential chaos coming from farmers in town, while the peasants' presence would stimulate economic growth. But after a decade or so of experience many leaders individually continued to hold steadfast to the notion that for the future, where possible, peasants had best stay out of town.

· · ·

In this chapter we have seen the genesis of the connection between the state and those who would one day become Chinese peasant migrants. By situating this relationship in light of the differing projects of the various states that have ruled China, the dynastic, the Republican, and the pre- and post-1978 Communist ones, the chapter showed how the Communist state after 1949, with its new power and aims, shifted older policies in order to transform the farmers of China into an industrial reserve army. The principal way in which the leadership achieved this end was by altering the stance of the state toward geographical mobility, installing a form of largely state-managed migration. It first set boundaries around peasants, marking them off as a separate, ascribed status group—almost a pariah class—and then barring them from entering urban areas. Or if they did come in, it was just as subjects, never as citizens.

Unlike either the late dynastic state or its Republican successor, the pre-1980 Communist state sought to manipulate rural-to-urban migration, making it illegal. Soviet-Marxist goals of unimpeded industrialization and regime-controlled growth through central planning made for municipalities run cheaply but provisioned sufficiently so that urbanites, the holders of the privileged urban *hukou,* would be peaceable and suitably productive. Peasants were drawn into the towns occasionally through the lure of urgent manufacturing often taking place there; they were pushed aside when supplies grew scarce or growth targets were scaled down.

On the surface the post-1978 reform-era measures appeared to transform the policies of the socialist Chinese state toward its wanderlusting agricultural producers. Its politicians' gradually expanding permissiveness toward peasant movement off the land suggested a novel approach toward migrating peasants. And yet in important ways the content of its connection did not shift so much after all. By denying the ruralite the right to urban citizenship, the *chengshi hukou,* the state was able to resolve the contradiction that had befuddled it since the 1950s: peasants could now enter the cities and contribute to the productivity there, but the state need not provide for them.

3 Urban Bureaucracies I
Migrants and Institutional Change

State policy that converted urban-dwelling peasants into industrial drudges was only one prong in the production of the floating population. There were also the powerful state bureaucracies that executed this policy. But these offices—though obviously a critical component in the structure shaping farmers' stay in the cities—did not jostle with the transients and emerge unscathed. In this chapter, we observe the process whereby rural outsiders became unintentional agents of institutional transformation for the managers of the state.

The process had three dimensions, all involving the bureaucrats' gradual accommodation to the presence of migrants, along with officials' increasing acculturation to the transition from a planned to a market economy. But, despite the state's introduction, with time, of rhetoric about law, as of the late 1990s none of this had added up to enhanced chances for genuine urban citizenship for transients.

The first dimension of change occurred once markets (for food, jobs, housing, and basic services) appeared in the cities. The strangers who simultaneously took up residence in town and offered their own cheap, unentitled labor for sale soon brought to the fore fundamental value contradictions among both functional and geographical bureaucratic offices. These were conflicts—among the values of order and economic growth—that had been more or less latent under the regime of the state plan, when officials had urgently worked to meet quotas and achieve their common objective of plan fulfillment.

With the coming of peasants, some bureaus and areas initially emphasized the priority of forestalling the potential chaos with which their cadres associated outsiders. Others, backed up by the permission granted by the state's new promarket policies, became more blatantly geared toward economic development and income generation. Thus, migrants' existence in town intensified internal divisions within the state. These divisions led to new implicit coalitions and alliances for and against migrants, as well as to a newfound market-driven competition not just among bureaucratic offices, but also among various provincial and urban jurisdictions, and between administrative echelons within the same bureaucracy.

Second, the combination of markets and migrants, both—from the perspective of bureaucrats—operating seemingly spontaneously and unpredictably, exposed the futility of attempting to plan and direct geographical movement that answered to supply and demand. This mix also forced the members of the bureaucracy to face the fruitlessness of trying to coordinate their disparate objectives—once these had emerged—in the hope of bringing some control over the sojourners moving into or stopping within their jurisdictions. So migrants and markets revealed the incompetence—really, the failure—of planning in this general realm.

Third, the upshot was that urban state officials, still intent on taking hold of the situation, and remaining in command of substantial resources while hoping to claim ever more of them—despite or in response to the progress of marketization[1]—managed in time to turn at least some among their region's transients into commodities. They commodified not just the itinerants but the acquisition of citizenship itself. Because of the excessive amount of rules and regulations in once-socialist China (those pertaining to the *hukou* at their core), anyone with power could charge for helping an applicant implement or evade them. Opportunities for rent-seeking, in short, were legion.

Thus the prior exaggerated state of bureaucratization in China laid the groundwork for commodification to become the chief mode of migrant-manager interaction once markets came onto the scene. In the language of Karl Polanyi, speaking of change in a society that was previously agricultural,

> ... the transformation [to industrial capitalism and production with the help of specialized machines] implies a change in the motive of action ... all transactions are turned into money transactions. ... [It] involves in effect, no less a transformation than that of the natural and human substance of society into commodities. The conclusion, though weird, is inevitable.[2]

The effect was all the greater where inchoate capitalism collided with a governmental structure laced up and down with minute directives and prohibitions, all anchored upon the *hukou* barrier against peasants in cities.

With time even those units—such as the labor and public security bureaucracies—which typically placed a premium on stability, started to see the promises of payoffs in the new environment. Accordingly, they began to appeal (even submit) to the guidance given by the forces of supply and demand, in lieu of their old dependence on compulsion alone. This altered perspective no doubt was at least in part a product of their recognition of something crucial that Hein Mallee suggests: without the "strong state control over daily life" that the regime enjoyed before the incursion of market forces, the impotence of simple administrative intervention became obvious.[3] Other commentators, discussing places as disparate as Western Europe and Mexico, concur in this observation.[4]

For managers and for those transients with the requisite funds, both citizenship and the state of being unsettled became potentially marketable products that bureaucrats and people in motion (or, at any rate, away from their original homes) could sell and buy in exchange for an artificial, substitute (and, surely, inferior) form of citizenship. As the two groups joined in this trade, once-Communist cadres participated in a form of institutional change: in permitting the commercialization, the purchase, of what was previously and simply city people's inalienable birthright, they altered the exclusivity of urban citizenship.

One more alteration occurred as urban public agents became party to the market. Their discourse began to feature notions such as services, interests, and even legal rights and obligations between themselves and their "foreign" charges.[5] But these shifts in their leaders' speeches and documents appeared just in the methods regulators were told to adopt (or to mouth) in managing migrants, not yet in the methods they really employed. As, in the absence of an effectively operative legal framework in China, simultaneous instructions and practice went in the other direction, it is quite possible that the intention, at least at the start, was more to achieve better control than it was truly to let legality determine behavior.

So in all three respects—the creation of cracks within the bureaucracy; the recognition that the old and customary plan was flawed; and the construction of a consciousness in officials of market processes (useful, they discovered, both for enrichment and for enhanced mastery)—we see fundamental alterations in the regulatory framework. But, despite the eventual resort to a rhetoric of legality in the early 1990s, in the absence of actual lawfulness, true city citizenship for country people stayed strictly off-limits.

INSTITUTIONAL CHANGE

The old planned economy, like any social institution, afforded the bureaucrats who ran it a stable predictability, a sense of order and organization, reliability of expectations, routinization of procedure.[6] The conformity of conduct it engendered made it possible "to coordinate many simultaneous activities so as to make them mutually consistent," in the words of James G. March and Johan P. Olsen.[7] Its mandate to meet output targets clearly defined working assumptions and goals, even in times of upheaval. Command, and the expectation of obedience to instructions, structured incentives at both official and mass levels and thereby provided harmonization to general societal activity. Thus the plan, even when relatively loose, subject to switches, circumvented by elaborate subterfuges, and set at local echelons, remained the key institution in China for decades, the source of social cues, at least where economic behavior was concerned.

Scholars often treat institutions as fixed consensual modes of conduct that are fairly impregnable. True, some recognize that what Ronald L. Jepperson calls "reinstitutionalization"—"exit from one institutionalization and entry into another institutional form, organized around different processes or rules"[8]—may occasionally occur. But the general assumption is that the massive redistributive effects such a shift portends must involve a massive power transfer.[9] In this view, revisions in the rules of social life occur just under conditions of—and as the outcome of—open competition over power.[10]

In recent years political scientists interested in transitions have focused their research on transformations purely within the *political* realm, where official redistributions of political power take place, as if changes in the explicitly political "rules of the game" alone make a difference. But the Chinese leadership's initial decision to unleash market forces—a move that gradually decimated the institution of the economic plan[11]—also ushered in a "reinstitutionalization."

Yet this change was one not brought about—as such studies imagine are necessary—by any open or explicit contestation among political groups or social forces (nor did it lead, even over nearly two decades, to overt alterations in the political rules or structures). Representative of the more conventional perspective on such transformation is this surmise of Jack Knight's:

> In a nondemocratic state . . . the structure of institutional bargaining is mainly between the state and powerful interest groups and formal institutions are the product of private contracts between the state and those groups.[12]

In China, to the contrary, this decision of state leaders to allow, even encourage, the operation of market forces to attract farmers into the metropolises was a resolution leaders reached on their own, in the interest of invigorating productivity, and in the absence of any open expression of preference by the actors involved. For surely the actors most affected, the powerless peasants, could never on their own—either by explicit word of mouth or by public demonstration—have engineered the outcome.

Thus the rearrangement of power relations, both among groups and between groups and the state, unfolded through the logic of the forces of supply and demand, rather than through any open political negotiation.[13] Indeed, the market forces, once set into motion—of which peasant movers took advantage—led to an essential impotence of the bureaucracy, as this quotation from an official source indicates: "The old system [of the planned economy] is no longer effective in holding back the city-bound population flow."[14]

Similarly, a district official in Beijing, facing massive numbers of businesspeople who came from other parts of the country, remarked: "We had to retreat all the time. There was no other way, for the situation is always developing beyond reach."[15] We go on to examine the effects of migrants' collision with the institutions of the planned economy, as they combined with markets to undermine it.

THE PLANNED ECONOMY FALTERS: SPLITTING UP THE BUREAUCRACY

Soon after peasants began making their way into the cities, a regulatory structure emerged to cope with them. It appeared place by place, not all at once, and its particulars were designed by individual cities, not by the central government. But it was stamped everywhere by the institutional modalities of the planned economy.[16] For all these local regimes for handling peasants in town shared that institution's penchant for specified and exacting procedures, preordained quotas, and prohibitory provisions, paired with punishments for violation. In general, in the early 1980s cities turned most of their attention to issues of ensuring that firms engaging "foreign" (*wailai*) workers first obtain approval to do so from the city's labor bureau, and that their quantities be kept within specified bounds.[17]

Nearly all the major offices at the urban level quickly became involved in the administration of transients' affairs: among those whose work was most affected were the ones in charge of labor, construction, public security, the Industrial and Commercial Administration (ICA), civil affairs, family planning, taxes, public health, housing, commerce, transportation, and grain. In addition, the Ministry of Agriculture, as the advocate for peasants' interests,[18] increasingly spoke in favor of allowing farmers to move into cities and repeatedly insisted that the negative impact of their doing so would be negligible.[19]

What all of the urban bureaus and commissions—already laden with obligations lent by their primary job of overseeing ordinary, permanent residents—had in common was, first of all, that they each found their functions multiplied just by the presence of new numbers in town. All of them found as well that their roles often also became hopelessly complicated by the fundamentally capricious nature of the migrants' daily existence.

But the old pursuit of departmental interest in the various offices, along with the unwillingness of cadres in any one unit to submit to the authority of those in another, kept them divided, unable to forge a cooperative, united front.[20] So when it came to migrants, the various agencies each had their own perspectives and corresponding objectives, some actually welcoming the visitors as potentially lucrative elements, others wishing rather to whisk them away as disruptive intruders encroaching on the urban turf. Additionally, the influence of market forces activated splits among both the functional and the geographical divisions of the state bureaucracy, creating latent alliances for and against migrants, as new opportunities brought to the fore and heightened the differences among them that their disparate missions had already long ago fashioned.

Most fundamentally, the contrast was one between those offices (and their officials) who continued to hold fast to the order goals that were ultimately paramount under the planned economy, and those who turned their efforts toward revenue generation and profit making, apparently even at the cost of possible social instability. Migrants served as a metaphor for markets, and the stance of a particular office toward the migrants mirrored its receptivity to markets. Before noting the bureaucracies' reception of migrants, I draw on interviews to sketch their respective responsibilities. My interviews took place in Wuhan and Tianjin, both of them large cities that are commercial entrepôts and became homes to many migrant peasants.

The Bureaucracies: Functions

The labor bureau mainly had authority over the members of the floating population who became factory workers.[21] For these it set hiring quotas, on both a per factory and a per district basis; gave permission for hiring; issued permits; authorized contracts; and carried out periodic inspections. The bureau was also charged with limiting the numbers of outside laborers in the city—which could involve forcing the dismissal of outsiders hired in what it determined was "excess," or exacting fines for their presence. The priority commitment to servicing local labor, a guarantee that meant skimping on nonnatives, was summed up by an official in Tianjin: "We tell the factories just to use local labor, if they can get enough of it." Only when local labor could not fill the need would bureau officials accept alterations of the annual quota for outsiders, at least through 1992.[22]

In Wuhan, the planning commission and the labor bureau jointly set targets for the city's permissible intake of outside workers. The overall city quota was then broken down by sector and area in conjunction with the various firms' and districts' applications. In fact, into the early 1990s the city sported two employment plans, one specifying the number of outside workers and one for the regular workers for each state-run factory. Wages were issued for the plant by the bank in accord with this plan. In the late 1980s and in 1990, the quota for outside labor in Wuhan was 90,000 per year.[23]

The construction commission was responsible for the subcategory of manual laborers engaged in the many aspects of building and renovation, from the simplest digger to the sophisticated electrician and interior designer.[24] Like the labor bureau, its role for its own clientele was to issue work permits and ensure the validity of contracts.[25] Under the commission, the construction management section supervised the outside teams, while its various subdivisions oversaw bidding, the behavior of the teams, and the quality of their work. Another subdivision set the prices and standards used in the imposition of fees. The commission, however, left the internal management of the teams, including the wages paid the workers and the level of their welfare benefits (if any), to the bosses of the teams themselves.[26]

Under the ICA two sections were concerned with the migrants, an office for individual and private entrepreneurs, and one for the open markets.[27] Both offices had the right to determine, within nationally set limits, the level of management fees assessed for various types of nonfactory labor (in general, fees for labor were higher than those for doing business) and for different kinds of produce; they also dispensed business licenses. The ICA eschewed direct supervision over the outsiders, turning them over to the Individual Entrepreneurs' Association to watch.[28]

Those planning to open restaurants or to be barbers needed only a sanitation certificate from the public health department; those who would be doing business needed a location. In spite of the power of these offices to certify and legitimize—theoretically, a local *hukou* was required to do business in a city—their officials took a surprisingly casual attitude toward entrepreneurs whose firms were too small in scale or whose labor seemed too insignificant to manage, such as nursemaids, carpenters, cobblers, helpers in restaurants and stalls. As one commented,

> Coming without a license is illegal, but nursemaids, helpers in restaurants, and helpers at stalls don't need it. Carpenters, laborers, and shoe repairpeople can do without it. Some carpenters get a license and some don't; they should have it, but if not, it's hard for us to control. There's no way to force them.[29]

Market management committees also admitted to having found no way to gain control over peasant garbage-pickers.[30]

Civil affairs departments were responsible for the vagrants among the floating population. For the most part, they handled those luckless wanderers caught by the public security in a state of "three withouts": that is, those without legal certificates, proper professions, or fixed living places, the classic category of the *mangliu*, or "blind wanderers."[31] Civil affairs officials sought to clarify where the vagabonds had come from (the officials I met had become experts in discerning the dialects of the home counties of many of them); to cure their illnesses, if any; to preach to the young people among them; and to provide them with a minimal quantity of sustenance and clothing.

But the civil affairs bureaucracy was not really geared toward welfare, properly understood. Its members directed their energies to detaining itinerants (in custody, at hard labor on farms or in centers called *shourongsuo*), until they could be sent on their way back home.[32] This dispatch was accomplished either by handing them a free train ticket or by personally escorting them. If the persons were deemed to hail from a nearby place, they might be sent on their way in a matter of days; if they came from within the same province, the period could be up to two weeks, or as much as a month if they came from further away. Although this department's personnel went to substantial effort to connect with the wanderers' home governments, writing letters and phoning, their work was largely thankless, for recidivism was rife.

Officials of the Tianjin family planning commission had a threefold task: dispensing birth-history cards; propagating policy; and helping with problems of daily livelihood.[33] It is likely, however, that insofar as transients were concerned, more of their time was spent on ferreting out the delinquents—those giving unauthorized birth in the city—than in serving the law-abiding. "We go and check on changes in their situation, and there are a lot of these," confided one official. Like the officers in civil affairs, these bureaucrats also needed to keep contact with the home townships of the transients: ideally, any births were to be recorded in the place of original residence. But as late as the end of 1995, the *Chinese Population News* reported that "because of the lack of unified and coordinated actions by units concerned, the principle of joint control by the place of permanent residence and the site of current residence of the floating population can't be enforced effectively."[34]

In an attempt to bind them—as the members of the "regular" urban population were bound—within and under the watch of some sort of "unit," every workplace was to have someone managing birth control; every landlord who rented to an outsider was responsible for reporting to the local street committee; managers from the ICA were to superintend those in the open markets; families were to watch over the nursemaids they hired; street and residents' committees were to oversee the unattached and those in hotels; and the counters in stores where they sold were also to keep track. But usually these charges went unmet: tacit agreements between landlords and their tenants stymied these intentions, for instance;[35] and those sleeping in construction tents (generally as the workers' cooks), shantytown shacks, and in the open were largely beyond anyone's reach.

National regulations fixed business taxes for licensed businesspeople at 3 percent of business volume, thereby limiting the discretion of city tax bureaus. But the city tax bureau could flexibly set the temporary business tax (*linshi jingyingshui*) in its open markets, a tax targeted mainly at the unlicensed, within a margin of 5 to 10 percent, as decreed by the central government, and this tax was collected locally.[36] Thus the migrant merchants' markets offered a definite prospect of boosting the city's tax intake.

The public health department was to address the infectious diseases to which the frequently filthy conditions in floaters' communities made their inhabitants susceptible. Its functionaries were charged with attempting to vaccinate the preschool children of the migrants; with inspecting the sanitary conditions among caterers and barbers and compelling the ill among them to cease working; and with regulating the sterilization of cooking utensils and the cleanliness of the areas' surrounding stalls. They were also kept busy investigating and taking preventive measures at construction sites, in the markets, and in any other places where transients congregated.[37] But the constant arrival of new outsiders and the frequent mobility of those already in town undermined the efficacy of their efforts.

Up until the early 1990s the housing department enforced a mid-1984 national regulation against renting state-owned housing to outsiders.[38] By 1991, however, policy was changing, though the bias toward ensuring dwelling space for permanent residents was still overriding, as this comment evinces: "Residents' housing is very tense, so we can't let everyone [from outside] rent, or the situation for the regular residents would be even worse [than it now is]."[39]

Moreover, the housing officials were tasked with confiscating housing if a private homeowner were to sell or rent to a nonlocal without first obtaining official permission. As policy gradually became more lenient, however, it became permissible in Tianjin—to give one example—to rent in a private home so long as one held a business license from the ICA, a ruling reached explicitly to encourage outsiders to come to Tianjin to do business.

It was also up to the housing bureau to examine rental contracts and to verify that all was in order. That entailed obtaining clarity as to ownership, the condition of the housing, the amount of the rental charge, the potential renter's possession of the identification card of the renter, and the intended use. But those in cities' outskirts—where huge numbers of transients were located and management personnel scarce—usually escaped the net of the law.

This brief overview of the duties of the dozen or so agencies concerned with the transients suggests that a gamut of viewpoints existed among them in regard to how to handle these outsiders. The respective divergent long-standing objectives of the various offices helped dictate this range of perspectives. But the presence of the market and its incentives gave them a new focus.

The Bureaucracies: Perspectives

The disparate stances of the various units were a function of the extent to which an office's chief objective was to enhance revenue or maintain order, and also whether its work combined the two goals. Where the duties of the unit's officials afforded rent-seeking opportunities, the two objectives were both brought into play. In these cases, even though the bureau's primary business was the maintenance of discipline, revenue and order aims became blended. I lay out their objectives in table 2.

Units whose chief concern was generating income (revenue and/or rent earning was their goal) expressed—and in their behavior evinced—unreserved approbation for the floating population in their cities. For instance, social scientists in Harbin described a dynamic demonstrating the support of industrial bureau heads—those in command of production in the individual industrial sectors, who directly supervise the firms—for outside labor:

> The city government believes that too many people is a kind of pressure. But the production departments hire them and the government doesn't know about it. After time passes, the production departments go to the government for permission, saying we're dependent on these people to accomplish our task, so the government then acquiesces.[40]

A case in point was a conflict that had surfaced in Tianjin in the early 1990s between one of those individual industrial bureaus, the textile bureau, and the individual plants it oversaw, on the one side, and the city's labor bureau, on the other. The increase in enterprise autonomy and the attendant profit-mindedness that came with market reform[41]—along with the refusal of city people to perform many kinds of industrial work once mandatory job assignments were relaxed—disposed plant managers to yearn for the formal authority to hire the number of peasant workers they required to keep their machines humming.

But the city labor bureau's leaders, in conjunction with the city government, clung into the early 1990s to their customary aim of maintaining the full or nearly full employment of city residents and so wanted to keep down the numbers of outsiders, in the interest of ensuring jobs for the local populace (and social stability within the city).[42] Here the clash between the productivity and revenue-generating objectives of the producers and the order orientation of the quota- and security-minded labor bureau is apparent. There is a definite parallel here with capitalist countries, where employers are more favorable to migrants' entry than are states, which must take up the burden if unemployment ensues.[43]

Table 2. Chief Duties of Urban Bureaucracies
Concerned with the Floating Population

	Order as Goal	Revenue and/or Rent Earning as Goal or Possibility
Individual industrial bureaus	No	Yes
Commerce	No	Yes
Grain	No	Yes
ICA	No	Yes
Public security	Yes	Yes
Labor	Yes	Yes
Construction	Yes	Yes
Taxation	Yes	Yes
Urban transportation	Yes	Yes
Railways	Yes	Yes
Family planning	Yes	Yes
Public health	Yes	No
Housing	Yes	No
Urban appearance	Yes	No
Civil affairs	Yes	No

As for other agencies whose chief concern was generating income, in both Wuhan and Tianjin the commercial commission—probably because its mission (even under the state plan) was to expand circulation and capital turnover—was among the most enthusiastic boosters of the transients.[44] According to Wuhan informants from that bureaucracy,

> There's no pressure on us because of the floating population. They buy a lot and help us expand our sales. Through their TV ads we learn where to buy things, so they give us economic information. And they come here to sell things we don't have, increasing our own local supply.[45]

The city grain department was in agreement with this posture, despite the potential pressure on its own stocks that more residents might bring to bear. For, more important, peasants carried in with them grain to sell.[46]

The ICA's workers had the same general perspective. Though they knew of unlicensed entrepreneurs operating in Beijing's outskirts, they often simply "keep silent."[47] Indeed, deputies from the Tianjin ICA proclaimed,

> We welcome them; they invigorate the economy, bring in the whole country's products and take our products to other places. We don't fear their competition, but just want the market to be active.[48]

Moreover, because of the fees this agency was in a position to assess, the opportunities the outsiders offered them for rent collection were countless.

Members of these four agencies, all trained on furthering economic activity and maximizing receipts, perceived that they had either no or minimal conflicting aims that could interfere with their approval for the transients. This implicit migratory coalition among once socialist organs (though there is no evidence of specific collaboration) served as a functional equivalent to alliances of social groups in industrial democracies whose members benefit from immigration, such as business owners or middle-class households needing nursemaids.[49] For in both sorts of societies—regardless of the formal political structure—those whose interests are primarily in finance, in commerce (whether licit or illicit), or simply in convenience, can, through commodifying them, make common cause with aliens. They thereby help frustrate at the point of execution the government's exclusionary policies.

The duties, and related perspectives, of the seven units who sought order and might also generate revenues were more complex. For their role as regulators positioned them to impose levies, usually illegally or at least well beyond the legal levels, and, at a minimum, to charge for services. Just as a writer on the private, informal sector in Sri Lanka explained, since the transgressions of informal business present chances for bribery, officialdom may sometimes prefer to allow instances of minor wrongdoing to go on, as its members rake up lucre in the process.[50] For the most part, however, these agencies' ultimate commitment to public order and to full command over the administrative terrain under their charge placed them at the forefront of any campaign to control the flow.[51]

The following statements illuminate the essential ambivalence of the public security's situation. The first bluntly sums up its customary official reaction to the migrants:

> Local people of various walks of life all appreciate them; only the public security disagrees. "What's good about them?" its officials ask.

"They upset social order, create a lot of criminal cases, are hard to handle, and keep us constantly on the run!"[52]

This public security perspective—that unmanaged migrants were a sure recipe for havoc—was evident in a 1995 article in the *Legal Paper*, quoting a "senior responsible person from the Ministry of Public Security," who warned ominously,

> If we let go completely, i.e., give a green light to the free choice of employment, [to] blind and disorderly flow of population, and [to] free migration within the country, we will see nothing but chaos.[53]

This horror of disruption harked back to older official Chinese modes of coping with outsiders. In mid-nineteenth-century Hankou, for instance, the chief method of handling destitute outsiders was to offer them the funds for getting out.[54] At the same time in Shanghai city authorities repeatedly essayed to obliterate the crude dwellings of migrants.[55] Later, in the Republican era, police again tried to tear down what they viewed as the "illegal shacks and sheds" of urban transients then in the city, but, as before, to no avail.[56]

Behaving in just the same way, during the recession of 1990, Beijing and Tianjin, among other big cities, sent away migrants in the thousands;[57] Guangdong's and Hainan's battles to round up floaters and chase them out were multiple.[58] There were many, though remarkably futile, accounts of attempts at flattening lean-tos, coming in particular from Guangzhou and Beijing.[59] An especially flagrant example was the case of the demolition of the migrant courtyard structures in Beijing's well-established Zhejiang Village in late 1995.[60] Within a few months of this dramatic destruction, however, many of the transients were back in place.[61]

But this hostile viewpoint must be pitted against the manifold chances for payoffs—and probably even collusion—with which the public security was constantly presented, as well as opportunities for garnering money when its personnel employed their power to intimidate and fine. Such occasions are described in this floater's account:

> Control? If they want to control us, what do they get for it [*yao guanle women, tamen chi shemma*]? Don't mention that on ordinary days we pay all kinds of tribute. At New Year's time, the upper levels send down orders to the police stations that there should be no incidents. They've no choice but to request that we help give them cover. If there are big or special cases, it depends on us brothers to grab the culprit and send him to them, let them gain merit.[62]

There were also side payments available for overlooking *hukou* irregularities, gossip held.[63]

I alluded above to the labor bureau's exclusionary bias toward outsiders; it was matched by the attitude of the construction commission. In the latter's case state officials were not just wary about competition from the cheaper outside diggers and builders; they also alleged that labor done by what they viewed as a rural rabble of unqualified builders was sure to be poor in quality.[64]

And yet certainly some of the officials in both the labor and the construction bureaucracies were not only negative toward the peasants, but also enmeshed in webs of illicit and lucrative payoffs connected with them. Indeed, a volume edited by the Wuhan Labor Bureau contains charges that the labor department itself was rife with embezzlement, favoritism, malfeasance, and dereliction of duty; and that it often operated in contravention of the control figures for outsiders decreed by the city government. The implication was that its staff accepted bribes in exchange for approving the unauthorized (extraquota) use of outside labor.[65] Graft-laced subcontracting was common in the construction trade, as we see in a later chapter.

As for tax officials, certainly they suffered frustrations from the easy mobility of the outsider peddlers, whose skill at evading taxes was legendary.[66] But when queried directly in 1992 in Tianjin, those working there maintained that, as suggested above, the take overtook the vexation: "The state's tax income increases from their presence. In the state's view, tax receipts increase."[67]

Urban transport and other bureaus responsible for city infrastructure, along with the railways, though clearly subject to heightened pressure from the crush of new residents and visitors, did not appear as victimized as one might expect. For, though their administrative problems multiplied, they could count on governmental subsidies should they really fall short. As public utilities, their function was to "serve the people," so they received priority treatment and were thus frequently able to parlay the pressure from peasant riders into extra funding.[68] In Tianjin, the passenger transport office of the public utilities bureau had figured out that outsiders' use of its minibuses earned the unit a lot of income.[69]

Officials in charge of family planning lamented the stresses and complications brought to their work by peasants who arrived in their cities, whose compliance with birth control norms was generally nearly impossible to monitor, since they were not attached to any local unit. "This is the most difficult point in birth planning work, because they have no fixed unit managing them and they frequently move about," admitted staff at the family planning office in Wuhan.[70]

But here too, when caught, such malefactors could be assessed for their misdeeds, to the extent that in one Hebei township, a large part of local revenue derived from fines on births outside the plan.[71] A woman giving birth without permission there could be subject to a fine as high as 10,000 yuan. Though this was a rural area, urban counterparts must have existed. And because the city's own supply of contraceptives was planned in accord with the numbers of the permanent urban population, the pills family planners pushed on the peasants had to be purchased, with the transients' outlay supposedly reimbursed by their rural home governments.

Only the units tasked with upholding decorum in their disparate ways, but usually without much means of drawing rents beyond occasional and petty bribes and fees—public health, housing, urban appearance, and civil affairs—had simply to labor in the service of public order. Thus, while the balance of the agencies could be said to consist of a "regulatory coalition," this coalition, more latent than explicit, contained a definite diversity of interests among the bureaus within it.

Interprovincial Conflicts

As if replicating the tensions between migrant-sending and -receiving countries that exist internationally, the interprovincial movement of migrants in China was definitely perceived to be to the advantage of the sending regions and to the detriment of the receiving areas. Since the decentralization of economic responsibilities that went with the program of economic reform put new financial pressures on local governments, economic accounting came to dominate their reckonings.[72]

So the appearance of market relationships aggravated economic disparities among the provinces in new ways. As we will see in chapter 5, and again as is the case internationally, the places from which peasants departed were poorer and woefully short on both arable and rural industry. Consequently, their rulers felt distinctly disadvantaged and deserving of relief. By contrast, those to which they flowed were flourishing and more able to furnish jobs, although, their leaders complained, surely not an unlimited supply of them.

Fiscally strapped provincial and urban units in the interior determined that they could go some way toward solving their problems by exporting excess labor power: "We consider migrant labor to be a kind of cooperation between eastern and western parts of the country," said Xie Shijie, a

Communist Party secretary in populous Sichuan province. "They leave empty-handed and return rich—it's like making money from nothing."[73] As one scholar explains, poorer provinces quite consciously "use labor export and contracting out labor as an important breakthrough point in getting rich."[74] Sichuan's governor, under pressure at one point, still blatantly refused to cut off the outflow from his province, claiming that the harm to the local economy would be too great. Other cadres in Sichuan similarly demurred, on the grounds that they simply lacked the funds to provide social insurance and unemployment benefits for the province's own surplus rural labor.[75]

But for their part, those in charge of the wealthier areas saw things differently. The planned economy had accustomed those in command of each geographical administrative unit to compete for superior achievements in economic growth and output value, but also to keep down their population size and unemployment levels.[76] For decades their work had been assessed in terms of their ability to meet designated targets in all of these regards. Demonstrating the ongoing power of the plan to define local perspectives, a pair of Guangdong researchers outlined some of the specific interests of the wealthier provinces in a baldly exclusionist essay that appeared as late as 1989.[77] They wrote of how the population pressure posed by the peasant interlopers clashed with national targets for Guangdong's population control by the year 2000: "Incoming people will cancel the effect of our planned birth control program."[78]

They also bemoaned that in-migration would "block the bridge" for the transfer into cities of Guangdong's own rural population, thereby preventing Guangdong from reaching the national average urbanization level. And they complained that what they perceived as intruders were intensifying the contradiction between the supply and demand for labor that the province was already grappling with internally. Together, new influences from market incentives and old inclinations instilled in them by the plan made provincial officials averse to hosting and having to support excess labor power, especially if from the outside.

The conflict between two types of regions periodically erupted in publicized incidents, as at the time of the 1990 Asian Games, when Beijing City authorities peremptorily expelled two hundred thousand outsiders, in the interest of beautifying the environs for foreigner tourists. This imperious initiative roused protests against the capital city's "local protectionism," which the leaders in sending provinces, Shanxi, Hebei, Henan, Shandong, and Anhui, sent up to the central government.[79] Another instance went in the other direction when, several years later,

Sichuan's governor, Xiao Yang, came under an attack from the receiving areas. This time the grievances were those of Beijing City, along with a group of coastal provinces, for Xiao's failure to curb the outward movement of migrant workers from his province.[80]

Certainly in the 1980s, but into the 1990s as well, at times of economic stress peasants could become a kind of "rubber ball," as two journalists characterized them, bounced away by the interior places, but parried by the coast as well.[81] A most graphic account of this comes from a piece of reportage literature, probably describing a scene at New Year's time, when sojourning peasants going to and from home were always on the move in the millions:

> In Dalian station, the peasant workers are stopped as soon as they get off the train, then are quickly driven toward the cars for Beijing and Shenyang.
>
> A batch dispersed away from Beijing are chased to the train for Harbin.
>
> Some, greatly puzzled, inquire: "But we want to return to the south, so why do you make us go north?"
>
> The work personnel in the station, impervious to reason, howl: "When we tell you to get on the train, just get on, and go where you want; as long as you leave Dalian, we've fulfilled our task!"
>
> For those who couldn't afford the fares, Dalian issued a short-distance ticket to Haicheng. So the peasant workers ask, "After we get there, then what?"
>
> The dispersion personnel bellow in response: "We don't care, going a section [along the route] is a section [further from here] [*mei banfa, zou yiduan shi yiduan ba*]!"[82]

In general, as a result of the divergent interests of poorer and richer provinces, migration and regulation were supported, respectively, by the inland and the coast. The paradoxical upshot was that those places most thoroughly partaking in the new market economy were also the ones most loath to let it operate where the mobility of peasants was concerned. Meanwhile, some of those benefiting least from the new open policies of the central government leaned most heavily on the market's promises where they portended a thinning out of their own surplus labor.

This irony is illustrated by a spokesperson from Sichuan, who clamored for central governmental policies that would stimulate the market, but in a direction tilted toward Sichuan, instead of, as they had been, toward the coast.[83] In another example, in early 1995, arguing directly in favor of the market, at least for labor, Xiao Yang criticized Beijing's efforts to limit the inflow of outside workers as "contrary to the laws of a market economy."[84] Other poorer provinces whose officials spoke out for permissiveness toward peasant labor mobility included Hunan, whose party chief was vocal on this score at the 1993 meeting of the National People's Congress;[85] and Henan's governor, Li Changchun, at the following year's session.[86]

Meanwhile, the magnet regions "even resort to local protectionism, discharging rural laborers [who could not find work in their areas] and forbidding the free movement of farmers," according to the official *China Daily*.[87] As examples, at the end of 1994, while Beijing imposed strict measures intended to halt the flow of migrant workers to the cities, the authorities in Guangdong proclaimed an end to the hiring of labor from outside the province (rulings that, of course, could not stick).[88]

That there existed an at least latent alliance between rich provinces and the chief functional components of the "regulatory coalition" may be seen in a joint action undertaken by Guangdong in March 1992. The province was reported then to be working in close collaboration with the ministries of public security, railways, labor, and civil affairs to establish "public order" among job-seeking arrivals.[89] In Haikou two years before, the public security and civil administration organs, and the departments of transportation and communications and of labor, were actually ordered to act in close coordination with army units to "fight against the influx"; in Guangzhou in 1994 the People's Liberation Army was also called in to assist public security officers, the armed police, and the railway police in maintaining order.[90]

And yet, like most of the other members of this undeclared alliance, Guangdong officials were not unambivalent. They too were well aware of the debt they owed the outsiders. According to two traveling journalists:

> At all levels of the Guangdong party and government, right down to the heads of the town and village enterprises, everyone highly praised the contribution of the peasant workers. Provincial Party Secretary [as of 1989] Lin Ruo said, "Without the peasant workers, Guangdong's prosperity wouldn't exist. . . . The tide of peasant workers is an indispensable component part in the drama of Guangdong's, especially the Pearl River Delta's, takeoff drama."[91]

So, given these contradictory pulls on the province, it was not surprising that when the poorer regions extolled the peasant laborers at the 1994 session of the NPC, Guangdong's deputies had what the news media labeled a more "mixed reaction," as they called for "strengthening administrative measures."[92]

Urban Variation in Receptivity

In addition to this direct conflict among provinces wishing to push peasants out and those reluctant to take them in, there were also intercity disparities whereby cities differentially used tax and fee schedules, in order either to attract or to repel nonresidents.[93] Even within fairly narrow limits, a great deal of variation obtained as of the early 1990s.

Some cities were more exclusionary than others and therefore set their charges at higher rates; this was the claim of interviewees from the labor system in Tianjin, where local unemployment was uncomfortably high, as compared with other cities. The work of Hans Hendrischke suggests that an important factor in Tianjin's bias toward order may have been "pressure from Beijing, which did not want political unrest near the capital."[94]

Probably tied to this pressure, in 1992, Tianjin factories had to pay the city labor bureau 10 percent of each peasant employee's wages per month;[95] in Wuhan, where the market orientation was much stronger, the rate was only 5 percent. Also undoubtedly related was the fact that a full 8 percent of the workers in the textile trade in Wuhan were sojourners at that point, while in Tianjin, the corresponding percentage was 0.8, even though the textile trade in Tianjin was then employing more peasant labor than was any other sector in the city.[96] Tianjin, perhaps not just by chance, won acclaim that year for reducing its unemployment rate for local (as opposed to outsider) job seekers more than any other Chinese city had done.[97]

Even within the same city, however, various bureaus worked at cross-purposes, some distinctly more welcoming than others. Again, a Wuhan-Tianjin contrast is instructive. In Wuhan, where, it seems, the public security was more hostile to outsiders (as compared both with the labor bureaucracy there and with Tianjin's public security), factories had to pay this bureau 38 yuan per year for each outside worker in 1992. In Tianjin, the rate was then just 2 yuan per worker per month, according to textile bureau representatives.[98]

Another instance where cities differed was in the management fees, taxation rates, and charges for licenses that outsiders were obliged to pay and purchase. As the first transients made their way into the towns, urban administrations quickly forged a rich structure of exactions, at first in hopes of limiting the numbers of newcomers. With time, this essentially xenophobic approach to the use of levies developed in more marketlike directions, as some city bureaucrats consciously competed for migrants, while others intentionally used high costs to render their own municipalities less attractive.

For instance, cities varied in the level of their management fees assessed on individual and private entrepreneurs doing business (jingshangde). The national rule as of 1992 was that localities were free to set their rates from 0.5 to 1.5 percent of sales volume. Wuhan used the full range of rates permissible, while Tianjin had a fixed rate of 1 percent. This permitted Wuhan to be a haven for the very petty businesspeople, those with incomes of under 500 yuan a year.

Individual entrepreneurs in industry or in the service or repair trades paid management fees in the range of 1 to 3 percent (as of 1992, those earning less than 250 yuan paid at the lowest rate; those with intakes higher than 3,000 were to pay 3 percent) of income in Wuhan. That this city's officials felt free to set the rates higher seems to indicate that, as a major commercial entrepôt, it had little difficulty attracting persons in these professions. In Tianjin, however, the rate was pegged at just 1.2 percent of total income for all comers. This lower rate may have been chosen out of concern about competition with close-by Beijing (which was, comparatively, packed with peasants from outside), in order to draw in more of such workers.[99]

Conversations with floaters along the streets and in the markets revealed further discrepancies, when the management fees that were actually exacted in practice exceeded the official rates. For instance, the vice chairman of the Individual Entrepreneurs' Association in Hanzheng Street, Wuhan, reported that those doing business in his market paid a management fee of 2 percent; and yet the rate set by the ICA for the city as a whole was just 0.5 to 1.5 percent.[100] A butcher, encountered on the street in another area of the city, was also being made to pay at the rate of 2 percent, despite city regulations.[101]

The central government also granted urban officials leeway in determining the tax rates and license fees charged their migrants. And in this realm, as with management fees, localities purposely reduced or increased the costs to incomers in the interest of encouraging or discouraging certain kinds of produce and particular types of traders from entering their towns. Wuhan, for instance, charged no tax at all on vegetables, as an observer might guess from the sight of its open markets, especially lush with leafy greens. Also, aquatic, meat, and egg products were subject to taxes in the range of 3 to 6 percent, considerably below what the capital had specified.[102] Tianjin's rate was, variously, 4 or 5 percent, but for rural sideline products it could be as low as 2 percent. Since city officials preferred to protect their local vegetable farmers, however, a higher tax was put on outsiders' wares in this category.[103]

The amount charged for temporary residence certificates was also distinctly variable among cities. In Wuhan, the public security again showed its vigor: entrepreneurs from the outside had to pay as much as 5 yuan a month in 1992 to hold temporary residence, and nursemaids paid 3 yuan, also on a per-month basis.[104] In Tianjin, however, the temporary certificate cost just 10 yuan for the whole year, though it had to be repurchased annually.[105]

Different sources give widely disparate data for separate municipalities within Guangdong province: in Guangzhou, according to local scholars, the fee for registering was as low as a one-time 5 yuan in 1992;[106] but journalists in Shenzhen assert that for a temporary residence certificate in that city transients were forced to hand over a full 100 yuan in 1990.[107] If true, all this suggests great variability not just among cities or just among bureaucratic agencies but also in regard to the same bureaucracy's stance toward different classes of outsiders.

But however the fees were doctored at the scene, the important point is this: by the early 1990s official municipal rate-setters were fully conscious of—and in interviews explicitly articulated—the potential for manipulation offered by the flexible rate schedules received from the upper levels. In some instances local labor authorities pegged their fees at the high end, expressly to keep down the numbers of outsiders that would be hired by local factories. Meanwhile, in other cases the ICA or its sections might choose to set the lowest rates—even in the very same municipality—in order to attract more itinerant businesspeople into their cities' markets.[108]

Because of these discrepancies, it is impossible to make general statements about the stance of any given city. And given the grave difficulties in counting country folk transient in cities, there is no way to determine accurately the effects on migration of these various tamperings with assessments. What is clear, however, is the influence of market principles upon the operations of local bureaucracies in handling migrants, sometimes in line with, but sometimes acting to reshape, the former missions served by disparate offices.

Interechelon Disputes

Another kind of divergence was the result of disagreements among bureaucratic levels, with officials at the higher echelons of administration usually standing on the side of order, those below striving for market advantage. A good example was identified by Yuen-fong Woon, who determined that in Guangdong there was "a major tug of war" going on between local governments and employers on the one hand and the provincial and central governments on the other during the spring festivals of 1989 and 1990. According to her data,

> The Guangdong provincial government enlisted the support of the central government to push the long-distance migrants back, as it wanted to protect its citizens from unemployment, which would cost the government food and other welfare subsidies . . . [while] local governments and employers found it cheaper to employ long-distance migrants than local workers.[109]

The *Southern Daily* noted the same sort of conflict between Guangdong province and the enterprises there: "The province issues notices forbidding hiring but the factory hires [anyway]," it reported.[110] Similarly, also writing from the Guangdong area, the traveling journalists explained:

> Many city and county governments are caught in the narrow space between the provincial government's ban and the enterprise's rebellion. On the one side they are forced to copy and issue red documents [sent down by the province] strictly banning private hiring; on the other hand, they give tacit consent toward various units' private hiring, keeping one eye open and one eye shut.[111]

Stated in the words of factory managers, "Orders to dismiss come from the upper levels, but if we let them go, we're afraid of having heavy jobs with no one to do them."[112]

This same sort of clash of perspectives cropped up in late 1995 in Beijing, when central government and city leaders ordered the demolition of the large courtyards constructed by wealthy merchants in Zhejiang Village (noted above). Since the city's Fengtai district government relied on the migrants for as much as 40 percent of its revenue, its officials stood on the side of the outsiders. Meanwhile, rancor ran against them just at the higher levels, where worries of disorder overrode any thought of economic benefit.[113]

Here again, as in the case of differences among bureaucratic offices, we find that the mentality introduced by the market economy (combined with the incentives it activated)—a mind-set geared toward generating revenue—operated enthusiastically on behalf of migrants in some areas and at some bureaucratic echelons, but at best just with ambivalence at others. In general, the coming of markets superimposed a frenzy for fund-raising atop the old administrative system, promoting a competition for revenue among those who became participants in these markets plus a new ambivalence about their mission among those in many of the other units.

The battles between those areas where the market was thriving—which became places attracting more outsiders than they could handle—and those pushing them out found echoes among the functional components of the bureaucracy and among its tiers. But managers' old fears of disorder and instability, which the planned economy had instilled in them, gradually succumbed to the lures of the market, especially as the plan itself seemed to crumble from the onslaught.

INADEQUACIES IN ADMINISTRATIVE APPROACHES

Among urban bureaucrats who had been skeptical of or hostile toward transients—such as the officials of the public security, the Ministry of Labor, and the administrators of some major cities, key components of the "regulatory coalition"—there emerged over time a growing recognition that there were definite limits to the capabilities of the static, fundamentally inflexible planned economy. As the bald incapacity of planning to harness interregional mobility became evident, it very likely disposed city managers to experiment with allowing the forces of supply and demand to substitute their novel incentives for those of preordained commands. The inability of local bureaucracies to coalesce around a common goal—managing migrants—and the extent to which rigid official missions, assigned by the planned economy, isolated agencies and worked to push some of them back into the past must have helped shape this awareness.

The Futility of Discipline

By the end of the 1980s, the bullying and regimens that had characterized most urban bureaucrats' first confrontations with in-migrants had given way to other tactics. Many public officials who had felt the pull of the possibilities for making money were also often too frustrated and over-extended, too overwhelmed, to pay city-dwelling peasants' behavior much heed, as this quotation demonstrates:

> Some departments only see the floating population's beneficial aspect
> for developing the commodity economy and not its negative aspect.
> They think they shouldn't limit its scale. Some think their mobility is

so great there's no way for government departments to control them. So they let them drift on their own. Under the direction of the planned commodity economy, the management of the floating population then loses control, and produces many problems.[114]

One example of this incapacity was the behavior of the managers at the housing bureau in Tianjin, some of whom displayed a passivity bordering on paralysis. This became evident as they admitted that peasants failing to follow city regulations on housing rentals would not be punished but simply sent back home. It was useless to fine them, "because they don't necessarily have money to pay. And besides, they have no unit managing them [which could force them to obey]."[115] Just the same tone of resignation marked the words of an official in charge of produce markets, who explained,

> According to regulations, it's not allowed to sleep outdoors at the market. If you do, you'll be criticized and educated. But there's no specific rule on the amount of fine attached to this offense.[116]

Other examples of similar surrender on the part of the bureaus were the Wuhan ICA's admission that "people who set themselves up on the sidewalk [outside the proper marketplaces, without renting stalls] can't be made to pay taxes or fees";[117] and Tianjin tax bureau leaders, who acknowledged that "those who can't be reached can evade their taxes."[118] A wonderful image is that of the nimble peddler, appearing in several different places every day. Meanwhile, the management officer, standing put in a certain time and place, and collecting his or her fees from everyone he encountered once a day, constantly failed to net the peasant. Between the two raged a tense game of match.[119]

The common position of the Tianjin women's federation, labor, construction, and ICA officials represented one more variation on this theme of abdication. Uniformly, one by one, they boasted of having no relations with the "spontaneous labor exchanges" that served the transients, variously terming such markets "too easy to lead to problems," "too full of abuses," or "too hard to manage."

And even when real hostility overcame cadres' ineptitude and contempt, to the extent that some action was attempted, it was usually at best half-hearted and singularly ineffective. As one observer noted,

> Though the public security and the women's federation, along with other concerned departments, jointly banned a black market in nursemaids and posted the ban on the walls near the market, so far it's just a warning, not real interference.[120]

Similarly, when Tianjin's public security employed over 150 officers to clear out an unofficial labor market in Guilin Street in early 1989,[121] it was soon reconstituted by its participants at another spot in town.[122] And a 1994 move to bar peasant job seekers from a site near the Beijing train station (by cordoning off their original locale) merely drove them off a block or two.[123] Indeed, though these markets outside the scope of the law met intermittent harassment from the police, the attempts of the latter to efface them were always ineffectual.[124]

The distaste the outsiders engendered and the disarray that appeared to mark their ranks left the ICA indisposed to set up any form of organization for them at all.[125] And in Shenzhen, according to a Beijing-based news agency,

> Though the local authorities have taken some measures to disperse and repatriate beggars, they seem to be at their wit's end. The traditional measures of detaining, dispersion and repatriation are to no avail.[126]

These various responses were all distinct from the relations that obtained between officials and the ordinary urban population in the days before the command economy was dismantled. They all delineate the increasing impotence of a functioning bureaucratic framework in the face of seeming hordes of outsiders irregularly moving into and about the city—people whom, after all, the urban system was never designed to handle in the first place. This predicament often left officials at a loss and must have educated them eventually in the inefficacies of managing drifters and hawkers by decree.

Problems with Permits

The initial effort to rein in what much of official urban China viewed as roving ruralites entailed setting up rigorous procedures for the registration of their temporary residence in cities. These rules were grounded in the 1958 NPC regulations on household registration, which specified the process for people to follow in establishing their presence legally in a place that was not their site of *hukou.* Its article 16 pertained to temporary residence, though without using that term: it stated,

> If citizens leave their permanent address and go to another region on private business and reside at that new place for three months or more, they must apply for an extension of their residence visa. . . . If there is no valid reason to grant an extension or no basis for an application for permanent residence, they must return to their permanent residence.[127]

Individual cities drew on this ruling and also modified it as they saw fit.[128] For instance, when migrants first appeared in Guangzhou, they were compelled to register after just three days; later, when numbers increased and the authorities began to take outsiders more into stride, they were allowed to wait a full week before reporting in.[129] In late 1994 Beijing, the requirement was to register with the police after just three days and to apply for a temporary residence license after a month.[130] Municipalities all demanded that peasants obtain certification and approval from their home governments—whether through a permit to enter cities (*jincheng-zheng*) or, less commonly, through a letter of introduction[131]—before venturing into town.[132]

Beyond the fact of getting transients to make known their presence in the city, labor permits were a second major concern of the localities, as they are—but just for genuinely *foreign* workers—in Western Europe.[133] Additionally, further procedures existed for working, varying somewhat depending on the trade one wished to enter.

The cumbersome nature of the process into the 1990s is illustrated by the procedures Wuhan's administration dictated for construction teams.[134] Each team had to hold both an operating license granted by the Wuhan ICA and a construction license from the city's construction commission. Obtaining the construction certificate required that the labor boss present a portfolio of prior achievements; a note of approval from the team's own local government for going into the city (*jinchengzheng* or *waichu zhengming*); proof of the possession of a certain amount of liquid and fixed assets; and an entrustment letter (*weituoshu*), showing who would represent the manager in his absence. The construction license then passed to the city's labor bureau, which, if it approved, then issued an outside labor forces' temporary work license. Only then did the team have the legal right to do its work.

For those planning to go into commerce or services, the steps were similarly unwieldy. First the individual had to acquire a certificate (*jingying zhengming*) for doing business from the home government's industrial and commercial management bureau, in addition to the permit to enter the city. Bearing these two documents, the prospective business-person was to approach the city's ICA, and apply there, through an application report (*shenqing baogao*).[135]

The ICA office also required a certificate telling where the person would work (*jingying changdi* [or *changsuo*] *zhengming*); then finally, and only after payment of a fee (about 25 yuan in 1992), it handed over the license for business. Holding this license from the ICA, the individual

had to show that license—along with the home place's letter of introduction—to the city's public security or a neighborhood committee, whose
personnel would then extend a temporary residence permit (*zhanzhu-
zheng*).

If a factory's leaders wished to engage peasant laborers, they needed
to deal with the city labor bureau. First the workers or their group had
to be in possession of a certificate from the home place's government
allowing them to leave and go into the city. Then, the workers had to be
issued a temporary work permit (*linshi gongzuo xukezheng*). Next factory officials were to take this permit to the public security bureau, which
would dispense a temporary residence certificate before the workers or
group would be entitled to sign a contract with the enterprise. No individual was allowed to change jobs without retracing these steps.[136]

In order to comply with the state's policy on birth control, a married
woman migrating into the city had to bring along a pregnancy certificate
from her home government, indicating both that she was married and
the number of offspring she had. This document made her eligible for
the urban version of that certificate, usually in the form of a card, which
she could acquire at a city neighborhood's family planning commission.
Should she arrive without the necessary documentation from home, she
would be ordered home to take care of the procedure.[137] Should she
attempt to remain in town without it, she was to be denied a residence
certificate and any sort of work license.[138]

Hence, the entire system of permits was meant to produce a situation
in which every farmer occupying city space would be not only accounted
for in official records (potentially subject to supervision and control) but
also busy at a registered workplace (thus, it was assumed, not prone to
foment disturbances). But both of these old assumptions were in the
course of losing their foundation, even as the rules were enunciated and
their enforcement commanded.

In fact and increasingly over time peasants became far more likely to
circumvent the rules than to comply with them.[139] In a 1996 survey done
by the Ministry of Agriculture, as many as 69 percent of the movers did
not notify officials in their hometowns of their decision to leave, while
even more—79 percent of them—did not register their arrival in the
cities.[140]

In part this slippage was a function simply of the growing numbers of
outsiders in given locales, and of their ability to overwhelm the government: for instance, from 1986 to 1990, the number of migrants in Beijing's
Zhejiang Village shot up from 12,000 to 30,000 and after 1990 continued

climbing at the rate of 50 percent a year. But a mere 5,000 of these had registered their departures with the Leqing county's Administration for Industry and Commerce back in Zhejiang as of the mid-1990s. Perhaps this uncontrollable delinquency was why, in 1992, the state Administration for Industry and Commerce conceded that merchants going out of their native places to do business no longer had to produce certificates issued by the local branches of this agency in their home areas.[141]

Another problem, probably the core one, was that the logic behind all of these practices hinged on connections that were either never very dependable or, alternatively, that grew progressively less reliable as the reform era unfolded. One was a link between those exiting the villages and their governors, which had necessarily weakened with the termination of the communes, an event that occurred more or less simultaneously with the peasants' acquisition of the right to migrate. Another was bonds among administrative agencies in different locales, or even in the same city. As we have seen above, the disparate missions and jealousy over turf of the different bureaucracies in dealing with migrants did not dispose them to cooperate. As a result, migrants learned that they could often skirt the gatekeepers and yet go about scot-free.

Failures of Coordination

Difficulties of coordination led to a notable failure among city offices to coalesce their concerns into a committee at the level of the municipality as a whole, one that would be charged with containing the strains caused by migrants. The familiar frustrations with horizontal coordination that had always plagued the planned economy—in which hierarchically arranged bureaucracies responded only to vertical commands—confounded the already complicated task of checking migrant labor through administrative management.

Thus, as long after the flow had begun as 1990, many cities were still unable to compose a joint committee to handle their migrants, despite frequently expressed intentions to do so. A researcher in Guangdong finds "no central agency [in place] to plan, administer and supervise the work on the floating population" as of that point.[142] At the same time, Haikou, the capital city of neighboring Hainan, and also a magnet for migrants, obviously had made no headway in creating such an organ, for its radio broadcasts bemoaned the "lack of a unified command and leadership and close coordination of [concerned] departments." The same can be documented for many cities, including Harbin, Wuhan, and Hangzhou.[143]

Tianjin put a small leadership group in place in late 1990 to administer the business of the temporary population. According to the explanation of an official from the city's public security's *hukou* management office, as more and more floaters arrived there, city authorities eventually recognized the need to cooperate to solve the transients' problems.[144] He also admitted, however, that bureaucratic languor and ineptitude had delayed the achievement of such collaboration in Tianjin, and probably in all these other cities as well.[145] The job of the group was to protect public order and to try to ensure that outsiders registered. But despite the formation of the committee, each department involved in it continued to manage its own affairs.

In Guangdong, it was not until 1992 that such an organ was finally formed, by which time that city had started to recognize the utility for controlling migrants of aligning its efforts with, instead of against, the ongoing flow. Its charges indicated this switch in objectives: they were not just to supervise the implementation of regulations on *hukou*, but also to authorize contracts between employers and workers, and to coordinate the interregional movement of migrants with the sending areas.[146] Similarly, by the time Shanghai announced its success in finally setting up an organ—a Shanghai municipal office for managing the external labor force—to manage its outsider population in 1994, its sole responsibility was not repression; it was just to issue labor certificates.[147]

As for Beijing City, upon confronting in early 1991 what was labeled "a drastic increase in the number of immigrants from other parts of China," a capital committee for the overall management of social order was drawn up in response.[148] It appears, however, not to have stuck. For in less than a year, municipal officials had proposed the establishment of "a powerful and authoritative administrative organ to handle this population."[149]

Not again until the middle of 1995 was the city reported to have been able to bring together a special group in charge of managing the transient population.[150] And again we see an alteration in emphasis. At that point, Mayor Li Qiyan and Vice Mayor Zhang Baifa issued a progress report on establishing organs in charge of the unified management of migrants, along with a pronouncement that the city had been accelerating the application of legislative measures in dealing with migrants over the previous two years. They also called for "upholding the principle of doing things in line with the law."[151] It is notable, however, that such a bow in the direction of legality was followed within less than half a year by the sudden razing of the housing of the hundred thousand residents of Zhejiang Village.

This shift to couching management in terms of legal tenets, and in harmony with markets, was made in the wake of a national forum sponsored at the end of 1994 by the highly anti-immigrant public security bureaucracy, under the aegis of its Central Committee for the Comprehensive Management of Public Security. Its security-minded conveners who were then affirming a lawlike rhetoric seemed by that point to be at their wits' end, as this quotation from the meeting evinces:

> For the time being . . . because administrative and other related work is unable to keep pace, the mobility of migrant workers is more or less in disorder, seriously unsettling the administration of public order.

While—in a very old refrain—making "public order the focus and residency registration the groundwork" in handling the migrants, and possibly in light of the frustration suggested above, its message also asked localities with an inflow of peasants to coordinate their work with those with an outflow and told relevant departments to enhance their cooperation, in order that work be "brought within the jurisdiction of the law."[152]

MARKETS TAKE OVER: THE COMMODIFICATION OF MIGRANTS

Taking this legalism with some skepticism has a few justifications. For legalistic rhetoric not only accompanied continuing brutality (as in demolishing dwellings), it occurred along with a growing effort on the part of officials to make money from the appearance of migrants. This was quite feasible now, with the lure of lucre present on a far grander scale than in the time of Mao (not just because the pursuit of profits—and sometimes even of loot—was sanctioned now, but also because market activity generated so much more cash). This climate enshrining enrichment, along with the multiple opportunities for commodification that noncitizen migrants incessantly offered to the agents of a still-standing and regulation-rich bureaucracy—and in the absence of actually operative law—disposed many official functionaries to join in this process of plundering urbanized peasants.

Irregularities and Graft

To begin with, as we have seen above, transients were assessed fees and made to pay taxes on their business operations that benefited urban bureaus. But there was more to the story than that. Precisely because socialist China's bureaucracy under the planned economy had been so heavy with rules, orders, and directives, and also because the persisting *hukou* barrier rendered farmers in town particularly vulnerable, these peasants in the cities made ready victims for any agency—or individual official—offering a service or managing a function. Beyond the legally designated taxes, "many provincials have to pay several dozen different taxes" in Beijing (just as they did at home in the countryside), according to a Chinese scholar.[153] In the view of the floaters themselves, "so-called management is all money collection, and no assistance or service."[154]

One account illustrating the situation comes from a shoe repairer whom two journalists encountered in Lanzhou in 1989:

> Each month we put out 45 yuan for the industrial and commercial tax, the environmental protection fee and the public security fee, but we still can't buy tranquillity.
>
> Those people wearing a red badge on their sleeves are always tossing down a "pay-a-fine-bill," wanting 8 or 10 yuan. In fishing out the money, if you're too slow, it's no good. If your expression is slightly cool, after several days they'll look for an excuse for revenge. These bills are written by the people themselves; they can fine you 2 yuan and write down 1 and then give you no receipt. Heaven knows where the fine money goes. They've taught us gradually, when they come for shoe repairs, it's like a solicitation: if they can collect a little money, then afterward it will be easy to manage your affairs.[155]

This kind of corruption was rife throughout the construction trade as well. At the individual level, this peasant construction worker's plaint to these same reporters was typical:

> In Shenzhen, some units signed one-year contracts with outside construction workers, so they make them obtain a work certificate, a border certificate, a temporary *hukou*, and personal insurance. These documents are not all necessary, but some people depend on certificates to get rich.[156]

Bureaucrats and cops on the beat in the public security departments, whose responsibility was really to maintain control and order, were officially opposed to the incursions of outsiders. But these people also found their own ways of commodifying the act of physical movement. Rules on the books, combined with the utter defenselessness of the transients and the unavoidable slipperiness and irregularity of their quotidian existence, often turned innocent peasants into easy prey for corrupt officialdom.

A case of a very common phenomenon was provided by a father and son collecting scraps on the streets of Nanjing in 1992. They told of trying to register, hoping to purchase their temporary residence certificates and a business license, so they could operate according to the law. But the police, advising them rather to go home to tend the fields, preferred repeatedly confiscating their cart to selling them the certificates—an act that, by contrast, would net only the one-time fee.[157]

A poor migrant worker in Shenzhen also encountered police intent on making money from inspecting even those who tried to follow the rules, according to this story from 1989:

> In Shenzhen, a temporary *hukou* costs 100 yuan, insurance is 350 yuan, and the management fee for laboring is 48, so in one year you must pay 498 yuan to work. If you don't carry all your documents with you, a disaster will befall you [he broke a traffic rule, and police fined him 5 yuan; when he complained a little, they upped the fee to 10]. Carrying all your documents is too troublesome; especially for those bare-backed coolies, meeting this demand is just too arduous. But without the papers, you'll be thrown into the detention center. In the center, it's very crowded, you eat pig's food, are surrounded by flies, get bitten by fleas, the commode spills, excrement flows, it's dirtier than a toilet. Once in, you have to buy your way out, and that will cost you at least several tens of yuan, at most several hundred.[158]

Repetitious official attacks on hiring practices tagged as illicit point up the irresistibility of the impulse in factories to profit from employing low-wage peasants. Infractions included recruiting without first getting approval from the city labor bureau; hiring beyond the quota allotted, in the hope of raising an enterprise's output level;[159] posting advertisements at the train station (rather than through official channels); or failing to solicit local workers before engaging outside ones. Some firms reported the outside labor they recruited as being members of the city's own unemployed; this they achieved with the tacit concurrence of their supervisory departments, which profited from the management fees on outside labor that they in turn could collect.[160]

As in the 1950s, some plants were brazen enough "actually [to] go out and find their own workers and in the process casually to accede to peasant demands [to arrange] urban household registration certificates [for them]."[161] Underreporting—or even not reporting—the use of extra-plan labor, done in the interest of escaping management fees,[162] could reach the range of 80 percent of that really hired.[163] Bank personnel, who ought to have served as a check on such behavior, but who were themselves eager to solicit savings accounts, winked at firms that set up several different accounts in order to evade quota controls.[164]

By the 1990s, those investigating the wrongdoing found a way to benefit as well: the official fines for these offenses themselves rose steadily. According to Linda Wong, in 1988, Guangzhou regulations on hiring in the city had specified a fine of only 20 yuan per worker per day for offending. But by 1990 provincial regulations in Guangdong called for 100 yuan per day to be paid by enterprises for any "native" Guangdong peasant laborers recruited if the employer failed to get permission for hiring them, but 300 per day if the workers were from outside the province.[165] In extreme cases, the charge had even climbed to 2,000 yuan per worker in some cities by the mid-1990s.[166] In all these instances, migrants represented for managers not just the abstract market but actual money as well.

Urban Citizenship for Sale

As the commodification process wore on, urban administrators also got into the act, as they began to charge the newcomers "municipal entrance fees." Here was an easy chance to earn money not just by charging for entry, but sometimes by actually offering the precious local *hukou* for sale. At first they intended that the monies so collected could be used simply to rebuild old, worn-out infrastructure and to refurbish city facilities.[167] We might note that these were costs for which the permanent residents, long since enjoying the installations gratis, had never been asked to contribute; perhaps the logic here was that the outsiders, as trespassers, hastened the degradation of what were meant to be just the city's proper citizens' private public goods.

At least by the second half of the 1980s, the authorities in a number of the bigger cities—Shanghai, Guangzhou, Wuhan, and Beijing, to name a few—had recognized the potential the transients presented for income generation for the city at large.[168] Eventually these city officials realized that this effort would also be useful in presenting a more attractive, competitive, and user-friendly milieu to much-sought-after foreign investors, as the get-rich-quick mentality fostered by the market generated a pell-mell style of rapid modernization.

Perhaps because of the ongoing smaller-scale bribery in which individual public security and labor officials had been engaging continuously, it was often unclear, even in the official media, whether or not the practice of levying fees for access to the city (or the related one of selling *hukou*) was licit or not. Journal articles spoke of both black market and official prices with the amounts varying with the prestige of the city.[169]

According to Kam Wing Chan, in county-level cities and towns in Jiangsu and Henan, an urban household registration cost from 8,000 to 15,000 yuan in the early 1990s; in Shenzhen buyers were already paying up to 30,000 yuan on the black market just for a temporary residence permit in 1992.[170] Allegedly 25 billion yuan had accrued to local governments nationwide by early 1994 as a result of the sale of three million of these documents.[171]

On the other hand, regulations forbidding the sale of the *hukou* were published in late 1988 and again in mid-1992, under the orders of the State Council and of the Ministry of Public Security, respectively.[172] And in late 1992 the official *China Daily* stated,

> Since March, money has been collected by some people in certain localities to handle the procedure of "changing agricultural household registrations to nonagricultural household registrations," which is not permitted under the government's plan.[173]

Despite the legal ambiguities, by the early 1990s, it had become open and common practice for both the larger cities and the smaller towns as well to institute a "blue seal" *hukou*, with a licit price varying with local conditions, from 3,000 yuan in the smallest country town to 10,000 in the large cities, as of 1993. In line with the other sorts of competitive bidding among municipalities aimed at attracting (commodified) migrants, some cities lowered the price of this new *hukou*, in the hope of soliciting more takers.[174]

Urban leaders chose the level of treatment they wished to accord the purchasers of this city-specific certificate. In some cases licenses permitted their holders to send their children to high school, to get regular (state-involved) employment, and to enter the army. As of May 1993, ten cities had instituted the program and nearly ninety thousand people had partaken of it. Eventually, in early 1994 an official source even announced that this business, for that it surely was, had been endorsed by the Beijing authorities.[175]

Given the costs, obviously a calculating, market-tutored mentality was feeding a decidedly snobbish preference for admitting to a merchandised citizenship only the wealthy and the skilled among the outsiders—those who could afford the exorbitant prices of registration papers, or those whose individual presence could clearly embellish the city. These were reckoned to be "the superior from the peasantry," "those who have won out in the economic competition of economic reform," a Chinese publicist explained. Such people could be expected to settle, invest, sponsor industry, even purchase commercial buildings, construct housing, and bring in foreign capital.[176]

In Shanghai, the blue certificates were specially extended to foreigners operating enterprises for at least two years with an investment surpassing 200,000 yuan; professionals; domestic investors; and senior management personnel in enterprises, so long as the individuals could invest more than 1 million yuan in business for two years or more. Despite the costliness of their sponsorship of the city, these patron/peasants were initially permitted to become just "provisional citizens." But they were promised the right to become permanent ones "with time," even able to vote in the city one day![177]

Beijing authorities, displaying the same proclivity to admit only what one journalist (referring to recent Canadian policy) termed "designer immigrants," instituted a "city construction and appearance fee" in late 1994.[178] But they soon reduced the enormous fee of 100,000 yuan (billed for urban residence in the center of the city)[179] by 80 percent or more for highly skilled technical workers, or for those holding master's or Ph.D. degrees.[180] Rather less elitist, but still evincing a definite preference for the best, in the early 1990s a handful of cities reserved urban citizenship as a bonus for a tiny minority of outstanding peasant workers.[181]

USING MARKET FORCES FOR CONTROL

What we have seen is that Chinese urban officialdom was forced by the mix of migrants and markets to confront the failings of the plan—its utter incompetence in the face of a continual, yet uneven influx of farmers—matched against the magnetism of the market. Bureaucrats' collective response, over time, was twofold, in both instances market driven: they not only commodified the migrants, they at the same time essayed to accommodate themselves and their offices to this flow, in the hopes of achieving greater command over it.

Take the role of the State Council. In early 1992, at Spring Festival, a time in the year when enormous crushes of country workers always converge, going to and from the coast, this body issued an urgent circular to nine provinces. It demanded that provincial officials adopt forceful measures to stop the "blind wanderers" (*mangliu*) from going south [to the coastal cities].[182] But only two years later, the emphasis at the same season shifted (perhaps in a sort of despair) from banning to "guiding the flow."[183] Besides, rather than directing municipal administrative organs simply to push peasants out (as it had, for instance, five years before),[184] the document encouraged "all regions and departments to provide necessary services" for them.

It also called on them to "develop the labor market," coordinating the labor, railway, communications, and public security departments—all prior regulators—in this endeavor. Later, at the end of 1994, the State Council was even more accommodative, appealing to local authorities to hold at least 60 percent of their outside workers at their place of occupation for the duration of the holiday, and charging employers along the coast and in big metropolises such as Beijing, Tianjin, and Shanghai with suspending recruitment just for the month following the festival period.[185]

While the State Council involved itself with the more macroissues of admission, limitation, and expulsion of migrants, designing more specialized measures was the charge of the localities.[186] Here too there was development. As noted above, early in the 1980s cities turned most of their attention to ensuring that firms engaging "foreign" workers first obtain approval to do so from the city's labor bureau, and that they keep their usage within specified bounds.[187]

But by the mid- and late 1980s, urban administrators had recognized that workers from the rural areas were at a minimum short-term residents, who were staying at least a while in their jurisdictions. Accordingly, the rulings about them became more differentiated. Already in 1985 Wuhan's ICA, public security, and Individual Entrepreneurs' Association collaborated in authoring regulations controlling the births of their transients;[188] around 1988 Tianjin and Beijing began to publicize official decisions on a range of matters pertaining to the daily lives of these people.[189]

It was not just the breadth of concerns, but also the nature of management attempted, that shifted after 1990. In Tianjin, for example, there was a switch from simply sending them away to calling for greater toleration of their presence on the premises. This new approach also aimed explicitly at setting up state-sponsored labor markets for them in lieu of chasing them out, in the interest of preventing aimless vagrancy.[190]

And by the middle of 1995, Beijing City was proclaiming its policies in the form of laws, produced, at least in form, after deliberation by the Standing Committee of the Municipal People's Congress.[191] The Beijing City Regulations on the Management of Transient People Seeking Jobs in Beijing, for instance, required employers to secure not just employment permits but also temporary dwelling places for their charges. Also, much more transparently than decrees that had gone before, it listed services migrant workers were to perform, protections they should enjoy, the fees they would be expected to pay, and the legal responsibilities to which they would be held accountable in the event of violating regulations.

By early the next year, the city had even established its first migrant worker service center, which was to help resolve labor disputes and guide recruitment.[192] Nonetheless, the contemporaneous leveling of Zhejiang migrants' living places must make us suspicious of the motives here; certainly it suggests that these new laws were just a new experiment in keeping control over outsiders.

There was also a marked change in the management strategy of the Ministry of Labor—one of the principal members of the original regulatory coalition—around the end of 1993. At that point this agency began to define its scope of activity—at least at the verbal level—as encompassing not just the affairs of city workers but those of peasant laborers as well. Accordingly, the ministry set forth an Urban-Rural Employment Coordination Plan, which called for labor-exporting rural localities consciously to organize their efforts in guiding the exodus and in composing "legitimate channels" for the movement. It also challenged the urban importers "to formulate necessary labor market rules and management systems to manage laborers and services" for them.[193]

Similarly in the spirit of the late 1992 fourteenth congress of the Communist Party, which heralded the nation's economy as a "socialist market" one, a commentary in *Shichang bao* (Market news) advocated the "formation of an information system and a service network suited to a market economy to facilitate the transregional labor flow."[194] A year later, in 1995, efforts of the same sort by the labor ministry continued, as the director of its employment department, Zhang Xiaojian, argued for fostering an orderly transregional flow of workers, designing legal channels, establishing market rules and services, and building up coordination within distinct regional labor markets.[195] The ministry also strove to synchronize its actions with—one might even say capitulating at last to—the actual situation of supply and demand obtaining in the market.

This it did by stipulating that where there was "an extremely large labor surplus, away from home employment cards should be issued, based on accurate data on demand for labor in other places"; "where there was a labor shortage, a migrant employment certificate should be issued based on the actual needs of the hiring units."[196] By 1996, this ministry was collaborating with the Ministry of Agriculture—the migrants' patron—in attempting to open new employment avenues, and in designing a unified migrant employment certificate management system, with the aim of aligning supply with demand.[197] By early 1996 three regional information networks for labor markets had been set up in South, East, and North China, respectively, linked up by computers with a labor market network center, based in the Ministry of Labor. Allegedly, it connected 21 provinces and claimed, incredibly, to account for some 500 million workers.[198]

In addition, a network of labor employment service organs was said to cover much of the countryside, at least in the relatively developed areas. These were units equipped to issue registration cards to be presented upon a peasant's arrival at an urban work unit. And major population centers that attracted migrants in the millions had also by the early 1990s devised their own means of better managing the inflow. Their methods were reminiscent of the bilateral contracts used in France and Germany throughout the 1970s that aimed at cooperation with the principal sending countries. Probably they shared the same intent: to bridle rampant worker in-migration.[199]

Perhaps the most remarkable shift in a locality's stance was the one taken by Guangdong province, one of the most popular destinations of peasants and initially among the staunchest supporters of the regulatory alliance. In late 1991, this province—which in the late 1980s was sending high-level delegations to neighboring provinces to dissuade them from letting peasants leave home and demanding their leaders' help with leading the peasants out of its own territory—apparently under the direction of the central government, organized a program of interprovincial labor cooperation. This new program was arranged in conjunction with bordering provinces Hunan and Guangxi and with one of Guangdong's other major suppliers of surplus labor, Sichuan.

The program, or "agreement plan" (xieyi jihua), that they devised involved setting up labor coordination centers in each of these provinces, responsible for channeling and modulating the outflow of workers. The compact was a form of macrocontrol in some sense guided by plan, to be administered either by labor departments in each locale or by separate management offices set up under labor departments specifically for this purpose.[200] By the spring of 1995, a Center for Information Exchange on the Labor Needs of South China, created to provide estimates of demand and to integrate information on regional supply and demand conditions, was at work, with the support of ministries and commissions under the

State Council, as well as with the cooperation of nine southern provinces that were involved in the network.[201]

By the end of 1993 Shanghai, another prior regulatory receiver, was appealing to the provincial governments in the areas of its own main labor sources—Anhui, Henan, Jiangxi, Zhejiang, and Sichuan—for a similar kind of cooperation. In this case, Shanghai—which earlier in the very same year was sending "urgent telegrams" to Jiangsu, Anhui, and Jiangxi to keep people from going out and to help in sending them back home[202]— pledged to notify its neighboring provinces about the state of the city's labor market, in the interest of avoiding an inappropriately immense influx; and to create more job markets. Apparently officials in all these host regions had at least to some degree resigned themselves to adapting to market forces—but, clearly, they did so to utilize these forces as a new method of control—in order to cope more effectively with in-migration.

DEBATES OVER REFORM OF HOUSEHOLD REGISTRATION

As the notion of genuine (if guided) labor markets was becoming ingrained, talk of alteration in the old registration system also started to appear. It had begun already in the mid-1980s with the gradual introduction of individual identity cards. As of mid-1989, cards had been issued to 420 million people, with a projection that by October that year, 500 million persons (all adult citizens) were to be equipped with the certificates and would be required to use them in every sort of official exchange, from marriage registration to applying for a business license.[203] Not until 1992, however, had "the majority of places . . . shifted from relying on the household *hukou* to the personal identification card."[204] Thus, these cards,[205] which were both permanent and portable, had effectively replaced the home government's introduction letter and its specific grant of permission to go away.[206]

Further transformation was in the offing. In line with the analysis above, a January 1994 commentator's essay in the *People's Daily* admitted that the gatekeeping role of the *hukou* system had been shattered once policies of reform and marketization had made essential urban goods that were once unavailable to ruralites—such as food, jobs, housing, and schooling—accessible to anyone with the funds to pay for them.[207]

With such a recognition becoming common, by the mid-1990s an uneasy consensus had developed around the notion of eliminating the system of household registration altogether. To judge from the public media, the main discussion was chiefly one between two units, the

Ministry of Public Security and the Chinese Academy of Social Sciences (CASS). Both took as their point of departure the Decision on Some Issues on the Establishment of a Socialist Market Economic Structure, approved by the third plenum of the fourteenth party congress, which was held at the end of 1993.

That statement included a pledge that "we should . . . gradually reform the residence registration system in small cities and towns, [and] let the peasantry work in factories or do business in small cities and towns."[208] The two sides agreed with its view that the ultimate objective was to abolish the *hukou* system, "wiping out the distinction between agricultural and nonagricultural residence and removing obstacles standing in the way of reasonable mobility."[209]

Beyond that basic shared position, the stance of the public security was decidedly less lenient than that of the scholars at CASS. Like the passport bureaucracies and the city of Moscow in the Russia of the early 1990s, they seemed determined to retain their system.[210] Indeed, four crucial points that separated the two participants to the debate indicated how far apart they really were. The first, that only the public security researchers emphasize, was legalizing the entry of the peasantry only into small cities and towns, a position hardly different from what had been authorized a full decade earlier;[211] and the second was timing the change, with the public security speaking of "a relatively long process of social and economic development."[212]

Third, as in the first promigration documents of the early and mid-1980s, the public security group preferred to restrict permanent settlement to those who had jobs, housing, and sufficient funds to sustain themselves in the city;[213] and fourth, the public security advocated limiting the privileges for peasants, only allowing their children to get inexpensive schooling, but permitting them to inherit the residence status of either parent (thus implying a continuation into the future of status differentials, at least for peasants with two peasant parents).[214]

More than three years after the first announcement of radical change, no alteration had taken place. In mid-1996, a new initiative for reform emerged but, again, without any immediate sign of implementation. This was one, notably, more tied to markets, as it promised "tighter regulations and controls [that] will be carried out through market mechanisms, such as the price of land, the price of housing, and the price of labor."[215]

The slowness of execution could well have been tied to continuing bureaucratic contradictions. In particular, whatever its movement toward markets, at bottom it was surely the powerful public security—the agency charged with ultimate responsibility for the registration, surveillance over, and order keeping among the population—which had the greatest stake of all in the old *hukou* system. And it was that ministry's opinion, in the words of one of its "senior responsible persons"—despite his decorating his declaration with a reference to law—that:

> There is a need for the reform of the residence management system and more work on the related legal front. But one cannot assume we can do without the residence registration system and that the role of the residence booklet is no longer significant.[216]

Thus, ongoing reluctance to effect fundamental change in citizenship rights, even in the face of widespread marketization, seemed to signify that the most pressing influence was a persisting and even heightening paranoia in the face of moving peasants. For, beginning in the middle of 1995, the issue of the floating population was termed

> No longer a question of the transfer of surplus rural labor, but a major economic and political issue which has a direct bearing on economic development and social stability.

This was a formula that was repeated thereafter for some time to come.[217] In one formulation, this stark statement of apprehension was, suggestively, combined with a warning,

> Infringements on the legitimate rights and interests of migrant workers and businesspeople are serious and signs of migrant workers becoming a source of trouble have appeared in some places.[218]

Apparently an enhanced anxiety about public order by the mid-1990s had hastened a movement toward legal rhetoric; it seems this fear had become explicitly paired in leaders' minds with the notion of using the law.

. . .

Under the joint press of market forces and mobile farmers, institutional transformation got under way in the Chinese bureaucracy during the decade or so after farmers first began to drift voluntarily from their domiciles into the metropolises. The change implicated state policies and official bureaucracies' and their cadres' understanding of their missions, as well as the intrinsic worth and restrictiveness of a central institution of the state, the urban *hukou*.

The state socialist bureaucracy, as one of the three structural factors (along with migration policies and the urban public goods regime) that confronted the farmers as they entered and while they stayed in town, acted as a bar against their acquisition of citizenship, in spite of economic liberalization with its incipient markets. Even though state institutions did change, the phenomenon of capitalism-cum-incomers did not lead, at least in its first decade and a half in Chinese urban areas, to political liberalization. Instead there were two very different results: one, the commodification of transients, and two, an effort to find new forms of control through conforming to market forces.

For this socialist bureaucracy—like all administrative apparatuses of this type—was replete with regulations and prohibitions, the household register, which undergirded them all for the peasants, being the most prominent for the purposes of our discussion. When the market's enticements appeared, they did far more than spur competition among receiving areas. In addition, bureaucrats, each armed with the particular endowments that their own units bestowed—the rules and powers attached to their unit's past procedures—used these properties to fleece the transients. And second, that bureaucracy proved so ineffective that officials found themselves forced to seek out new modes of control and coping, through manipulating what they were hoping could be regulated markets and a rhetoric of rights.

We have seen the three phases in this process of transformation. The first entailed internal repositioning within the official bureaucracy, a system whose cadres had been fairly uniformly oriented toward the incentives set up by the planned economy—rewards for following commands to maintain order, to produce returns for the upper levels, and to fulfill specified quotas.

When markets, combined with state policies authorizing them, moved peasants out of the countryside, initially the various functional and geographic subunits of this administrative apparatus responded differentially to having these unentitled strangers in town.[219] Some wholeheartedly embraced the transients for the revenue their presence promised, and others, geared toward the planned economy's norms of predictability, order, and regimentation, turned ambivalent, enticed by graft but still wedded to rigid "guidance."

A second phase soon overtook the first. Before long, frustrated by the plan's constant missteps and malfunctions on confronting—and failing to control—migrants, and enticed by possibilities for financial gain, almost the entire array of officialdom began to find ways to take advantage of the peasants newly in their midst. The commodification of migrants, migration, and, eventually, of the institution of urban citizenship itself meant that the chance to earn wealth had in less than half a decade set up a dynamic whereby the former exclusivity of urban existence had become degraded. This was the result of the nearly simultaneous arrival in municipalities of markets, and of outsiders willing, even anxious, to be counted as appropriate residents there, or at least to hang onto a toehold in town.

And third, the increasing clarity over time of the incompatibility between a bureaucratic management of migration and a more and more marketized economy and society brought a despairing awareness of the difficulty of ruling by diktat over the cityward movement of emigrating farmers. Even those administrative and regional organs that had been most doggedly regulatory and that had struggled at first to contain and control the movement of ruralites onto their turf by means of commands had found themselves progressively more impotent. With this, their customary approach to their jobs was shaken.

The alternative the leadership chose at this point was to make a fundamental reorientation in policy, one in which it began to recognize the potential that synchronizing officials' efforts with the forces of supply and demand might hold for attaining some degree of stability and order. The outcome, by the mid-1990s, was the adoption—but just at the level of rhetoric—of the concepts of law, service provision, and reciprocal rights and duties. That this particular change was largely just cosmetic appeared clear when proposals to revamp the *hukou* system—and along with it, city citizenship—seemed suspended in midair.

4 The Urban Rationing Regime I
Prejudice and Public Goods

In its impact on the cities and their residents, the floating population—a visible, palpable product of the transition of the socialist state from plans to markets—became a metaphor for the market. As such, it served as a target for the release of the many frustrations and anxieties that urban dwellers experienced during the sunset of the planned society. Thus, this set of sojourners can be understood as a specter: in the eyes of the urban citizens and their officers, it stood as both the symbol of and scapegoat for what, for them, was the often ominous cessation of the urban socialist economic order, as economic reforms and rural transients simultaneously gathered force in the cities.

That these reforms delivered anxiety as well as material prosperity has been documented: according to Frank Pieke, an anthropologist working in China in the late 1980s, by 1985 the majority of urbanites already felt endangered by the threat they perceived that the reforms posed to their privileges and security, in short, to the sense of certainty about daily provisioning that they had long taken for granted.[1] Similar fears attended the thought of the loss of the privileged position the urban *hukou* gave city dwellers. As the Chinese scholar Han Jun comments,

> The household registration system isn't just a system of popular control, it's also a welfare system. If we get rid of the various kinds of social and economic benefits attached to the urban register, could urban residents tolerate it?[2]

As just one example of urbanites' conflation of the program of economic reform and its offshoots with the coming of country people, by the mid-1990s there existed protest groups such as a Union Front, which lumped together the issues of inflation, unemployment, and the influx of peasants into the cities.[3] Then-Premier Li Peng, in meeting with deputies to the third session of the eighth National People's Congress in March 1995, jointly addressed the two themes of price stabilization and the management of transients, in response to the concerns of the deputies.[4]

A survey of five hundred households in Shanghai's Pudong New District in the mid-1990s found that residents commonly perceived the floating population to be "bringing negative influences," with 97 percent of the respondents alleging that outsiders aggravated at least one of the following four problems and 74 percent of them blaming floaters for as many as three or four of them: employment, the environment, security of property, and traffic and transportation.[5] In general, "urbanites blame the floaters for a lot of urban problems," concludes one set of Chinese researchers in 1995, problems, as it happened, also linked to economic reform and marketization.[6]

This chapter considers the third structural feature of China's socialist statism that shaped the rural transients' process of urbanization: the former, fading regime of planning and rationing that privileged urbanites. I examine the ways in which the effects of markets got mixed in municipal dwellers' minds with the migrants who accompanied these markets. Markets spelled disruptions to old, trusted patterns of privilege, of what for decades were the institutions framing urban citizenship—what I have called the "urban public goods regime."[7] The daily behavior of peasants trying to labor and survive in cities also unavoidably clashed with the several elements of this regime. Thus, as a pair, together they shook up many of the various forms of existential security to which city people had long been accustomed.[8] Migrants, though the lesser party to the process, got a great deal of the blame.

The planned economy, with its preordained portions and mandated allocations, had bred in city folk and their officials a mentality of apportioned entitlements in finite quantities, stasis, and predictability. This inclination biased urbanites' assumptions, perceptions, and expectations in ways that prejudiced the reception they accorded the outsiders. In any context, when natives encounter outsiders, many fear and loathe them. The "hosts" generally suppose that newcomers will rob the public pot— which citizens see as containing a fixed sum of goods—of a portion of its shares with no adequately compensating payoff for the original recipients. That citizens trained for decades by the rules of the planned economy would entertain this assumption must be even more likely.

Indeed, the disbursal of the benefits (and thus citizenship itself—as defined by membership and by the receipt of public goods) to which urbanites had become accustomed had been contingent for decades precisely upon the *absence of markets*. Administratively allocated, guaranteed jobs; underpriced and highly accessible transportation and water; cheap food and electricity available at stable cost; and the near nonexistence of crime had become the perquisites of citizenship—law and order, full employment, low-cost utilities, and price stability[9]—that residents, in effect, treated as public goods. Like public goods, all these benefits were not allocated through markets; they were publicly provided; within the walls of the city they were largely nonexcludable; and they were jointly supplied (one person's consumption would not reduce the amount available to anyone else).[10] These properties clearly applied in the cases of price stability and law and order and, given the provisioning commitments that the socialist government undertook toward city people, appeared to do so for employment and utilities as well.

So, as the markets brought in the migrants and simultaneously weakened urbanites' guarantees of state-supplied benefits and welfare, the badges of their city citizenship, the ills associated with incipient markets—competitive labor markets, inflation, crowded transport vehicles, crime, and scarcer water and electricity—not surprisingly became linked to migrants as well. As a result, the simple presence of the migrants (even without their voicing any demands for benefits) meant to the regular residents the dying away of what had been. What city folk perceived as a floating mass easily assumed the place of scapegoat, the target for resentments born of what regular residents felt were diminutions in their rights.

Though the managers of the local urban state (which must pick up the tab) clearly preferred to exclude the members of what they viewed as migrating rural hordes from enjoyment of cheap and gratis services and amenities and, at least well into the 1990s, to deny them jobs that could go to native sons and daughters, the other amenities we address in this chapter appeared in the city openly, more or less for the taking.[11] Like any other public goods, they proved frustratingly difficult to deny to interlopers.

The mind-set that city dwellers developed in the midst of these changes in the urban public goods regime—when pitted against the backdrop of their habitual modes of thinking and receiving—must have worked to enhance the discrimination against farmers moving into their midst to which the other two structural features of urban state socialism in China—state policies against migration and domineering bureaucrats—

had already disposed these people; none of this boded well for outsiders' acquisition of urban citizenship.

I look first at the mind-set, then at the impact of markets and migrants, respectively, on six public goods, both in reality and in light of that mind-set. Finally, I consider two ways in which migrants' own behavior did contribute to the subversion of a way of life.

URBANITES' PREJUDICES IN A TIME OF TRANSITION

Citizens' Attitudes and Anti-"Foreign" Bias

Distaste for the alien is common across the globe. Robin Cohen writes of a "demonology" frequently surrounding immigrants in the twentieth century, whereby the most negative traits of some individuals among them—criminality, tax evasiveness, welfare gorging—are extrapolated to describe them all.[12] Here we want to pinpoint the specific factors that shaped Chinese urbanites' prejudice against incoming peasant "others" in the 1980s and 1990s.

A clue comes from a study of the cosmopolitan port city of Hankou during its nineteenth-century phase of industrialization. Then squatters, whether laborers or beggars, were denigrated as rootless people who summoned up distaste and even alarm among the town's permanent residents. According to William Rowe, the local hostility they attracted resulted

> in part because their unsettled status made them appear prone to criminal and deviant behavior [but] most basically they were outsiders who, by staying, had *violated the rules of the game*.[13]

This reference to rule transgression provides a start in distinguishing one context from the next. In particular, if we want to differentiate the reasons natives offer to explain their resentment of incomers in one place as against another, two aspects of rules are important: those about who deserves to be a citizen (here, a recipient of goods from the state); and those about what natives have—and care about retaining—at the time that outsiders enter. I label these two types of rules "rules about the principle of deserts" and "rules about expected benefits," respectively.

Problems of xenophobia and restrictionism become unusually salient when the structure of benefits is under threat for everyone, or when the principle of deserts is being challenged. As Kitty Calavita notes in writing about the United States, such moods appear during times of economic uncertainty, dislocation, and transformation or when there is crisis or a threat to the national security.[14] The charges natives level about what they imagine migrants are attacking at such times reveal a great deal about what natives care most about and believe they are losing; their claims also illuminate what the significant public goods in a society are at such times.

My discussion of state migration policies—policies that Chinese urbanites under the P.R.C. took as norms of justice—suggested three customary rules about deserts and benefits that peasants floating into Chinese metropolises infringed upon, rules different from those in most other "host" environments around the world. These were, first, that one's household registration delimited one's sole legitimate area of habitation; second, that a distinctive and unalterable structure of rights and benefits was attached to each area and belonged to its legal dwellers alone; and third, that the goods of the city, since they were granted by the state plan, were finite and should be allocated only according to status distinctions set by the state. Neither economic factors such as financial contributions to the common good through paying taxes, nor cultural factors such as ethnicity, but simply possession of the urban *hukou* was the maxim of inclusion, the principle of deserts.

In the United States in the late twentieth century, to give one counterexample, the socially constructed principles of deserts and benefits, and thus the widely accepted implicit rules, were quite different. In that country, "deserving" people would ideally be tax-paying, naturalized citizens or (best of all) full-blooded natives. Manuel Garcia y Griego notes that nativism was rooted in a fear of the dilution of services available to citizens in the United States, plus in "a perception that 'nonmembers' do not contribute to the public coffers from which such services are funded."[15] This understanding that paying for public goods by meeting one's tax obligations can, along with citizenship, legitimate the use of the goods, is common in capitalist economies.[16] But in socialist China's cities, where the personal income tax was altogether nonexistent before the rebirth of the private sector in the 1980s (and still paid by only a tiny number of people even long afterward),[17] simple legal residence was the basis for deserts.

Moreover, the goods at stake were different. Because of decades of expectations formed around the welfare state, and because of governmental efforts to take responsibility for citizens' employment after the Second World War, people in the United States expected that welfare benefits and jobs would be ensured by the state for the "deserving." As this changed in the 1980s, the most salient antiforeign issues in the United States became the drain immigrants were believed to put on welfare funds and their apparent snatching of jobs. Probably this mentality reflected the neoliberal philosophy then accompanying globalization, and the menace that philosophy and that process were posing to the welfare state and to jobs in the advanced industrial states.

Julian Simon, writing in the late 1980s, remarks that the issue of job "displacement" of natives "was the most emotional and politically influential fear about immigration" in the United States then and includes various forms of welfare services as among those that "most often catch the public eye."[18] In France and Germany public concern in that period also centered around the demands that immigrants appeared to place upon welfare services and unemployment programs.[19] In these cases, though, it was just those who actively asserted themselves—by drawing on welfare services or by applying for jobs—who disturbed these unwritten rules.

But in China, by contrast, it was literally impossible for migrants on their own (unless employed as temporary labor within state-owned firms, some of which automatically offered outsiders a modicum of services) to encroach upon the sort of benefits that citizens in the capitalist West most fiercely guarded, such as welfare, retirement, and medical care. For under China's socialist economy, up through the early 1990s, such services were totally excludable, as they were arranged by state-owned work units and generally closed to any but the employees of these units. Moreover, up to that point, since the urban state generally essayed to guarantee jobs and benefits for its citizens, these particular benefits were not yet an issue of concern to most city people.

Thus, in the mid-1990s survey of Chinese urban residents cited above, 91 percent of respondents were anxious about floaters' influence on transport, 81 percent about security of property, and 77 percent about transients' impact on the environment, all issues unrelated to welfare benefits or jobs. They were instead worried about the basic dimensions of an exclusive urban existence, closed to outside influences and disruptions. Only 36 percent were apprehensive about outsiders' effect upon employment.[20]

Another difference between China and elsewhere in the reaction to migrants had to do with outsiders as scapegoats. Unlike in more static societies, where outsiders may help "legitimate dominant norms" by serving as the target for societal grievances,[21] the floaters of China's reform era in no way reinforced established rules and mores; rather, their presence served to elicit nostalgia for rules being thrust aside. For their entry into the cities was simultaneous with the withering of those rules. Thus their existence acted chiefly to call attention to the fading of cherished norms; peasants in urban areas more often provoked urbanites than helped them to reaffirm extant values.

The elemental nature of the rules peasants' arrival challenged is apparent in the responses noted both in scholarly journals and in the more popular "reportage literature":

> Beijing people act crudely toward the gold diggers from outside, and there's a reason: the amount of financial subsidies the city government uses in public transportation, supplies, and social welfare is nearly an astronomical figure. One person in every six is an outsider. This money will proportionately increase, so that Beijing people, having lived a comfortable life for a long time, feel they've been subjected to various kinds of inconvenience, crowding, and trouble because of this.[22]

> There are many people, especially those urban dwellers whose everyday lives are affected by the tide of laborers who reproach the laborers for not "being good and staying home," and who reproach the government for not controlling these outsiders who are wandering everywhere.[23]

> Their thinking, morality, language, and customs are all different, their quality is inferior. The places they inhabit are very likely dirty places. ... They lack a concept of public morality ... so that behavior that harms prevailing social customs occurs time and time again. City residents are dissatisfied because they disturb normal life and livelihood.[24]

> City people are biased against them ... they disdain their words and behavior, hate their enjoying advantages that originally only should be enjoyed by locals.[25]

> Urbanites feel they're a threat to their iron rice bowl and their situation of living in ease and comfort. In a lot of places this is a reality.[26]

Their grating discontent surfaced in petty harassment:

> When they ask the way, Beijing people intentionally send them in the opposite direction; if they carelessly bump someone getting off the bus, it can lead to a brutal attack. When they enter a restaurant, the waiter creates difficulties. When they knock on the door and ask for old things to buy, the owner might fiercely spit![27]

Thus, urban citizens in China participated in a universal dislike for the outsider. Their particular scorn, however, intertwined with their sense of the end of a way of a life and the withering of the norms of propriety about benefits and deserts in the bond between native and state that had attended that former style of life. The floater embodied their loss.

Managers' Perspective on Chinese Transients

Faced with a flood of floating peasants, urban participants in a late 1980s research forum in Shanghai concluded that

> The cities, already bearing too many outstanding accounts, have seen their burden increased. . . . This is hard for the permanent residents to tolerate.[28]

And according to a government report, these supposed interlopers "influence [that is, adversely influence] the permanent population's normal life" by overusing electricity and water;[29] they caused the administrators of the city of Guangzhou, who felt forced to provide additional supplies of a range of goods and services to accommodate the influx, to "declare that they are overwhelmed."[30]

Just as in the United States, Chinese cities must bear much of the cost of the migrants but have little leverage over their influx. In China, the municipalities are tasked with providing their own infrastructure and basic services (as for transportation, water, and sanitation), and also are allocated from the central government quantities of grain (and, up until 1992, subsidies to keep down its cost) in amounts meant to serve only their permanent residents. The cities themselves must pay extra to meet any surplus demand beyond these basic amounts.[31]

But the core of the problem went beyond a rational calculation of expenditures. The chief issues were two: the drastic shortage of urban infrastructure as the period of economic reform began and peasants started to arrive, and the mentality of the planners. First of all, services and facilities in the cities were grossly inadequate, already seriously over-strained even before the peasants arrived.[32] Analysts speak of decades of overcrowded housing, inadequate water supplies, insufficient transport, and congestion in traffic; of shortages of fuel in cities at all levels, and of urban areas with weak infrastructure "originally nearly saturated" long before the time when floaters began to fill and crowd them further.[33]

R. J. R. Kirkby identifies several causes behind this poverty of urban amenities.[34] Most important, in the days of Maoism, and even more so beginning with the Great Leap Forward, when the State Construction Commission and the Ministry of Urban Construction were both gutted,[35] investment in the cities—as in all orthodox Marxist-Leninist systems[36]— was geared just toward industrial production, while nonproductive expenditure was given short shrift. By the time of the third and fourth Five-Year Plans (1966–70, 1971–75), he shows, such spending amounted to a mere 16.2 and 17.5 percent, respectively, of all state basic capital construction investment.[37] Additionally, a lingering distrust of urban ways provoked central party leaders to strive to limit the scale of large cities.[38] As one Chinese commentator describes the result:

> Over several decades, cities became dirty, chaotic and lacking [in infrastructure and amenities], while capital, energy and land were seriously wasted at the same time.[39]

Second, there was the mind-set of the bureaucrats. As we saw in chapter 3, the arrival of the peasants exposed a confrontation between a static society governed by the state plan, on the one hand, and the expansive, dynamic principles of the operation of the market, on the other. Two of the most central tenets of the planned economy exemplified how the plan managed this stasis: one, that the numbers of a city's permanent population formed the basis for the planned provision of urban public goods to ensure the satisfaction of the official residents' minimal daily needs;[40] and two, that the charges for the basic necessities of urban citizens—their household water supplies, their housing, their transportation, gas and electricity, and foodstuffs—would be kept low and stable, through heavy subsidization by the state.[41]

The propensity of urban officials in particular to think in terms of such fixed sums is apparent in a governmentally sponsored study undertaken at the end of the 1980s. There the calculation was made that in 1987, in the twenty-five cities with native populations of over one million, if the floating population were added in, the amount of various urban services available to residents would drop by 16.62 percent.[42] That markets have multiplier effects, that is, that new demands beget their own supplies, was as foreign and odd a notion to many Chinese urbanites of the 1980s and 1990s as were the outsiders themselves.

Indeed, a central reason why the planned economy relied heavily on the *hukou* system, with its compulsory registration of the urban population was this: the records of that system enabled city managers to provide for—and not just to police—households.[43] In 1990, as one Chinese scholar notes,

> At all levels and in all localities, administrative management agencies plan their work and projects in accord with the size of the registered permanent population within their respective jurisdictions.[44]

Up through the mid-1990s, more than a decade after peasants first made their way into the towns, where they, like any other dweller, drew upon the electricity, sewage, water, gas, food products, and transportation of the city, there was never any urban planning done that took them into account. Yet even as late into economic reform as at least mid-1992, under this pressure urban bureaucrats continued to attempt to supply the full gamut of urban amenities and foodstuffs at a level that would be certain to satisfy the registered permanent population living within the city.[45]

Concentrating so much on ensuring these services for set—and very predictable—numbers of people, city bureaucracies often could not cope with newcomers' problems as well. As a Chinese commentator, worrying about the impact of the floating population upon the cities, adds, "Concerned departments are only prepared to manage the permanent population, and some even lack the strength and numbers for that."[46] The practice of subsidization still stood even as market prices became more and more prevalent;[47] yet bureaucrats perceived that

> They [the floaters] increase the supply burden. They can't do without eating, wearing, living, and traveling. With the dual-track price system, the difference [between the genuine market price and the low, state-set price for urbanites] must be subsidized by the government. [This means that] the floating population fraudulently . . . partakes of the advantages due [proper] urban residents. . . . So the more floating population, the greater the subsidy burden.[48]

And, as financial officials in one large northern city explained in mid-1992 in speaking of subsidized grain,

> The floating population enjoys subsidies illegally. We don't know who gets the grain, but we need to guarantee enough of it for city people, so the amount of grain coming into the city must increase. . . . We're actually subsidizing the floating population.[49]

The upshot was that city officials reasoned that they were suddenly compelled to provide grain at a higher level than before because of the socialist state's obligation to provision all proper urban residents (*hukou* holders), and because there was no way of identifying interloping consumers. Thus, floaters were perceived to free ride on the supply. For one example, in 1988 it was estimated that the Beijing city government spent 100 million yuan in subsidies for outside laborers without ever meaning to do so.[50]

According to officials from the Finance Bureau of Tianjin, in 1991 the city still offered fifteen types of "hidden subsidies" (*anbu*) at that point, not given directly to staff and workers but paid to the provider units out of the city's budget to ensure the availability to urban dwellers of the good in question at prices far below cost. These included subsidies for grain, oil, coal, water, electricity, buses, meat, vegetables, milk, soap, and lumber.[51] So, given urban bureaucrats' continuing mentality of planning and subsidizing locals, since floaters—especially those resident in the city center—enjoyed urban residents' subsidies just by virtue of living in the city, they ipso facto boosted the urban financial burden, even without demanding a thing.[52]

Although subsidies were reduced through the 1980s, as late as 1990 those for urban food supplies alone were calculated as amounting to 32 percent of all local government expenditures.[53] They were said to add up to 1.5 billion yuan a year in Guangdong province. When grain prices were freed up in 1992, the national state expenditure on their subsidies was reduced by nearly 15 billion yuan nationwide.[54] Clearly, if the state did not spend such a great deal on urban residents, the incoming peasants would not have been such a threat to urban bureaucrats. Thus, planned-era management, plus the poverty of the cities, positioned urban officials to join ordinary city folk in disfavoring "foreigners."

SIX PUBLIC GOODS

Rivalrousness and Elasticity

Given the extent to which the prejudices of city residents—ordinary citizens and managers alike—were structured by expectations left over from the regime of planning, a few simple truths about markets, peasant newcomers, and these people's own public goods were lost on them. For one thing, the potential long-term, multiplier effects of markets, which perhaps would even be enhanced by including migrants in the markets, might actually work to expand some of these goods over time; this possible *elasticity* of the goods went unnoticed. And, second, the true extent of the burden on and the competition for goods that migrants would be apt to create, even in the present (the *rivalrousness* of the goods), was in most cases likely to be far less than perceived. Fears and anxieties brought in by the transients, in conjunction with the threat of the loss of the planned economy and its urban public goods regime, obscured such insights.

I analyze the rivalrousness and elasticity of five of the six public goods (all except the crime-free environment) allegedly under assault by the migrants (but also by the markets of economic reform). This exercise underlines these misperceptions by estimating the actual amount to which each good was really *rivalrous* (such that additional users would decrease the benefit derived from the good by the original consumer).[55] Thus, the more rivalrous, the more the presence of floaters would truly be a threat to urban citizens' enjoyment of the good.

The exercise also points up the extent to which the good in question was present in a variable versus a fixed sum; if the former, there was the possibility of increasing its stocks, that is, its supply was in some sense *elastic.*[56] It is here that markets come into play. Encroachers would diminish the supply of only the very inelastic goods—those completely immune to the multiplier effect of demand stimulation (or to any other mode of engendering their increase).

In short, if the good is either relatively nonrivalrous, or if it exists in a variable-sum state (its supply is responsive to markets or to some other stimulant), the chances for congestion (at least in the medium and longer term) would be considerably less than if the reverse were the case. Both rivalrousness and elasticity influence not just the supply of the good but also the price level at which it becomes available to the original users. These five public goods—full employment, water, electricity, transportation vehicles and road space, and food (and prices for it)—vary in their rivalrousness and in their elasticity. But for the most part none of them was fully as rivalrous or inelastic as urbanites imagined. To illuminate the gap between prejudice and reality that urbanites' confusion of migrants with markets caused, I indicate the disparities in table 3 and in the discussion that follows.

Employment

A key question concerning employment and migrants anywhere is whether, on balance, migrants take jobs from citizens.[57] This issue, complex in any context, was further complicated in reform-era China by the ongoing transition between economic systems. Economic reform brought new pressures to urban enterprises to earn profits, and market competition (from nonstate and rural town and village enterprises, and from abroad) and rising prices for raw materials and labor (factors whose costs were once controlled by the state) forced urban firms to find ways to save or else suffer losses or, eventually, even face bankruptcy. As time went on, many urbanites were losing or in danger of losing their jobs.

Full employment in the cities had been treated as a public good by the

Table 3. Rivalrousness and Elasticity of Five Urban
Public Goods in Large Chinese Cities

Public Good	Rivalrousness	Elasticity
Full employment	Medium	High
Water	High	Low
Electricity	High	Medium
Transportation	Medium	Medium
Stably priced food	High	High

state in the time of the planned economy. Thus cities had created new jobs even when there was no real need for them, with the result that much hidden unemployment had kept city residents in work.[58] When in the 1980s market forces began pressing enterprises to improve their performance and reduce their expenses, just as farmers simultaneously arrived to fill urban factories in growing numbers, the actual agent behind the unaccustomed unemployment of urbanites became quite ambiguous. The intermixing of causes is apparent in this remark by a Chinese scholar:

> The layoff of some local workers is not the result of labor market competition from the in-floating population but a consequence of economic reform.[59]

Thus, what was really occurring was not just a competition between individual workers, but a clash between labor allocation mechanisms. As analysts in a jointly edited governmental study pointed out, four of the principal features of the "traditional" (or planning-era) employment system came under assault with the use of country labor in the cities. These were (1) its aim at high employment; (2) its single-stranded channel; (3) its arrangement of job placement according to plan; and (4) its normal exclusion of workers from the fields.[60] Thus, in its major role in the demolition of all of these patterns, the floating population neatly symbolized the commodification and commercialization of the economy as a whole that came with reform.

Many urban citizens saw a menace in the marketization of labor, and in the peasants it pushed into their midst. As late as mid-1995, editors at the pro-farmer *Peasant Daily* felt compelled to defend their constituency by making the following points:

The fact is that allowing peasants to find jobs and enterprises to hire people on their own will not turn the world upside down. . . . The market has its own built-in operating principles and restraint mechanisms. One is the principle of supply and demand. . . . If mobility does not lead to jobs or if its payoffs are less than its costs, peasants will stay home. These two principles determine that as far as peasant mobility is concerned, the market mechanism is both an incentive and a constraint.[61]

City folks' insecurity mounted in the face of market pressures, as many factories, especially in labor-intensive lines of manufacture such as textiles, more and more began dismissing older urban workers and taking on peasants instead.[62] In this milieu, a mid-1990s survey in Shanghai showed that a substantial segment of those 36 percent of the respondents who believed that the floating population damaged their chances for employment were motivated by the fear of this, even though they had not yet lost their jobs.[63] The pairing of these phenomena—incoming peasants and disappearing posts—in the public mind was enunciated by a senior official from the Ministry of Labor in late 1993, who asserted that the rise in the nation's urban unemployment (to four million, officially, at that time) was

> caused partly by the unrestricted influx of rural residents to the cities . . . [and by] job cuts as state enterprises seek greater efficiency.[64]

There was surely a reality behind the anxieties of city workers. After more than a decade of migration, growing numbers of migrants were entering state factories while these factories steadily reduced benefits for all, as the move to comply with markets—and the attendant competition from cheap migrant labor—steadily gathered momentum.[65] In early 1995, the Ministry of Labor predicted that between 1996 and the year 2000, as many as 3.5 million urban workers would be laid off;[66] beginning in 1992, Beijing City was already seeing about 15,000 lose their jobs per year, with only 56 percent becoming reemployed.[67] Relatedly, the numbers of permanent workers, at just under 135 million, was down nearly three-quarters of a million at mid-1996, as compared with a year earlier.

Meanwhile, the number of temporary, generally peasant workers—who, over time, were increasingly hired in state factories without full compliance with the regulatory regimens, welfare obligations, or financial management systems under which state workers were supposed to be employed—had risen by over a million, to almost 12 million over the same period.[68] In Wuhan, city workers in two urban state-owned construction companies saw their share of the work force in their teams drop from over 90 percent in both of them in 1986 to 65 and 42 percent, respectively, by 1989, as outside teams from the countryside seemingly poured into town.[69] If these figures seemed dire for state workers, the truth was probably far worse: the government is notorious for understating the figures in such matters.[70]

But to what extent did city jobs really became *rivalrous* with the insertion of these two new forces; and what factors might have rendered the new urban labor market(s) sufficiently *elastic* to accommodate the influx? Looking at the employment of two competing sets of labor in terms of three kinds of stages helps me clarify the issue of rivalry. These stages are first, that of the level of economic development of a particular economy; second, the period in the business cycle during which a set of outsiders is arriving; and the third, the stage in the settlement pattern of a specific group of immigrants.

Thus, where the economy in question—as a function of its level of development—has a demand for the kind of labor for which the foreign workers are well suited, problems of competition would be less severe, for there would be a ready niche for outsiders.[71] Second, when migrants seek entry during a boom as opposed to a recession, there is not likely to be as much difficulty.[72] And, third, generally speaking, when migrants have newly arrived, they are more likely to be relegated to lower-wage, lower-skill, high-turnover, ethnic enclave-based businesses, where their very segregation poses less of a threat to the native worker. Where some measure of assimilation occurs (which is by no means a certainty), second-generation migrants are more apt to compete successfully in the primary labor market than were their parents.[73]

For several reasons, there was a special space for migrants in the urban labor market during the developmental stage in China when they entered it. For one, the country's socialist economy contained serious gaps, bequeathed by years of radical politics. Maoist planning, with its unflinching bias toward heavy industry, had fiercely eschewed markets, consumer goods, the service sector, and investment in infrastructure. And many of the migrants were versed in crafts (such as carpentry, garment manufacture, and tailoring) or performed services (such as shoe repairing and barbering) for which there were unmet needs.

Even as late as the end of 1995 a government publication explained that "migrants can ply their own economic skills because a 'structural blank' has long existed in the service industries."[74] Others among them possessed the brawn needed to power the nearly relentless urban construction surge of the 1980s and 1990s. So, since parts of the city's economy called precisely for people with the abilities migrants possessed, there would be some rivalry, but its incidence would be confined just to the sectors where newcomers could fill jobs that urbanites had held in the past.

When we turn to the second stage, the one in the business cycle, we find that as in developing economies elsewhere, rural workers were the first to be dismissed in times of tightness. Here, however, bureaucrats were applying a specific policy that lasted up through the early 1990s of specifically protecting urban-born employees in recession periods. This policy countered the advantage the country firms and peasant workers would otherwise have commanded. One instance in Beijing during the state-induced recession of 1988–91 was the order to reduce the city's work force by 29,000; this goal was achieved by clearing out peasant labor in order to make way for at least some of the 137,000 regular laborers newly added to the work force of the city that year.[75]

But this policy bias was not just confined to economic downturns. Even in normal times, partly as a lingering residue from the days of state planning, local bureaucrats in the labor administration (as opposed to some enterprise managers) gave priority to guaranteeing the employment of the urban populace within the boundaries of their own jurisdiction, at least for the first decade or so after migration had begun. As officials from the labor bureau of the city of Tianjin explained in mid-1992,

> The local unemployment rate is an important element in deciding on the use of outside labor. . . . The floating population is a burden on the city and for the city's stability it's important to employ local labor. If the numbers of the unemployed [urban] young reach a certain amount, they can easily become a problem.[76]

Indeed, as late as 1994, some cities were still instructing all the institutions under their charge not to hire any new laborers from other provinces and to expel migrant workers currently on the premises;[77] a few years later, private entrepreneurs were being pressured to employ former state workers who had been dismissed, instead of rural migrant laborers, in the city of Shenyang.[78] And at the end of 1997, as pressures mounted on large- and medium-size state firms to meet market demands or go under, "every locality [was] scrambling to adopt a policy to impose restrictions on the hiring of rural workers."[79]

These reactions were in part a reflection of city managers' having operated for decades under a highly controlled system in which the supply of local labor was carefully calculated and administratively allocated to fill the needs of local enterprises. Preferential treatment that locals as a group received during the first flush of the transition—especially during recessions—as beneficiaries of the old system helped them recoup the losses they may have suffered because of the incursion of rural-run firms and peasant sojourners. This dynamic cut down on the rivalrousness of urban jobs.

The third stage that bears on the contest between local and migrant labor involves the settlement of a particular migrant group. Here we find that ethnic enclaves in which many migrants congregated on the outskirts of cities,[80] typical of the urban dwelling spots of first-generation migrants around the world,[81] were so nearly self-sufficient communities that they were unlikely to produce any larger multiplier effect in jobs for urbanites as a whole.[82] Many of the businesses—in marketing, crafts, and services, in particular—started by migrants did generate new employment.[83] But the employees the enclave entrepreneurs recruited were virtually always their own co-provincials or other outsiders and not urban natives. Another kind of job that attracted many outsiders was the dirty, low-skill, exhausting posts—in textiles, elementary building jobs, sanitation, and scrap collecting—that native urban workers, especially younger ones, had disdained.[84] Like the first two stages, the third applies universally.

So in China as elsewhere, initial transients are isolated not just into separate markets, but often also into distinct enclaves, yet one more factor that significantly reduces the rivalrousness with natives over jobs that their entry into the cities might otherwise have injected into the urban labor market. But in China the floaters were frequently relegated to separate "villages," self-started enterprises, and unpleasant jobs demanding only rudimentary abilities not just because, like migrants around the world, they were first-generation migrants, but also because, unlike their counterparts elsewhere, the mainstream labor market was totally inaccessible to them. This factor reduced rivalry between the two labor groups.

Given the steady incursion of market-oriented behavior and mentalities as the 1990s wore on, however, the preference of many city industrial plant managers for peasants, along with these managers' inclination to dismiss or cut back on the benefits for urban workers, augured a graver scenario for the city population as a whole. As this process unfolded, progressively rigorous pressures for cost-cutting were bound to stimulate—and to intensify—rivalry between citified farmers and city labor.[85] Competition was likely to become keenest between urban employees whose skills most resembled those of first-generation ruralites, those, that is, whose abilities and training best fit the earlier stages of economic development, such as construction workers, or basic production workers in the older industrial sectors, such as textiles.

Besides considering stages and their aid in explaining the rivalrousness of city labor market(s), another way to weigh the impact of migrants on urban employment is to analyze the elasticity of these markets. Many urbanites were blind to the possibilities that the marketization of labor might promise, in part because their assumptions were so fully tied to those of the planned economy, with, as noted above, its full employment, single channel, placement by plan, and exclusion of peasants. On the whole these assumptions operated to bolster a view that is frequently encountered around the world that migrants are job-displacing.[86] Over the years when the state was responsible for the jobs of everyone in the municipalities, it seemed logical to imagine that there was just a finite supply of jobs in the economy, such that the successful entry into the labor market of new job seekers would reduce the total stock of jobs open to natives.

But the operation of a true labor market would undermine these assumptions. Instead of displacing rivals for a limited number of jobs, migrants themselves created more jobs, in several ways. For one thing, their very presence yielded a multiplier effect, as their demand for additional goods and services must have stimulated new productivity in the economy overall.[87] Additionally, they were more apt than natives to become self-employed or to begin their own businesses.[88]

But most crucially, the entry of peasants led to the collapse of the former unitary market, as their exclusion from that one and their own new occupations produced a segmentation within the old single-stranded market. Indeed, the reform period ushered in city labor markets that were multiple and complex, with manifold separate niches segregated one from the next by the geographical origin and trade of those in them.[89] As groups with varied competencies, belonging to disparate networks and new occupations appeared, the economy expanded to absorb them. As Ronald Skeldon concludes, "Given the nature of the segmented labor markets, it is unlikely that there is much direct competition between migrants and nonmigrants for individual activities."[90]

In fact, the numbers of regular city jobs for city workers were not only not fixed in reform-era China, as urbanites had long been schooled to assume; they were in fact declining, as state firms released surplus workers to the market or cut way back on their workloads and their wages.[91] But the numbers apply only if we take the point of view of officials supervising the state sector. Whereas state-owned enterprises accounted for 78 percent of the nation's industrial output value in 1982, the state firms' contribution had plummeted to just 53 percent 10 years later;[92] and permanent workers in the state sector accounted for only just over 50 percent (77.6 million of a total of 144.8 million) of the total industrial work force by 1992.[93]

The story is quite different if we take the nonstate sector into account. Beginning in 1982, according to the government's own count, over 10 percent of job seekers were taking up jobs in the private sector yearly;[94] as of the end of June 1994, the 18.87 million registered individually operated firms represented a 22 percent increase over the same period a year before and were employing over 30 million people, according to government figures.[95] The same point is apparent in the statistic that the growth of state-owned enterprises accounted for a mere 6.6 percent of national industrial productive growth, while 93.4 percent came from non-state-owned enterprises at that time.[96]

Besides, there was the foreign-invested sector, unknown to the socialist Chinese economy before 1979, which contained over 174,000 firms as of mid-1993 and was employing millions of rural migrants, particularly in the processing and assemblage plants along the southeast coast.[97] Thus, the steady swelling of the economy under the influence of market forces rendered the notions of a finite supply of jobs, a unitary labor market, or an inelastic one—concepts that may have had some validity at various junctures during the era of the plan—totally obsolete.

From another angle one scholar, sympathetic to opening up the cities to farmers, hopes to pacify his urban-biased opponents by playing to their prejudices toward what they saw as superior skills among city folk:

> Even if we establish a unified urban-and-rural labor market and let peasants freely migrate to the city, there won't be many rural workers who can enter because of the limits of their own abilities and of their information about employment, so they'll be at a disadvantage in the employment competition.[98]

Thus, since city people often could not simply be replaced by migrants, the appearance in town of the latter was more apt to mean the creation of additional jobs than to cause inroads into an extant pool of posts, at least up to the late 1990s.

In sum, this incipient market was only moderately rivalrous and also highly elastic. The macro-level transition between systems in which the new markets in labor operated—a transition that in some ways gave the edge to migrant firms, in other ways preserved the privileges of urban citizens, and in yet other ways isolated natives from migrants and some migrants from others—best explained the changing operation of urban employment allocation. But many urbanites, educated by the planned economy, were particularly wary of the incursion of outsiders, who they believed were the fundamental cause of their potential posting problems.

City Services: Water, Electricity, Transport, Cheap Food

> Other than public transportation, water, and electricity, peasant workers don't use any of the amenities of city dwellers, yet urban residents don't need to pay any fees whatever to use them, while peasant workers must buy a "green card."[99]

> The urban environment is ruined. Wherever there's a large concentration of mobile population, shacks are erected at will, cooking is done outdoors, the streets are used as public toilets, structures are soiled, and public facilities are destroyed.[100]

These two quotations, one by Chinese expatriates abroad, commiserating, the other from a Shanghai resident, censorious, evince the murky understanding of what "foreign" farmers really do to the cities: the first acknowledges that they used at least some facilities but excuses this; the second accuses them of behavior, such as defecating in the open or stir-frying on the sidewalk, which clearly implies inadequate access to municipal amenities.

Still, the entrance of peasants into metropolises in the 1980s—an environment where market principles had not yet really penetrated— suddenly made city people (especially managers) feel that the supply of their urban facilities was quite finite. And yet, among these amenities, only water was both seriously rivalrous and severely inelastic. For the others, short-term rivalry and long-term inelasticity were probably much lower than what urbanites presumed.

Moreover, the attempt to exclude migrants from the use of the city's own supply of these goods sometimes even became counterproductive. For instance, in Beijing's Zhejiang Village, which the city refused to service (and perhaps in other migrant communities, with time), by the early 1990s community elites had already begun to provide water and electricity (along with their own transport and sewage facilities, and other public products). Obviously their private systems—especially if run by rules entirely of their own—would only further deplete the original city residents' stocks.[101]

Water   Of the four city services, water was the most impure public good, that is, the most rivalrous: additional users clearly cut down on the amount that could be enjoyed by the original users. Moreover, in the short run, it was the one whose supply was the most difficult to replenish, thus, the most inelastic. Water, therefore, posed the most difficulties when hordes of outsiders suddenly arrived. But a more likely explanation for shortage was a far longer-term one: the underpricing that had attended urban socialist planning, which had encouraged habits of excessive consumption despite scarcity.[102]

Perhaps the most important point—for water as well as electricity and buses—was that the concurrent process of economic reform, with its unrestrained economic development and rising standards of living, rapid industrialization, and heightened pollution—itself generated vastly increased demands on the urban infrastructure and its resource supplies.[103] Indeed, the fact was that the extremities had first appeared simultaneously with the coming of country people in the early 1980s, and not just later on as a result of their presence.[104] Here again we encounter a confusion of cause and a convenience of blaming.

The shortages of water were readily apparent. Already in 1987 the twenty-five cities with over a million people each could only allocate 174.8 liters of daily-use water per (urban) person per day, without counting in the floating population in these cities. In economically developed countries, by contrast, people use 400 to 600 liters per person on average. Once the floaters were included, the average dropped down to only 145.7 liters.[105] By 1990, large cities were experiencing frequent water supply cutoffs;[106] and over 180 cities nationally were short of water.[107] As of the mid-1990s, the vice minister of construction publicized the alarmist information that more than three hundred of China's major cities had actually "run out of water."[108]

In the country's fifty cities suffering from acute water shortage in the early 1990s, of which Beijing was one, the guaranteed rate of water supply was only two-thirds of full supply during peak consumption periods. In Beijing's case, this meant a daily gap of 150,000 to 200,000 liters in such periods.[109] Even in normal times, the capital's supply could satisfy only four-fifths of the need in 1990.[110] One governmental announcement claimed that its citizens received a per capita amount of water equal to only one-twenty-eighth of the world norm![111]

Problems were serious in Shanghai too. There an environmental scientist revealed that the Shanghai Tap Water Company had predicted the daily demand for tap water in that city would be 300,000 tons more than the company's production capacity of 5 million tons in the summer of 1994, causing the people to use 300,000 tons of unclean water a day.[112] In 1988, when the number of floaters was probably half what it was six years later (estimated as 1.25 million in 1988),[113] their presence was allegedly requiring an increase in livelihood water of 159,000 tons per day.[114] If these figures were correct, the nearly three million floaters in town by 1994 seemed to be using the missing 300,000 tons.[115]

Those concerned about water tended to focus their dismay on the floaters. Officials estimated, for example, that outsiders in Beijing were utilizing more than 60 million tons a year.[116] They assumed, however, that the transients were consuming at the same per capita rate that urbanites were, a most questionable proposition.

For in fact, many sources reveal that huge numbers of in-migrants in Chinese cities were living there critically deprived of water. There are reports of people squeezed into shacks in Beijing, where one toilet served more than six thousand people;[117] of a shantytown in Shenzhen housing fifty shelters, in which hundreds subsisted without running water;[118] of peasants putting up in Shanghai's Pudong Zone in "simple, unhealthy, unauthorized structures built by themselves," which offered no shower or toilet facilities;[119] and of those living on the streets of Guangzhou who washed up at the public faucets or even in the ponds of public parks (figure 1).[120] A 1995 survey in Shanghai revealed that a mere 11 percent of nearly four and a half thousand migrant households actually possessed a toilet.[121] Surely farmers in the city used some of its water, but certainly not at the rate that an average urbanite did.

Whatever the root of the problem, its solutions were costly, time-consuming, and sometimes counterproductive. Beijing City's method of dealing with the quandary, for instance, was to extract 100 million to 200 million cubic meters of underground water per year. As a result, the underground water level had dropped more than 40 meters below sea level by 1995, from just 5 to 10 meters below in 1950.[122]

Other northern cities, such as Harbin and Taiyuan, were similarly constricted: in Harbin, as of 1985, 420,000 people of a total population of about 2.3 million, or nearly one-fifth, had no access to running water, and the average daily usage was just 98 liters per person, a full 52 fewer than in other big cities.[123] In Taiyuan, the only hope rested in a multi-decade undertaking begun in 1987, an effort to divert water from the Yangtze to the Yellow River. Even its first phase was not scheduled for completion until 2010.[124]

Other large-scale projects, such as the proposed South-North Water

Figure 1. Showering at a faucet on the sidewalk, Wuhan.

Diversion project that was to expand a reservoir in Hubei province and deliver its water to Beijing, was a project that promised to be contentious, high-priced, and lengthy.[125] Given all these difficulties, in the short term, while utilizing impure water, scrounging for funds for treating sewage water for re-use, or simply suffering shortages, urbanites tended to blame the peasants, who seemed to be pouring in much faster than water was.[126]

Electricity   Electricity ranked as the second most troublesome public good, being somewhat less challenging to replace rapidly than water (more elastic in supply) and yet nearly equally competitive as to usage (rivalrous). Still, with high-speed and ubiquitous economic growth under way throughout the country, the extent to which floaters caused the problems in cities must be questioned. For as with water, large numbers of them lived without.[127] Few of the chief occupations in which they were engaged required the use of energy—not nursemaiding, most basic construction work, or the sale of produce, and surely not scavenging or begging. Factory work and garment manufacture were exceptions, but only the latter was actually initiated and supported by the transients themselves. A 1992 study in Guangzhou discovered that most of the transients lacked a kitchen, so they cooked by using some bricks and collecting firewood (figure 2).[128]

Nonetheless, urbanites jumped to the conclusion that migrants were

Figure 2. Cooking on the street, Wuhan.

the source of the shortages. A 1990 report in the *Beijing Evening News*, for instance, complained that the 4,000-plus garment firms in Zhejiang Village's Nanyuan district, by consuming more than 20,000 kilowatt hours of electricity per month, had wrecked the area's electrical transformer. On a nightly basis, the thousands of sewing machines running together routinely interfered with the domestic lamps of the local residents—the proper users: the lamps "went pale as a candle," while city folks' television screens "got all messed up."[129]

Power use was obviously a serious issue in Beijing, where electrical power was already short by 300,000 to 400,000 kilowatt hours at peak time in 1987.[130] In other cities, the problem was hardly less severe. In Wuhan, where the giant electrical gorger Wuhan Iron and Steel Company was consuming massive quantities on a normal basis, the extra 450,000 kilowatt hours of electricity per year that detractors figured the floaters were using "made the city's originally tense supply even more tense," in the words of an official report.[131] In Guangzhou, the same researchers conclude that migrants were responsible for an increase in the use of electricity by 2,353,600 kilowatt hours annually. Maybe they reason this way because of the high participation rate of migrants in the work force of the foreign-invested, small-scale processing and assemblage plants located nearby.[132]

Certainly new transformers, dams, and power stations could be and were being built, and alternative forms of energy developed; electricity, which can be generated, had some elasticity. But this would take time, plus massive sums of investment.[133] In the meantime, the visible target of the floating population, much more than the cherished modernization stimulated by the market, became the scapegoat for frustrated urbanites and their officials.

Transportation   Scholars in two cities in the early 1990s—Harbin and Wuhan—consider the squeeze on their city's transport facilities to be the most irritating type of pressure caused by the floaters.[134] The mid-1990s survey of Shanghai residents' attitudes noted above indicated that people in that city concurred with this viewpoint, with 91 percent of the sample expressing strong feelings on this issue (and 30 percent stating that the effect was a serious one), a full 10 percent more than on any other topic.[135] Reporters sympathetic to the peasants tried to explain to urbanites that it was really the rural transients who were inconvenienced by inadequate transportation, as in the statement below:

> When train or ship tickets sell out, a departmental cadre or factory
> manager can stay at a guest house or hotel and wait a couple of days.
> In contrast, peasants on the move will be stranded at the pier or train
> station, with no place to stay and no meals to eat. The key is to
> accelerate the development of the transportation system so that it can
> keep up with the economy. That's the only way to solve the problem
> at its root.[136]

As one reporter complained, Beijing's subway system was operating 40 percent beyond capacity as of the mid-1990s; 70 percent of its passengers, it charged, had come from out of town.[137] In Shanghai, whereas only 35.2 percent of the natives were depending on the public transport system, with the bulk of the population either walking or bicycling, a startling 72.3 percent of the floating population (a term that probably included tourists or people in town for business or work for only a few days) used the system.[138] Each outsider (a word probably used in the same way) in Hangzhou on average allegedly rode buses an average of 369 times a year, almost 150 percent of the patronage by a typical urbanite.[139]

Moreover, those among the large numbers of floaters working in the markets who adopted a "pendulumlike" lifestyle, daily going and coming to and from the city's suburbs with their produce for sale, created an extra strain on the buses and trains.[140] More complications for urban management departments arose with the peaks and troughs of sojourners' seasonal adjustments, as bureaucrats strove to arrange their work in accord with a constantly rising and falling burden.[141] Cities trying to cope with the crush calculated the numbers of extra buses they would need to meet the new demand. Administrators in Chengdu, for one, believed in the late 1980s that they were facing a need for another 473 buses; in Wuhan they figured the city was suffering a diminution equivalent to 689 buses because of the numbers of intruders.[142]

And yet as a public good, transportation modes were only of moderate rivalrousness and also could be expanded (were elastic). Indeed, where urbanites' passions ran deepest (i.e., on the issue of transport), there was actually relatively less objective foundation for alarm. Certainly the plight of urban transport, just like that of the rest of the municipal infrastructure, was grim even before the advent of the floaters. As of late 1979, it could still be said that many cities were laboring under a road network dating from the 1930s.[143] Reeitsu Kojima infers that investment in fixed assets for this sector in cities—as for all types of consumption— had been insufferably low for years; and government researchers note that road construction had been in the red long before the early 1980s. Kojima calculates that in 1983 there were 2,640 people per bus in China, compared with just 1,000 internationally.[144]

Nationwide, the number of bus stops per 10,000 people in 1987 declined from 6.77 to 5.64 once floaters were counted in.[145] And as with other urban amenities and services, city bureaucrats kept fares low to match workers' low wages, in the name of "serving the people"; this tactic was possible only with massive subsidies. But offering cheap rides stifled investment in improvements, as local transport companies struggled under deficits.[146]

At least three qualifications need to be made to this pessimistic picture, however, two of them revealing that, as a public good, transportation was considerably less rivalrous than either water or electricity; the third suggests that its facilities were relatively elastic. First, many of the peasants in town (unlike the tourists, who were also considered as part of the floating population in some accounts, and who certainly did arrive in throngs with the opening of the country to foreigners and markets) simply did not use public transport.

Construction workers, for instance, who represented a substantial proportion of the floating population, tended to stray little from their workplaces; the majority of them even slept in shacks they erected right on their building sites. "They exist in an environment totally isolated from the city," according to one 1995 study in Beijing.[147] Factory workers and garment manufacturers similarly resided in their workshops as a rule.

Moreover, most types of migrants were busy laboring, with only very minimal breaks, at least ten hours per day.[148] Nursemaids as well rarely traveled within the course of the day. Scrap collectors and beggars alike operated on foot.

Second, the peak usage times for the two gross population segments—residents and outsiders—tended to be staggered. In Tianjin, the peak times for regular urbanites were 6 to 8 A.M. and 5 to 6 P.M., whereas even those floaters who did use public transportation, because of their more irregular jobs and more varied schedules, usually rode just between 8 A.M. and 4 P.M.[149] In Shanghai, investigators found a similar pattern: there the early peak for residents was between 6:30 and 7:30 A.M. and the late one between 4:30 and 5:30 P.M. The floaters, on the other hand, had their early peak between 8 and 9 A.M. and their evening one between 4 and 6 P.M.[150] Both of these points—about minimal usage and nonconcurrent usage—challenge the notion that urban transport was a highly rivalrous good or, as a correlate, that peasant migrants' intracity movement truly competed with that of the natives.

The third qualification is that peasants brought income to the transport system, which could surely be used to upgrade it.[151] A short-term solution along these lines was undertaken in the early 1990s in a number of cities, including Tianjin. There transportation bureaucrats, relying on the market, hired minibuses with superior accommodations that made fewer stops and had special routes just to service outsiders, and they charged higher fares to ride in these vehicles.[152] If this type of practice, which entailed painlessly expanding supply, were widespread, it would become clear that transport facilities were not just not terribly rivalrous but also reasonably elastic; in this case markets could clearly overcome problems wrongly associated with peasants.

Food   As with respect to the other public goods, there was no shortage of grieving backlash against migrants for allegedly depleting the stocks of food on the urban market, along with creating the inflation that this supposedly occasioned. One example is from a 1991 Beijing source, complaining that each day the city was compelled to supply outsiders with 1.2 million *jin* of meat, 6 million *jin* of vegetables, and 5.4 million *jin* of grain.[153] Governmental researchers in Beijing conclude,

> This influences the permanent population's daily consumption, makes the prices rise on the free markets, nurtures a rampant black market exchange of grain ration coupons, and increases the burden of financial subsidies.[154]

Another accusation of the same complexion, focusing on prices, held that,

> As outsiders pour in, in places teeming with fruit, fruit becomes expensive; at the seaside one can't eat cheap fish. The tension resulting from the supply of consumer products not meeting demand goes against the personal interest of the local people.[155]

In Shanghai in the late 1980s, one account held that if the floaters consumed at the same rate as citizens did (0.8 *jin* of grain, 0.9 *jin* of vegetables, and 0.3 *jin* of meat per person per day), every day the city would have to provide incoming construction workers with 117.6 tons of grain, 132.3 tons of vegetables, and 44.1 tons of meat, "a great pressure on our market supply." And one scholar estimates that, since residents were receiving 8 yuan' worth of food subsidies per resident per month in the late 1980s in that city, had the floaters become permanent residents under those rules, state expenditures would have risen by well over 100 million yuan a year.[156]

In a mid-1992 interview an anthropologist at Zhongshan University claimed, in a popular form of reasoning, that "food is more expensive than before because more people are here."[157] Already by 1988 in the Pearl River Delta, the 3.2 million peasants from elsewhere were seen as responsible for grain shortages and an attendant price climb.[158] Calculations of the ordinary residents' norm varied with the city, but, since this norm was always taken to constitute the standard at which floaters also consumed, everywhere there was alarm.[159]

The logic appeared simple: more people, less food; less food, higher prices. As two Western journalists pointed out, "As long as they're in the city consuming grain rather than on the farm producing it, migrants contribute to galloping increases in prices of dietary staples."[160] And yet, as with all of the other city services, this reasoning contained a few flaws. First, as scholars studying migration comparatively note—and as some Chinese researchers also admit[161]—migrants, living a spartan lifestyle, tend to underconsume, saving and remitting much of what they earn.

Numerous sources comment on the miserable diet of the hordes of transient workers in the foreign-invested firms, often consisting mainly of gruel; the same was roughly the case for many construction workers, and for beggars and scrap collectors, all of whom tended to subsist on steamed buns and vegetables, practically never swallowing any meat.[162] Indeed, this pattern has been attributed as a prime cause for migrant labor's contracting the communicable diseases they were then charged with spreading. In fact, with their consumption rates generally well below those of average permanent residents, and with their relatively high productive levels, migrants actually work to reduce inflationary tendencies.[163] Considered in this light, food was by no means as rivalrous as was assumed by many critical Chinese analysts, that is, floaters did not diminish the stock enjoyed by original residents nearly as much as urbanites believed—if they even did so at all.

Second, with the start of economic reform, China's grain and produce supply gradually became governed much more by market forces than by the arrangements of the state plan.[164] Instead of the majority of output being strictly controlled by state purchases at state prices as it had been under the plan, higher demand in the cities stimulated greater output on the farms, even if many of the former farmers had deserted the fields. Indeed, local officials in Tianjin explained in 1992 that subsidies had been reduced during the reform period, as production of food rose in response to the liberalization of prices.[165] Thus, because of the new markets, food became much more readily and rapidly elastic than it had been, or than water, electricity, or even transport vehicles ever were.

And the third point is that the real weight of outsiders' eating did not fall on urban residents anyway, but instead—through the continuing subsidies they paid—on the grain and finance departments of municipal administrations.[166] There was also pressure placed on the urban departments charged with transporting the extra supplies into town.[167] The sticking point here was that cities, in accord with their customary concern to satisfy the demands of the proper, registered, urban citizenry, perforce subsidized food products improperly (in their eyes) but unavoidably enjoyed by the floating population.[168]

In the early reform period (at least up until 1988 or 1989), floaters intruded on urban supplies by illicitly obtaining ration coupons through black markets or barter and then buying grain or other rationed goods at the cheap prices meant just for residents. In 1989, city researchers in Wuhan estimate, a hundred eighty thousand transient people had bought and exchanged residents' grain coupons, which amounted to the city inadvertently handing over to massive numbers of outsiders subsidies meant just for the locals.[169]

Alternatively, sojourners acquired food licitly through their work units at higher, "negotiated" (*yijia*) prices, sometimes at their own and sometimes at their work unit's expense, or bought it at state stores, also at *yijia* prices. But despite the higher prices transients paid or the private transactions in which they engaged, the city was nonetheless inconvenienced. For its officials perceived that they were forced to amass these extra stocks and arrange for their distribution.[170]

As more grain and other foodstuffs appeared on the open markets, the city's burden was reduced but not eliminated. Urban governments continued to be concerned about the presence of adequate and inexpensive stocks for the urban citizens.[171] As of 1992, Guangzhou's officials in charge of grain tried to expand the acreage sown to food crops or contracted with other provinces or imported grain from abroad. In trying to raise the acreage for food, they still relied on orders based on planning, plus some material incentives, to require peasants in the surrounding countryside to grow the necessary crops. All this meant that city bureaucrats had to lay out funds to encourage peasants to plant more food, bring the extra food into town, and subsidize the price city people paid for it, once it was on the spot.

Bumper grain harvests up to 1985 (and after 1990), along with copious supplies of nonstaple foods, however, combined with heavy state subsidization, eventually seemed to state leaders to render ration coupons unnecessary and even burdensome as compared with times of scarcity in the past. Consequently, the low-price grain, edible oil, and other produce once available just with coupons for permanent urban residents were made completely accessible on open markets, with rations and urbanites' exclusive right to them eliminated nationally by the end of 1992.[172]

As—beginning with Guangdong in April that year[173]—one city after another dispensed with issuing coupons, state subsidies for grain and edible oil decreased by 13.84 billion yuan in the first 10 months of 1992, compared with that period the year before.[174] By that point, over 400 cities and counties had more or less freed up their grain market systems, though some localities linked this liberalization with a continuing, if reduced, provision of subsidies to help urban residents cope with the attendant price rises.[175] But even before all that had occurred, most urbanites, enjoying higher incomes with the onset of reforms, had already rejected the lower-grade grain that came with coupons and were themselves, just like the floaters, buying on open markets.

These several types of information on food supply suggest three conclusions: that cheap food was the least rivalrous of the four public goods; that it was the most elastic; and that the chief and most severe constraint that floaters placed upon urbanites' enjoyment of it was neither one of supply nor one of price. It was rather the burden bureaucrats felt forced to assume—and which they continued, even in an era of extensive marketization, to carry—as part of the baggage of the planned economy.

Thus of the four city services of which urbanized peasants partook—water, electricity, transportation, and cheap food—only water, and to some extent electricity, was sufficiently high in rivalrousness (here meaning that more consumers diminished the amount available to others) and/or low in elasticity (capable of being restocked in a reasonable period of time at reasonable cost) to merit the concern that urban managers, ordinary metropolitans, and the media expressed about migrants' seeming usurpation. I conclude that the discontent and grumbling were more a product of the city populations' unease with all the associated unsettling effects of incipient markets, and their unfamiliarity with the possible returns from these markets, than of the actual threat to their public goods that peasants (as opposed to markets) posed.

In many cases (certainly for food and transport), the newly functioning markets could even have solved the problems, if only bureaucrats had been able to unbind themselves from the mentality of mandatory subsidization that had guided their governance for decades. Here once more we encounter peasants, caught in the interstices between two systems, and accused of the consequences of the clash between them.

Public Order

The public good of peace and order was surely one notable by-product of the rigid and repressive regime that had ruled China as a socialist country for thirty years as of the start of the reform era. Neighborhood committees and work units maintained close watch and tight rein over urbanites almost all of the time (the major exceptions being the long years of the Cultural Revolution, the brief interlude of the "hundred flowers" in 1957, and the time surrounding Mao's decline and death in the mid-1970s). For the most part, the average citizen could count on a crime-free, quiet, and stable city environment.

Many urbanites believed that the coming of rural transients to town was responsible for wrecking their typically harmonious habitat. One sensationalistic expression of this assumption appeared in the volume *Seeing China Through a Third Eye*, published in 1994:

> Urban people's income has risen at a speed nearly commensurate with
> that of economic growth. But this hasn't been the case for peasants'
> income. So when peasants enter the city there will be jealousy, a sense
> of inferiority, even hatred. This kind of mood not only undermines
> their becoming urbanites, but will be expressed in crime.[176]

In early 1995, a majority of the deputies to the National People's Congress reportedly bitterly about the "huge migrant population swarming into Beijing, and the consequent social order problems."[177] And a mid-1990s opinion poll of residents in Beijing, Guangzhou, and Shanghai found that poor social order had become the "number one public enemy," as respondents held the floating population to be the "root cause" of their feeling of insecurity.[178]

In another study, 34 percent of Beijing residents said that the most important cause of their new sense of insecurity in the 1990s was that the city had attracted too many migrants.[179] After transportation, security of property ranked as the second most troubling effect of the floaters' presence, according to the Shanghai survey noted above, with 81 percent of the sample emphasizing its importance, and 14 percent even terming it "serious." The main reason these people felt threatened was that they had personally experienced theft in the recent past.[180]

Here, as in the case of all of the other public goods under challenge, the new role of markets was at the very source of the problem. With economic reform, wealth became elevated as the symbol of status and achievement among a population denied (and trained to denigrate) material gratification for decades. Moreover, marketization led to an increase in income gaps and new opportunities for free movement and encouraged the mushrooming of "underground economies" and rampant corruption. As a result of these influences, crime of all sorts was on the rise in the 1980s and 1990s. As one indication, by the mid-1990s the numbers of serious crimes committed with firearms were rising at the rate of more than 20 percent a year.[181]

Accompanying the pull of market incentives was a definite dwindling of administrative controls, which not only enticed criminals but also liberated bureaucrats to join in, and so blatantly increased the incidence of misdemeanors. And certainly those on the move, suspended in a sort of management vacuum, were apt to escape whatever controls and discipline were still being wielded by any jurisdiction or work unit.[182] In short, as the process of marketization progressed in tandem with a withering of planned forms of business, it opened up lacunae where clever folk could take advantage of gaps in the mesh between market and plan. The process in itself made space for malefaction of many sorts.

Under these circumstances, roving habitual criminals took cover among innocent mobile peasants, and in the eyes of urbanites one became confounded with the other.[183] This confusion helped foment ignorance as to the actual extent to which ordinary mobile country folk committed infractions. No doubt the figures were inflated, reflecting the courts' inclination to come to speedy verdicts and the ready tendency of biased police to arrest people appearing obviously misfit in urban settings.[184] In illustration of the bent of the law in China, a Chinese criminologist, pointing to the high rate of outsiders among the arrested, when asked how he could be sure that peasants had actually committed the crimes in question, responded guilelessly, "Why, because they were arrested!"[185]

Just as with other disparaging data about the behavior of peasants on the move, figures on criminal activity were not just high, but also inconsistent and erratic, both among cities and for the same city, even at the same time.[186] For instance, for Beijing, one allegation claimed that migrants committed 70 percent of the crimes in the busy areas of the city;[187] and that they represented 37.6 percent of all criminals arrested there by 1992 (up from 22.5 percent in 1990).[188] Another, by an official from the capital's household registration section of the public security bureau, held that migrants amounted to 50 percent of the criminals arrested there in 1993.[189] But a 1993 survey indicates that outsiders were responsible for as much as 80 percent of all criminal offenses in the city![190]

The same disparities among data appeared in research on other cities: for Guangzhou, criminal cases by migrants reportedly made up 80 percent of the total as of mid-1994, if one source is to be believed;[191] but writing in late 1994, another cited a figure of only 50 percent of all local crimes.[192] In mid-1994, outsiders in the nearby Shenzhen Special Economic Zone were said to be the cause of 80 percent of criminal cases, but four months later, according to a different source, for 97 percent.[193]

A criminologist at the Tianjin Academy of Social Sciences confides that in 1990 Tianjin's migrants had committed just 13.1 percent of its crimes;[194] yet a published source from just four years later claims that their cases accounted then for as much as 50 percent of the total in that city.[195] Its researchers find that the criminal rate among the floaters was over double that for natives in Shanghai in 1989: 2.64 percent for the former and only 0.9 percent among the indigenous population. But six years later, the supportive *Peasants' Daily* attests (without presenting any data), "Ninety-nine percent of the rural migrants are law-abiding."[196]

In several respects the position of outsiders in the urban areas in the 1980s and 1990s recapitulated that of Chinese sojourners in the cities of the 1930s and 1940s, the last time that markets and migrants had been operating freely in China.[197] Then, as a half century later, transients were scapegoated as the perpetrators of any unsolved criminal activity. Then too gangsters drew upon native-place networks to organize protection rackets, in order to take over labor markets; and secret societies of different sorts seduced innocent and destitute new arrivals in town to sign up for or be sold into degrading labor, principally prostitution.

Tales of all of these practices also appeared in the published sources of the late 1980s and 1990s, with references to regional gangs and their cumulating sway, especially in the corners of urban areas where peasants concentrated, such as the Zhejiang Village.[198] For instance, the author of *Seeing China Through a Third Eye* asserted that in this region,

> Theft from rich merchants takes place twice every three days. The armed robbers are peasants from Wenzhou. They form a clique and create a "production plan": they can't go home to the countryside until they've stolen a million yuan.[199]

Allegedly, gangs made their inroads by organizing and promising to protect the newcomers from the police and other troublemakers—for a price from both sides—or else by offering to find them jobs.[200] One source even recounted that Chinese sociologists had judged it likely that some 10 to 30 percent of the migrants were being drawn into a criminal underworld, "where they provide both the muscle and the prey of crime and vice-gangs," in the journalists' words.[201] In some of the informal labor markets of the city, the bosses were said to succeed in controlling both the prices and the labor for take.[202]

People from the outside were credited with many other forms of delinquency. In the late 1980s, larceny was labeled their chief specialty.[203] They were believed to steal cash, electrical wires and cables, precious raw materials, bicycles, motorcycles, plastics, and home appliances.[204] Supposedly, wrote a popular journalist,

> Crimes take place between construction sites and illegal procurement points. Theft, transportation, procurement and the sale of stolen goods form a continuous "dragon." Wherever there is a construction site, there will be illegal procurement points nearby, and many gleaners with their pull carts. There are many gathering points where out of town so-called garbage collectors assemble, which are actually hiding places for stolen goods.[205]

In 1990 in the areas just outside Beijing, outsiders were said to have staked out more than ten "black markets," where they illegally peddled lumber, iron and steel, and old used goods, presumably obtained illicitly, according to a survey by official sociologists.[206] By the mid-1990s, transients' two principal types of booty were sewer covers, to be sold as scrap metal, and automobiles; one source alleged that the frequent car thefts in urban areas were mostly the work of the migrants.[207]

But already in 1991, larceny had receded from its prominent place. Serious and vicious crimes became more numerous, as the incidence of incidents involving explosives, poisons, rape, murder, the illegal manufacture and sale of guns and explosives, counterfeiting, and kidnapings doubled in just the one year, 1990 to 1991.[208] Other offenses associated with outsiders included pushing "lewd products," a trade in which 95 percent of the practitioners in Guangzhou were said to be from elsewhere;[209] and committing arson, 25 percent of the losses from which were laid at the feet of the floaters in 1988 Shanghai.[210]

People without local registration were often caught practicing prostitution (to the extent that in mid-1989 in "a certain southwestern city," all of the more than 100 prostitutes were nonlocals);[211] dealing in drug trafficking and taking, and gambling;[212] and scalping boat tickets, a pastime supposedly so popular with transients in Shanghai that 80 percent of those arrested for this infraction were from somewhere else.[213] Smuggling and speculation were also thought to be favorite misdeeds of the floaters. In Shanghai in 1990, 80 and 66 percent of each of these types of crimes was said to be the handiwork of strangers to the city.[214]

But all of these data and sundry charges must be understood in light of three crucial facts: first, most obviously, they highlight the bias of Chinese urbanites to pin the cause of disquieting changes upon the persons of the incoming peasants, an inclination toward migrants common around the world.[215] Second, if some, probably minor, portion of the peasant migrants really did commit crimes, the circumstances undoubtedly reflected their status as outcasts, their exclusion from the mainstream. And third, often enough the floaters were victim more than perpetrator of crime.

Among the features of their circumstances that may have accounted for misdemeanors were the empty lives of those engaged in grinding toil without recreation or cultural relief.[216] According to two Chinese journalists describing the lot of the migrant laborer in a foreign firm,

> At work they're like a machineman, off the job, like a wooden man, almost without any leisure or cultural life. So they gamble, seek refuge in pornography, and grow degenerate.[217]

Other factors that may have been responsible for a higher incidence of crime among migrants (in China as elsewhere) were the difficult conditions under which they labored and existed day after day—inferior shelter, inadequate amenities, insecurity, and in many cases, low incomes—and their gender and age structure.[218] Since the great majority of first-generation immigrants are everywhere young men, the same group among any population from which criminals are always disproportionately drawn, migrants too will be responsible for a larger percentage of the crime in society than their percent of the total population alone would seem to predict.

And third, a significant but often slighted side of the picture is the role of the transients not as agents but as victims of crime. Indeed, in their encounters with city folk it is likely that the more frequent instigators of injustice and injury were not peasants at all, but instead their urban neighbors or employers, or the police. A volume of muckraking interviews with dozens of mobile ruralites provides many instances of what was clearly robbery and assault visited upon the farmers themselves. The book is rife with tales of abuse—delayed payments and denial of wages, harassment, physical aggression, and petty theft—and doleful musings by the injured parties, such as the following on being pickpocketed:

> "We people who drift about suffer a lot of loss . . ."
> "Why don't you inform against them?"
> "Who dares use an egg to strike out against a rock?"
> "Then why not report to the public security?"
> "We'd rather suffer one fist than 10 feet. If a person 'borrows' from you, you know that behind his back there are a lot of brothers."[219]

Asked of another, who had been attacked by a local competitor to the point of requiring hospitalization:

> "Did you report it?"
> He replied, "Report? They're local bullies, in league with the authorities. Where would we go to report?"
> When the officials at the industrial and commercial bureau heard about it, they said: "Whatever happens to you people who go out, you must cede a little. You shouldn't tangle with them, they're local villains."[220]

And on being hoodwinked by their employer and labor boss:

> The police say: "You outsiders come to work in Beijing in the several hundreds of thousands. We simply don't have enough force to protect you. So you people just have to pick yourselves up from where you fell."[221]

Probably some of these aggrieved outsiders turned to forms of revenge that then showed up as part of the criminal statistics.[222]

As in the 1930s, there were reports of gangs that robbed, cheated, blackmailed, and stole from the peasants within Beijing's Zhejiang Village, where criminal and victim were fellow "villagers";[223] indeed, among Henanese, Hebei, and Anhui migrants, fellow-native-place sojourners frequently became the object of harm.[224] There were more sensationalist stories of "vampire gangs that prey on unemployed young peasants, pretending they will find them jobs, who go on to force them to sell their own blood";[225] and tales of thousands of young peasant transient women kidnaped and sold by criminal gangs.[226]

And yet despite the many occurrences in which farmers were the prey, they rarely showed up in the data. Scholars investigating their plight explain that peasants who had been attacked rarely relayed the news of the crime to the authorities, both because they didn't trust the organs of the law and because they thought the costs would be too high.[227] If involved in a fight, it was no good going to the police for help; if the conflict was with a native Beijinger, regardless of the individual who was to blame all the outsider could hope to do was get away quietly after it was over.[228] In fact, in a survey of over thirty-five thousand migrants nationwide undertaken in 1994–95, 31 percent of the respondents reported that they felt their property or their persons to be unsafe in the cities.[229] That itinerant peasants themselves may be more prone than urbanites to be the injured party had not occurred to most city residents, to judge from surveys and the press.

I reserve for the last a troubling and enigmatic portion of the floating population, those people who seemed truly to be wandering aimlessly, perhaps in the city's roads or else by train from one municipality to the next, perhaps putting up temporarily at a train station or out in the open. These were the famous *mangliu*, the "blind drifters," who appeared to lack a destination, a purpose, address, steady occupation, or documentation of any sort—the "three withouts" mentioned in chapter 3. At New Year's 1994, Xinhua News Agency lamented over "what worries people most," which was

> those roving peasants who can't find jobs after experiencing many
> frustrations in recent years. Many peasants had to linger at train sta-
> tions, ports, or other public places after the Spring Festival, having a
> negative impact on normal social life.[230]

It was chiefly these elements who stirred up a chill of dread of the unknown among the settled urbanites. And, as the identity of these vagrants somehow became tangled in the public mind with criminals on the one side[231] and ordinary mobile peasants on the other, their very presence in the streets seemed to city people to convert floaters of every type into their fellow travelers. It conjured up for the "decent" citizens visions of hordes of homeless folk, dispossessed and ready to descend. As described by researchers from Henan, many of these people went out of the countryside on their own, ran out of money, and then could not find work. Unable to tolerate their situation, they turned into the *mangliu*.[232]

In truth, a governmental study done in late 1989—at a time of recession, when many construction projects had been suspended and private business was in disrepute—found that even at such a time the homeless represented a mere 3 to 4 percent of the total floating population.[233] In Guangzhou at that time, when the total floaters in the city district were counted at 900,000, only 9,390 persons, or about 1 percent, were discovered to be sleeping outside.[234] One study in late 1988 Shanghai came up with a total figure of 2.09 million migrants, but just 28,000 of them, or 1.03 percent, were found to be *mangliu*.[235] Again in 1993, Shanghai public security forces detained or repatriated 30,000 of these people, a figure, once again, equivalent to 1.5 percent of those considered part of the floating population of the city.[236] So once again we find urbanites' fears embellishing their perceptions with exaggeration.

This review of the types of and reasons for crime, the consideration of floaters as victims, and the look at the low proportions among them of "blind drifters" that surveyors found (at least as of the late 1980s recession) all expose the muddle of fact and fiction in which objective information about the floaters was often mired. Much of the problem—and of its perception by city people—seems to have its origin in the exclusionary and discriminatory practices and stances that surrounded the persons of the peasants as unregistered outcasts, noncitizens.

If city dwellers could have allowed the suspicious markets to operate in an untrammeled fashion, and if they could have allowed outsiders to participate and advance in them without prejudice—if, that is, they had recognized the migrants as being less competitive to their interests, and seen the markets as being more elastic as in fact they were—at least some of this crime might have disappeared. Though this would have heightened the rivalry between labor groups that undergirded municipal prosperity, it might also have enhanced the elasticity of urban peace and order as a public good. But such a scenario was impossible while city people's own benefit structure appeared to be crumbling around them.

MIGRANTS' CONTRIBUTION TO THE ERADICATION
OF THE URBAN PUBLIC GOODS REGIME

I challenge the grounds for much of the reaction of urban residents to the migrants because many of the effects attributed to migrants were really much more the result of markets. But in two ways migrants themselves did indeed contribute to the eradication of the urban public goods regime. This they did by engaging in behavior that was subversive of the framework of state planning and by undertaking activities that stimulated the market economy.

Undermining the Framework of the Plan

Made into outcasts and blamed for the decline in public goods that was often really the work of the market, many of the floaters scraped by through tactics—bribery, trafficking in false documents, tax evasion, labor market and job-related malpractices, and failure to register their residence—known to people in informal economies all over the world. They find themselves relegated to a second economy because they have been deemed unqualified or unsuitable for entry into the formal one.

The uncertainties of their lives encourage these practices; thus they cut corners and invest in subterfuge in order to survive, hustling for a foothold in an often unregulated and hotly competitive market.[237] From this perspective, the bribes they offer—the wages of outsiderhood—could be said to substitute for the taxes paid by members of the formal economy;[238] they could even be viewed as a form of insurance, as if these outsiders were thereby purchasing "security from prosecution."[239]

In that perspective, many among the floating visitors underwrote the current system of control. Rather than undermine or try to break the barriers they could not legally cross, those with the means to do so endorsed them. These floaters put their money into the status quo, as if tacitly acquiescing in the value of extant legal papers and procedures.

This they did by buying their way into the city and its procedures: they illicitly traded in forged documents (much as undocumented Mexican migrants do in the United States),[240] purchased *hukou*,[241] bribed to gain entry, and sent gifts to bureaucrats to obtain the right to do odd jobs. In the late 1980s, "obtaining, forging, and altering temporary residence certificates was very convenient," in the words of one Chinese social scientist.[242]

Reportage literature, official studies, and social scientific research are full of examples. Two Chinese journalists quote a repairman from Anhui temporarily working in Shanghai,

> Especially when you go out to find work, you must be a smiling child, deliver a carton of Marlboro cigarettes to the boss at 95 yuan a carton, give him ginseng, shrimp, and so forth, all amounting to several hundred yuan.[243]

A 1989 study by the Wuhan City Construction Management Bureau uncovered 192 cases of bribery, of which only one-fifth were attributed to state enterprises, the rest to rural teams.[244] In a sense, such corruption could be said to have reinforced the weight of official documents and patterns, by implicitly ceding to their authority.

Sojourners lacking official household registration in any city were supposed to register their presence there within three days; after three months they were obliged to obtain a temporary household certificate.[245] Failing to do so was not exactly breaking the law. Or at least there was no clear official consensus on the seriousness of this breach, one that lurked in the gray shadows between illegality and "noncompliance with regulations (*bu fuhe guiding*)."[246] But licit or not, the more important subtext was that this lapse spelled out the stateless limbo within which the urban interlopers lived. By 1989, as even state-sponsored researchers conclude,

> The temporary residence certificate [which one acquires in registering] is not very tightly linked to the floating population's personal interest, and the regulations are not strictly implemented, so they gradually have lost their binding force.[247]

This failure was acknowledged to be widespread, but not uniformly so across cities.[248] In 1988 one investigation found that only 30.5 percent of outsiders in Beijing either laboring or doing business were not registered, while nearly 75 percent were.[249] But by way of contrast, around the same time as many as 44 percent of those floating in Shanghai had not registered, and up to 70 percent of the laboring migrants in Guangzhou were in that category.[250]

We might conclude that this infraction was just an analogue to the behavior of those in informal economies elsewhere who had determined that the costs of becoming formal—paying taxes, following institutional procedures, keeping accounts, submitting to work regulations—surpassed the benefits derived.[251] A similar explanation holds that informal status is

chosen where the "government makes it difficult and expensive for them
to register their business or difficult and expensive to abide by the
rules."[252] Some of this analysis did fit the Chinese case; and one researcher notes that Chinese investigators believed that the excessive demands of officials were intentionally aimed at forcing the floating population into breaking the law, for that would enable them to rake in
fines.[253]

But there was more to the story in China's case. For the blanket
deprivation of the urban *hukou* to all rural incomers meant that the
certain impermanence of most floaters' stay in town, combined with their
labor bosses' recognition of this fact, made the bosses reluctant to invest
the energy and resources to enroll them on the books. This instability
also nurtured purposelessness among the transients and increased the
chances that they would not possess any fixed address or occupation that
could serve as their requisite credentials and thus as the foundation for
their identities in registering.[254]

In the produce markets, they nibbled away at the sanitary standards
designed for the official shops and stalls, desperate to wedge their way
into the business. They could be caught shifting their site and trading by
dark, all in the interest of bypassing the interrogations, inspections, and
collections of the bureaucrats.[255] Trash-pickers' take shaded into valuables,
and they raised their profits by tampering with their scales or repackaging
their booty to enhance its weight. In the Zhejiang Village, where there
was a sales volume of 1.5 billion yuan in 1995 according to official
statistics,[256] Beijing Vice Mayor Meng Xuenong complained that the city's
revenue from the businesses in Dahongmen (in Fengtai district, where
the village was situated) had dropped from 6 million yuan in 1994 to just
1 million in 1995.[257]

Not only that; the extensive tax evasion within the village that this
drop implied was often backed by armed resistance to city tax collectors,[258]
obviously an expression of the illegitimacy the outside merchants attributed to the assessments made by these officials.[259] I might note, however,
that the city administration's provision of fewer than ten agents for an
area housing nearly a hundred thousand residents demonstrated its own
failure to absorb the area into its framework.[260] The result of this evasion
plus maladministration, in popular perception, was that the transients in
the village "enjoy the subsidies of the Beijing permanent population,
while they benefit from what is in effect a tax-free 'priority treatment.' "[261]

In all these ways, the floaters' delinquency expressed an awareness of a relationship in flux. For it was where the controls from the old system remained tightest, as in the capital, that registration rates were relatively higher in the early 1990s.[262] Another important factor was the degree to which a local economy had become marketized; in Guangzhou, for instance, or in the heart of Beijing's Zhejiang Village,[263] where systemic rules had changed the most, the bureaucratic power of the old urban state over its intruders had become the weakest.[264] And as the economy opened wider, any benefits registration had once afforded, either in locating work or in obtaining food, had diminished substantially.

Along this line of thought, though ignorance was sometimes attributed to floaters to account for their lack of respect for the city's rules, another interpretation may fit more aptly. The cocky and alienated independence of some peasants in the face of the declining clout of the state and the emergence of a new economic form seem more to the point. The fearless confidence of some floaters in confronting a state and a community that, while ostracizing them, was also of no use to them, is captured in this conversation at a spontaneous labor market:[265]

> Asked why they don't register, some say: "I didn't know about registration." Others say: "Registration requires paying money and it restrains you." The reporter then asks, "Aren't you afraid of violating the law acting this way?" An eighteen- or nineteen-year-old with a Henanese accent responds, unconcerned: "Afraid of what? Come to check on us, and we'll run away. Catch us, and we've no money."[266]

There was also a view among the urban-dwelling farmers that registration fees just functioned as one more form of local bureaucrats' coercive extraction of fees, and so not abiding by the rules served as their silent rebellion.[267]

Taken together, the overall impact of these transgressions thus had a far more powerful meaning than just making do in the status quo (although that was true as well, at least for the short run). The catalogue of violations recounted above stood as a mode of denying the right of the old state and its plan—a plan that anyway had excluded them—to order the migrants' lives.

Thus, in buying temporary safety to shelter their condition, the floaters wore down old systems by nonobservance. And their "chaotic" infractions ate away at the plan and the lifestyle it supported.[268] Circumstances may have provided the need for them to act as they did, but they also offered opportunity to open up new space. And as their substitute practices accumulated, they corroded the bedrock on which the patterns of the past were built.

Stimulating the Market

But if the migrants refused to participate in the plan, they surely partook of the market; and they did so on terms that were vastly different from the economic conduct that had gone on in the city in the past. For one thing, they produced a fair measure of revenue for their places of destination without any guidance or directives from the state. In addition to the taxes turned over on their sales, the sundry fees coercively collected by urban bureaucrats, and the purchases of household registration permits mentioned in chapter 3, they made other kinds of payments to urbanites and other contributions to the urban economy. For instance, there was their rent for rooms let out by city residents, their own daily livelihood expenditures, their savings deposits, their industrial output value, and the foreign exchange their products garnered. In addition, they also contributed supplies of various sorts, plus their own labor power.

There are several types of information available on migrants' taxes, though little by way of aggregation. In 1987 in just one district of Chengdu, open markets netted 1.1 million yuan of taxes and 700,000 of fees.[269] In Tianjin in 1991 more than 5 million yuan in taxes came from one industrial market alone where outsiders prevailed.[270] Wuhan's financial offices found that in 1989 migrants contributed 40 percent of the taxes collected from the whole city's markets and private entrepreneurs.[271]

One researcher estimates that in Shanghai, the total rent that could be received by Shanghai residents would reach 1 billion yuan per year, assuming that two million floaters were renting rooms from local residents at an average annual rent of 500 yuan per person.[272] But my survey of housing in chapter 7 will suggest that if, as officially announced, the floating population in Shanghai was about three million in the mid-1990s, it was quite unlikely that as many as two-thirds of these people were living in legally rented rooms at such a fee.

The daily expenditures of sojourners were calculated variously by different cities. An analyst in Wuhan judged that outsiders spent 8.67 yuan per day as of 1988, from which the city obtained nearly 7 million yuan; another study yielded a figure of 10.3 million a year later.[273] Shanghai estimated at the end of the 1980s that outsiders' consumption amounted to one-fifth of the city's social commodities' retail sales volume.[274] It was not indicated in these figurings, however, how much peasant floaters themselves spent, as distinct from all nonresidents (including wealthy tourists). For this I have just a single datum, from 1989 Hangzhou: each peasant worker there paid 4 to 5 yuan for one day's consumption needs.[275]

In Dongguan City in the Pearl River Delta, outside labor was estimated to produce U.S. $37,440 worth of foreign exchange earnings in 1990.[276] As for savings, one source noted that in 1988, in one township of Guangdong's Bao'an county, outsiders remitted over 30 million yuan to other places; however, they also placed more than 90 million yuan in local savings banks.[277]

In addition to their contribution to revenue, which by itself must have stimulated local markets, migrants also brought or arranged for the delivery of stocks—industrial commodities, food, and other supplies—to sell to the cities' populaces. The best measures of this contribution came from the produce markets that proliferated so energetically once peasants were allowed into the urban areas. In Wuhan in 1989, of the total people in business at the city's 159 industrial products and produce markets, the 21,300 of them said to be from the outside accounted for 57 percent of the total.[278] In that year, these transients supplied 74 percent of the meat, 85 percent of the eggs, 62 percent of the aquatic products, and 73 percent of the vegetables in these markets, to be exact![279] And in Beijing, in 1990, 75 percent of the 4,230 people known to be engaged in private business in the open markets were counted as being peasants from the suburbs and other provinces.[280] A frequently encountered refrain in the texts on this issue was this one: "They've solved the problem for the people of Shanghai [or any other large city] that it was 'hard to eat vegetables.'"[281]

As for their input as labor, the jobs peasants filled were often ones crucial to particular sectors and sometimes, as Cockcroft notes in writing of illegal immigrant labor in capitalist economies, vital even to the entire local economy as well.[282] For instance, in Zhengzhou in the 1980s, they "resolved the enterprises' pressing need for labor," in the textiles, steel, chemical fertilizer, and coal brick industries.[283]

In the construction trade in a range of cities—such as Chengdu, Zhengzhou, and Hangzhou—temporary contract labor from the countryside already amounted to more than 60 to 66 percent of the number of the regular workers by 1989. Some of the most important types of work, like foundations, concrete mixing, and interior renovation, were all assigned to them. Each peasant builder was estimated to create 22,000 yuan of output value per year in Chengdu around that time.[284] And as we have seen earlier, as time went on, substituting peasant labor became a deliberate choice—as opposed to using it just as replacement when urbanites refused to work in a trade—as a means of producing great savings for cities.

The textile trade was the other one where peasants had already made a critical difference in several cities by the end of the 1980s. In Chengdu, though rural contract labor only accounted for about one-fifth overall, in the spinning and weaving workshops, two-thirds of the laborers hailed from the countryside. In Hangzhou's famous silk trade, one-third of the workers vital to the sector had to be recruited from the rural areas, while in the most arduous work, in chemical fiber production, over half the workers were floaters.[285] This assistance to the more traditional sectors was matched by floaters' creation of trades totally absent from the cities in the days of austere socialism, such as tailoring, shoe and bicycle repair, barbering, catering, and the like.

And, as scholarship on migrant labor elsewhere in the world states, it is not just that "foreigners" come cheap as compared with standard city workers in state-owned firms. The flexibility of such workers, as expressed in their docile willingness to work night shifts and their resignation to employment insecurity, allows plants to respond to financial crises and recessions with ease, to keep the machines running overtime, and to make do with substandard equipment.[286] Though this outcome is very commonplace in other countries, for post-1949 China its incidence on such a large scale was something quite new.

Moreover, their acceptance of a lack of benefits could save factories literally millions, and Chinese management was quite cognizant of the possibilities. For instance, here are the so very precise calculations performed in 1989 by the Zhengzhou Textile Industrial Bureau:

1. no wage subsidies (labor insurance, half-price medical care for family), for one person/one year saves 216 yuan;

2. no maternity leave (three months), or award of three months' vacation for having just one child, for one person saves 500 yuan; and

3. no family dorm: if the 6,000 peasant workers in the plants lived in factory housing at the rate that regular staff do (60 percent), we would need 20 million yuan to house their families.[287]

For all these reasons, the mere availability of floaters prepared to work—at least at first on any terms—offered not only all of these several financial and material returns noted above. Besides all that, the very presence of the peasants assisted in the evisceration of all the old, benevolent management rules, an emasculation that was going on at any rate as a result of market reforms.

This process, certainly without the transients' expressly intending it, ultimately furthered the alteration of former urban industrial and employment structures that, in the pro-marketization milieu of the 1980s and 1990s, was occurring in Chinese cities anyway.[288] For not only was there a breakdown of old conventions: migrants' very urban existence in itself also stimulated and accelerated the progress of this marketization, as they participated in new forms of ownership, management, and employment; as they presented a competitive force; and as they furnished market information and linkages with other places.[289]

. . .

With this chapter, I fill out the threefold structure—including state policies about geographical mobility and urban bureaucracies—that thrust floaters into a realm where they were totally unqualified for citizenship once they became resident in urban areas. Even though their hitting up against the public goods of the city made it seem to urbanites that they were partaking of many of the goods of the once-socialist city—jobs that city people could have had, low-cost water and electricity, bus space, and stably priced staple foods—as they appeared to ruin its previous public peace, in fact in most cases the newcomers themselves were barely competing with citizens or even interfering at all.

But since they emerged into the municipalities, and into city dwellers' consciousness, at the same time markets did, they fell subject to a peculiar dynamic. In this dynamic, both bureaucrats and citizens perceived them through lenses on reality lent by the old state plan, so they appeared particularly chaotic, threatening, and disorderly; their spontaneity and potential for disruption became exaggerated, along with that of the markets. As the apparent rivalrousness and inelasticity of every public good they drew upon became amplified because of this confusion, discrimination intensified against them. The outcome could not be positive in terms of the prospects for peasant citizenship in town.

What peasants symbolized for city people, then, was the sense that what urbanites had considered their birthright, the urban public goods regime—according to which only they could deserve the benefits of privileged city living—was in transition, in decline. So as migrants became a metaphor for the markets they accompanied, their seeming assault on perquisites got much more attention than what was probably more important: their genuine contribution to the erosion of the administrative side of the planned economy and the model they provided of a new mode of economic activity. For as the transition to the market in the municipalities advanced, the mundane, daily activities of the floaters themselves—working at their trades, trading in the fairs, and struggling to survive—pushed the process onward.

PART TWO

Agency

5 State Policies II

*The Floating Population
Leaves Its Rural Origins*

I now reverse my focus, upending the kaleidoscope. In this next part the argument pivots on the same three institutions whose effects on the migrants chapters 2–4 examined: state migration policies, urban bureaucracies, and the rationing regime in the cities, again placing each at the center of one chapter apiece. But I shift to gaze from the structure of the institutions to the floaters as agents, though surely not as fully unbounded ones. I also switch from analyzing the impact of policy, bureaucracy, and discrimination upon the migrants as a uniform group to exploring variation among them, and the sources of that variation.

In addition, in this part I consider the expanding range of agency for mobile peasants as they moved from countryside to city. The previous two chapters demonstrate that migrants and markets, in confronting state institutions—the urban bureaucracy and the rationing regime—twisted and even partially remade them. Yet the actions and reactions of metropolitan officials and residents toward newcomers severely undercut outsiders' opportunities for acceptance and inclusion among the city folk as citizens on regular terms.

Here I return to the subject of chapter 2, the first institution, state policies about and affecting migration, but I ask explicitly whether these policies left much space for agency. Beginning in the early 1980s, as we saw in chapter 2, the leadership's reactivation of markets throughout the economy progressively relaxed the rules about, vastly enlarged the scope of, and recast the course and content of the geographical movement of the population, especially that of peasants. But clearly the marketization that politicians thereby unleashed materialized against the backdrop of a powerful statism that by no means evaporated all at once. Even as millions of ruralites exercised their agency in choosing to relocate, their options as they did so were very much the product of forces far beyond their reach. The continuing clout of the state (and its prior policies) in shaping what happened in the markets reduced transients' agency, even if the impact varied across the countryside. Moreover, these policies, in conjunction with economic forces, deeply influenced both the motives and the traits of the bulk of those who moved, and also where they went.

So, overall, this chapter elaborates upon the ongoing subjecthood (a concept I alluded to in chapter 2) of the sojourners as they exited the countryside. The discussion implicitly reveals the limits of agency and the truncated role for rational choice, as it elucidates the larger, often at least partially state-determined, factors that bounded farmers—even in an age of raging marketization—when they formulated their choices. The following two chapters address the development of the transients' agency, as they engaged in the production of alternative forms of urban citizenship, once they settled down in town.

The floaters' decision to migrate raises three specific questions: why, precisely, did many peasants want to leave the countryside in China in the postsocialist period (i.e., after 1982); what recruitment processes assisted in prying them out; and what was the ongoing linkage between the leavers and their native places? In order to grapple with these queries, I first look at three models of rural-to-urban migration, showing how the Chinese situation calls for their modification in order to explain the peasants' departure; and then I appeal to modernization and dependency theory to consider the persisting bond between ruralites and their home villages.

THREE MODELS OF MIGRATION

The first of these three models about migration weighs "pushes" and "pulls" and usually focuses upon purely economic factors. Its assumptions are those of the neoclassical economist, as it tends to be based upon the atomistic, rational-choice, cost-benefit calculations of the individual actor.[1] The second is a macromodel of historical-structural interpretation, and the third a meso model of social networks.

The push-pull model takes as its premise that ruralites considering an exit from the countryside face a choice and are in a position to weigh and select from the pertinent features of the homeland against the supposed allures of the city. Samuel Huntington and Joan Nelson, for instance, believe that farmers will choose escape, given bad or deteriorating conditions at home, so long as exit is a possibility.[2] John Connell and his colleagues specify the chief economic factors motivating geographical mobility away from the fields: lack of income-earning opportunities; high person-to-land ratios; generalized economic depression; and inequalities in the distribution of and access to land and other resources, between regions, villages, and families.[3]

Other analysts, who also employ a microeconomic model but emphasize more explicitly a rational-choice perspective, postulate that individual migrants (presumably fully cognizant of their total situation) react to spatial imbalances in the basic factors of production and resultant disparities in wages.[4] The best known approach of this type is Michael P. Todaro's; he puts "rational" "considerations of the relative benefits and costs"—mainly financial but also psychological—and the "expected" "urban-rural real wage differentials" at the heart of his explanation.[5]

But proponents of the second, macrostructural, mode of reasoning, find that simply listing comparative conditions in the places of origin (the country) and the sites of destination (the towns) is too simplistic. Their fundamental criticism is that this is a static, superficial perspective that ignores both the underlying causes that confront migrants and the dynamics that molded the alternatives of actors' calculations.[6] Rational models, say the structuralists, presume a role for conscious deliberation and choice where in fact there is sometimes little space for maneuver between starvation and departure.[7]

According to these critics, an historical-cum-structural approach, by contrast, would pay heed to the forces that have shaped markets, constrained information, or otherwise biased migrants' decisions.[8] Such a model shifts the investigation away from the moment of choice toward, instead, the origins of the particular costs and benefits that face the farmer, such as the pressures that have altered the organization of production, those that have reordered the spatial demand for labor, and those that have affected modes of recruitment and compensation.[9]

One such structural explanation puts migrants' relocation in the larger context of deliberate labor recruitment and forced labor extraction; another, relevant to the attractions of China's foreign-invested special economic zones, ascribes it to the impersonal penetration of the periphery by the international, capitalist economic system.[10] All of these analyses negate the narrowness of a focus on the autonomous choices of the individual actor.

But some find this structurally oriented framework wanting, because it ignores the principal variable prominent in a third model, which is the social networks that connect potential leavers with those who preceded them into the cities.[11] Migration is not the simple outcome of poverty, however induced, but rather grows from previous bonds, both economic and political, between the locales of origin and destination. It is, two scholars of this persuasion hold, "a network-driven process."[12]

Network theorists also fault an economistic push-pull approach not so much for being shallow as for being unable to explain migratory patterns that have nothing, or little, to do with economic explanations.[13] For instance, according to Manual Garcia y Griego, "About 70 percent of the flow of Mexican migrants into the U.S. departs from only eight Mexican states, which are not the poorest regions in Mexico."[14]

One chief value of the network approach is that, as opposed to the rational-choice model, it examines streams of itinerants, as opposed to atomistic individuals on the move.[15] Thus, it forces the investigator to unearth earlier flows of mobility—whose cause is not necessarily prejudged by reference to economic motives alone—that laid the foundations for those transfers we witness in the present.[16]

Despite these critiques, the network approach is by no means necessarily antithetical to the other two; utilized in light of their concerns it can actually subsume them. For, as Richard Mines argues, "The migratory network receives its signals from the larger society [the macro- and historically fashioned environment], and in turn creates options [opportunities provided by social contacts] for its members [the micro-, choosing actors]."

These "options" certainly constitute one type of "pull" and so are compatible with a theory of rational action, and thus of agency and choice.[17] The major difference is that network contacts are not just one more factor in a list determining rational actors' decisions. For they have an independent influence: they moderate the signals sent by the macro environment, reducing the associated costs and enhancing the benefits. And they do so in accord with potential movers' membership in particular networks. The contacts, therefore, may shape the options available to the affiliates of the network in very significant ways.

As this material indicates, the proponents of three at least apparently disparate models contend. But in an analysis of the Chinese floating population the models themselves do not compete; instead, they collapse, under the weight of the state—a state much more involved in regulating its populace's mobility than most other states. For the policies of the Chinese state either created or exacerbated the push factors that drove poorer people out of the less promising rural areas; state initiatives also allowed more fortunate and skilled migrants from other sorts of areas to take advantage of opportunities elsewhere.

Over the long term, the state was responsible for many of the macro-structural conditions causing certain areas to deliver transients and others to receive them; and the measures it mandated—and its bureaucracy enforced—often created some of the networks that guided itinerants' movements. Deliberate recruitment, too, was often the work of state personnel and state agencies in China. In short, decades of planning, policy, and bureaucracy—some of which continued even into the era of reform—helped fashion much of the macrostructural parameters, as well as set up (or reinforce) many of the social networks within which Chinese peasants made their "choices" about moving.

Moreover, in a negative sense, the state stymied the development of nonstate-related social networks. Its substitution of state-plan-driven, vertical commands for marketized connections over decades must have acted during the years of socialism to break down (or at least attenuate) once extant urban-rural, interregional, and enterprise-job seeker horizontal relationships, as well as to block new ones. And once state planning was retracted in the early 1980s, this long history of privileging only vertical ties must have made Chinese migrant labor even more dependent on primary social relationships than in other societies.[18] This process, accordingly, left hiring practices for migrant labor in many ways as fully personalistic and often authoritarian as they were sixty years ago.[19] Here I refer to recruitment through local ties; the centrality of gangs and labor bosses; and the flimsiness of contracts, supplemented or replaced by the use of guarantors, plus deposits as a condition for securing a job, funds that fall under employers' arbitrary control.

In grappling with the three questions in this chapter—about why peasants leave, the nature of their recruitment out, and the roots of their persisting ties with the villages—we find parts of their explanation in the theories outlined above. Notions of pushes and pulls at the individual level and of macrostructural conditions do help explain the forces that press (or draw) peasants out of their homes; and network theory is suggestive in understanding the nature of recruitment in the Chinese labor market. Two other competing theories—modernization and dependency—shed light on the influence of migration on the countryside. But I must make one major adjustment to them all: in China the clumsy prowess of the government has particularly skewed the operation of all of the factors to which the theories point.

WHY LEAVE THE COUNTRYSIDE?
PUSHES, PULLS, AND MACROSTRUCTURE
Push Factors I: The Political Economy of State Policies

In a large-scale survey of 985 households conducted in 10 provinces in summer 1988, the principal reason peasants cited for why they left their homes was that their income from agriculture was too little (59.3 percent); the second most frequently offered cause was that they lacked an adequate supply of land and that the surplus labor in their areas was too great (13.9 percent).[20] How can these factors—common in rural, urbanizing societies around the world—be explained in the Chinese case?

The seemingly microchoices that individual floaters made to exit from their countryside homes clearly occurred within a definite macrocontext, one that was simultaneously determined on two levels. The first of these was the political economy established by state policies, from which all rural areas suffered; the second was the specific ecosystem formed by the geography of their native places, which was more a product of purely economic forces and of sociocultural traditions and therefore varied across the countryside.

State Policies Leading to Scarce Arable Land and Surplus Labor A crucial issue was that of the increasing gap between available arable land and proliferating population. By the time the communes began to come down in 1980, the peasant population had grown by more than 60 percent over what it had been when rural collectivization started in 1953, a growth to no small degree the result of three state policies: the explicitly pronatalist stance of the leadership over most of this period;[21] the official prohibition upon the departure from one's village; and the provisioning regime in the communes, whereby, according to James Lee and Wang Feng, "peasant families no longer had any incentive to plan their demographic behavior."[22] Besides, such families craved multiple offspring in the absence of any rural old-age security provision by the state. The central state saved itself expenditure on such welfare in the countryside by counting on the communes and especially on traditional customs that dictated that children were to care for their parents.[23]

As a result of these policies, the number of people in the countryside increased, while (according to official calculations) arable land dropped from 107 million hectares in 1957 to only 99 in 1977,[24] a decline of 7.5 percent.[25] By the end of the 1980s, the population was increasing by over 115 million and acreage decreasing by almost 10 million *mu* per year, leaving an average national acreage of 1.29 *mu* of cultivated land per person, "less than one third the world average," according to a Chinese scholar.[26] A popular ditty, doubtless an exaggeration, had it that "many peasants spend three months doing farm work, one month celebrating New Year's, and eight months idling about."[27] A survey conducted by the Ministry of Labor in 1995 showed that a full 20 percent of respondents in eighty villages across the country reported that they were forced to make do with less than one *mu* of arable land per laborer, too little to provide an adequate living. Nationally, even the average two *mu* per laborer represented a drastic shrinkage from the 12.5 *mu* average of 1952.[28]

Primarily the outcome of these steadily worsening person-to-land ratios, the numbers of what the state perceived to be rural "surplus" labor accelerated, even as the central government's statisticians lost all track of their magnitude, wildly estimating them to be anywhere in the range between 100 and 200 million in the mid-1990s.[29] In some places where the problem was particularly severe, such as China's most populous province of Sichuan, the official *People's Daily* had already announced by 1987 that over 50 percent of the labor force was "redundant."[30]

Preferring to see the peasants remain on the land even after freeing them from it, the regime proposed to them various modes of transfer out of agriculture other than departing from the countryside.[31] But what seemed the most promising of these avenues—participation in town and village enterprises (TVEs)—was able to occupy less than half the surplus labor as of the mid-1990s. A typical governmental analysis held that in 1994, while the TVEs had absorbed approximately 100 million peasants, nearly 200 million remained as surplus, three-quarters of it in central and western China.

According to the Chinese demographer Gu Shengzu, even after some 60 million had left the farms to labor elsewhere, more than 100 million remained.[32] The problem of local absorption of surplus labor into TVEs was exacerbated with time, as the technical level and capital intensity of the firms rose: each increase of 1 percent in gross value of industrial output had led to a 0.57 percent growth in employment in these firms in the years 1978–84, but that increase had fallen to 0.15 percent by 1992.[33]

The words of traveling peasants interviewed by two Chinese journalists in 1989 bring life to these data:

> A nineteen-year-old junior high graduate from Xianju county, Zhejiang, seems delicate, like a student. His group of seven people all recently graduated, had just read a notice saying that people are

needed at a construction work site in Changchun. They quickly dashed from Hangzhou to Shanghai and bought their tickets . . . much better than staying in the rural areas with nothing to do.

There's a lot of scrap collectors in Shanghai's outskirts; saw some at dusk, pulling a cart full of junk, an old man from Anhui's Feidong county, with his son. . . . Reporter asks about their family situation—why he has to go out to do this bitter work. He candidly answered: "Feidong county is a suburb of Hefei City . . . it's densely populated and the land is very infertile. Our family has seven people and only 8 *mu* of land. No matter how hard you work, can only fill your stomach, not as good as going out to work to make some money. . . . I'm afraid this vile spawn [indicating his son] will become a bachelor in the future—this is why at a ripe age I go out to Shanghai and do this work that other people despise. . . . We live near the big city, so we don't need a bride price, but wedding is expensive—even rural young girls marry want color TV, radio, furniture set. Without 10 thousand yuan, can't do it."

A village construction team from Wusheng county, Sichuan, composed of thirty-one people, now working in Haikou, Hainan. Their leader said the produce at home is plentiful, eating is no problem, but because people are many and land is scarce, the average per capita arable is only half a *mu*. If the wife and kids till it, that's enough. Young, strong people have nothing to do at home; only can go out to work and don't care how much they earn, if they can save a little, that's fine.[34]

My own 1992 interviews with peasants encountered on city streets and factories in Wuhan, Tianjin, and Nanjing corroborated these tales. As one example:

A twenty-two-year-old female from Huai'an in Subei, now a restaurant worker in Nanjing, is paid 80 yuan a month and gets her meals free, with no rent to pay. She sleeps in the restaurant, on a chair; works 5:15 A.M. to 10 P.M., with no days off. The job is unsuitable, she laments, and she wants to go back home. But there's nothing to do there. Her older sister, unmarried, sits at home, completely idle.[35]

Once the commune was no longer present to dictate the content of people's workdays, there was a vastly more efficient deployment of peasant household labor in the countryside. Other sources of the labor surplus were increases in the level of mechanization and in the application of electricity, chemical fertilizer, and pesticides per *mu* of arable over the years, which eventually—if not at first—worked to reduce somewhat the need for sheer manual effort.[36]

One outcome of this sense of being unneeded at home was a mood of aimlessness, as young people without a specific plan made for the urban areas:

> In a township of Dongguan, Guangdong, there are 540 Sichuan girls from the far suburbs of Chengdu; because their spirit is very strong, local people call them "Sichuan peppery misses." Three came to chat with the reporters; are junior and senior high graduates, working in processing enterprises. . . . Speaking of their future plans, these lively young girls at once change to being at a loss: "On the one hand, go on as we are, on the other hand look around; wherever we end up, we'll figure it out there."[37]

Two young men I interviewed expressed similar thoughts:

> A scrap-paper collector in Nanjing, twenty years old, also from Anhui, has a wife and nine-month-old child who have already gone back home. He's attained just five years of primary school education. Why is he here, I asked? "We have 2.5 *mu* a person to till, which is rather a lot." "But," he complained, doubtless repeating a local ditty, "tilling the fields is meaningless . . . if it isn't drought then it's floods" [*mei-yisi zhongtian . . . bushi han jiushi yan*].[38]

> An eighteen-year-old shoe repairer from Zhejiang left home after primary school and came directly to Tianjin, five years ago. He came to make money, since he can't make any tending the fields. I asked, "Why come so far?" "The further the better," was his rejoinder. "Why not go on to Tibet, if that's the case?" I wondered. He ran out of travel money, was his only excuse. Does he have future plans? "Live one day, write off one day" [*huo yitian, swan yitian*], he quips.[39]

Policies Making Agricultural Work Unprofitable and Rural Incomes Low   The state was an important culprit as well when it came to the unprofitability of agriculture in many regions, especially in recent years. The fundamental explanation lay in Communist theories of economic development. According to ideas first raised in the 1920s in the Soviet Union, agriculture was to serve as the source of primitive accumulation. Returns from this sector were to go into industry, chiefly heavy industry.

The state garnered high returns from taxes on the output of agriculture, as well as a price structure that squeezed the peasants between low procurement prices for their produce and high prices for their inputs.[40] At the microlevel of the peasant household, profits no longer mattered anyway after 1955, when the process of collectivization thrust each family into larger and larger working units with time, so that the labor of the individual had less and less direct impact upon what he or she was paid.

When family farming first replaced the communes after 1982, it seemed that the incentive structure for the peasant family might shift significantly. Each household was allowed to operate a plot contracted to it by the local authorities. The dissolution of the commune coincided with a decision to raise the prices for agricultural products in early 1979; combined with the reopening of rural produce markets, both in the countryside and then in the cities, these changes spurred peasant initiative, and incomes on the farms at first rose faster than those in urban areas. Over the years 1978 to 1987, real per capita income growth for city households climbed at the rate of 6.9 percent a year, while for peasant households the rate was 11.5 percent.[41] Another telling figure was the real consumption gap between cities and country, which narrowed from 2.9:1 in 1978 to only 2.2:1 by 1985.[42]

But after 1985, when a bumper harvest led to government changes in grain procurement policy and a reduction in the marginal price paid for above-quota grain, overall farm prices dropped by an average of 9.2 percent. At that point, consumption in the countryside slowed down, while that in urban areas picked up.[43] Also a result of these measures, the closing of the gap between rural and urban incomes (which had stood at a ratio of nearly 2.4:1 in 1978) begun in the early years of the rural reform, had already started to open wider in the mid-1980s. By 1990 the 1978 ratio had reappeared. In table 4, which covers the period from the initiation of legal migration to the noticeable shift in the ratio of incomes, I illustrate these trends.[44] By 1994 the gap had widened to 2.6:1.[45]

Behind these gross summary statistics lie far more arresting anecdotal data. A writer in *Society*, a Shanghai journal, for instance, claimed in 1991 that a peasant could make a mere 150 yuan a year from one *mu* of land, but 1,000 as an urban migrant.[46] Another case comes from Alan Liu's research, which reveals that in a hilly region of Shaanxi province, the differential in annual income between a migrant construction worker and a peasant was already as much as eight to one in the mid-1980s.[47]

State-set prices (in addition to inflation in these years) had a great deal to do with these declining trends in agricultural profitability and differential incomes after 1985. By 1987, for instance, the costs of agricultural production—because of official prices for the necessary inputs—were clearly growing more and more unfavorable for farmers; in that year alone, they rose nationwide between 20 and 30 percent over the year before. The effect was that the net profits from each *mu* of grain fell by

Table 4. Per Capita Annual Income in Rural and Urban Areas, 1982–1990

Year	Rural	Urban	Urban (rur=1)	Rural (urb=100)
1982	270	535	1.98	50
1983	310	573	1.85	54
1984	355	660	1.86	54
1985	398	749	1.88	53
1986	424	910	2.15	47
1987	463	1012	2.19	46
1988	545	1192	2.19	46
1989	602	1388	2.31	43
1990	630	1523	2.42	41

SOURCE: "Income Distribution Statistics Analyzed," *Jingji yanjiu* 1 (1992): 53–63, translated in Joint Publications Research Service CAR-92-043, June 22, 1992, 14 (original table was based on 1981, 1983, 1986, 1989–91 Statistical Yearbooks of China and the National Economic Statistical Abstract for 1984).

18.1 percent from 1986.[48] Conditions continued to worsen for the peasantry thereafter. Compared with 1988, the price index of farm products rose by only 10.87 percent in 1992, as relative prices on the grain market dropped in late 1992, while the price index of capital goods used on the farms rose by 33.59 percent.[49]

State investment policy must also bear part of the responsibility. The leadership, hoping that reorganization in the countryside would by itself stimulate a major upsurge in productivity, cut back investment in agriculture over the course of the 1980s.[50] Over the years 1981–85, the government slashed the percentage of investment given to agriculture in total investment from a thirty-year average of 11 percent of total investment in capital construction to only 5.1 percent; in 1986–88, the rate was a mere 3 percent.[51] Peasants, recognizing the mounting insecurity under which they were struggling, shrank from making their own long-term investment in the land but instead plundered the soil in the short term.[52] The resultant drop in the fertility of the soil and in its ability to resist natural calamities fed a vicious circle of accelerating unprofitability.[53]

Peasants who had left the land expressed their keen awareness of this unprofitability, as in these quotations:

A Shanghai neighborhood with black, polluted water and stench. Subei people [those from northern Jiangsu] live on boats there, come to the city to do transport work. Reporter went to speak with them. They are peasants from the Yancheng region, carrying bricks, tiles, sand, and rocks from Zhejiang to Shanghai, a mobile transport team. Reporter asks if they are satisfied. They reply: "Though the mosquitoes and flies are five times more on this black water than on the shore, and the stench of polluted water is such that we can't get our food down, but our life is guaranteed . . . life on the boat is bitter and tiring, one boat full of bricks is 50,000 jin [2 jin equal a kilogram], sometimes spine all worn out. Last year only earned 4–5,000 yuan." "If it's like that," the reporter queries, "why not go home and till the soil?" "Agriculture today is also very hard," they reply. "The prices of things the peasants use go up, we can't hold our own."

One hundred twenty girls from Suiyang county, Guizhou, working in a processing enterprise producing Christmas flowers in Dongguan in the Pearl River Delta. One, who had been a primary school teacher at home, had helped her parents with their burdens since she was young. "To lighten their load, I went to the mountains to collect pig feed, and then fed the pigs and the ducks; at harvest helped in the fields, all day in the mud, like a mud monkey; still couldn't buy a decent piece of clothes."[54]

By the mid-1990s, according to Croll and Huang's work with data from eight villages, declining agricultural incomes meant that where funds could not be garnered from nonagricultural activities at home, income from activities outside the village became essential simply to sustain agricultural production itself.[55]

Another significant element in state-induced disparities between the two sectors was the policy of state subsidization of urbanites, especially when pitted against the taxes peasants must pay. Azizur Rahman Khan and his colleagues calculated in the late 1980s that while 39 percent of urban income was provided by the government in net subsidies, the average rural household was at the same time handing over 2 percent of its income in taxes. In fact, this work exposed the alarming information that the average per capita urban subsidy of 720 yuan in 1988 amounted to 95 percent of the total rural disposable income per person that year (760.1 yuan).[56]

The data cited above, however, represent only the official inequities: yet another source of peasants' grievance was the unofficial local, often arbitrary exactions—sometimes because cadres were venal, but often because rural officials, themselves underpaid and their work underfinanced, were simply unable to meet their budgets—which made for much higher levels of inequality.[57] In one moving example, a peasant floater and his wife conversed in front of two journalists in 1989:

> "I've lost money in the city, but I'm not thinking of returning home . . . to avoid subjection to further injustices . . . electricity is often turned off at harvest time, so we can't draw water, then the crops die. The supply and marketing co-op comes with fertilizer, but the township, village, and brigade cadres take the lead and there's not much left for ordinary people. By the time it reaches us, we have to pay a high price. Whatever the state supplies the cadres take first advantage."
>
> His wife, shy at first, at this point can't hold back, rails about cadre corruption and favoritism, bribery, rapacity.
>
> The husband quickly stops his wife and warns: "A few more months without work and we'll have no money for rice and even this small room will not belong to us; where will you escape to then?"[58]

Moreover, the leadership was slow to take note of the grievances in the inland areas, apparently only fully awakening to the anger accompanying these imbalances with the two hundred or so scattered rural uprisings of 1992 to 1993.[59] In the summer of 1994, the government's *China Daily* quoted a "senior official" as recognizing the regime's responsibility for the imbalance, in admitting that "the central government excluded the inland region from opening to the outside in the late 1970s, leaving it lagging behind."[60]

By early 1993, the State Council had adopted a policy intended to speed up the development of rural enterprises in the west. But it was still another two years before the leadership even announced "plans" to install a revenue transfer system to narrow the gaps in economic development among regions, urged that foreign investment be made in the underdeveloped areas, and arranged for an increase in special loans for TVEs in the central and western areas.[61] David Zweig notes that it was not until November 1996 that party chief Jiang Zemin called on central and local officials to "strike a balance between industrial and agricultural development."[62] The effects of these initiatives would be slow in coming.

And yet interview data suggest that these push factors were not the whole story. Other migrants in the city were not so much pushed to sojourn there but rather pulled by opportunity to do so, some of them sporting quite a positive and future-oriented outlook:

> At a silk weaving factory in Tianjin, I met three young women. Two were from Henan, chosen to work in the factory because they had just graduated from high school. If they didn't come here, what would

they have done, I inquired? There's some handicrafts work [making rope] and town and village enterprises in their area, or they could have gone into business there. The other one was from Hebei: her parents would like her to stay in the city in order to get some training.[63]

Five young men from Hunan villages, in their early twenties, were selling shoulder bags on the street in downtown Hankou. All are high school graduates. They came there because they had heard business was brisk. They prefer Wuhan to Changsha, because there's too much competition for their product in Changsha. One plans to stay another year, then go home to study electronics.[64]

A twenty-four-year-old woman, unmarried, from Changzhou, Sunan (southern Jiangsu), was at work in a Nanjing produce market. She sells vegetables to help her older sister, who married a Nanjing man sent to their village during the Cultural Revolution. Living with them, she pays no rent. A middle-school graduate, she worked in handicrafts before coming here. Her home is economically developed, and a lot of people there work in town and village enterprises. But her family is poor, and she can make more money in Nanjing than at home.[65]

How can I account for differences such as these?

Push Factors II: The Ecosystems of Labor Export Provinces

Surveys concur that, on average, 12 to 14 percent of the labor force in sending regions across the country had departed to live and work outside the village—that is, these workers were absent at the time of the survey.[66] But despite the unfavorable state policies documented above, in most regions of China most peasants were not forced to leave home. Most significantly, as distinct from the situation in most developing countries, once the household responsibility system was implemented in the course of rural reform, every household had a plot of land.[67] But even if their departures were not coerced, there was more to their "choices" to go than just a free and individualistic calculus of costs and benefits.[68]

I approach the issue of costs and benefits by looking comparatively at a number of factors across the provinces. The use of the province as a unit in analyzing the variables that promote migration is problematic, granted. Surely there is regional variation within China's thirty-one provincial-level units. But the concentration of transients from particular provinces—plus the persistence of at least significant pockets in these provinces from which peasants continuously departed over the span of more than a decade—should justify the use of provincial figures. More-over, roughly comparable data on a nationwide scale are available just at the provincial level, despite an array of sample surveys.

Two more caveats: first, the analysis that follows employs official data, which are known to be fraught with errors and often based on insufficient information. Still, similar errors across areas, or errors that cancel out other errors, make the relationships I posit—and thus comparative differences, even if not the data themselves—more or less approximate. Second, I present the factors under analysis one at a time for the most part, rather than constructing multivariate tables, in order to clarify the specific nature of the impact of each factor.

The following eight inland provinces all appear in most lists of the major population-exporting areas compiled from the mid-1980s into the mid-1990s: Sichuan, Henan, Anhui, Hunan, Guangxi, Guizhou, Hubei, and Jiangxi.[69] Hebei and Gansu appear in some lists. One source estimates that Sichuan, Guizhou, Guangxi, and Hunan alone represented over half of the extraprovincial net migration nationwide.[70] Another asserts that Sichuan, Jiangxi, Hunan, Hubei, Henan, and Anhui were responsible for about 24 million of the population that was mobile year-round as of 1993, calculating at the time that the total of such persons was in the range of 50 to 60 million.[71] If this last source is correct, these six provinces (about 20 percent of China's 31)—places where population was especially high relative to land, for they held a full 35 percent of China's population as of 1992—were responsible for as much as 40 to 48 percent of its migrants.[72] Even worse off than these places, where people left in large numbers, were a set where, desire to go not withstanding,lack of access to the outside and a dearth of capital for making the trip stymied any movement at all.

A set of statistical measures based on the discussion above, which situate these provinces comparatively within the national context, illustrate the most pressing ecological problems with which those "choosing" to exit had to contend. The data in most of the tables that follow come from the period 1989–90, a time of nationwide recession, when the state's credit cutoffs and monetary tightening forced millions of bankruptcies nationally—in both the urban and the rural areas.

The figures below, therefore, could be skewed, though if so the direction of the bias is not obvious.[73] In any event, the data demonstrate that the problems that fostered migration—which we have reviewed above—had already congealed by the end of the first decade of rural reform.

Additionally, in the absence of any central governmental measures that successfully combated the difficulties, these problems continued and, I show, in some cases even grew into the mid-1990s.

The problem of an exceedingly high person-to-land ratio was particularly severe in a set of twelve provinces, in which, as of 1989, the average per capita of cultivated land was less than 1.6 *mu* (table 5), as compared to a national average at that time of 2.11. Six of our eight provinces are on this list (all but Henan and Hubei).[74]

Besides the six provinces on our list of labor exporters, another six provinces appear in table 5: Jiangsu, Guangdong, Hainan, Zhejiang, Fujian, and Shandong. But unlike the first set, which are in the inland, these six are all situated along the eastern coast. The crucial point here is that all the provinces in this second group differ from the former in that they contain areas where town and village enterprise is flourishing. So in these areas, similarly crowded rural people were less inclined to leave.[75] In such areas the possibility existed for surplus laborers to *li tu bu li xiang* (leave the land but not the native place), the preferred option in the eyes of the leadership, as noted above.[76]

For to develop these firms required proximity to cities of some scale; capital (or the means of accumulating it); and a modicum of transport infrastructure, so that supplies, technology, and market information could reach the inhabitants. A littoral location, topography, and climate combined to produce an ecosystem in which it was much more often the case in this second set of six provinces that places existed boasting these conditions.[77] In most of western and central China, by contrast, one scholar notes,

> Because reform has been slower and the geographical environment is different, resources are scarce, energy is lacking, transportation is difficult, communications are backward, information travels slowly, the industrial base is weak, and capital is lacking, and town and village enterprises develop only slowly, so that, despite reform, the economy hasn't developed.[78]

Thus, as of the mid-1990s these enterprises were found overwhelmingly in the eastern section of the country: of the total output value of the firms nationwide, those in the east accounted for 65 percent, those in central China for 30 percent, and those in the west for a paltry 4.2 percent.[79] The research of two Western scholars, Louis Putterman and William Parish (and his collaborators), collaborates these findings. Putterman points out that TVEs were overwhelmingly situated

Table 5. Provinces with Average per Capita of Cultivated Land below
1.5 *mu*, 1989

Province	Per Capita Cultivated Land	Province	Per Capita Cultivated Land
Jiangsu	1.41	Hunan*	1.17
Guangdong	1.00	Zhejiang	.98
Guangxi*	1.16	Anhui*	1.59
Hainan	1.19	Fujian	.93
Sichuan*	1.13	Jiangxi*	1.33
Guizhou*	1.20	Shandong	1.52

SOURCE: Guojia tongjiju bian, *Zhongguo tongji nianjian 1990*, 355.

*Provinces frequently cited in the literature as sources of the floating population (I omit Beijing and Shanghai, where average per capita cultivated land was also below 1.5 *mu* at 1.02 and 1.06, respectively; though they are provincial-level units, they are not provinces but large cities).

> near cities and in developmental pockets in eastern China . . . [repre-
> senting more] an expansion of existing cities . . . than a broad diffusion
> of industrial activity to rural China as a whole.[80]

And similarly, Parish et al. write,

> High transportation costs and continuing dependence on subcontracts
> from state enterprises means that rural nonfarm employment has ex-
> panded rapidly only in pockets near the coast, near major urban cen-
> ters, and where prosperity in agriculture provides ample local markets
> for nonfarm products.[81]

Two additional reasons disposing areas within these provinces to build
TVEs emerge from research on the prefecture of Wenzhou, Zhejiang, a
place especially famous for its rural enterprises. These were long-standing
traditions of crafts and marketing, and a wealth of commercial crops such
as tea, fruit, sugarcane, and lumber.[82] But these traditions were themselves the product of locational, soil, and other resource endowments. As
G. William Skinner points out,

> The potential for success in business specializations was largely a func-
> tion of the local system's location with respect to cities at different
> levels in the economic hierarchy and to the transport routes linking
> the cities within an urban system. Local systems disfavored on both
> counts were simply in no position to maximize by exporting business
> talent of any kind.[83]

Once the post-Mao regime permitted the peasants again to cultivate commercial crops and crafts, many peasants in areas blessed with a history of producing them found lucrative occupations at home. Meanwhile, other craftspeople and traders traveled from their home regions, where their specialties were quickly in surfeit and competition intense, to find clients and buyers.[84] Returns from these itinerants then became the start-up capital for local enterprises, thereby fueling a virtuous cycle of income generation.

In such cases, commercialization and industrialization flourished dependent upon, but also facilitating, the migration of specialists, even as the presence of these processes meant that a smaller proportion of the population would actually depart. One 1994 study of twenty-eight counties in fifteen provinces, for instance, demonstrated that while an average of 13.3 percent of the total labor forces from these counties had migrated out of the county as of the time of the survey, in the fourteen low-income counties studied, 17 percent had gone; in the four middle-income counties, 12 percent left; and in the ten well-off counties, only 8.3 percent had departed.[85] These findings clearly point to differential departure rates, depending on the resource base at home.

In addition to the urban-rural income gap noted above, the cumulative effect of these interlinked processes was evident in an increasing income gap among regions (table 6) that developed between 1985 and 1990.[86] At the end of 1994, the differences had even widened.[87] Turning back from regional to provincial comparisons, we can target more sharply the correlation between income gaps, the presence of TVEs, and migration (table 7). First, we compare the percentage of rural laborers working in TVEs in various provinces with the national average as of 1989–90, which was 10.93 percent. The percentages working in these firms in provinces generally held to be the chief places of origin for the floating population all fall below 10.93, as do the percentages in the poverty-stricken far western provinces (places, however, probably too remote and disconnected from transport, informational, and market linkages to send out many migrants).

Without TVEs and therefore relying mainly on the land for income, peasants in the central and western areas found that their disadvantages only increased. In these relatively backward, less prosperous areas, official statistics on the productivity of labor[88] showed the difficulty of earning a living just by working on the land.[89] Indeed, the eleven provinces in which each agricultural laborer, on the average, created less than 2,000 yuan of agricultural output value in 1990 (table 8) matched very closely

Table 6. Differences in Rural per Capita Incomes, by Region,
1985, 1990, 1994

	1985		1990		1994	
Region	Income	Index	Income	Index	Income	Index
West	355	100	497	100	856	100
Center	343	97	538	108	1,087	127
East	497	140	812	163	1,617	189

Table 7. Percentage of Rural Laborers in Town and Village Enterprises,
Various Provinces, 1989–1990

Province	% of Laborers in TVEs	Province	% of Laborers in TVEs
Hebei*	9.57	Hubei*	11.29
Shanxi	14.19	Henan*	7.39
Liaoning	21.63	Hunan*	8.07
Jiangsu	24.14	Guangxi*	2.90
Zhejiang	17.32	Sichuan*	6.20
Anhui*	7.35	Guizhou*	1.80
Fujian	13.80	Gansu*	6.16
Shandong	16.11	Yunnan	4.25
Guangdong	14.29	Qinghai	4.56
Shaanxi	7.67	Ningxia	5.61
Xinjiang	6.49		
National average	10.93		

SOURCES: Guojia tongjiju nongcun shehui jingji tongjisi bian, *Zhongguo nongcun tongji nianjian 1992*, 46; and Zhongguo tongjiju bian, *Zhongguo tongji nianjian 1991*, 312.
*Provinces frequently cited in the literature as sources of the floating population.

the list of provinces popularly believed to be the principal homes of the floating population: seven of them appear on that list.

The lack of ability to earn a comfortable income on the land, then, combined with the paucity of other income-earning possibilities at home, must have disposed peasants from these provinces to leave, even though those from these places usually went without particular skills or products to market. The remaining four provinces in this table are all in the far

Table 8. Provinces with per Capita Agricultural Output Value
Below 2,000 Yuan, 1990

Province	Output Value per Laborer
Anhui*	1,940.4
Henan*	1,806.2
Hunan*	1,746.4
Guangxi*	1,582.1
Sichuan*	1,512.4
Guizhou*	1,154.3
Yunnan	1,401.9
Gansu*	1,508.7
Tibet	1,974.8
Shaanxi	1,717.5
Ningxia	1,925.1
National average	3,931.8

SOURCE: Guojia tongjiju nongcun shehui jingji tongjisi bian, *Zhongguo nongcun tongji nianjian 1992*, 195.
*Provinces frequently cited in the literature as sources of the floating population.

Table 9. Provinces with Average Rural Net per Capita Income
Below 560 Yuan, 1990

Province	Average per Capita Net Income, 1990
Anhui*	539.15
Henan*	526.95
Sichuan*	557.76
Guizhou*	435.14
Yunnan	540.86
Shaanxi	530.80
Gansu*	430.98
National average	686.31

SOURCE: Guojia tongjiju nongcun shehui jingji tongjisi bian, *Zhongguo nongcun tongji nianjian 1992*, 217.
*Provinces frequently cited in the literature as sources of the floating population.

west, where prohibitive topography must seriously have obstructed departure.

The effect of the variables is cumulative. For low per capita income, which is also a mark of the provinces migrants leave, is an outcome of low labor productivity and lack of TVEs.[90] In 1990, only the following seven provinces, five of which are often cited as places migrants leave, had average per capita incomes under 560 yuan (table 9).[91]

Differential regional rates of transferring out of agriculture reflect the presence of local options besides agriculture or leaving, and thus the relative prosperity, of the east: as of 1987, only 68.8 percent of rural workers were engaged in agriculture in the eastern part of the country, while in the central and western regions the figure was 85 percent.[92] In 1994, figures not much different from these were still being offered: according to the former minister of agriculture, He Kang, the nonagricultural labor force in the east accounted for 35 percent of the total rural labor force, for 23.5 percent in the central areas, and for just 17.9 percent in the west (thus, the agricultural labor force was still 65, 76.5, and 82.1 percent, respectively, of the total labor forces, nearly a decade later).[93]

If we examine the situation in individual provinces, we find that those provinces where agricultural laborers represented more than 65 percent of the total workers in the countryside in 1990 (table 10) were, again, the very provinces often cited as the origins of the floating population: Yunnan, where topography makes travel generally prohibitive, is the only exception.

Still other indicators reinforce these differences. If we look at a set of ten provinces for comparative purposes (table 11), we find that those where the gross output value from agriculture accounted for more than 50 percent of gross output value in the countryside, and where the output value from rural industry amounted to less than 33 percent of gross output value in the countryside, that is, those where alternative income-earning chances were scarcer, we find that these were, once more, the provinces whose population outflow was reportedly highest. Summary statistics for the three regions did not show any improvement a few years later: in 1992, the proportion of output from TVEs in gross social product in the rural areas amounted to 76.9 percent for the east, 63.48 percent in the central area, and only 38.2 percent in the west.[94]

Two years later, in 1994, the situation had become even more polarized, if figures cited by the former minister of agriculture, He Kang, are accurate and calculated on a basis commensurate with these. He claims

Table 10. Provinces with Agricultural Laborers Forming
65 Percent or More of Rural Work Force, 1990

Province	Agricultural Laborers as % of Total Workers
Anhui*	68.8
Jiangxi*	66.1
Henan*	68.4
Hunan*	72.3
Guangxi*	76.5
Sichuan*	72.5
Guizhou*	78.2
Yunnan	78.2
Gansu*	65.4
National average	60.2

SOURCE: Guojia tongjiju nongcun shehui jingji tongjisi bian, *Zhongguo nongcun tongji nianjian 1992*, 35.

*Provinces frequently cited in the literature as sources of the floating population (I omit Tibet, where the percentage is 80.1, but from which migration must be very difficult, and Hainan, where the percentage is 70.2 but where, since development is rapid, there would be less incentive to leave).

that rural industry as a percentage of total social rural output value surpassed 80 percent, on the average, in eastern areas, but was as low as 15.5 and 19.5 percent, in the central and western regions, respectively.[95]

Moreover, where rural industry was lacking, peasants had an additional, related incentive to leave. Local officials, having few or no profits-generating industrial firms to tap for funds, were apt to burden peasants with exactions as they struggled to cover the costs of local infrastructure and services, no longer provided for communally since the end of the commune after the early 1980s.[96]

A most spectacular instance of this phenomenon occurred in poverty-stricken Renshou county, Sichuan, a place where sweet potatoes and cotton were staple crops and where, reportedly, taxes and other fees were running at the rate of 100 yuan a year per peasant in the early 1990s![97] If true, this could amount to as much as one-third of per capita income in that county[98] and would go a long way toward explaining the outbreak of a major riot that occurred in this spot in the early 1990s.[99]

In China, then, the state—through its policies with respect to rural

Table 11. Output Value of Agriculture and Rural Industry
as Percentage of Gross Rural Output Value,
Various Provinces, 1990

Province	Agriculture	Rural Industry
Anhui*	58.13	26.76
Jiangsu	28.00	60.40
Zhejiang	29.55	58.06
Henan*	48.81	31.87
Sichuan*	59.59	26.93
Gansu*	60.72	21.65
Hunan*	61.34	24.68
Guangxi*	76.49	13.09
Shandong	36.58	52.34
Liaoning	38.88	49.00
National average	46.00	40.43

SOURCE: Calculated from data in Guojia tongjiju nongcun shehui jingji tongjisi bian, *Zhongguo nongcun tongji nianjian 1992,* 56.

*Provinces frequently cited in the literature as sources of the floating population.

organization and to investment, population, migration, welfare, and pricing—made a substantial contribution to the outcome produced by the natural economic situation throughout the countryside—both through its action and through its inaction. The result was that, by the 1980s, arable per cultivator was pitiably inadequate, and doing agricultural activity woefully unprofitable. When peasants "chose" to leave, it was in large part in reaction to these state policies that had so structured their home environments.

The Outcome: Three Kinds of Places, Two Kinds of Migrants

Alongside the conditions that characterized the peasants' environments in all twelve of the low-arable-per-capita provinces listed in table 5, there were crucial variations in geography, ecology, and custom that rendered the inhabitants of some very densely populated places better able to cope than others.

New state policies after 1978 brought these regional differences into play. Migrants left these places as well as they left the less fortunate ones, but they did so in smaller proportions. And, to generalize, the types of migrants who did so, the kind of work they tended to perform in the new location, and the destinations chosen all differed for those in the former places from what they were for those in the latter. In gross terms, the data we have just examined indicate that there were three sorts of rural places, each with its distinctive population-exporting situation.

The first was blessed with connections to transport routes and markets and was woven into urban networks; many former full-time farmers in such areas commercialized their agricultural output in the early 1980s, and many of those with capital plus craft and marketing abilities sponsored nonagricultural enterprises or took to the road.[100] Peasants who left these areas were not only pushed by ecosystemic and politico-economic circumstances; they were also pulled by the state's play to their skills.[101] Coastal provinces, such as Jiangsu (particularly Sunan, its southern part), Zhejiang, and Shandong, are the best examples.

One story of entrepreneurs from such areas comes from the very early days of reform. Beginning in 1978, just as the economic policy changes were beginning, a group of Zhejiang carpenters discovered that there was a market for their abilities in southern Inner Mongolia.[102] The news of their success quickly traveled back to their hometown, and large numbers of other craftspeople and small merchants followed in their wake. By 1987, these people from Jiangnan made up over one-third of the private entrepreneurs in one city in this far western province, according to incomplete statistics. At that point, the sojourners principally hailed from Zhejiang's Wenzhou and Jiangsu's Taizhou, places where land was scarce but commercialization well developed.

Quite different were the somewhat isolated and resource-poor villages, where near self-sufficiency was more the norm, and where conditions and opportunities for nonagricultural investment were scarce. For these less fortunate areas, where not just capital and natural resources were scarcer but residents with skills were few, migration was more a question of the state and the environment's push than of any specific pull. Here our examples would be the eight or ten central China provinces identified above as the most typical sending areas.

A few counties illustrate these points. Miyun county is situated in a mountainous region outside Beijing City; despite its proximity to the capital, in many ways its people's living situation was typical of that of China's mountain folk population at that time. With inferior resources and soil, and a rugged topography, this county is also cursed with frequent natural disasters. Only 8 percent of its land lies in the plains, and the average acreage per person is just over one *mu*. As Beijing's largest county (housing nearly four hundred thousand people), its problem of surplus labor is severe and, given its relatively convenient access to the big city, it sends out many workers.[103] Were it not so near the city, it is not difficult to imagine its people would be stranded.

Another typical example is Longshan county in Hunan, a place with few talented people.[104] While the national average was sixty university students for every ten thousand people, in Longshan in the mid-1980s there were just nineteen per ten thousand. Illiterate and semiliterate people here amounted to 29 percent of the population, as against a national rate of 23.5 percent at the time. The lack of skilled and technically able personnel was considered an important factor in the failure of industrial efforts and even of attempts to develop husbandry there. Poverty, a low rate of high school attendance, poor health care, and little commercialization, with grain planting and pig raising the chief occupations, meant there were few options for the surplus labor, except simply to leave.

Yet one more case comes from the eastern coast but from a region where, unlike much of the coast, the natural conditions are inferior. Living near the sea, the peasants here tried their luck at processing aquatic products and at fishing but still were plagued with problems of employing their surplus labor. Next they experimented with township enterprises but found that their lack of capital, isolated geographical position, and the absence of any market towns nearby stymied the attempt. Finding great limitations to transferring the idle workers out of agriculture by creating work at home, their only solution appeared to be to send their laborers out to do construction.[105]

But beyond these two types of regions, in both of which people found a road outward, were the truly destitute and remote locales. According to one study, "Most migrants come from several central provinces and from within those provinces, it's not the poorest areas or households that send the most migrants."[106] By contrast, regions of the third type were places where leaving at all must have been out of reach for many. At the provincial level, these areas would be mainly the poorest parts of the northwest and the southwest, places

> characterized by poor natural conditions, a low level of productive forces, poor transportation, a lack of information, straitened government finances, low living standards, and backward culture, education, and science and technology.[107]

That few migrants emerged from places in this third category can be inferred from several kinds of data.

First of all, migration theory concludes that those individuals most apt to migrate from unfavorable regions are those who possess the resources necessary for transportation away from home and for the fees that will be assessed along the way (with the caveat that the truly well-to-do have no particular incentive to leave); and those with contacts and information that can assist in locating employment opportunities in the place of destination.[108] At the level of individuals, it is the "rather poor and the rather rich" who migrate.[109]

Surveys in China tended to support this point. One conducted in late 1994 and early 1995 that investigated over 300 "typical" villages from a nationwide sample, tapping a sample of over 35,000 people, established that most of those who left were indeed within the middle-income range: 49 percent came from households with incomes between 3,000 and 8,000 yuan. By contrast, 15 percent had incomes under 3,000, and 18 percent over 12,000. The remaining 18 percent could be called upper-middle, with incomes in the range of 8,000 to 12,000 yuan.[110] These figures could be compared with an official statement in late 1995 that nearly 7 percent of the population (80 million peasants) was earning under 530 yuan per capita annually, 65 million of whom were living in western China.[111]

Second, migration theory also pinpoints proximity to transport routes as an important factor in people's proclivity to exit.[112] Indeed, in China, of the 318 villages that this survey investigated, 79 percent were situated in areas where transportation was either "very convenient" or at least "rather convenient"; another 20 percent were in places where respondents simply claimed that it was only "not too convenient."[113] This leaves just 1 percent who moved from places where transport out was admittedly difficult.[114]

Another study in the mid-1990s showed that 92 percent of a sample of Shandong migrants had paid less than 50 yuan (the equivalent of about U.S. $6.00) for their transportation out; 98 percent of the total had spent under 100 yuan.[115] This statistic suggests that only those for whom mobility was financially feasible and convenient would depart. It implies that peasants in the third, poorest sort of areas, for whom both finances and logistics stand in the way of moving, would be unlikely to depart.[116] Thus, we are left with just two large categories of migrants.

A Chinese scholar labels these two categories "classic surplus laborers" and "investing emigrants," respectively. The former, such as vegetable hawkers from Anhui, practice "cyclical migration," remaining farmers half the year. These people "flow into the city because they cannot be sure of making even enough to eat from farming alone." They would be our group from the inland.

His latter group, those who typically come from Zhejiang (our coastal set), bring both material goods and human capital to the city and "come to create rather than seek employment opportunities."[117] Another way of distinguishing these types is to separate those who are self-employed or employers on the one hand (capitalists, if petty ones) from wage earners, on the other.

It is the coastal group who became "investing emigrants": the able handicraftspeople, the service and management specialists, and the commercial entrepreneurs. There is evidence that people from the coast disproportionately engaged in the secondary and tertiary sectors.[118] For instance, in a late 1991 and early 1992 sample survey of almost 300 migrants in Beijing, the investigator found that almost two times as many entrepreneurs came from the economically developed coastal areas as from elsewhere; and that those from such regions brought capital with them, unlike those from the inland. Such differences must be at the root of the respective incomes of the two groups: 30.9 percent of those from Jiangsu, Zhejiang, Fujian, and Guangdong were earning more than 400 yuan a month, while only 3.6 percent of those from Hebei, Henan, Sichuan, and Anhui made that much.[119]

Inland floaters—the "classic surplus laborers"—came from the rather remote, somewhat mountainous areas inland, places with underdeveloped or single-product economies. Alternatively, they hailed from the terribly crowded sections of central China. These people moved toward the Yangtze and Pearl River Deltas. Once in town, they became the manual, wage-earning laborers.[120] According to one report from the late 1980s, half of the migrants from Sichuan had become workers in the construction trade, while the others were all involved in other sorts of labor-intensive jobs.[121]

To a certain extent, this twofold categorization is a caricature. One piece of research finds that "ordinary" laborers represented 64 percent of those departing from the east, 69 percent of those from the center, and 71 percent from the west.[122] Yet another states that, while 80 percent of the total surplus rural workers nationwide who left home performed simple, principally physical labor during their sojourns, those of this type leaving the central and western regions represented 90 percent.[123]

At the same time, despite their own statistical data, the authors of this second study reinforce the stereotype in adducing this "general law": "Where the economic level is low, it's ordinary surplus labor forces going elsewhere to do nonagricultural work: where the level is high, the proportion of those who belong to the category of skilled business labor is high." As for those who returned home, they conclude, "research shows that workers from the developed areas mainly become skilled management in enterprises or set up their own businesses."[124]

Two large points emerge from the data that shed light on the differences we have found among regions and migrants: first, two macro factors—the ecosystem and the political economy produced by state policy—set the parameters for the micro "decision" to migrate. Thus, the most basic dimension of variation was really regionally, not individually, determined. For the Chinese case, the best way to differentiate the types of regions that produced two disparate kinds of migrants is whether or not a given area had built up town and village enterprises.

And second, since varying regions generated variable kinds of migrants, the exodus is best explained as being overall a result of a blend of market forces and state policies, and thus of agents' choices differentially affected in disparate locales by different sorts of macro factors. As these factors operated together, peasants on the move built up and drew upon networks their neighbors had knitted, networks formed with particular migrants who shared with them subjection to the same regionally based, macro influences.

RECRUITMENT PROCESSES:
THE IMPACT OF SOCIAL NETWORKS
Micro, Macro, and Networks: Sometimes a Seamless Web

Surveys of Chinese migrants have repeatedly concluded that the majority of them—just as others around the globe—were drawn out of their home places by friends, relatives, and fellow villagers. One group of researchers states that in Wuhan in the late 1980s, three-quarters of the outside laborers in the city had located their urban jobs through relatives and friends.[125] Other research based upon nationwide samples comes up with varying percentages, but they are always well over 50.[126] The figures given for those recruited through official agencies, state-owned enterprises, or governmental professional offices were routinely below 10 percent.[127]

Heavy reliance on ascriptive bonds and on go-betweens is the norm in any society where people are uprooting themselves.[128] Networks cut the transaction costs of both selling and engaging labor—the migrant's in finding funds, emotional support, sustenance, and a job, the employer's in locating reliable personnel. And such bonds enhance the confidence of the employer in underlings as well as facilitating control over the work force.[129]

In one typical example from the Chinese floating population, journalists spoke with a group of transient workers from Guangxi whom they encountered in the Guangzhou train station at New Year's time in 1993. The laborers' leader admitted he had escorted them from their village "on orders from the boss."[130] A job hopeful at a Nanjing neighborhood-managed labor introduction station, resigned to working in construction, wistfully mused that "you need to know someone to get a temporary factory job [meaning in a state firm]."[131]

Both the scholarly literature and informants made frequent reference to the preference of employers for the friends and relatives of current staff and workers, and for current workers' assistance in ascriptively based recruiting.[132] Many interviewees insisted on the necessity of "knowing someone." For instance, officials at the Wuhan Labor Bureau explained that "a factory has to know about a person [being considered for a job] through an introduction";[133] and bosses of a county-owned construction company from a Hubei county insisted that "in hiring from outside, we use only people with whom we have personal relations or else we won't hire them. We're strict about this."[134]

To fit this story to the three models of migration outlined above, deciding to go with one's friends and neighbors represents an individualistic, "rational," micro-determined choice. And state officials' machinations to obtain particular movers could ultimately skew somewhat the macrostructure of the labor market. Thus the networks along which and by means of which peasants traveled were often enough the result of a mixture of micro choices and macro placements.

Such a construct calls into question the opposition between recruitment forms (direct engagement by employers against social ties between sending and receiving areas) invoked by some analysts.[135] What mattered in this postsocialist period in China was not that the state determined the bulk of relocation as it did in the past, for it did not. It was that its bureaucrats kept the mentality and some of the modes for guiding those who went, and that for some migrants the impact was decisive. Deliberate recruitment, then, often drew upon and was the product of networks knit one way or another by the state and its agents.

The problems that arise in not recognizing this overlap are illustrated in a 1986 study, which claims the following: of 1,657 transients who came from the countryside to Beijing, 29.7 percent were organized by local labor contractors; 42.8 percent were influenced or actively recruited by relatives or friends; 27 percent decided to move entirely on their own; and 3.4 percent were recruited by state corporations.[136] The trouble with these categories is that, empirically, they were not distinct: both local labor contractors and state corporations drew almost exclusively upon their own or their employees' relatives, friends, and fellow villagers in their selection procedures. In short, bureaucratic and ascriptive modes of recruitment were by no means competing strategies; rather, they formed a seamless web.

Government Policy

In at least two ways explicit policies of the state laid down the pathways along which peasants later moved into town. The first of these went back to the 1950s, when Shanghai was directed to deliver thousands of workers and technical specialists to develop the western border regions. As a result, of all China's regions, those from the northwest accounted for the next to largest group of migrants (of whom presumably many were return migrants) in Shanghai in 1988, second only to those from eastern China, Shanghai's immediate neighbor.[137]

Second, in recent years a State Council directive ordered that hiring firms should recruit from areas where the masses' livelihood was difficult and labor power in excess.[138] In accord with this policy, a city document indicated that the Wuhan city government had designated particular counties of Hubei, such as the poor old Soviet bases of Hong'an and Dawu, for this special treatment.[139]

State Agencies as Recruiters

In addition to explicit state policy, state agents assisted (and superintended) floaters in finding employment. These agents included geographic units, local-level labor departments, branches of the women's federation, and state factories. Though doubtless a gross exaggeration, in the mid-1990s an official claim was put forward stating that as many as one-third of the laborers emigrating from the countryside of ten major labor exporting provinces, or six million out of eighteen million emigrating individuals, did so under the organized sponsorship of governmental labor departments.[140]

A State Council circular attempted to institutionalize this practice in the early 1990s by approving a decision of the Ministry of Labor. It called on whole provinces to establish "stable supply and demand relationships with construction industries and service trades in key cities," by which the provinces were to supply labor to units in need of it in an organized way. The objective was to strengthen macro control over agricultural labor forces entering the cities, by designating fixed-point linkages between specified urban and rural areas.[141]

Whatever the figures or the success of central-governmental pronouncements, labor department personnel did act as intermediaries in several kinds of transactions that brought rural labor to the cities. Some personally traveled to government offices in the countryside to arrange the importation of nursemaids for their cities' residents.[142] Others invited bureaucrats in county governments elsewhere to organize the export of their surplus construction labor into the towns.[143] In Dongguan City, in the Pearl River Delta, a study in the early 1990s found that 22 percent of the workers employed from outside had been located by urban labor departments contracting with counterpart departments in poorer locales, as in Hunan and Guangxi provinces.[144]

Connections created by the copious conferences held over the years by bureaucratic functional "systems," such as the women's federation, created a foundation for finding faraway Sichuanese nursemaids for Tianjin families. Beginning in 1987, and into the 1990s, Tianjin's women's federation staff was writing letters, making telephone calls, and sending delegates to draw upon such ties in its search for groups of housekeepers.[145] Substituting its agency for the yet inchoate market, it targeted the indigent, underdeveloped areas of Sichuan province, where idle women were known to be numerous.[146]

Urban state-owned factories were also directly involved in recruiting workers. One way they did so harked back to the time long before reforms began: some firms subcontracted their simpler production tasks to collective rural work units.[147] Alternatively, factories worked through state-organized labor recruitment agencies to draw large groups of workers from the countryside.[148] Perhaps the most prevalent method urban factories used to engage outside labor was, as in the 1950s, signing collective contracts with county governments. In the Dongguan study cited above, as many as 50 percent of the workers had arrived through such direct contacts between the firms and the labor departments of their home counties.[149]

Official Agents as Labor Exporters

Just as destination-area officials recruited labor from surplus areas, those in the sending regions organized to expel it, completing this ersatz market. As two journalists explained, "Many cities and counties have made labor export into an economic property."[150] This practice got a quick start as soon as the central government relaxed its prior restraints on geographical labor mobility. In one early case, in the first part of 1984, the party committee of Miyun county near Beijing (mentioned above) urged every household to send out one of its members to work.[151]

Within another two years, local governments in the Jiangsu country-side had already contracted with other provinces to "export" over a million of their workers.[152] And the economic departments in over-populated southern Jiangsu's Nantong prefecture struggled to compete in the migrant labor market; its leadership was able to open new markets so successfully that between 1978 and 1987 they had boosted the area's output of sojourning laborers from a mere 8,000 to 154,000 and had taken in 819 million yuan in income in compensation, not counting remittances coming from the migrants.[153]

By the late 1980s rural governments' preparation of peasants to leave the land had become widespread and sophisticated. Kazutsugu Oshima details the activities of village construction agencies and labor service companies in the Jiangsu countryside, which organized and arranged labor export, dispatched it in groups, and demanded fees for the workers from the firms that took them on.[154] By the mid-1990s provincial author-ities in the sending regions were reportedly stipulating in their economic plans the number of extra hands in their areas and setting out measures to urge them to go.[155]

In many areas village party branch secretaries selected, trained, and set up contacts for their villagers before letting them depart.[156] Sichuan, the master of the strategy, created labor service development leading groups at the county level, training bases, and labor service exchange markets. Its rural officials also transported peasants out in groups.[157] One report in mid-1996 stated that the provincial government claimed that up to three-fifths of its migrants were officially recruited and organized, with the provincial administration's taking labor orders from other provinces and then recruiting in response.[158] As of the end of 1993, the official Xinhua News Agency asserted that "most local governments adopt policies to encourage the migration of farmers."[159] Higher up, provincial officials across the inland had set up offices in Guangzhou, a key destination point, to coordinate the transfer of their surplus rural labor with that city's labor bureau.[160]

Interbureaucratic Bonds

Apart from such conscious management, bureaucratic networks also emerged almost automatically from the linkages between units entrenched years before by the state plan, even in the midst of the rapid dissolution of planning itself in the 1980s and 1990s. Such ties, which engendered trust between firms, were not readily undone, regardless of market reforms.[161] They rested on decades of particularistic dealings, informal by-products of the state plan.

In one version, peasants could be found in towns in the early 1990s laboring on long-term contracts that had not yet run out, left over from the days of the rural communes, agreements signed between city governments and the former communes' "brigades."[162] A volume published by Wuhan's labor bureau explains that "the basis for recruitment of rural construction teams is this: if they haven't already worked for the unit in the past, then they are the firms' cadres, staff, and workers' friends and relations."[163] In an interview in 1992, that bureau's officials explained that a full two-thirds of the construction labor employed in the city then had come from outside the province of Hubei. When asked how the managers of a firm knew where to find such labor, the answer was simple: "They hire those they trust, with whom they have worked before, whom they understand."[164]

Similarly, the Tianjin construction trade developed "brother provinces" from which it selected teams for its contract work.[165] These teams, from the neighboring provinces of Hebei, Henan, and Shandong, were originally sent to Tianjin in an arrangement between the construction commissions of Tianjin and these provinces following the Tangshan earthquake of 1976, to help restore the city's shattered architecture.

What began as an official (*guanfang*) relationship blossomed into an informal one. Some teams stayed on, with their provincial bureaucrats setting up offices in Tianjin to manage them. The Tianjin construction authorities in the past had picked out thirty-two counties, all rich in labor power with superior skills and sound organization, which then became Tianjin's special "labor bases" (*laowu jidi*). Thenceforth, Tianjin construction officials always called on these bases, and a long-term relationship of cooperation was born.[166] Thus we see the lingering effect of statist arrangements.

In a number of ways, a portion of migration was mediated intentionally by official agencies and policies of the state, even if the numbers of peasants so relocated did not account for the dominant proportion among all the movers. Moreover, false distinctions drawn by researchers may well lead to a misappraisal of the extent of this mediation. It operated to shunt what could be termed the troops of China's rural labor reserve army from places where local bureaucrats considered them a useless burden to spots where their cheap toil was a valued good.

The data presented here offer no clear verdict as to whether the processes entailed represented micro choice, macro structuring, or networks; they are often best described as an intermingling of two or three of these modes. For example, often what was started by the state for purely bureaucratic ends acquired a measure of trust and, therefore, became a social network over time.

Marketized Modes of Recruitment

As against more purely ascriptive or official forms of recruitment, there were other ways in which peasants found urban employment. These included dependence on labor recruiters, contractors, bosses, and agents; spontaneous labor markets and labor introduction stations; and advertisements, which all appear to have represented alternate, more market-oriented modes of locating work. But none of them had emerged as separate or competing avenues of job placement as of the mid-1990s.

First, labor bosses did not constitute a distinct mode of recruitment. The typical pattern was for a recruiter to hear that a certain place needed labor. He would repair to the area to sign a work contract and then go home to bring back his co-villagers.[167] A steely and imperious boss encountered at a Nanjing work site in 1992 was managing over a hundred workers, all but ten from his home village in Anhui. Even the mere tenth of them who were drawn from other areas also came from Anhui and were mostly relatives of the boss's fellow villagers.[168] Other contractors signed agreements with city governments.[169] But whatever the channel of job information, labor bosses too operated through kin and comradeship, the bonds of which sometimes stretched into state agencies.

True, the manager of a Nanjing neighborhood labor introduction station run by a district women's federation claimed that labor contractors found their workers at her station. But young men waiting there admitted that they could only reasonably expect to find construction work on the strength of their connections with hometown friends.[170]

What were called "spontaneous labor markets" cropped up in major cities across China throughout the 1980s (figure 3).[171] There hopeful, unconnected itinerants waited, often all through the day, for a chance to negotiate with potential employers and get hired for short time spans if

Figure 3. Looking for work in Beijing.

they were outstanding or lucky. Several studies found that only a tiny minority of workers found their jobs this way.[172] But construction teams coming into the city needing extra hands—especially those desperate enough to engage "even those collecting scraps on the street"—did sometimes take on low-paid, unattached personnel in such marts.[173] This slipshod sort of marketplace could not, however, commend itself to the serious job seeker.

By the late 1980s advertisements for labor had appeared "everywhere in the Pearl River Delta," particularly around the time of the New Year, when thousands of new migrants arrived in the area.[174] Their efficacy has not been systematically charted, to my knowledge. But a rough indication of how well they were working as of mid-1992 may be the experience of the Nanjing neighborhood labor introduction station mentioned above, whose manager boasted of its use of newspaper ads and television spots. In spite of these efforts, none of the clients waiting on its steps on the day of my visit had heard of the introduction station in any way other than through friends or relatives.[175] Another bit of information comes from a study by Mobo Gao, who claims that "management doesn't usually advertise for new workers but waits for employees to introduce their friends to the factory."[176]

In the Dongguan study, where employed workers were the object of investigation, only 4 percent had come on their own, consulting ads and looking around for a while.[177] In the words of the staff at the Tianjin branch of the women's federation, "Individuals have relatives here or have heard about jobs from fellow villagers. They don't come blindly. Very, very few arrive as strangers."[178]

In short, in the first decade and a half of China's post-1980 migrant urban labor market, bureaucratic arrangements and personalistic networks—not infrequently interconnected—were still the effective placement avenues.[179] The presence of many sorts of networks, combined with the macro ecosystemic and state policy factors described in the previous section, undercuts the explanatory power of an appeal to the individual agent's "choice" alone, despite the incipient emergence of a labor market of sorts.

DEPARTED MIGRANTS AND THE NATIVE PLACE

The most controversial issue about the impact of migration on the sending areas is not so much whether successful sojourners enrich their own home places. Instead, since the custom of sending remittances is a universal one (even if not every single migrant engages in it), the answer to that is obvious.[180] At the very least, some families benefit, no matter how the money is spent; at best, the sending villages as a whole experience some improvements, whether directly from migrants' families' investments in community infrastructure and welfare or from the multiplier effect that comes from their new consumption. What is uncertain is the effect of migration and remittances on regional polarization and income gaps.

Modernization or Dependency?

One approach to this question is to appeal to the conflicting theories of modernization versus dependency.[181] Adherents of the former see the process of out-migration as leading to development in the countryside, spreading skills, information, and new ideas about the larger world, generating jobs, and providing new sources of income and motivation.[182]

But dependency theorists dispute these claims. Dependency analysts of migration in the Philippines and Mexico maintain that migration, as a function of the spread of the capitalist market, has as its principal effect on the rural areas of origin of the migrants a depletion of these areas' talent and capital. Those of this persuasion acknowledge that migrants acquire skills outside but allege that what they learn cannot be used at home should they return. They also charge that the employment absorption capacity of the enterprises they may set up will be limited as well.[183] Others note the dependent state into which migration thrusts the village, as it comes to rely on outside jobs and purchases for its well-being, instead of generating indigenous productive forces.[184] There is also a judgment that with the departure of the most capable laborers, agricultural production will suffer.[185]

Scholars writing on China echo some of these worries. Jeffrey Taylor suggests that "the greatest threat of out-migration may be to farming communities," as the young and best educated abandon the fields. Since some of these émigrés value the land more for insurance than for subsistence, they permit it to fall fallow.[186]

In order to resolve this dichotomous assessment of impact, we need to understand more about what kind of peasants return to what sort of rural areas, what they do upon returning, the size of the remittances they send, and changes in incomes in different areas over time.

A Continuing Tie to the Land

The intention to return to the land is one that migrants hold around the world,[187] perhaps most vigorously in places like pre-1990 South Africa, where for most of the twentieth century black migrant laborers—like China's peasants in the Mao period—were not granted the right of permanent residence in cities.[188] The bond to one's fields is also a theme in Chinese history, as the work of Myron Cohen reminds us. For the traditional pattern in pre-Communist China was to maximize the rural family's income by instituting a division of labor among family members. Accordingly, some members were sent out of the villages to earn their income away from the fields.[189] But even after lengthy absences they never cut their tie with the village.

But in reform China two factors particularly disposed migrants to go back home, both of them products of major state initiatives. Indeed, with the exception of most of twentieth-century South Africa, similar motivators have been absent in other societies: these were the pull factor of the "household responsibility plot," allocated to each farm family in the early 1980s with the breakup of communes, and the persisting power of the *hukou* to reduce the time of many peasants' stay in the cities.

In 1984, when the State Council permitted peasants who supplied their own grain to enter market towns, its directive required that they first transfer their fields to other cultivators.[190] And yet, though this directive permitted them to register their households in the town, the great majority of the farmers refused to give up their land at home, many outwardly effecting a turnover but covertly retaining the fields within the family.[191] Keeping their own land, floaters had a guaranteed grain supply, before grain became available at reasonable prices on urban markets. A 1989 report stated that over 50 percent of the migrants in the Shanghai suburbs were still getting grain from their friends and families at home.[192] But a survey of twenty-eight counties in fifteen provinces as late as 1994 found that even by then, with affordable grain fully accessible in cities, fewer than 3 percent of those queried had given up or even contracted out their land.[193]

This bit of security remained as a fallback when the urban job search was unsuccessful; thus, on the few occasions when state economic policy meant that city jobs were cut back, many rural workers repaired to their native villages.[194] According to an official from the Tianjin Public Security Bureau, "If they don't find a job, they go home." And, similarly, in the words of a Chinese researcher, "Some can't tolerate the situation and quickly leave."[195] The implication is that a definite place to return to exists.

The second factor is the lack of an urban *hukou*. This denial eventually operated as a push from the city for many migrants who had made their way there, as researchers point out as late as 1996:

> Why do they return home? Although the restrictions of the *hukou* are lessening, still there's been no fundamental change in its visage. If peasants want to live in the city and buy a *hukou*, that requires a lot of money. So more than 90 percent in our survey [of Anhui's Fuyang prefecture] would rather use that money to go home and set up an enterprise.[196]

Further evidence comes from the findings of other Chinese scholars, one writing in 1994 that "because of the *hukou* system, most go home to marry and don't return";[197] and the other reporting in early 1992 that, at a psychological level, "the household registration system strengthens [peasants'] feeling of a bond [to the countryside]; they won't take the initiative thoroughly to throw off their ownership power over the land."[198]

Thus, in reform-era China migrants maintained their rural affiliations at least partially in response to the policies set by their state. Most prominently, the land a peasant household was allocated in the decollectivization movement of the early 1980s took on a symbolic significance apart from its value for livelihood; far more than a supplier of sustenance and a form of income insurance[199]—given peasants' exclusion from urban citizenship—it was a means of psychic security. This, plus the continuing power of the *hukou,* meant that Chinese peasants were probably more apt to retreat to their home than their counterparts in other countries.

Return to the Countryside

Given this continuing attachment to the home villages and the land—combined with the precariousness of peasants' status in the cities—many peasants at least intended to return home after a few years of earning the money for a dowry, a house, a wedding: in one study of nearly 200 migrants in Beijing in 1991, 44 percent hoped to go back after earning some money.[200] According to the *People's Daily,* whose journalists may well have had the state's objectives at heart in reporting it, 66 percent of the people from Guizhou who had traveled to Guangdong to work in the late 1980s returned home out of a feeling of "sentimental attachment."[201] Using data from the 1993 public security sample survey of Shanghai, Roberts and Wei found that the proportion of migrants in each duration cohort remained the same in 1993 as it had been in 1988, leading them to assume stability in the distribution of migrant duration in that city over time.[202]

The question then becomes what migrants did upon their arrival back at their old homesteads. The Chinese official press of the first half of the 1990s lent support to modernization theory, which would predict newly prosperous and retooled laborers coming back to inject scientific, technological, marketing, and management skills into their villages, creating new jobs and generating wealth. Stories of this sort abounded in the papers, as in news of Fuyang prefecture, Anhui; Dazhi county, Hubei; Jiangxi's Ganzhou prefecture; Gansu's Zhengning county; and Guanting county, Anhui.

In Ganzhou, for instance, in just ten months of 1993, returnees set up 1,200 factories and business companies at home, investing a total of 40 million yuan in them, and providing employment to an impressive number—a hundred thousand—of the local people. There were also the ten thousand rural workers from Gansu's Zhengning county who reportedly brought back a phenomenal "1,200-plus pieces of economic and technical information." All these data sparked the creation of thirteen shops and plants, increasing local peasant income by over 30 million yuan.[203]

But stories of such successes often contain crucial supporting information about the kinds of migrants acting in them: in Dazhi county, to take one case, the pioneers who set up TVEs on their return were people who had worked outside for five to ten years and had mastered one or more skills while away. In Anhui's Wuwei county, some of those coming back had set up thirty firms, but it was the half of them who had acquired skills in their sojourns. Anhui's Guanting is a mere 40 kilometers outside the provincial capital, Hefei, where finding a market for the area's six new firms must have been much easier than in the truly remote hinterland. Finally, 81 percent of Fuyang's new entrepreneurs had at least a junior high education, all had a skill, and 60 percent had worked as technical personnel during their stint in urban units.

These examples suggest the self-evident. Where the more educated and skilled departed, the outlook was decidedly more propitious for promoting prosperity if they returned home. But prosperity was possible only if the requisite infrastructure—electricity, roads, communications facilities—was present at home, and if reasonably close and accessible markets made investment worthwhile. Able businesspersons had to be paired with a fertile soil for their ventures to allow these auspicious outcomes to emerge.

As for the blanket assumption that migration facilitates a transfer of skills and knowledge, there is the flat testimony of a poor and unskilled woman, age thirty-four, camping on the outskirts of Wuhan with a construction team, and serving as its cook. We encountered her squatting among the mosquitoes and with no electricity or water, her pig rummaging at the tent's side. She came from Yingcheng county, Hubei, a mountain district to the west of Wuhan, with her husband, an ordinary excavation worker, and her brother, the boss of the team of workers. Her home was easily flooded and very poor. These were her words, when presented with the modernization theorist's optimism:

> Here we don't learn anything; there's no techniques, no news or information, no machinery. Everything is physical labor. When we're done each day, just go to sleep. How can we transfer any culture back home?[204]

We might also ask how the young rural women abducted by labor recruiters from the inland to act as prostitutes and masseuses in the Pearl River Delta would use the skills they acquired once they returned to their villages. One sorry tale of such abductees, as told by two Chinese reporters, concludes with these lines:

> At home, the pure only can be unemployed or forever chase oxen, and join with the poor and the bored. Going to Guangdong as masseuses, though it's a break with the world of morality, still one can earn and

spend a lot of money, live a life of debauchery, join with the rich and prosperous.[205]

A governmental study of female rural textile workers temporarily employed in Zhengzhou in 1990, people who indeed absorbed some skills, brings to life this yearning to stay on in the city, especially in the absence of possibilities in their native place:

> Their home villages have no textile factories. What they've learned can't be used at home. . . . They're no longer strong enough for rural labor. They try to think up a way: (1) they . . . place their hope on changing their *hukou;* if it were formally proclaimed that no one could ever do this, more than one-third of them would leave at once; (2) they strive to extend their contracts but worry that many personal problems will be hard to manage; and (3) they wish that the factory would create employment opportunities for them for their return home, such as running some classes in tailoring, sewing, barbering, or growing plants, so they could acquire some skills practical in the countryside.[206]

So, along with the tales of success, there were surely also many cases where migrants failed to gain valuable knowledge by laboring outside. There was also the agony of those who tasted the big city but—because of various prohibitions related to lacking an urban *hukou,* and because of the difficulty of renewing their contracts or finding new work—with skills or without any, had no real options other than returning to a home place that was still not equipped to satisfy their needs. Some of them, though their outlets were closed off, were said to cry, "Kill me! I'll never hold a hoe again."[207]

In such cases, many of those compelled to return found it painful to readapt. Often the land could not absorb more laborers, and, with investment opportunities at home no better than before, they struggled to go out once again. Others hung about, increasing the unemployment burden, and became an unstable force, stirring up problems of social order.[208] Alan Liu writes of a Jiangsu county government official who complained to the *People's Daily* in 1990 that returned migrants were causing disturbances with their "frequent visits and appeals to authorities."[209]

Thus, surely marvelous results came to parts of the countryside when its most able members migrated out and came back. But, as the theoretical literature explains, the results depended on the fit between the skills of the returnees and the investment potential of their native places.[210] Where there was none, suffering must have been common. Hard statistics for determining the relative prevalence of one kind of situation as against the other are not yet available. But the less savory sequel to sojourning should not be overlooked.

Remittances and Their Impact upon Regional Polarization

Did remittances from migrants lead to an accumulation of capital in the villages of origin, reducing poverty there and fostering a balance of productive resources and assets and an interregional developmental convergence among districts? Modernization theorists, from their neoclassical perspective, say they do.[211]

But others instead see migration as "the father of inequality," generating new wealth just for the families or the villages of the initially better-off, those with the funds to undertake migration in the first place.[212] In a study of northern Jiangsu's Nantong, "migratory birds" constituted a mere 2 percent of the population, but all hailed from the same small area. Their community alone got rich by investing the migrants' remittances (a portion of which, apparently, was collected by local officials) in electrical power, transport facilities, roads, and schools. Meanwhile, this intercommunity polarization threatened social stability in a region accustomed from prereform times to a modicum of local equity.[213] As Charles Wood suggests, the macroeconomic effect could be "cumulative backlash" if "migration decisions accentuate rather than reduce regional and sectional disparities."[214]

The financial gains for home areas when migrants remit money can be of astounding proportions. Yongjia county, Zhejiang (one of the two chief counties whose itinerants populate Beijing's Zhejiang Village), sent only 15 percent of its total agricultural labor force out in the early period when migration first began, in 1985. Yet the earnings these people were able to garner right away, which they "donated" (presumably under some duress) to the county amounted to 48.9 percent of the total agricultural income of the county for that entire year.[215] Even poorly situated, mountainous counties in Guangdong exporting labor in the late 1980s were able to derive income from their migrants in the amount of 30 to 40 million yuan, the equivalent of 25 percent of a county's total annual income.[216]

By the first half of the 1990s the most prevalent reports were of remittances in the billions, aggregated at the level of the province. For instance, the more than five million Hunanese surplus rural laborers who found jobs outside the province brought home an income of about 5 billion yuan in 1994;[217] according to one account, Anhui sent out the same number of workers and received as much as 7.5 billion back in 1993.[218] If these figures are accurate, what Hunan's migrants contributed amounted to about 3 percent of gross domestic product (GDP) in the province for that year, and what Anhui's gave was 7 percent there.

There are a number of difficulties with such statistics, however. For one thing, they are notoriously hard to verify. To illustrate the point, two news releases about Sichuan's remittances for the year 1993 were quite discrepant: one claimed that five million laborers had gone out, sending back "more than 5 billion yuan," or what would have been about 2.4 percent of the province's GDP that year; the other asserted that ten million had migrated, returning 10 billion yuan, or 4.7 percent of GDP.[219]

But there are other difficulties making sense of the figures, even if we could determine which set was accurate. Consider that Henan's transients allegedly sent or brought back cash and wages in kind equal to "more than 2 billion yuan" in 1992, amounting only to 1.5 percent of provincial GDP, as against Anhui's intake worth 7 percent of its GDP the very next year.[220]

One major problem is that these aggregate data offer no clues about critical components of the comparison. They say nothing, for instance, about which regions of the province were sending migrants, where they were going, or in what sort of work paying what wages the workers were involved. It may be that all else is equal, and that the income-earning opportunities for rural migrants simply improved from one year to the next. Also, we know nothing about the allocation of funds once they reached the village. How much could families appropriate, how much went to general fees and collections for the benefit of the locality, and how much simply disappeared into cadres' pockets?[221]

As just one example of the sort of disparities that must have influenced the results, one source states that the Shenzhen Special Economic Zone government estimated that every migrant worker there sent home an average of 4,000 yuan in 1994, whereas those in Shanghai remitted just 1,800.[222] Differences of another kind are apparent in the finding that workers in the Pearl River Delta in 1993 exhibited a range of behaviors in remitting salaries, with over half sending under 1,000 yuan, but just under a tenth sending over 2,000.[223]

Surely the various factors affecting an individual's level of sending money cannot be captured in aggregate provincial comparisons. The remarks of random informants encountered on the streets of Nanjing and Wuhan in summer 1992 illustrate the complications in coming to a final judgment about what happened to urban earnings. Some migrants averred that they found it hard even to save any money at all;[224] others sent anywhere from 60 to 200 yuan home each month.[225]

Did migration, in alleviating some of the strains on the countryside—along with generating funds to be sent back by migrants—as enthusiasts insist, work toward eliminating the split between urban and rural China, bridging the gap between the rich cities and the poor hinterland, and reducing regional income inequality?[226] Because of the serious ambiguities in data aggregated provincially (not the least of which is that the overall figures include both urban and rural components), it is difficult to answer these queries decisively. But it is still striking to find that per capita income in the ten chief labor-exporting provinces (table 12), with only one exception (Guangxi), actually *declined* as a percentage of national average per capita income over the years 1978 to 1994.

Moreover, all of these provinces continued to show rural per capita incomes below the national average for the countryside in 1994, despite a decade of out-migration. They all also still had per capita GDPs under the national average as of 1994.[227] So for the main provincial homes of migrants, we must conclude that, after a decade of migration there had not yet been a victory for modernization theory.[228]

· · ·

The Maoist state before 1978 created a noncitizen class in the countryside, a project greatly bolstered by its elimination of markets. The new leadership after Mao's death restored the workings of supply and demand and permitted peasants to depart from home. But much of the state's impulse to shape macrostructural patterns persisted, and rural residents and sojourners could no more escape the imprint of macro-structural determinants set by state policies, institutions, and strategies than they could avoid the macro influences of the ecosystems of their homelands.

Therefore, when peasants migrated from their villages, they were hardly fully decision-taking free agents. Instead, the pushes and pulls activating them were the results of an admixture of statist initiatives and market forces. For this reason, one cannot claim that individual choices, rationally taken on economic grounds—or even ascriptive ones—were free of the state. Thus we find blended networks, partly bureaucratic and partly personalistic; a poverty of functional, impersonally constituted horizontal linkages; ecological features mediated by differential governmental measures; and a varying applicability of modernization and dependency theories, in accord with increasing state neglect of needy

Table 12. Average Provincial per Capita Income as Percentage
of National Average, 1978, 1989, 1994

Province	1978	1989	1994
Hebei	100.00	93.61	89.52
Anhui	70.48	77.12	66.56
Jiangxi	77.14	70.82	68.45
Henan	65.08	70.90	64.86
Hubei	94.29	99.41	87.48
Hunan	78.73	76.20	71.00
Guangxi	60.00	61.06	73.60
Sichuan	67.30	68.38	65.97
Guizhou	49.52	53.07	40.14
Gansu	92.70	72.58	50.58

SOURCE: *Provincial China: A Research Newsletter* 1 (1996): 71.

regions over time. These were the conditions under which Chinese migrants enacted their rural exodus. Given these factors, it is hard to assert
that simply invigorating markets was producing citizens from peasants.

This chapter, in searching for transients' agency, challenged generalizations and dichotomies in migration theory. First, it showed that individual migrants' "choices" to leave sometimes involved macro (bureaucratic)
structures of recruitment, at both the state and geographical levels. Second, it established that networks in postsocialist China drew on both the
micro (ascriptive) and the macro (bureaucratic) connections in which the
individual was enmeshed, so that networks alone do not constitute an
explanation.

And third, the chapter suggested that modernization theory is accurate, at least in the short run, but only for the better endowed individuals
coming from the more favorably situated regions. At the same time,
dependency theory's concern for the poor, the manual laborers of the
labor reserve army, is very likely well placed, certainly for the near term,
for those who departed from the hinterland. But for the truly destitute,
those peopling the most poverty-stricken and inaccessible western part of
the country, even exit was not an option. I now ask how the various
sojourners fared, once they arrived in the municipalities.

6   Urban Bureaucracies II
Peasants Enter Urban Labor Markets

Having reviewed how state policies and ecosystemic effects cut up the countryside into three gross regions and the transient population into two stereotypical groups—those from the poorer inland, more likely to bank on their brawn, and those from the coast, equipped with craft and capital—I can ask the next important question. What happened to this distinction when these people entered the cities and inserted themselves into urban labor markets? Did they remain just subjects, at the mercy of economic forces and state designs? Certainly peasants' meeting with markets in the cities was once again mediated by influences and practices of the state and its agents.

But this mediation by no means made the peasants passive. Returning to the municipal bureaucracy, the focus of chapter 3, I show that the outsiders' arrival in cities reshaped what had been a crucial institution within this urban bureaucracy, the urban labor market, and contributed to a breakdown in the state's exclusive ability to affect the disposition of the metropolitan work force. Reciprocal interactions with markets helped many migrants find a niche in the city, as bonds with the state smoothed the way for others.

Even those migrants thrust back on their own devices found their way to new modes of belonging and of distributing goods, and thus to new sorts of citizenship in the city, a subject pursued in more depth in chapter 7. In what follows I first examine what influences the state in transition from socialism was able to exert on migrant workers and their work environments; and then how specific types of demand and supply structured the new, emergent labor markets. In the last, largest section, I develop the implications of migrants' mixing with markets and the state by exploring the dynamics of operation in the labor markets of each of the six chief occupations typically taken up by transients in town.

THE STATE IN TRANSITION: MACRO, MESO, AND MICRO EFFECTS FOR MIGRANT LABOR

At one level, the state's mediation came from the macro fact of the transition from socialism. Here several features were relevant, some left over from the former regime, others a function of the transition itself. Some of these features appeared on the surface to be much like those that characterize the "secondary sector" of the classic dual market model, conceived to describe labor segmentation under capitalism.[1] Examples were a high level of competition, frequent turnover, and exploitation of the workers.[2] But the origin of the features in this case lay not in capitalism, but in the macro phenomenon of state-socialism-in-transition.

The state still mattered at the micro and meso levels as well, where social networks operated. Here there was the micro question of whether given migrants (or, the meso question about a group of migrants, through its leaders) had connections with state personnel and institutions in the city. The nature—or the absence—of such ties had quite variable consequences for individuals and groups. Here we see the effects not of system change but of institutional residues, of the "stickiness" of the socialist state. Indeed, through the mid-1990s the character of individuals' brushes with officialdom—or the lack of any—overlay and could even substantially modify the impact of the traits (linked to native place) that were associated with the two categories of migrants delineated in chapter 5.

Thus, we will find that our ideal-typical eastern, or skilled, business-person migrant in some ways suffered from having minimal (or only indirect) links with state agencies. Meanwhile, some of the manual laborers from the central and western regions—the foot soldiers of the labor reserve army—gained some benefits from having such bonds. While the former type of transient created alternate communities that developed forms of citizenhood outside the state, the latter became incorporated—but in a distinctly inferior manner, at a decidedly lower level—into the framework of state-sponsored citizenship that served proper, city residents.

At the macro level, we find effects that had an impact upon all city workers. With the transformation from socialism, urban-based labor, once simply designated jobs by bureaucratic allocation for the most part,

began undergoing commodification.[3] And as placement by state assignment waned, the monopoly of the single-stranded, state-dominated labor
"market" collapsed.[4] In its place, novel modes of recruitment, along with
an unprecedented (for the P.R.C.) mix of ownership systems, started to
structure a new multitude of markets, all of them subject to a range of
competitive pressures unknown in China since 1949.[5]

For instance, in some trades (such as construction), outsider faced
native, and state firm confronted informal one; in others (such as carpentry) migrant group contended with migrant group; in yet others, foreign
investors came up against anonymous rivals in the world market at large.
There were also cases in which sojourners from a particular region cornered the market—as in the case of Zhejiang tailors—and where,
therefore, competition was for the most part absent within a trade. But
in the main, the scale and scope of competition was both sudden and
compelling, fed by the release of a massive surge of pent-up energy, as
farmers, first freed from their fetters to the fields after 1983 and then
frustrated by the downturn in the terms of trade for agriculture in the
middle of the decade, headed for town and were confronted by the vast
array of disparate enterprises there. The release of new labor on a colossal
scale, joined with the rapid emergence of novel types of ownership, lent
a special lawlessness to the flurry of market contention.

For at the same time that powerful competitive pressures mounted,
pushing employers into unsavory practices, state regulatory forces were
weakening and corroding, another product of the transition to markets,
and of the all-too-abrupt insertion of cash into the economy. All this
occurred under the joint onslaughts of a newfound, overriding market
mentality; a demise of party/state-sponsored collectivist ideology and
values; and explicit efforts by the central leadership to generate wealth
throughout society by deregulating economic activity and by decentral-
izing economic decision making, finances, and responsibilities.[6] Increased
bureaucratic discretion for lower-level bureaucrats and managers, all anxious to amass income, plus diminished supervision, were the result, particularly in the continuing absence of any firmly grounded and reliable
legal infrastructure.[7]

A widespread and increasing decline and, in some cases, total absence
of the functions of control and regulation once mightily provided by the
socialist regime, along with new and increasingly powerful competitive
pressures from the market, led, with time, to a reduction in the provisioning for and security of workers, even in firms once dominated by statist
regimens.[8] But all this was much more pronounced in enterprises—in the

private and foreign-funded sectors—wholly outside the framework of the archetypal urban, state-owned factories, and it occurred there earliest.[9]

Another aspect of the transition was that, where the state and its regulations were not disappearing, the enshrinement of enrichment untethered by norms or operative official canons meant that many lower-echelon state personnel quickly acquired the unsupervised clout and the will to bend the still extant—even excessive—rules of a regime that yet retained pretensions of commanding society. In this bending, bureaucrats struggled (and often managed) to gather rents. For both these reasons—the atrophy of some controls and the manipulation of others—irregularities and corruption became the mark of much of the state's bureaucracy. As described by a Western journalist in 1994,

> After 15 years of Deng Xiaoping's reforms, China remains stuck half-way between the command economy and the market. The result is a painful neither-nor existence that combines the worst of both worlds. On the one hand, there are no central controls; on the other, bureau-crats wield strong administrative powers and dole out market-distorting price subsidies for favoured state enterprises.[10]

But at the same time that the ability of the central state to control economic activity from the national echelon declined, other features of its power at the macro level lingered. For one thing, in a number of trades the state continued to determine, and so distort, price and profit structures; this power affected trades taken up by, and raw materials necessary for the occupations of, some groups of migrant labor. Much more crucial and just affecting migrants was the ongoing force of the urban *hukou*, which interfered with rural workers' entry into urban trades, confounded their obtaining work contracts, and hindered the chances of remaining in town for many.

So, in sum, at the macro level, tens of millions of rural newcomers, bent on finding work in China's cities, were permitted to do so by a switch in the rules of the state (and the coming of the market) soon after the 1980s arrived. But they were subjected in the process to a set of large forces, present in any developing society, but all the more potent when merged with a very abrupt shift from a state-dominant economy to a proto-market one. These were competition, deregulation, and—given China's yet feeble legal structure—lawlessness. To these forces were added the lingering clout of the state, as seen in its manipulative, rent-seeking cadres, its residual price-setting, and in its use of the *hukou* to skew the labor market and, accordingly, to determine formal citizenship and economic rights in cities.

At the micro and meso levels, however, the effect of the state was not necessarily so negative. The continuing occupation of the heights of power by the state and the party into the 1990s—even as the role of the state (as against the market) itself was shrinking, the party bereft of prestige—was such that the world of officialdom could still be benign for some, if divisive overall. For the old prerogatives attached to official agencies and agents meant that state workers, and outsiders connected to state institutions and their leaders, were still placed at an advantage at least up to the mid-1990s.[11]

The result was that linkages with officialdom—whether direct, for individuals in the employ of or under contract with a state-owned unit; or more indirect, for members of some native-place-cum-occupational groupings through the personal network connections of their leaders— could soften the effects of excessive rules and their corrupted application and at least marginally overcome the disadvantages of a rural *hukou*. Through the early 1990s, a tie with state units and with the weakened but not yet obliterated regulatory force of state paternalism could diminish the exploitativeness of migrants' employment and also enhance to some degree the stability and security of their work.[12] Indeed, it could offer a kind of citizenship, if much watered down and clearly lower class.

Again we return to that key state institution, the *hukou*, which structured not just the macro division of the population into peasants and urbanites, but also the meso level of social networks. Because the *hukou* set peasants apart, disqualifying them from ordinary labor markets, the status of their respective networks outside these dominant markets made all the difference to the line of work in which they became engaged, and thence the treatment they received. The meso traits of networks (with the state or with one's native-place group) also differentiated, as well as sometimes significantly improved, the lot of the peasant laborer in urban China in the 1980s and 1990s. If this account sketches the effects state institutions had on migrant workers in cities, what was the job market itself like?

THE URBAN JOB MARKET: DEMAND AND SUPPLY

Demand Factors

Thomas Faist connects the employment outcomes of migrant workers in Germany and the United States to the demand produced by public policies and state institutions on the one hand, and to supply, based on immi-

grants' resources, on the other.[13] For China, the state's policy of marketizing reform, combined with a sudden commitment to rapid, no-holds-
barred economic growth, both of which began in 1979, set in motion
fundamental changes in the country's urban employment structure.
These policies had enormous implications for city-bound peasant workers.

Reform dismantled the monopolistic, domestically oriented, urban-
centered, heavy-industry-biased statist, socialist frame for employment
(as I noted in chapter 4).[14] Freeing urban job seekers from their dependence on job allocation by labor bureaus, the policies gave them a range
of opportunities.[15] Reform policies permitted work outside the state
and collective sectors, in the newly revived privately and foreign-owned
and -operated enterprises; greatly expanded the opportunities in light
industry; and legitimized the previously proscribed commercial and service sectors.

Since the mid-1980s, as urbanites increasingly opted for jobs in new
sectors, state firms became pressed to find substitute labor.[16] And with
the end of the several-decades'-old bar against peasants working in cities,
urban firms, charged with achieving high output, turned to rural labor—
labor not entitled to most of the benefits historically granted urban
workers in the P.R.C.—who were suddenly available for this work in
massive numbers, for the first time since the 1950s. In addition, a vast
variety of low-tech jobs in building and services called out for casual
workers. Thus, in this arena loaded with opportunity, even semiliterate
farmers could find an opening.[17]

Certainly, the occupations these trends offered to peasants—in construction, marketing, services, textiles, sanitation, transport, and scrap
collecting, to name a few—are ones allocated to transient labor the world
around, from the migratory laborers and guest workers of Western Europe to the shantytown peasants of Latin America.[18] But even if Chinese
migrants filled the same lowly jobs as migrants elsewhere, the structural
causes—the roots of the demands—were different. The very existence of
many of these jobs and occupations in transitional-era China resulted
from crucial gaps in the old economy, finally exposed with the progressive
collapse of the former state-dominated, heavy-industry-biased frame.[19]
The prior single urban labor market, led by the state—which was, in fact,
far from being a "market"—developed fissures, and peasants poured in
to fill them. But the important distinction from many other places was
that the state was not gone, and its presence continued to structure the
lot of the sojourner in a number of ways.

Supply and Networks in the Labor Market

A huge army of surplus peasant labor, eager to stop up these gaps, then, was the obvious source of supply. But how to tap the supply? In fact, there were several answers to the question, each corresponding to different types of migrants. Here I distinguish these types in accord with the network resources of each, as opposed to the broad regional division into just two types in chapter 5. Because of our addition of state connections, we expand to three Piore's designation of two groups of migrants. Piore finds only "free-floaters," those who come to the city with no particular job in mind and have no specific destination, and those who, planning to join relatives and friends, do have a particular goal in mind.[20]

To bring together the two types in chapter 5 with the three here, we can say that the resources of value possessed by (some) migrants from the inland areas were more apt to be ties with the state, whereas coastal migrants' beneficial bonds (if they had any) came primarily from their native places. Piore's "free-floaters," those with no urban ties—or with ties of no special worth—were either wholly on their own or might have been scraped up as extras and sometimes found themselves connected, usually very briefly, to one of the other two sets.

Since the state-sectoral frame was still extant, a bond with it of any sort constituted a valuable resource. Those who received placement in a state-owned unit could expect to be granted a contract;[21] it afforded some modicum of state-sponsored protection (low exploitation in terms of hours and pay, and some welfare benefits), and at least some minimum of job security (stability). State connections brought migrants a second-class citizenship, compared with the greater array of benefits and more extended security for urban workers (at least up through the early 1990s). The state programs to recruit peasants from poverty areas noted in chapter 5 meant that transients from the interior were the ones most likely to work under state contract. So the first set of migrants were the state-tied.

The fate of a second set of migrants was a function of features of their place of origin. Elsewhere, where the state is not an active, bureaucratically organized employer of transients, such connections are the only ones available.[22] But in transition-era China, ascriptive ties had the most salience for those who were unconnected to the state and who worked in the private, entrepreneurial sector. As suggested in chapter 5, a ubiquitous regionally based, historically rooted diversity dominates the Chinese landscape, one that is so salient to the Chinese themselves that they typically perceive those from elsewhere as almost ethnically disparate.[23]

Fortunate were those whose own local area held rare and popular products that could be marketed, or who were heir to a tradition of special skills or occupations;[24] such goods and abilities could be parlayed into a resource for urban life.[25] Just as in pre-1949 China, peasants from the eastern provinces south of the Yangtze—especially Zhejiang and southern Jiangsu—ranked at the high end of the prestige scale for outside labor, in part because of the talents passed down there over generations, in part because of the capital many of that area's sojourners tended to bring along to town.[26]

People with networks stretching back into their home areas in this region were most likely to bank on ascriptive linkages and to rely on their fellows and on their area's skills or products to become private entrepreneurs or their employees. Unlike the private entrepreneurs native to the city (the urban-registered), the overwhelming proportions of these folk were quite unlikely to establish ties with urban officialdom.[27] As a result (or perhaps as a preference), they withdrew into a realm of their own, one devoid of the state-sponsored benefits and belongingness even of the second-class citizen, where they counted instead just upon mutual support.[28] Here was a basis for a new form of community and, potentially, a kind of extrastate citizenship, in postsocialist China.

Thus, in processes of chain migration, set into motion after earlier arrivals had settled, Chinese migrants just like those anywhere else depended on their respective fellow townspeople for news of openings, for placement, and for assistance on the job[29]—so much so that researchers estimate that, because of prearranged appointments, mainly the doing of family and friends, as few as just 5 to 10 percent of newcomers to Chinese cities could not find work within a week of arriving.[30]

In terms of welfare and well-being, for those whose ties were just to their fellow villagers, the nature of the treatment migrants received on the job—how exploitative, how stable—was a function of the group's profession, and of their own status within that group. Their situation depended on the degree of authority and hierarchy within a given trade, and on the competitiveness, prestige, and strength of the networks in that trade. So the competition, deregulation, and lawlessness that characterized the transition by no means had the same impact on all groups or on all workers within the private sector.

Three points should be made about the effect of the regional specialties upon which this nonstate-connected group was thrown back. In the first place, connections between traditional skills or products for export and current careers gathered strength from chain migration, as the weight of successive streams of movers cumulated over time; at its best, such synergy could issue in near trade monopolies in the places of destination. Under these circumstances, conflicts of interest and competition among regional groups must have greatly diminished.[31] Thus, in these trades, at least for the bosses, such as the wealthy merchants of the Zhejiang Village by the 1990s, exploitation resulting from cost-cutting pressures was minimal.

Second, these ties, more a tendency than a categorical fact, were neither fixed nor rigid, as Bryna Goodman found for an earlier age.[32] Thus, an informant in Wuhan commented, "In no one trade is everyone from one place of origin."[33] So competition was present, though to variable degrees in different trades. Moreover, it increased over time, as more and more peasants sought to make their way in the city.[34]

And third, not all groups benefited from their association with their native places. For the late twentieth-century "ethnic division of labor," akin to the one G. William Skinner analyzed in the late imperial period, was by no means grounded in skills that were equally valuable.[35] Indeed, those from poorer, less wealthy, and less cultured regional areas often suffered as the victims of subethnic biases and attendant discriminatory recruitment patterns in town resulting from their geographical heritages. For example, Henan women looked down on Anhuinese and Sichuanese women for becoming *baomu* (nursemaids), and Sichuanese disparaged those Henanese and Anhui people who gathered trash; Anhui scrappickers were generally despised by all.[36]

All told, regional stereotypes did have validity. Reportedly, as many as 95 percent of the maids in Beijing were from Anhui's Wuwei county in the early 1990s.[37] Shoe repairers left Zhejiang and could be found around the country plying their trade.[38] Also from Zhejiang, especially its Leqing county (within the famous Wenzhou prefecture), came both ordinary garment workers and expert tailors who serviced city dwellers nationwide.[39] Purveyors of a potpourri of other, more distinctive, even esoteric, professions were all commonly linked to one region or another.[40] Natives from Rui'an, Zhejiang, for instance, were skilled at repairing eyeglasses, helped each other obtain the necessary licenses for this trade, and dominated it in Beijing. And Anhui's Fuyang county's peasants specialized in frying rice. Both Zhejiang and Jiangsu provinces were widely acclaimed for practicing a range of miscellaneous crafts, including cotton fluffing, umbrella repair, and furniture making; and were also known for peddling plastic goods, purses, and jewelry.[41]

Non-Han minority peoples from Guangxi province brought jewelry and silver to market. Those from Henan collected old things and sold them, and in some cities simply picked up trash. And one writer claimed that in Chengdu, for instance, migrants from one region or another gathered different waste products, depending on the place from which they came; beggars, too, divided up into regional gangs.[42] Those who bought women and children tended to be based in the southwest, especially in Sichuan and Guangxi.[43]

Only those migrants of the third type, the hapless "free-floaters," those coming to town without craft, connections, or competence, wandered altogether aimlessly, at loose ends. Though they mainly ended up as beggars and scrap-pickers, their type could also be found plying other trades. A simple vignette illustrates their vagrant mode of operation:

> At Nanjing station, peasants were asked where they were going. "Whatever, doesn't matter [*suibian*]," was the casual reply. "We sent people to stand in line to buy tickets. . . . Whatever place they can get tickets for is where we'll go."[44]

Each separate trade category analyzed below potentially had either one, two, or three of these types of migrants within it, depending upon the nature of the networks, or tracts, that laced through that trade, and the degree of dominance of each (table 13). In some trades (construction, nursemaiding, crafts and services, or begging) it was possible to get a job with no connections; in others, such as manufacturing, that was generally not possible. Those in construction or serving as nursemaids could have gotten their work through any one of three kinds of channels. The balance between the tracts within each trade varied with the degree to which the trade in question was tied to the state, and the extent to which the labor of its practitioners was more or less specialized and internally coordinated. In general, lack of coordination meant places for "free-floaters."

Networks, whether state- or group-based, created in China's cities a multitude of separate markets for transients, since the regular one was largely impenetrable to them, rather than delineating a simple, bifurcated, dual market into whose secondary portion migrant labor elsewhere is generally portrayed as being consigned.[45] According to the chief theorist of the dual market model, Michael J. Piore, this market is one that is

> divided into two essentially distinct segments, termed the *primary* and the *secondary* sectors. The former offers jobs with relatively high wages, good working conditions, chances of advancement, equity and due process in the administration of work rules, and, above all, employment stability. Jobs in the secondary sector, by contrast, tend to

Table 13. Types of Networks within Six Trades

	State	Home place	None
Construction	X	X	X
Manufacturing	X	X	—
Nursemaiding	X	X	X
Marketing/services	—	X	X
Garment processing	—	X	—
Begging/scrap collecting	—	X	X

be low-paying, with poorer working conditions and little chance of advancement; to have a highly personalized relationship between workers and supervisors which leaves wide latitude for favoritism and is conducive to harsh and capricious work discipline; and to be characterized by considerable instability in jobs and a high turnover among the labor force.[46]

Piore focuses upon stability and fairness versus instability, exploitation, and personalism to distinguish just two sectors. After Piore, a number of other scholars adapt his theory, still working with a double-sectoral model. In general, these authors, all of whom are describing relatively stable capitalist markets, adduce different factors to account for the presence of two distinct tracks in the labor market. But they all agree that migrant workers and other disadvantaged laborers unfailingly occupy the secondary one. They also all emphasize the same traits in distinguishing one track from the other: income levels, working conditions, the presence of contracts, adherence to governmental regulations, unionization of the work force, whether or not a firm pays social security for its workers, and, especially, job stability.[47]

But as Edward Telles, writing of Brazil, notes, "formal and informal sectors are each made up of diverse economic categories," such that within the informal sector there are some whose profits and incomes are dependably regular (affording the stability that is supposedly present only in the primary, formal sector), their incomes predictable and high.[48] Similarly for China, one set of researchers claims that scrap-pickers in the mid-1990s could collect a monthly income up to 3,000 yuan, several times that of an average Beijing resident.[49]

In China as well ascriptive traits did not neatly delineate primary and secondary markets. As Subbiah Kannappan, drawing on data from a broad range of Asian, Latin American, and African societies, astutely observes, "a relatively complex process of interaction [obtains] among the traditional society, the rural labor force, and urban employment," such that " 'traditional' factors and ties will cut across" the formal/informal sectoral divisions.[50] This finding held true for China, too; it refers, in different language, to what the Chinese call *guanxiwang*, or personal connections. Surely where networks "cut across" the borders between sectors, personalism and ascriptive factors entered not just the secondary sector as Piore holds, but the primary one as well. Thus, as we have seen in chapter 5, some peasants used network relationships to find temporary jobs in urban units. Moreover, in reform-era China how individual migrants fared in their work lives was not really dependent on being in a primary versus a secondary segment of the labor market, but on the nature of their network ties.

Some might assert that the urban *hukou* did act to split the urban Chinese labor market into two, differentiating urban *hukou*-holders from rural ones. But even if we grant this perspective, what we are looking at is not really a dual market in the usual sense. For in other environments around the globe workers could aspire to transfer out of the secondary market eventually, certainly if they were wealthy and belonged to the dominant ethnic group. But in China during the transition from socialism individuals could not cross the boundaries between the two halves, regardless of common Han Chinese ethnicity with the mainstream city population or level of wealth.[51]

So urbanized ruralites as a category, what is called the "floating population," though cast by the *hukou* into a large, excluded realm, only appeared to the casual observer to subsist as a unified group in a separate market of its own. For the very disparate nature of the respective social networks that sustained subgroups of country workers—some linked to state bureaucracies and units or to their leaders, some in grids of their own quite apart from the state, some without ties at all—belied such an assumption of simple duality. China's urban migrants, instead, were participants in a multitude of markets, each operating according to very different rules. As recent research in China asserts,

> Our country's current labor market is different from the usual concept of labor market. First, a peasant worker is not a completely independent individual entering a labor market. Second, labor does not completely rely on the influence of market prices but flows in accord with

traditional social networks. So it's a transitional labor market. And the market's span is unusually large, but market information to guide the flow of labor is lacking.[52]

Given these factors, I propose a framework that distinguishes between three ideal typical markets: state-administered or formal markets; informal, but ascriptively guided, nonstate markets; and what the Chinese label "spontaneous," or "blind," nonadministered, anonymous markets.[53] Migrant laborers could be found in all three. Guided by this breakdown, I consider six occupations taken up by China's transient urban "peasant" labor, and the sometimes as many as triple markets—statist, ascriptive, and anonymous—within each of them. We will find that these multiple markets each functioned with separate rules and recruitment strategies, catered to disparate pools of workers, and offered varying working conditions.[54]

SIX OCCUPATIONS

These six trades, ones in which floaters were frequently found in China's cities, are construction; manufacturing; nursemaiding; marketing and services; cottage-style garment processing; and begging and scrap collecting.[55] The first three contained statist markets and at least one of the other two sorts; the workings of the second three trades, all in the entrepreneurial sector, were dominated by either ascriptive or anonymous markets or by a combination of them.

Over the course of more than a decade, most accounts agreed that about 75 percent of the floating population entered cities with the objective of locating work or doing business.[56] But there was far less consensus as to the proportions engaged in particular trades. Even for one city, the estimates of those doing construction work varied from 350,000 to more than 800,000 over a six-month period, from late 1994 to spring 1995.[57] In early 1995, even the Ministry of Public Security, whose efforts at accuracy must have been better than some, could only guess that somewhere between 30 and 50 percent of all migrants were engaged in the building trade.[58]

Sometimes discrepancies resulted from researchers' use of different occupational categories. Three surveys done in the mid-1990s illustrate the problem. One, a study of twenty-eight rural counties in 1994, reports that 40 percent were working in industry but includes handicrafts workers among them; 42 percent were in construction; 11.6 percent in commerce; 5 percent in agriculture; and 1.5 percent in transportation.[59] Another, done by the Ministry of Agriculture also in 1994, notes that only 28 percent of the transregional migrants it surveyed nationwide were in industry; just 23 percent in construction; still 5 percent in agriculture; just 8 percent in commerce; 15 percent in food service; and 5 percent in transportation, leaving 16 percent in "other" categories.[60]

And a third, an investigation by the Rural Development Institute of the Chinese Academy of Social Sciences, shows that 22 percent were employed in industry; 33 percent in construction; 10 percent in transport; 31 percent in commerce, food, beverages, and services; and 4 percent in agriculture.[61] It is obvious from these three studies both that it is difficult to get consistent readings and also that researchers' use of disparate categories complicates any effort at comparability. Still, it is clear that construction, manufacturing, and services, broadly defined, were the major groupings.

If we look at gender breakdowns, we find that in the Pearl River Delta, where country women were preferred over males for the more precise and intricate assemblage work required in toys, plastics, and electronics,[62] they constituted about half the work force.[63] Elsewhere, though, they accounted for just a quarter or even less.[64] In general, males sorted into construction labor while women did household and other service work (including sales), as well as some forms of manufacturing.[65]

Construction

Of all the possible lines of work that peasants could transfer into, construction was probably the one demanding the least investment and the lowest risk, and promising the quickest returns;[66] for these reasons, though it has been termed the most bitter and tiring of the jobs floaters undertook, it was surely the most popular.[67] And given the minimal capital outlay required, and the low level of cultural preparation demanded to become an ordinary digger, teams outside the state sector anxious to work in the cities quickly grew in numbers.[68] One effect of large numbers was that, in the face of so many contenders, state management departments, for decades operating within a highly regulated, largely planned labor market and still obliged to uphold some barriers against outside irregular labor forces, found themselves overwhelmed in the transition to marketization, even as they essayed to keep the trade under control.[69]

Besides the numbers and continuing, if erratic, regulation by the state, the construction trade was beset by financial pressures from low state-determined profit rates and multitudinous surcharges, while depending for its raw materials on products whose prices were rising through the 1980s and 1990s. Overall, these factors, a mixture of state and market forces, made it difficult for anyone engaged in the trade to earn money legally in it.[70] To overcome all these obstacles against gaining entry to the city, obtaining work contracts, making money, and staying on in town, builders and their work teams turned to what critics targeted as "irregularities," which cropped up and flourished.[71]

Construction workers could be found in all three kinds of networks or markets: linked by contracts to state firms; operating in teams of fellow villagers; and completely on their own, as individuals; or in a combination of some two of these forms. Market liberalizations of the 1980s permitted rurally based construction firms to take the initiative in signing contracts, so that by the middle of the decade informal, peasant labor teams had already appeared as a challenge to the state teams.[72] In October 1984 the state council boosted the chances of these "outside" teams when it passed regulations urging state firms to recruit rural builders in lieu of the more expensive, permanent urban-based ones.[73]

One source states that by the end of 1985 rural builders and diggers hired by state construction firms nationally already amounted to nearly one-third of the permanent work force.[74] By the end of 1987, fully half of Guangzhou's builders were said to have come from elsewhere;[75] the same figure was given for Shanghai at the end of the decade.[76] In the early 1990s, one scholarly Chinese journal reports, "in recent years, construction teams from out of town have consistently made up two-fifths of the construction workers."[77]

In major cities, most of the rural construction workers came from nearby: in Shanghai, in 1989 for instance, 43.5 percent were Jiangsunese and 28.5 Zhejiangese, natives of the two provinces closest to the city.[78] Nanjing's builders from outside mainly hailed from northern Jiangsu, the province of which that city is the capital, since the natives of the wealthier, more fertile south of the province were busy with township enterprises and agriculture.[79] And in Wuhan, in the early 1990s between one-third and one-half of the outsiders were from that city's own suburbs and counties, or at least from the province of Hubei, of which Wuhan is the capital city.[80] That so many of the peasants working in this trade came from the cities' hinterlands laid a foundation for the informal, ascriptively based ties that characterized much of the business in this sector.

All construction teams, whether state-related or informal, were ranked by the official construction commission of their own locality, in accord with a national grading system.[81] Each team received a ranking from one to five: the first was for central government- and provincially managed, state-related teams that had reached a certain standard of excellence. The second rank pertained mainly to city-level teams and to some provincial and central ones.

Firms under the jurisdiction of township governments, at the third level, were the highest ranked rural teams, and so on down the administrative hierarchy. Whereas first-level teams could perform any kind of construction, second-level teams were restricted to buildings of thirty stories and below; third-level teams could build up to only twelve stories, and fourth only up to six stories. Fifth-level teams were not allowed to work independently, and could only supply labor power to supplement the work of other teams.

A third (or lower)-level team aspiring to work legally in a city had to get a work permit from that city's construction commission and had to register with the city's industrial and commercial management bureau, in order to obtain a business certificate to enter the city. Altogether, it had to acquire four documents in the course of setting itself up for work in town. These documents were to be presented to the managers of an enterprise in the city before they could legally sign a contract with and employ the team: a business license (*yingye zhizhao*); a certificate from the team's rural governmental office indicating that it could leave the countryside (*waichuzheng*); a permit for entering the city (*jincheng xukezheng*); and a quality specifications credential (*zizhi zhengshu*).[82]

Once at work in the city, officially connected rural construction teams were subject to supervision by an exhaustingly lengthy list of urban bureaucracies, including the construction commission; the labor, public security, industrial and commercial management, tax, environmental, and transportation bureaus; and the residents' committee. They also had to pay taxes to their rural home governments on the basis of the various expenditures of the project and deliver management fees on their estimated earnings.[83] In part these numerous payments were the result of the rent-seeking that a vast bureaucracy, especially in times of deregulation, fosters. In the words of a responsible person from a Shaoxing county, Zhejiang, construction team at work in Shanghai in 1989,

> Now for peasants, going out to work is very hard: first there are
> various kinds of fees. Besides paying taxes according to regulations, in
> Zhejiang, we must pay management fees to the province, the county,
> the township, the company, and the construction team, altogether five
> mothers-in-law, and separately pay other fees to the Shanghai project

quality supervision office and to the construction work site management. Altogether these amount to 30 to 50 percent of our wages.[84]

The bosses of organized construction teams generally only entered the city after having first established contact with city authorities.[85] In one pattern, urban-based, state-owned companies needing extra labor drew up three-year contracts with rural teams, usually ones based in the city's own suburbs and counties. Alternatively, teams might be identified by communicating with the local administrations of specified, mountainous poor areas in neighboring provinces. There were also the long-standing ties between construction offices in major cities and "brother provinces" noted in chapter 5. In these cases, team members were more or less incorporated into the urban unit, even if they got only some, but by no means all, of the benefits of the unit's urban workers.[86]

In the early 1990s Tianjin's Construction Commission was hiring peasant labor teams as reinforcements on three-year contracts; according to its officials, these workers were granted the same treatment as local, permanent ones. Commission officials contrasted the situation of these people with that of laborers in other outside teams, who, despite working on contract, were operating just on an ad hoc basis, rather than through a long-term arrangement. These latter teams' management was not bound by any regulations on wages.[87]

While those who became part of the state firm's ranks got regular days off—one rest day every two weeks (in addition to national holidays)—the ad hoc outsiders worked seven-day weeks, stopping only at harvest time (when they repaired home to perform field labor), at New Year's, and in the winter.[88] Other state-related construction workers were employees of rural teams owned by state administrations in the countryside, where, again, rules were followed, treatment was superior, and bosses were more humane, though the pay might be lower.[89]

Construction team leaders with ties to the local bureaucracy in the city they entered, if not necessarily holding contracts with state firms, could take care of their ranks to some extent by drawing upon such *guanxi*. At a minimum these bonds enabled them to arrange temporary registration without difficulties, and, when required, to find low-priced food or living space for their charges.[90]

The value of connections with state employees was especially apparent when a team (or worker's) contract came to an end: linkages with the right people allowed many to linger.[91] As explained in a Wuhan Labor

Bureau pamphlet, the "countless ties" that existed between outsiders and city people meant that dismissing these workers "has implications for personal relationships and affects people's interests, so that many [successfully, apparently] plead for mercy [to be allowed to stay on the job]."[92]

Indeed, most contractors would not even venture into a city without some kind of official connection. Asked who becomes a labor boss, an informant in Harbin explained that "if a person has personal relations here, he can do it . . . he must go through connections or he wouldn't come to the city with a group."[93] Sociologists in Nanjing agreed: "Construction labor uses *guanxiwang* in irregular markets" to find jobs.[94]

Unlike managers in state-owned firms who adhered to state policy, recruiting their peasant builders either by means of established linkages or in accord with state-designated anti-poverty plans, those operating with varying degrees of informality used more casual ways of finding their work forces. Many informal labor bosses simply gathered people from their own home areas, much in the mode of Larissa Lomnitz's Mexican foreman who "market[s] the unskilled labor of relatives and neighbors," and then went on to structure the internal management of the team in accord with blood and place relations.[95] The foremen who assembled gangs stood above them, not laboring themselves but moving about the city, making contacts, and presenting gifts and bribes. Often they had been resident in the city where they had won project bids for more than a decade.[96] Such bosses were often powerful at home as well, by the mid-1990s positioning themselves to dispense the patronage and petty bribes requisite to winning local village elections newly institutionalized at that point.[97]

In other cases bosses operated on a broader geographical scale, composing gangs made up of people from several provinces, by encouraging relatives to invite one another.[98] Yet others simply scouted around the countryside, searching for idle workers, and, having assembled a gang, went on the prowl, ready to relocate with the demands of the market.[99] My few encounters with these contractors convinced me they were an arrogant and peremptory lot, wielding enormous arbitrary and fearsome command over their underlings.[100]

In the most anonymous style of recruitment—where contacts counted for nothing—only the boss was contracted to the project. He switched his work force frequently, depending on the work abilities, obedience, and level of skill of the recruits.[101] Those "miscellaneous personnel" employed in this mode could be chosen quite randomly, at spontaneous labor markets; or hired from among the unemployed hangers-on camped around train stations or other sites where the jobless congregated.[102]

The personnel so recruited were often not registered for urban work or temporary residence, since private deals between construction entrepreneurs and the public security bypassed these official procedures, enabling the entrepreneurs to fire their workers at will and to pay lower taxes for purportedly smaller work forces.[103] Surely unregistered laborers were afforded no protection or benefits, a situation that typifies workers' declining level of advantages and protections as they stood further and further from the core of the state or, worse yet, from linkages of any kind.

All such teams, progressively more and more "informal" and less and less networked—whether to the state, or, internally, on a long-term relationship basis with a team boss—belonged to an intricate system of subcontracts.[104] Beginning after the early 1980s, state firms and urban collective enterprises drastically increased their subcontracting of rural labor power.[105] As the first step in the process, a state-owned firm would engage a rural collective firm or enterprise or hire individuals. The next step was to subdivide the task and follow a descending hierarchy of subcontracting.[106]

There were two forms of subcontract: the double contract (*shuangbao*), whereby both the tools and materials and the work team were contracted; and the *danbao* (or single contract), whereby just the work project itself was under contract with a labor boss (*gongtou*).[107] Generally, city-based *gongtou*, having urban connections, came with their own equipment and materials. The outsider bosses brought along nothing but their workers and bid just to carry out the work. The skill of the workers, their wage level, and the amount of regulation under which they toiled all decreased with successively lower levels in this hierarchy of delegation.[108]

Many outcomes attended the increasingly pervasive lack of regulation as the overall size of the urban labor market expanded and state oversight over its many strands diminished. One was the competitive edge that rural builders soon acquired over official urban ones.[109] In Wuhan, for example, by 1989 outside construction teams had already captured half the bids. And while the area of the projects they took on amounted to just under half (45 percent) of the total, their costs came to only one-third.[110] The simplest explanation was that their workers' pay was lower than that officially mandated for state teams.

But in fact, pay for peasant construction workers varied less by ownership system or over time or space than it did by task. Scattered data show that for the average peasant construction worker, a rate averaging around 10 yuan per day (or 300 yuan for a full month of workdays) was relatively constant across time and space between the mid-1980s and the early 1990s, while in the state sector, the average pay in 1989 was 180 per month (presumably before bonuses, which would have brought the figure up to something over 300 per month).[111] So the important difference was that the peasant workers toiled more hours for similar wages.

Other features of farmer-builder teams that attracted employers included their flexible internal structure. Unlike state firms' commitment to a work force, these teams held only a technical core and a minimum of administrative staff while recruiting temporary labor just as the need arose. And their production workers—young, strong, of farmer stock, and without other options—did without the dormitories state workers lived in, instead acquiescing in sleeping on site.[112]

The comparative cheapness of teams operating outside the aegis of the state was possible because of yet another effect of the transition: the decline in provisioning. Nonstate teams eschewed what the reform era dubbed the welfare "burden" long shouldered (but increasingly less and less so, as competition with outside teams mounted) by state enterprises (medical care, pensions, and labor insurance fees).[113] Also, as noted above, money was saved in that, unlike the regulars, temporaries were permitted to rest only in accord with the demands of the job instead of on a regular basis, as the permanents did.[114]

In the informal teams, the sole guarantee for the workers was a "safety contract," which, unfortunately for them, was accompanied by a "discipline contract." The latter specified that the worker himself had to pay the doctor if his accident resulted from "disobeying regulations." The hours of the outsiders were also highly unpredictable.[115] Thus, management in firms not linked to the state was labeled "chaotic": "When the task is tense and hands are short, some bosses press people to add on shifts and work sites, work all night, take no rest. Accidents and injuries abound."[116]

According to one source, the low cost and flexibility of these teams meant that "a lot of projects are undertaken by these peasant teams with an inferior technical level, backward equipment, and wanting quality."[117] Some, no doubt writing with an urban bias, attributed the poor results of many of these teams' work to what they claimed was the typically "very low cultural level" of their ranks, a scarcity among them of skilled personnel, and the "poor character" of the peasants. And yet, according to two surveys, over half of these rural workers in the cities had at least been to junior high school as of the late 1980s.[118]

Better explanations for low-quality work can be gleaned from the lawlessness under which they labored. Reportedly, "some teams get in without permission, using trickery and fraud," said a study of transients in Shanghai, written in the late 1980s.[119] Apparently the relevant bureaucracies had lost either the ability or the will to limit the entry of unsupervised groups and teams; or perhaps they received rents as a condition for allowing admission. In this environment, once construction team bosses got entry, they used whatever connections they could to obtain work contracts (often through corruption and cheating).[120] For instance, teams from outside the urban market may have bribed the hiring unit's first party secretary or state construction management personnel in order to secure a requisite credentials certificate, an operating license, or the right to open bank accounts.[121]

Another very common strategy was what was called *daoshou chengbao*, "inverted contracting," in which a bidder with an appropriate license and credentials accepted a contract and then passed it along, for a profit, to an unqualified or unregistered party.[122] This practice allowed teams without easy access to official agencies to work without properly acquiring the prescribed documents.[123] Other infractions occurred when unconnected teams, beset by competition, felt forced to bid low to win a contract. In this poorly regulated and competitive market they could still earn a profit, by turning out slipshod work, skimping on materials, ignoring safety measures, and exploiting and cheating their work forces.[124]

The result of these kinds of behavior showed up in the buildings constructed (figure 4). A 1989 quality check of 300 firms in Wuhan found leaks, uneven plaster, doors and windows that did not close properly, incorrect grades of concrete in use, stairs with inaccurate dimensions, and sinking foundations, threatening the safety of the buildings. Of 341 projects assessed, those undertaken by state enterprises had a 66.7 percent rate of meeting specifications; state-affiliated teams from other cities' rate was 45.5 percent, while those built by the informal, rural teams from the city's counties and suburbs was a mere 23 percent.[125]

Interviews, official accounts, and reportage literature concurred in describing the management of teams in the unregulated, nonstate channels as descending into an anarchic, semisubterranean world, one where shameless exploitation was common, no doubt a result of competition,

Figure 4. A break at a construction site, Wuhan.

deregulation, lawlessness, and disdain for the workers.[126] An official publication recounts the sorry tale of a ditchdigger, promised 5 yuan per
square meter, who had not been paid after working ten months. Since
the boss refused to let him quit, the hapless fellow was forced to escape
secretly, lacking even the funds to return home.[127] Such a story must
have been picked for publication because it was representative.

Four boys seeking work at a neighborhood labor exchange told me of
friends who were temporarily putting them up in the construction team's
workshed. The laborers were supposed to be paid 7 yuan per day for
thirteen to fourteen hours' work. But their boss delivered only 100 per
month, promising to hand over the remaining 110 yuan at Spring Festival. If these laborers worked too slowly, the *gongtou* scolded them, reduced their pay, and even fired them.[128] As a study of work site bosses
uncovered, "Various brigade leaders express lack of concern toward the
regulations [on treatment of workers] in the [1994] Labor Law; they
think what their workers most care about is making money."[129]

Another effect of competition, deregulation, and lawlessness was the
miserable living conditions of the work force, whose daily lives were
unstable and barren.[130] In major metropolises like Shanghai, where teams
from several provinces dug and built, they banded for mutual protection
into regional factions ranging from a dozen to several hundred members
each. Each team lived together at its work site, where living quarters were

stark. Many stayed in crude, temporary shacks that they threw together; after the structure they were building was under way, they resided in its lower stories.

Subsisting on twelve-hour workdays without family life, cultural distractions, or entertainment, or contact with the outside urban world (even as late as the mid-1990s), they took to gambling and patronizing prostitutes.[131] Easy targets of the law, in Shanghai in the late 1980s, they were charged with having perpetrated over half the criminal activity attributed to the entire floating population of that city.[132] Commentators frequently remarked on their restless mobility;[133] they roved from work site to work site, from city to city (throwing up and tearing down crude and simple shacks wherever they went), to and fro between job and their rural homes, and with the seasons.[134]

Thus, given the informality that came with reform—much as in other contexts where deregulatory processes and deunionization are under way[135]—the growing dominance of outside, peasant labor in the urban construction market was apparent, even by the mid-1980s. In China's transitional "reform" era, the possession of an affiliation with the state, and thus an incorporation into at least some of its systems, acted as the dividing line between a form of citizenship for some, and an increasingly pronounced exclusion from the urban community for others, as builders' ties became further and further removed from the oversight of state units.

Manufacturing

For purposes of simplification, I distinguish manufacturing in factories—as opposed to the cottage workshops of the garment processors to be discussed soon—according to whether the firm for which a migrant worked was state-owned (urban, large or medium-sized) or foreign-invested.[136] The material below describes the differences at these two types of labor sites as of the early 1990s.

The State Sector: Textiles   Many members of the floating population found refuge, if temporarily, within the confines of industrial enterprises, rather than being wafted adrift in the streets, stalls, shacks, sweatshops, and other work sites of the private sector.[137] Chinese peasants in urban factories were consigned to particular trades, as in any economy employing migrants: they principally labored in the manufacture of textiles, chemicals, and building materials, where working conditions were so inferior that urban youths shunned them. Even when outsiders appeared in other trades, they tended to be shunted into the jobs requiring hard physical labor.[138] For instance, an incomplete statistic listed more than two hundred thousand of them at work in Shanghai, laboring in over 60 percent of the state enterprises in the late 1980s, about 50 percent of whom were engaged in arduous labor.

Among the industrial departments within the state sector of the economy, the textile trade made the most use of peasant labor.[139] In the major textile center of Hangzhou by the end of the 1980s, they accounted for more than half the production workers;[140] and in some individual textile factories in Hubei province rural workers accounted for a similar proportion.[141] An official report from the mid-1990s claimed that two-fifths of the textile workers in Shanghai were by that time girls and women from the rural areas.[142]

In 1992, when queried as to whether peasants were concentrated in particular workshops within that trade, officials at the No. One Cotton Mill in Wuhan denied it. "They do about the same work as the regular labor does," they explained, because, after all, "the whole trade is nothing but tired, dirty, and bitter labor."[143] For this reason, in the late 1980s urban young people increasingly scorned textile labor, as they looked for more glamorous or lucrative jobs, often in the private sector. In Zhengzhou, by 1987 it had become harder and harder to get city youths to sign up for this work.[144] And as increasing numbers of older urban employees were laid off in this sector in the early and mid-1990s, cheaper young women of the floating population were taken in to replace them.[145]

Despite the verbal denial, documentary sources show that within this sector, rural workers were concentrated in the spinning and weaving workshops.[146] There the environment was particularly poor, deafening, dusty, and debilitating, with its intolerable clatter, high heat and humidity.[147] In these workshops, to give one example, temporary peasant contract workers constituted more than two-thirds of the staff and work force by 1989 at the Sichuan No. One Cotton Textile Mill. But in this factory as a whole, only one-fifth of the workers and staff were peasants.[148]

Still, placement in a decidedly unappealing milieu within the state sector gave millhands a privileged life as second-class citizens, compared with those of their floating fellows on the streets. Linked into the state sector first by recruiters who were either state employees offering contracts or their own relatives or neighbors[149] (or all three), and then by a guarantor[150] who was also state-connected; employed by work units subject to national regulations;[151] and supervised by the official trade unions,[152] even the

most unfortunate among them could count on at least some, and sometimes all, of the following benefits (through the early 1990s):[153] an employment commitment from their employer of at least one, but often up to
three years;[154] the benefit of a training course, usually in work methods
and in safety;[155] a modicum of hygiene and labor protection; steady wages,
sometimes supplemented by bonuses and subsidies; regular and limited
hours of work;[156] help with amenities such as housing and food;[157] and,
usually, at least minimal medical assistance while on the job.[158]

Peasant workers in state enterprises certainly did not stand the chance
of obtaining the income that some in the private sector could amass—the
usual wage for a peasant textile worker after several years, even in a
relatively profitable state firm, was in the range of 200 yuan per month
in the early 1990s[159]—while various surveys found that the average
annual income in the service trade for male migrants was about 270 yuan
a month in the mid-1990s; that the average floater's wage was 400 yuan
a month; and that the range went from less than 200 to 600 yuan per
month.[160]

But the substantially more secure existence that migrants' employment in state firms afforded them, compared with that of transients
outside the state, was one more indication that the labor markets' absorb-
ing migrant peasants in transition-era China was more complex than
classic dual labor market theory would predict. Thus, overall, though
peasant factory workers could contrast their working lives unfavorably
with those of their urban-registered state-affiliated co-workers,[161] the
benefits they did possess as employees of the state—at least in the better-
off firms as late into the transition as 1992—set them apart from other,
much more free-floating, members of the floating population. By mid-
1993, even as the official People's Daily was writing about how state
firms had "fallen in love with" peasant labor, because of all the money
this could save them, it still advocated offering peasant workers a certain
modicum of welfare benefits.[162]

Officials from the Tianjin Bureau of Labor listed a number of financial
advantages to the use of temporary outside labor: no insurance had to be
paid; the young people engaged were unlikely to become seriously ill
(and, with their limited-term contracts, would depart before they got
much older); no schools had to be set up for their benefit, since they were
required to be unmarried and thus childless; their housing, with half a
dozen or more squeezed into one dorm room, was remarkably cheap; and
no compensation was necessary when they were idle (as it was for regular
workers).[163]

Indeed, were temporary workers to refuse these jobs that urbanites disdained, the losses to the textile trade could have been substantial. According to the reckoning of the textile bureau in Zhengzhou, that city's six large cotton mills in the late 1980s were sorely dependent upon their outside labor from the countryside, as the following figures demonstrate. Reportedly, without these women, 30 percent of the weaving and spinning machines would have had to be stopped, and the annual loss would have been 230 million yuan in output value, 63.34 million yuan in taxes and profits. These same firms managed to increase their foreign exchange intake more than twofold because of the toil of the 5,800 peasant women they employed in the five years of the second half of the 1980s.[164]

In a government-sponsored report on the difficulties besetting rural women in the Zhengzhou textile trade at the end of the 1980s, a range of complaints was enumerated. They were being consigned to the outdated, worn-out machines, while regular workers got the modern ones; the regular, urban workers neglected to inform them of activities in which they ought to have been able to participate; some had to rent rooms at a high price far from the plant; and they lacked some of the welfare benefits, subsidies, holidays, and sizable bonuses granted to their urban colleagues. All of these things were problems, granted; but, as we will see, they surely pale next to the plight of the peasants in the foreign-funded sector.

The Foreign-Funded Sector   Migrant peasant laborers employed in foreign-funded firms—like those throughout the third world—struggled in conditions reminiscent of the gruesome scenes in Charles Dickens's accounts of early Western industrialization.[165] The nascent Chinese proletariat itself had also seen such times in the pre-1949 period.[166] With increasing energy after 1979 the central state wooed foreign investment for its potential to jump-start China's modernization drive and accelerate its growth, gradually slackening restrictions against foreign operators through the 1980s.[167] Nonetheless, the central government launched a massive media attack on the treatment that foreign-invested factories visited upon their transient labor. The data that follow come not just from that source, but also from reporters operating outside the state and in Hong Kong, local newspapers, and social science journals, which had begun documenting all the same abuses for some five years before the official campaign got under way.[168]

Hiring in this sector was not dissimilar to the procedures employed by the state-sector firms: personal ties and collective contracts were still the basis.[169] There were two important differences, however: if workers were recruited individually, the friends and relatives who invited them into or referred them to these firms were not themselves state employees but were instead other uprooted ruralites without social position or bureaucratic rank of any sort. And second, if they were engaged by a collective contract, their recruiters were more likely to be unreliable scoundrels than salaried factory officials drawing on long-standing interunit linkages.[170] The shoddiness, deception, and collusive graft built into the informal, nonstate induction process boded poorly for the treatment that was to ensue.

Once recruited, the chances that a rural migrant would be granted a dependable contract were slim indeed. According to a French source, 40 percent of those at work in joint-venture firms in mid-1994 had begun work without signing any contract. But an official Chinese account claimed that more than 90 percent of the laborers in Taiwan-funded and other "foreign" enterprises[171] in Xiamen at that time, and 70 to 80 percent of those in Shandong, had never signed employment contracts, making sudden dismissals easy to enforce.[172]

Even when firms did offer contracts, there was no guarantee that they would respect them.[173] Yet another 1994 report alleged that some foreign firms in Jiangsu and Liaoning prepared two copies of contracts, one in Chinese and one in English, each containing different terms.[174] Accordingly, Hong Kong bosses felt no compunction about casually firing their work forces or offering no wages during slack seasons, when the plant might shut down for a time. In one egregious case, several such firms in Bao'an county, Guangdong, let 2,500 go at one swoop when stocks from America failed to arrive.[175]

As another source quipped, "Most enterprises in the processing trade rely on outside laborers to 'come when beckoned and leave when dismissed.'"[176] Given the massive numbers of surplus rural laborers in search of jobs, and their acquiescence in low wages and miserable labor conditions, entrepreneurs outside the state sector placed no value on the individual worker; protesting pay cuts or the working environment could thus easily lead to immediate discharge.[177] Themselves subject to intense competition, hostage to the vagaries of the world market for their exports, and linked in a partnership with local officials anxious to attract foreign investment, "more than a few" foreign investors "come essentially to exploit," according to the *Wall Street Journal*.[178]

Though overseas firms were rumored to offer higher wages than state-owned ones, and by state regulation were enjoined to do so, they often did not.[179] Several reports attested that migrants employed by joint ventures actually received lower wages than state workers in the same region.[180] The comparison with Hong Kong salaries is far more shocking: an article from early 1988 revealed that migrant labor in Guangdong at that time was being paid less than one-seventh what the same kind of work could command in the territory.[181] Some, paid about 200 yuan a month (less than a state firm in Guangdong would pay), had nothing left for saving after meeting their costs for food and shelter; in another case, according to a disgruntled reader's letter to the *Southern Daily*, workers had to borrow money just to be able to eat.[182] Journalistic reporting alleged that most rural workers and their families were ignorant of these conditions when they set out from home.[183]

Other sources of outrage were the very common wage delays, deductions, and embezzlements. In mid-1993, for instance, the labor bureau and city federation of trade unions of Shenzhen received more than four thousand complaints on this general score (though they had no authority to offer redress), affecting nearly thirty thousand staff and workers owed some 5 million yuan.[184] Since workers would lose their wages and deposits if they were to leave, firms that could force workers to go had a ready opportunity for embezzlement;[185] many others held workers hostage by withholding their identification cards and deposits.[186] In the same category were the arbitrary registration fees charged workers in the Pearl River Delta, which could amount to more than one month's wage.[187]

Housing for the transients in the nonstate sector was, as for those in state firms, usually either in dormitories or in rentals arranged by the workers themselves. The difference was that here not eight but twenty women slept together, not infrequently two or three to a bed. Yet sometimes no dorms at all were provided, so that workers were forced to sleep right in the workshops themselves.[188] As for food, most reports commented on the brevity of meal breaks (twenty to thirty minutes, as in the pre-1949 days);[189] in some places workers received just two meals a day.[190]

Long hours without overtime compensation and seven-day workweeks received a great deal of official press coverage. Many reports noted that when a firm was overwhelmed with orders, its employees were toiling up to fourteen or even eighteen hours a day, with little or no overtime.[191] A poll in Guangzhou in late 1993 revealed that 61 percent of the workers were made to stay at their machines seven days a week; and 34.7 percent to remain there overtime, 20 percent without any overtime pay.

In addition to the long hours, employment in the foreign-funded sector was often physically treacherous as well. While conditions varied widely, some of these firms providing at least some kinds of social security and pension schemes,[192] substantial numbers of them lacked the medical coverage, accident insurance, and safety and hygienic protection offered in many state firms.[193] Fires resulting from hazardous conditions, combined with management practices of locking in laborers to prevent theft, appeared to be rather commonplace. In 1993, industrial fires caused 300 million yuan in losses; a full 60 percent of these occurred in foreign-funded firms.[194] And not only were precautions often ignored, accident victims had no guarantee of compensation. Statistics from official trade union surveys undertaken in 1993 provide an indication of problems of another sort: 18 percent of the workers at 20 firms surveyed in Guangdong told of regularly being beaten, cursed, or insulted;[195] 17.6 percent confided in another poll that they had been subjected to frisks and body searches.[196]

The explanation behind these phenomena, essentially the same as that for the situation of migrant workers engaged in domestically financed lines of work outside the state sector (such as in the nonstate construction teams), suggests a ready contrast with the lot of state firm employees. Because of the regulatory regime provided by the state and the financial protection afforded most state-owned enterprises (what is labeled their "soft budget constraint"), their managers well into the 1990s were shielded from the fierce competitive pressures and precarious returns that drove private entrepreneurs, rural construction teams, local officials, and foreign investors to various forms of lawlessness, exploitation, and self-exploitation.[197]

Perhaps most significantly, in the case of the foreign-funded firms, multiple petty alliances between local officials and foreign investors shored up these malpractices. On one side of the bargain were the profits-hungry foreigners; on the other the lately autonomous small-time bureaucrats who benefited from the taxes, stimulation to their own little economies, and employment opportunities that the foreign ventures could provide. In their eagerness to attract these operations to their jurisdictions, they "provide[d] 101 kinds of preferential treatment to foreign businesspeople," ignored safety standards and national regulations, and discouraged the establishment of trade unions, which if present, they feared, just might ward off the chance for engaging outside capital.[198]

Nursemaiding

In some cities as early as 1982 the local branch of the women's federation (a party-controlled "mass organization") set up labor exchanges for rural women who aspired to work as nursemaids (*baomu*).[199] In Tianjin, for instance, after a 1986 investigation showed that more than half of the five thousand cadre and intellectuals' households surveyed wanted to hire a maid, one of the city's assistant party secretaries organized the women's federation, along with the city's labor, public security, and propaganda bureaus and one city district, to create a Tianjin City Family Labor Market Leadership Small Group.[200] That group went to Beijing to study its women's federation's March 8 Family Labor Service Company. By March 1987 the Tianjin group had created a Tianjin City Family Service Introduction Office.[201] Also in the mid-1980s so-called spontaneous markets, unconnected with any official agency, sprang up, prepared to tap the reservoir of demand for such labor.[202]

Unlike in other trades in the private sector, demand appears to have consistently outstripped supply into the early 1990s. In 1985 Beijing, four of every hundred households were urgently clamoring for maids.[203] And even as many as seven years later in 1992, it was still "very easy to find work in the city as a *baomu*," since considerable need remained.[204] Social scientists in Wuhan in 1990 also spoke of unsatisfied demand, again because even in this inland, less sophisticated commercial center, city people refused to engage in this occupation.[205] Like construction work for men, nursemaiding suited young women lacking urban skills and knowledge.[206]

In nursemaiding, unlike the construction field, there was no competition for turf or for jobs between locals and outsiders. Instead, outsiders—migrants from a city's poorer nearby counties or often from Anhui province (where a tradition of specialization as domestic servants and maids dated back to the Ming dynasty)[207]—had a monopoly.[208] Therefore variation in the treatment of *baomu*, and the exploitation that obtained, was largely a function of the network with which a given woman became associated, and of the degree of regulation and lawfulness in that network.

Here we find three channels of recruitment, each with its own rules and practices. The official channel, under the charge of the women's federation or sometimes of a neighborhood residents' committee in a given city, included recruitment organs of various sorts.[209] These organs received women coming to town on their own, usually guided there by friends; drew them in by liaising with labor bureaus, sometimes in nearby village committees but, when necessary, from wherever poverty areas were known to have surpluses of idle young women; or they accepted charges sent by rural labor bureaus.[210]

These official agencies registered the maids, arranged contracts for them, collected fees from both maids and future employers, stabilized wages, negotiated conflicts, allegedly safeguarded the rights and interests of the women, trained them, and served as a vehicle for instilling trust on both sides.[211] Maids' contracts specified that they should be made to work only a six-day week of eight-hour days, and that they would remain in a given household from three months to three years, with six months to a year the norm.[212] A maid who lived in the employers' home, which was the custom in Wuhan, received free room and board, television privileges, and sometimes old clothes.

A second recruitment channel developed outside the supervision of the state agencies; it formed from the informal interactions of maids on the job. Sundays was their common day of rest; since most in a particular city came from the same home area, casual associations grew up naturally among them, first for recreational purposes, but eventually to provide extralegal regulation of their trade. In a number of cities, *baomu* associations had taken shape by the early 1990s, organized as loose networks based on hometown origin. These groups tried to improve their members' living and working conditions, to raise their wages, and to guarantee their economic rights, and they spread information on wage levels and job opportunities. Employers who hired outside these networks sometimes found themselves thwarted or saddled with a thief.[213]

But those working outside the channels created by state organs fell subject to the self-exploitation that characterizes unregulated labor markets among other types of migrant labor. In Shanghai, Beijing, and Nanjing a system entitled *jishi* (time-rate) *baomu* prevailed: maids worked by the hour at a number of different places each day and rented their own housing separately. Such women could force themselves to work up to twelve hours a day under this system, not taking a day off.[214] In this second, informal channel, wages might be higher and norms of good treatment sometimes enforced; still, individual women were tempted to exploit themselves.

In Beijing by the mid-1990s the job of *baomu* had become more a part-time or transitional occupation than a full-time, more long-term one, to be filled only when one first arrived in town, when one was temporarily between jobs, or if one had the energy for a second job. After several

years, most maids in the capital had accumulated sufficient social resources and skills to move on to more lucrative positions, or to jobs
offering more autonomy, such as working for a private entrepreneur,
marketing, or serving in a restaurant.[215]

The third channel, structured around the spontaneous labor markets
that became common in Chinese cities in the reform period, was the
riskiest, the least likely to afford decent treatment, and yet the one where,
for some, earnings could potentially be the highest.[216] It was in these
markets that "illegal elements" might prey on untended women and rape,
rob, abduct, cheat, or, at a minimum, force them into unsavory employment.[217] For instance, women could be made to work long hours, sleep on
or under tables, and accept low wages. Some employers frankly solicited
the more inexperienced, first-time servants expressly because they were
more obedient and more inclined to take on heavier tasks at lower pay.[218]

Pay for the *baomu* varied by level of experience and city. In 1992, 60
to 70 yuan per month was the average in a number of major cities, with
Guangzhou exceptionally higher: there, a maid could earn from 60 to 150
yuan, depending upon her proficiency, again with amenities included. In
Tianjin, the wages initially were as low as 40 yuan, but had gone up to
60 to 100 yuan by 1992.[219] Thus, though maids were not, like factory
workers or diggers, directly employed by the state, the presence or absence of state agencies and state-supervised contracts nonetheless left its
mark on the maids' working lives.

The Entrepreneurial Sector

We turn next to the entrepreneurial sector, including marketing, crafts,
services, garment processing, and begging and scrap collecting. All private-sectoral entrepreneurs and employees shared some degree of distance
from the state. But specific features connected to the nature of their
activities differentiated them.

Jobs in the private sector varied along several dimensions, all of which
had implications for the amount of exploitation and security migrants
could expect. The first variable was the presence of extensive networks
within the trade—for supplies and sales, as well as for building bonds of
mutual assistance. Those in trades boasting such ties stood in a better
position to achieve business success and to live tolerably. Other important
factors were the degree of competitiveness (horizontal pressures among
firms) in the trade; the presence or absence of a strict structure of authority within it (degree of hierarchy versus autonomy or amount of vertical

pressure within the firm for individual practitioners, a function of their position in that hierarchy); and the level of prestige of the trade within a status hierarchy of trades.

At one extreme were workers whose native-place network resources sorted them into trades only loosely linked internally if at all, and into highly competitive lines of work, where hierarchy was steep and prestige low; they experienced the most instability of position and the greatest amount of exploitation. And those whose resources sorted them into less competitive and internally cooperative occupations, where autonomy was substantial or hierarchy largely absent (or where they stood at the top of it) and prestige high, were exploited much less, if at all, and experienced correspondingly greater job security. Many private-sector workers, like those in construction, faced stiff competition. Where this was an issue, as for carpenters or butchers, their lifestyles depended a great deal upon whether they were part of a cooperative network that could bolster their position. For workers in private firms, their place in the firm's hierarchy also mattered.

Crafts and Other Services   A sizable portion of the floating population in the cities worked in crafts and performed services, whether buying and selling, fashioning and repairing objects of daily use, or provisioning the population. These were the proprietors and the rank and file of China's private sector, many of them peasants; disparate in skills and lifestyles, they generally worked without direct links to the state.

Only a tiny and terribly prosperous few of them had managed by the mid-1990s to gain acceptance into state-organized business associations devised for the urban private sector—the industrial and commercial federations (generally at the district level)—and could then go on to establish personal ties with district-level officials in the offices of tax, industrial and commercial administration, and public security; a minority of others obtained a modicum of city connections through such arrangements as offering to work for urban neighborhood committees, those official bodies responsible for regular citizens' welfare and security needs at the most local level.[220] But even these people required critical support from their home governments for leverage with local officials, which often did not come.[221] So ordinary private-sectoral sojourners' best strategy was to turn for protection to networks of mutual support from their native-place fellows. Though they were not even second-class citizens in the state, they were setting up alternative communities of their own, as we will see in chapter 7.

The numbers of private entrepreneurs grew rapidly when the central government allowed peasants to enter the towns. For instance, by early 1993, an official source reported that of all the workers at the stalls and booths operated by Beijing's more than a hundred thousand self-employed individuals (a figure that rose by 40 percent within two years, according to official sources), more than 70 percent were nonlocals.[222] Over the years, the wealth of a minority of individual merchants expanded exponentially, with especially talented individual businesspeople sometimes climbing from peddler to entrepreneur-owner of several sizable firms within just a decade.[223]

But the possibility for the great majority of these migrants to establish working relationships with the state or its officials was exceedingly slim. Comparison with native urban private entrepreneurs highlights the problems migrants faced. To begin with, a substantial portion of the transients perforce operated illegally because the process of getting business licenses of their own through official channels was prohibitively cumbersome, expensive or even impossible, especially when favoritism, nepotism, and corruption flourished in their issuance, and when the process required connections with local bureaucrats.[224]

Also, access to the highest levels of urban officialdom (including state factory and wholesale depot managers, as well as tax, industrial and commercial administration, and public security personnel at the municipal level)—and thus the chances for one's business success in the city—was difficult even for local businesspeople, unless they had something substantial to offer to government agents.[225] As Chinese researchers explain the situation, "Some people have a lot of capital but suffer from no 'go-betweens,' so capital in their pockets doesn't get any effective use"; also, they posit, "among merchants, pure commercial help is limited; only through relations with officials can one get things solved . . . and some resources can't be obtained without official approval."[226]

Besides these obstacles, even the native urbanites, if occupied in crafts or repair work, were stuck at the very lowest rung in the social prestige hierarchy;[227] how much lowlier still must have been the status of the outsider plying these artisanal trades.[228] Moreover, in produce sales, licensed urbanites had the advantage, since city district governments controlled stall space and as a rule would rent the best plots on open city streets only to their own citizens.[229]

A way around this problem of access to officialdom was through the mediation of native citizens: outsiders with some acquaintanceship with ordinary locals could rent the business licenses the latter had procured, in order to set up their own repair stands, book or cigarette booths, or, indeed, to start up any sort of small business.[230] When necessary, the natives would deal with the administrative authorities in the industrial and commercial management bureau on the outsiders' behalf. Though the basic-level authorities were aware of the deception, they agreed to keep silent—perhaps for a mutually beneficial price.[231] But the need to go through a middle-person in such arrangements, though it afforded a way to do business, also meant an additional layer of take and lacked the much more reliable provision for official protection that a citizen would have had. At any rate, only a small proportion of outsiders had established such ties by the mid-1990s.

Proprietors adapted to competitive pressures in part, as construction contractors also did, by paying low wages to their subordinates. For example, in a study of nearly 300 migrants in Beijing in late 1991 to early 1992, the investigator found that only 1.3 percent of employees received over 400 yuan per month (though 43 percent of the entrepreneurs themselves earned that much); moreover, 46 percent of those employed netted less than 150 yuan per month.[232] Another way of competing was by employing staff for appallingly long work hours. A late 1995 study in Shanghai found that the mean hours the respondents worked per week was 55.5, while as much as 25 percent worked 70 hours, and 7 percent even more than that.[233] Most employers in the private sector also offered no health insurance. This statement makes the point:

> Some employers say: "There's no one to take care even of our own health expenses, so how could we take care of theirs [the employees']?" When one worker got seriously sick after laboring for sixteen hours a day, the boss feared that taking care of her would waste money, and also feared that he would have to take responsibility if "something unexpected" happened, so he just fired her. So workers keep working if a little sick. This kind of thing is not infrequently seen among hired labor.[234]

In the case of the self-employed, competition—especially when the worker was not part of a network—could be countered only with merciless "self-exploitation," though at least the salaries of those working on their own might be comparatively stable. For example, the wages of handicraft workers, at about 300 yuan per month in Guangzhou in the mid-1990s, could be compared with those of casual labor in the employ of others, which fluctuated in the range of 120 to 300 yuan.[235]

Marketing   Commercial sojourners plied their trade in several different forms. Most of them operated autonomously, which exempted them from exploitation by others, though they increasingly had to contend with competition. One of the earliest styles, once peasants were free to travel, was to peddle home-grown products in major thoroughfares. Tianjin was one such node, for from there it was easy to transfer goods further north; Wuhan, favorably situated in the heart of central China, was another.[236] Often those who set up their own small retail businesses were connected by home-place networks with channels of supplies.

Another style characterized millions of periurban farmers who simply carted their produce short distances several times a week to a large city nearby.[237] Others, such as vendors dealing in rare specialties or nonperishables, journeyed long distances, even across several provinces, where they ensconced themselves for relatively lengthy periods, renting peasants' homes, living in cheap hostels, or sometimes even holing up under plastic sheeting behind their own market stalls.[238] Some began with simple two-way trading, which eventually graduated into wholesale businesses.[239]

Marketers had two chief modes of interacting with the state. The first of these was that some wholesale markets were still state owned in the early 1990s, so a minority of retailers worked out arrangements to acquire licenses from locals in order to obtain their stocks.[240] A different and more frequent kind of contact with the state for these small salespeople occurred when officials harassed them—charging excessive fees, appropriating tools of the trade, and helping themselves to produce, for instance—as they have been wont to do whenever marketing was sanctioned in the people's republic.[241]

Eschewing the state, others adopted a much more common and comfortable form of accessing supplies. They turned to fellow townspeople, as in the case of Henan "villagers" in Beijing, who shipped low-priced fresh vegetables wholesale from their rural homes to peasants waiting in the city; or traders from Yiwu county, Zhejiang, who controlled wholesaling in the small commodities manufactured back in their villages and then dominated the market in these goods in the Xicheng district of Beijing.[242] Merchants trading in produce who were a part of native-place cooperative networks eventually coordinated themselves to collaborate on prices and shared market information.[243]

A minority of outside merchants in big cities had become well enough endowed—and, consequently, well connected—by the 1990s to erect buildings and open large-scale stores, in which they even rented counters to local merchants and to more petty capitalists from other locations. Also, about one-third of the wholesalers and shippers in industrial products resident in Tianjin in the early 1990s were wealthy dealers hailing from Jiangsu, Fujian, and Zhejiang.[244] Thus, marketing was a trade buttressed by extensive internal, outside-the-state networks, whose prestige some years into the reform era had become sufficient to give its most successful members (those at the top of the hierarchy and who had won out in competition and achieved the wealth to employ others) the potential for stable and nonexploitative employment, at least for themselves.

Handicrafts and Other Service-Sector Activities   Unlike the produce traders, of whom most—more like commuters than migrants—stayed close to home, persons of skill were much more prone to range. In a typical pattern, they traveled first to regions where crafts and services were scarce and either set up their booths or stalls, soliciting jobs as they strolled through the streets, or appeared at "spontaneous" labor markets, offering their artifacts or their knack at repair. Since crafts are a tradition in the areas south of the Yangtze but not in the north, their practitioners were at first compared to migratory birds, moving to the north for the moderate season and then scattering back to the south for the winter. Some, however, with time settled down in strange locations, where they organized themselves into native-place clusters.[245]

Cobblers, for instance, mostly came north from Zhejiang and congregated together. In Tianjin, a large number (*yiwan*, or ten thousand, according to an interviewee) of them were making their homes in rented rooms around the north train station in the early 1990s.[246] In the most coherent form, they were linked by bosses who guarded the turf of the group and initiated or negotiated brawls over its invasion.[247] If the group was small and its hierarchy accordingly negligible, a handful of workers agreed among themselves on prices, and one of them acted as the leader. But in large groups, several heads, or "snakes," would take advantage of their power to control the turf and extort fees and gifts for the right to use a spot.[248] Since cobblers, like other artisans, were often organized into trades by place of origin, they were rarely subject to much competition. But only those who did not labor under the whims of a forceful superior could be assured of working stably and free of exploitation.

Moreover, though city folk marveled at the earnings of these cobblers, their prestige was only middling;[249] and their lot could be precarious because of the predations of officials, as noted in chapter 3.

Another kind of example is provided by the trade of carpentry, which thrived in the mid-1980s. By the end of the decade, however, competition and costs began to play havoc with the livelihood of these craftspeople. Incessant streams of tradespeople moving into the cities meant that the supply of workers began outpacing demand, while increases in the state-set prices of their raw materials drove some out of the market.[250] Many people from Zhejiang who had earlier landed in Lanzhou, for instance, found that they couldn't go on there and departed for Ningxia and Inner Mongolia.[251]

Besides the influence from official prices, there was another way in which these people operated at the mercy of the state. Carpenters carving on foreign turf sometimes fell victim to officials' highhandedness and cheating. In one story, reported by two Chinese journalists, a sofa-maker told of his co-villager, who

> made a set of furniture for a cadre from Lanzhou's industrial and commercial management bureau, but the official delayed paying. So the artisan brought his cousins to call at the cadre's house to demand the payment of the debt. But the cadre called out ten "brothers," who, grasping weapons, were laying in wait. When the carpenter's relatives saw this, they rushed away in fright. So it was as if they had worked twenty days in vain.[252]

Some small minority of craftspeople might have been fortunate enough to have a positive state connection, through bosses who were linked to city officials. But for the bulk of these proprietors and those in their employ, their best hope for support came just from informal native-place associations. As in the traditional *tongxianghui* (native-place associations),[253] they were joined by trade and by place of origin, sometimes simply in a comradely fashion deriving from the bonds established through chain migration,[254] sometimes in order to pass market information, engage in mutual assistance, or carry out joint business activities.[255] Failing this, though their earnings might have been satisfactory enough, in their work and in their lives they floated in limbo, vulnerable and on their own.

Garment Processing

A different life- and workstyle belonged to the sweatshop stitchers from the south, sojourning away from home. By about 1990, large concentrations populated Beijing and Tianjin, where they lived and worked in "Zhejiang tailor villages." These settlements began to take form by 1983. Then, as people from Wenzhou's Leqing and, later, Yongjia counties, which specialize in this line of trade, discovered the wide open market for their products, more and more of them began to pour in.[256] By 1987, over 33 percent of the legally licensed proprietors in the Beijing garment industry were ruralites, mainly from Jiangsu and Zhejiang, while as many as 90 percent of the employees were peasants from these areas.[257] Already by the late 1980s these outsider tailors had begun to take over the trade.[258] Observers' figures vary widely, but by the early 1990s Jiangnan peasants sewing in the Beijing and Tianjin outskirts numbered in the tens of thousands, if not a hundred thousand.[259] Over this time, individuals who had begun work as helpers in their families or for a fellow villager opened their own businesses; others graduated from small to larger stalls.[260]

In their urban "villages" (as in Beijing's Fengtai district's Dahongmen township), a coordinated division of labor prevailed, which had become perfected by the late 1980s.[261] This was a process of mass production complete with Wenzhou natives obtaining cloth from their Zhejiang villages, and then producing garments, which they then wholesaled, retailed, and transported exclusively through networks of fellow townspeople.[262] "They hire only their own," complained an excluded Anhui youth at a Beijing labor market in 1994.[263]

Eventually a huge wholesale market that Zhejiang people set up in the early 1990s became the main supplier for all clothing retail outlets in the city, while its sales network connected the migrant tailors to every part of the country.[264] This highly cooperative operation was essential to their success. For, as Hill Gates details, getting supplies, means of production, and transport vehicles through official channels and at state factories required a careful and quite cumbersome cultivation of state employees through the 1980s. The mastery of this process, difficult enough for local, urban petty capitalists, would have been next to impossible for outsiders.[265]

Following hometown customs, each household either acted as a workshop, turning out a particular kind of product, or else concentrated on marketing them (figure 5).[266] Where several households cooperated, they had come to town together, organized by the co-villager among them with the most capital or business acumen. Simple partnerships culminating into larger, mutually interdependent ventures undergirded the businesses,[267] with credit relationships sometimes reliant upon blood and geographical ties rather than interest payments and legal documentation.[268]

By 1994, a foreign journalist estimates, people from Zhejiang might have cornered up to 80 percent of the Beijing wholesale market in

Figure 5. Young tailors at their machines in the Zhejiang Village, Beijing.

medium- and low-quality garments.[269] This near monopoly meant that the poor treatment from which many of these firms' workers suffered was, like that endured by many private-sectoral peddlers, artisans, and merchants, not so much an outcome of the bosses' trying to undercut competition—for there was nearly none of that—as of a given tailor's placement at the bottom of a hierarchy of authority.

This poor treatment of the laborers manifested itself mainly in their living and working conditions. Within a number of similar areas in the Beijing suburbs, these erstwhile peasants undertook long-term rentals, mostly in sections of the homes of local farmers.[270] There anywhere from four to seven individuals crammed in, both sexes together working and sleeping. It was common to find four or five sewing machines, four or five adults, at least one infant, and only two or three beds within one ten-square-meter room. A foreign journalist interviewed a seventeen-year-old in such a clothing sweatshop in Beijing in late 1992, who told him,

> We simply work and sleep. I've never seen the Forbidden City or the Summer Palace and probably never will. I'm here to earn money and after I do I'll go back.[271]

One researcher finds proprietors employing five to ten workers, who worked into the night at low and unpredictable wages while their bosses might pocket from 200,000 to 300,000 yuan a year.[272] A more advanced form of exploitation involved layers of subordinates. What began as congeries of fellow townspeople, or at least fellow provincials, developed with time into mixed communities, or as one journalist characterizes the situation, the formation of "sub-ghettoes." In this case, teams of young women from Sichuan labored long hours at low wages for their Zhejiang bosses, stopping only to fall asleep on the floor beneath their sewing machines.[273] Given the shoddy, cramped, and ill-lit work sites, it is obvious that safety standards were regularly ignored.[274] This recruitment of non-Zhejiang people, and the particularly unsavory conditions of their employment, suggests that the benefits of being part of the in-group obtained not just for urbanites but within migrant communities too.

As for their relations with the state, in the beginning the first tailors to arrive were studiously compliant.[275] To be legal, these workers were first to obtain a business license at home and then to get it approved by the industrial and commercial administrative office in the city, regulations which they tended to follow. Increasingly over time, however, more and more of the newcomers felt free not to pursue this route, instead operating without a license. Thus they escaped the tax collectors, who progressively lacked the personnel and energy to track them down.[276]

In addition, an early effort by the Fengtai district party committee to mobilize some two thousand cadres from a range of bureaus to register the population there was repulsed. At one point in the early 1990s an official attempt to shepherd the outsiders into a district-managed market, the better to control them, was countered by the Zhejiang people's construction of a bazaar of their own, in response.[277] In the case of this trade, extensive networks, virtual monopoly, and growing status enabled its practitioners to confound, though by no means to best, the state by setting up an alternate community centered on a joint occupation.

Begging and Scrap Collecting

Not all beggars collected scraps; nor did all who collected waste materials also beg (figure 6).But the reportage on these two types of floaters often lumps them together, in limning their lifestyle, in delineating their internal organizations and their external relationships, and in excoriating their modes of amassing income. Here is a typical example:

> Some without real ability and learning can enter Shanghai to seek an income. Those beggars, scrap gleaners and collectors, waifs, mentally ill, and those disguised as street performers can all get a foothold in Shanghai by begging.[278]

Figure 6. Scrap collector, Guangzhou.

These people belonged to the portion of the floating population popularly labeled the *mangliu*, those who blindly wander about (sometimes also known as the "three withouts"), as noted in chapter 4. Despite the frequent use of this term to refer to the floating population as a whole, an official source claims that in the late 1980s they constituted only a tiny fraction of the total mobile peasantry.[279] Survey research from the mid-1990s yields percentages from under 1 percent up to 15 percent.[280]

Since vagabonds were on the move and often more stealthy than the average itinerant, their actual numbers must have been slippery. Still, official and scholarly China attempts to count them.[281] As an illustration of the difficulty of doing so, in Guangzhou, a "garbage kingdom" of five thousand was reportedly living along the edge of the river in the late 1980s. But another writer claims the number of beggars had already reached over twelve thousand in that city as early as 1985, while others count up to thirty to forty thousand vagrants of various sorts there by 1986.[282] Cheng Li reports that of the two to three thousand children apprehended in Shanghai annually in the first half of the 1990s, nearly 60 percent were surviving by begging, another 12 percent by collecting garbage.[283]

Just as their numbers are hard to calculate, their earnings are also the subject of inconsistent speculations. Some allege a Shanghai beggar could accumulate as much as 50 yuan by day and 100 by night in the late 1980s, but others report more like one-tenth of that, only 4 to 5 yuan a day, was the norm.[284] Though researchers may come up with different sums of daily takings, a common opinion is that such people got wealthy almost overnight, as their scrap gathering shaded into theft of such valuables as enterprise raw materials or electrical cables for resale at high profit. Others supposedly struck it rich just by panhandling, as they successfully preyed on the sympathies of passersby or the guilt of touring Overseas Chinese, sometimes by intentionally making themselves appear disgustingly pitiful.[285] All of these views indicate the very low esteem in which the members of these two trades were popularly held.[286]

And surely, many scrap collectors plainly subsisted in abject poverty. In a section of Beijing in the mid-1990s, a small group of Henanese picking through dirt for tidbits of paper, glass, and metal got by on just one meal a day and, selling recyclable waste materials, never took in more than 6 yuan daily. Living amid the flies, mosquitoes, and rats attracted by the heap of refuse they discarded after scavenging for scraps, with both stench and hepatitis running amok, they were soon to be pushed out by city officials.[287]

Migrants from Henan were especially numerous among urban trash-pickers (indeed, this particular group in Beijing had abandoned Henan's capital city, Zhengzhou, expressly because of the excessive numbers of scavengers there), but they did not monopolize the trade.[288] Rather theirs was a highly competitive occupation, and becoming increasingly more so by the mid-1990s.[289] The chief rivals of the Henanese trash-pickers were those from Anhui.

Moreover, for those in gangs it was also a steeply hierarchical occupation. Descriptions of the organizations that encased many vagrants hark back to historical prototypes. From the Qing dynasty, Republican-era Shanghai, and also from the Taipei of the 1970s we have accounts of beggar bands, based on regional origin, and headed by autocratic bosses, who themselves abandoned begging to rule over finely ranked subordinates arranged into specialized divisions of labor. These underlings daily brought back spoils to be shared, with the chief skimming off a major portion. In the Qing these chiefs cooperated with local officials in the maintenance of order; in the Republican period their ties with persons of clout entailed paying protection money to the Green Gang.[290]

Portrayals of the migrant beggar bands and "garbage kingdoms" of the late twentieth century follow this pattern very closely. They are

complete with references to turf, gang warfare among competing regionally based bands (and between local and outsider beggars), and chieftains
who lived in glory. Thus, we have competitiveness, autocratic hierarchies,
and low prestige, all bearing down on the beggars at the bottom of the
heap. Their bosses lorded it over frequently shifting and rank-ordered
underlings, who were compelled to placate them with booty, and over
scavengers from outside the band, who had to present them with gifts.[291]
An independent pollster in Beijing, working with Horizon Market Research, who surveyed the city's beggars in 1994, reports that nearly one-
third of them were members of such tightly organized cartels.[292]

In the 1980s and 1990s, the analogue to the 1930s Frenchtown police
of Shanghai (who were in league with the Green Gang) was the public
security. Its members, in one account, accepted bribes as a kind of tribute
and left the gangs to their own devices, provided they cooperated, both in
ensuring no troubling incidents occurred at New Year's time, and in
helping solve big cases so the police could "gain merit."[293] These deals
were the best tie to the state such underclass people could hope to arrange.

But not all the beggars and trash collectors were cozily knitted into
cliques or mutually protected by the police.[294] Stray individuals, operating
on their own, lacked the shield of a chief, as well as the seamy pacts
between gangs and state security officials.[295] In Nanjing, I encountered
one such pair of paper scrap collectors, an Anhuinese father and his
twenty-eight-year-old son from Hefei's rural suburbs, already in the city
for two and one-half years. The son, a primary school graduate, was
married with two children at home in Anhui and was saving money to
become a carpenter. But at that time, he had no money; his life, he
lamented, was "very bitter." Their joint monthly net was a paltry 150
yuan, or 1,800 a year, and they were dwelling in a rented room, for 30
yuan a month. Though there were many people in Nanjing from Anhui,
they had no contact with them, knew of them only to compete with
them.

They had not registered for temporary residence (at 107 yuan per
month) or for business (40 yuan per month), because the police, who told
them to go back home to tend the fields, refused to sell the licenses to
them. But without the certificates, they were highly vulnerable: their cart
had been confiscated by the police. To save expenses, they ate no lunch,
and yet they were toiling 10 hours a day, gathering bits of scrap. In this
way they managed to spend only 50 yuan per month on their own
livelihood and could remit the other 100 home.

"Why not join a construction team?" I asked?

"One needs *guanxi* for that, but I don't know anyone," was the sorry rejoinder.[296]

This account, along with the foregoing material, illustrates that trash collectors had one of two general modes of existence, paired with two different types of encounters with the state: ensconced in a gang, they relied on their bosses, who were sometimes well enough placed to be able to make peace with officials on their behalf. Or isolated and anomic, they passed their days uncertainly, at the constant mercy of marauding functionaries.

. . .

Six major occupations employed migrant peasant Chinese labor in the cities at the end of the century: construction; manufacturing; nursemaiding; marketing, crafts, and services; garment processing; and begging or scrap collecting. Those in each of these lines of work operated in separate and multistranded labor markets. Within each trade there might have been either two or three distinct types of labor markets, in each of which the norms and rules of business varied in accord with the connections possessed by those occupying it; and with the degree to which characteristic features of the macro-level transition to markets that China was undergoing—competition, arbitrary lawlessness, and corruption—governed its workings. As the *hukou* retained a lingering power to divide up the populace, the state still shaped a given sojourner's fate. In addition, sectors and subsectors with some connection with the state had very different experiences from those that operated wholly in the private sector.

At the macro level, the decline of socialist institutions and practices that accompanied the unlocking of market forces replaced state control over labor allocation and management norms with free-wheeling competition, a lack of regulatory oversight, and pervasive lawlessness. And yet inchoate capitalism operated in alliance (or concurrence) with remnant but still weighty features of statism that continued to govern some of these trades (or their sub-segments) well into the 1990s. And into the mid-1990s at the micro level, ties to the state could sometimes still mitigate the force of oppressive and unpleasant proto-capitalistic features.

The chief factor that accounted for the more benign regimen in the subsectors of certain trades—construction, manufacturing, and housekeeping—was the presence in them of contractual bonds with state firms or, in the case of nursemaids, contracts arranged by state agencies. But each of these trades also contained segments where the state was altogether absent; there, life was correspondingly unregulated and unpredictable.

In the other, more wholly entrepreneurially managed, trades—crafts, services, and marketing, garment processing, and begging and scrap collecting—we found the reign of the unencumbered private sector. Within that sector the cast of peasant sojourners' working life was determined by specific features of the trade itself—competition, authority structures, and level of prestige—as well as whether workers were part of a network or not. True, state connections in that sector—chiefly in the form of commercial ties or shared corruption, only rarely of protection[297]—for a minority of the newcomers (particularly the proprietors) surely eased the way in their pursuit of a profit. But even in such rare cases, the internal operations of their firms were free of any state oversight or benevolence.

For the private entrepreneurs with no links to officialdom at all—or, even worse, with no positive ties to any group whatsoever—though they may have become wealthy, they constantly lived on the edge of banishment and confiscation.[298] Overall, the coming of peasant sojourners to the cities helped pull askew the once very simple, single-track labor market; their arrival also worked to introduce a certain complexity into what constituted urban citizenship.

This chapter's material yields two large conclusions. First, with the winding down of its former systems, the socialism of the Chinese state, whether manifested in the clout of its cadres or in the paternalism of its enterprises, by no means immediately disappeared entirely; moreover, its force was still keenly felt at both macro and micro levels in the lives of peasants migrating to work in the cities nearly two decades after reforms began to chip away at its edifice. That is, the state's presence remained as a divider, separating into multitudinous channels—through its linkages and its regulations—that segment of the labor market that in other contexts is just the "secondary sector." For individual workers, the nature of the networks into which they were woven—whether with the state, with fellow townspeople, or with no one at all—made a profound difference, both for their treatment on the job and in the style of their lives.

And second, a subtheme buried in the data here carries forward the story of this book. The implications for officially sanctioned, proper urban citizenship were, paradoxically, better for some of the unskilled, less educated, poorer peasants from the inland (at least up through the early 1990s) than for those seemingly superior migrants from the eastern, coastal provinces, who came out with capital and competencies. For in the transition period, the former were most likely to be captured by state recruiters on the prowl for the cheap, surplus labor of the poverty regions, and unskilled workers were then able to sign employment contracts with state-owned firms. And too the administrators in the more penurious, interior rural places were anxious to arrange to ship out their excess country workers through deals with official urban agents. So we could say that some inland migrants ended up with a cheap and lowly version of urban citizenhood.

Eastern migrants, by contrast, formed their own, quite separate colonies once in town, enclaves wholly untouched by the regimens or values of the once-provisioning and paternalistic socialist state. Thus the ordinary transients may have stood a better chance at obtaining at least second-class citizenship (including some material welfare and some inclusion in state-sponsored systems and communities) if they were inducted into the labor reserve army of the simple ruralites than if they hailed from the talent-producing east. In the next chapter we track some of the implications of this second finding for different groups of migrants' daily lives.

7 The Urban Rationing Regime II

Coping Outside It and
Alternate Citizenship

Not only in their working lives but also in their daily lives—their housing, medical care, education, and welfare services—many rural migrants in the cities through the mid-1990s had to make do without the trappings of formal, state-bestowed citizenship. For they had to live outside the third institutional wall the socialist state erected against them, the urban rationing regime. Thus, except for laborers contracted to state-owned organs who, as we have seen, did attain a modest second-tier citizenhood, the official system refused to grant most outsiders membership in the legitimized urban community by barring sojourners from access to the city services remaining within its grasp.

Indeed, through the mid-1990s it was official policy that "citizens" not in possession of a local *hukou* were to be prevented from receiving education and health care treatment and were ineligible for state-allocated housing and grain allocation.[1] So, despite the imaginings and agitation of urbanites (which we reviewed in chapter 4), in fact most migrants subsisted in a style that did much less to challenge city people's privileges than the official municipal residents supposed.

Transients found their own mode of urban life, one that often clashed with or diminished regular urban services very little. One after another, markets for all the requisites of daily subsistence came into being, and many peasants in the cities found their own solutions to the problems of meeting their daily needs; in their market activities they also discovered the means for generating new, unofficial intermediary groups outside the state. As they did, and as, accordingly, the meaning of life without formal citizenship in the city was transformed, the exclusivity of urban citizenship was altered as well.

A common conception is that the rural newcomers to Chinese cities existed in an administrative vacuum, scavenging, hanging on without the urban citizens' rights to housing, education, and health care, and without any management responsible for their concerns.[2] And yet many of these people managed to stay on, some even to thrive. So the effect of their coming was a permanent collective urban presence (one, albeit, whose members were constantly shifting) of unlicensed sojourners not ratified by the regime. Over time, their joint success at survival without state endorsement posed a frontal challenge to the authority of the government and to its capacity to encompass and enclose the economic activities of entire municipal populations.[3]

But we cannot generalize their solution: as we have seen, transients included a set of laborers employed by the state, a hierarchy of native-place-based communities, and finally a range of stragglers—the state-protected; the community-connected;[4] and the anomic isolates. Where individual newcomers fell within this range was a function of the nature of their bonds. This chapter looks primarily at the community-connected and the isolates, referring only occasionally to the state-protected laborers as a point of reference. It asks how the two groups fared without any access to state-conferred services.

Those at the top of the hierarchy of noncitizens benefited from having cash[5] or other capital, a well-endowed community, and, most of all, informal connections with state cadres;[6] those progressively lower down the social pyramid lacked some or all of these sources of strength. Despite the continuing power of ties with officialdom, the novelty of market society recast the urban milieu, such that outsiders were not newcomers gradually assimilating into an established framework. Instead, they formed a patchwork of people in "parallel communities," plus some stragglers, all of them eking out existences for the most part outside the state.[7]

Thus, a layering of "citizenship" emerged among those not considered proper citizens. Some, mainly coming from the inland, found a second-class citizenship through official contracts; others, chiefly from the talent-generating east, carved out a separate belongingness as they accumulated resources and benefits of their own through what one scholar terms their "auto-integration";[8] and it was only a motley residual, totally marginal-ized mass that stagnated, abandoned and bereft.

This picture complicates standard (and, at a more macro level, entirely correct) formulations, according to which Chinese society of the late twentieth century was one with a "dual nature," whereby "urban and rural sectors operat[ed] under different economic systems and enjoy[ed]

different social and economic benefits . . . living in two different worlds";
or where "socioeconomic dualism" (urbanites and ruralites living by
different rules) characterized the city itself.[9] Once peasants entered the
city and interacted with state institutions and with the markets there, the
metropolis had no longer just one, but rather manifold modes of "living
on the edge," all "completely separate from local society."[10]

This chapter describes the solutions different groups among this population found to the everyday problems of housing, education, food, and
health care. It also explores the nature of organizational life among them.
It concludes by reexamining the situation of citizenship for the urban
transients. But first we ask about the gender ratio among these people,
their marital status, their success in landing jobs, and the level of satisfaction they experienced.

THE TRANSIENT COMMUNITY:
GENDER, MARITAL STATUS, JOB, SATISFACTION

Gender and Marital Status

Historically, Chinese migration has been predominantly male,[11] as is the
case throughout Asia and Africa, though not in Latin America.[12] This
pattern continued to hold in the reform-era migration. One tally, conducted in 1988, concluded that the percentage of men in various large
cities ranged from Wuhan's 60.8 percent to 87.5 percent in Beijing, with
Shanghai's at 70.8 percent.[13] A researcher in Guangzhou claims that as
much as 76 percent of his 1991–92 sample was male.[14]

But later data suggest a change in these proportions over time. A mid-
1990s study reports that only 63.5 percent of the capital's outsiders were
male,[15] and an October 1995 study in Shanghai concludes that by then
just 60 percent of the floaters there were men.[16] In support of such
findings, a study done under the auspices of the Ministry of Agriculture
in 1995 notes an increase in the percentage of women nationwide, from
30 percent in 1987 up to 40 percent just eight years later. Du Ying, vice
chairman of the ministry's Agriculture Research Center, attributed this
outcome to the increase in jobs in the tertiary sector, which tended to
employ female labor.[17] Moreover, in the foreign-firm-infested Pearl River
Delta, female labor accounted for half the work force in 1996.[18]

As noted in chapter 6, the occupations that engaged transient labor
were heavily gender-selective. In Beijing in the late 1980s over 91 percent
of the construction workers were men, while 95 percent of domestic
workers were women.[19] Women also predominated in the commercial,

catering, and service trades;[20] they often worked as factory hands—in textile firms in the state sector, and in manufacturing of toys, shoes, and electronic equipment for foreign enterprises.[21] One informant claimed that in the factories of Guangzhou in the early 1990s, 80 percent of the peasants employed were women.[22] There was also a preference for female hired labor among the private entrepreneurs.[23]

In addition, rural women accounted for a substantial proportion of the prostitutes in large cities: in one southwestern city around 1990, absolutely all of them were outsiders; in another southern locale, 70 percent of those located were transients.[24] And women on their own in search of work made easy prey for those who traded in human beings. Especially in the labor markets of the interior, women were kidnaped, then sold for sex, procreation, and cheap labor.[25] This abduction of women along the road who were initially intending to join the urban labor force may be another factor working, even if in a small way, to diminish the proportion of females among the transients who ended up in the cities.

The sex ratio shifted among those members of the floating population who remained longer in the cities;[26] as one 1992 study of 195 migrants in Guangzhou, Beijing, Fuzhou, and Xiamen found, males were significantly more inclined to return home to the countryside after earning money than were females.[27] Moreover, women may have had a greater propensity to stay on in the city because they found it easier to acclimate than did men. For the nature of their work—acting as nursemaids, serving food, and selling produce in the markets—involved contact with the resident population, unlike that of men, who were mostly eking out an isolated existence on building sites.[28]

Among the transients, not only did men dominate, but unattached persons constituted the great majority. In a random sample of nearly 300 persons conducted in Guangdong province in 1992, 40 percent were married, but 43 percent left a spouse behind at home, and a mere 16 percent came as couples.[29] One researcher in Guangzhou in 1992 notes that 66 percent of his male interviewees were unmarried.[30]

On the other hand, more female than male migrants were single in 1993 Shanghai, a reflection of their younger ages.[31] Among all the transients there only one-third had never married, but just one-fifth of the others had brought their partners with them to the city.[32] And in yet another study, married men—but not married women—coming to Beijing alone was common.[33] For most male ruralites became physical laborers in the city, whose skimpy wages could not sustain the livelihood of a whole household.[34]

Moreover, both the housing patterns (single-sex dorms or building sheds) and the regulations in many types of work demanded that the work force be composed of single people: this was true of construction work, the textile trade, and housekeeping. Thus, on the whole this was a largely male population, one for the most part living singly, probably more so than in societies where there was no legal blockage against peasants' becoming urban citizens and obtaining the schooling, health care, and city services that would enable supporting a family.[35]

Job Search

Though the transients were often unattached, a number of studies concur that, far from being at loose ends, they quickly got work. Five different research projects conducted in the mid-1990s all arrive at similar conclusions: several of them report that a mere 10 percent or less was not able to find a job within a very short span of time.[36]

Outsiders hanging around a large and typical migrant labor market in the center of Beijing in summer 1994 lent credence to this finding: most had short-term, odd jobs (*dagong*), if not a definite position (*gongzuo*), and had come to the exchange only to look for more work. Others were there because a work contract had just expired; while yet others wanted higher wages or more satisfying occupations. Those looking for any sort of labor planned to search for just a month, after which, if they did not succeed, they expected to return home to their villages.[37]

But the jobs ruralites landed in the city were always temporary ones. Thus, studies as of the mid-1990s indicate that migrants generally stayed in one city for no more than two or three years before moving on, though some might be away from home most of the year over a time span of anywhere from three to more than ten years.[38] Over half stayed away from home less than two years, and two-thirds had worked in more than two units.[39]

Various sources indicate, respectively, that somewhere between 20 and 40 percent of the peasants in cities were working just as seasonal labor in the early 1990s.[40] One survey in Shanghai in the mid-1990s finds that different kinds of jobs kept mobile workers away from home continuously for various stretches of time, but the average was well under a year: housekeepers stayed for 307 days; construction workers for 297 days; small business people and street peddlers for 225 days; and repair people for 207.[41]

Although mid-1994 research in eleven provinces concluded that the period of staying out was lengthening,[42] the summary figures from the mid-1980s had not changed much nearly a decade later: two investigators agree that only a little over half the outsiders in Beijing were remaining there more than six months at both times.[43] And just under a quarter had been residing in both Beijing and Shanghai for longer than a year, as of mid-1994.[44]

So while getting work rapidly was not difficult for the vast majority of migrant workers in large Chinese cities, the duration of the typical engagement was brief, marking the lives of many floaters in the city with disruption. Indeed, instability abounded, as their living site underwent frequent changes with shifts in job; their communities were subjected to continual alterations of inhabitants; and their numbers fluctuated, in accord with the season, the agricultural calendar, and traditional custom.[45] How did they themselves view this existence?

Satisfaction

Elsewhere in the world, rural migrants generally report a high level of satisfaction in their urban destination. For one thing, if they are members of squatter settlements as is frequently the case, they take comfort in their membership in a collectivity.[46] For another, those who have migrated into a society where the opportunity structure is relatively open tend to be contented in the present and optimistic about the future, not just for their children, but even for themselves.[47]

Additional variables are the point of reference of the migrants—whether they compare their situations with those they left behind, or with those of permanent urbanites they encounter in the new place; the length of time already spent in the city and where they came from; and their cultural level, income, and employment status.

Most migrants in other places reportedly believe their situation is positive;[48] it is better than what they left behind. But as they stay longer in town, those with greater skills and higher educational attainment become prone to dissatisfaction and cynicism,[49] perhaps an outcome of the disappointment of initially higher aspirations and a keener awareness of the discrimination they face and, consequently, their clearer sense of the low probability of their goals being met.[50]

Research among Chinese floaters concurs with some of these generalizations. For example, one scholar, conducting research among 195 floaters in Beijing, Guangzhou, Xiamen, and Fuzhou in 1992, finds that, within his sample, except for illiterates, as migrants' cultural level rose, their belief that they had a future in the city dropped.[51] Another, working from a sample of 300 migrants in Beijing in the same year, notes that those who felt satisfied did so only when their point of reference was people like themselves, which must have kept their expectations reasonably low.[52]

An indication of the congruence of Chinese transients' satisfaction level with general patterns of migrant adaptation elsewhere was that the inhabitants of Zhejiang Village (those more skilled transients from the southeast) grew increasingly frustrated with time: they might physically attack those who insulted them by the mid-1990s, something they would not have dared to do in 1986 or 1987.[53]

Other circumstances set rural Chinese apart from sojourners in other parts of the world. In Mexico City in 1970, by way of contrast, Wayne Cornelius writes that more than 97 percent were satisfied with having come, and 80 percent told him they never considered returning to their place of origin.[54] Similar conclusions apply to migrants in cities of Indonesia and the Philippines, where 78 to 96 percent of those queried did not expect to leave.[55] But a researcher in four Chinese cities reports a satisfaction level of just 64 percent in 1992 and notes that as many as 43.6 percent of his informants wanted to return to their homes in the rural areas, while only 14.9 percent were determined to stay in the city at all costs.[56]

Unlike the stories of in-country movements elsewhere in the late twentieth century, the Chinese accounts reveal that nearly 70 percent or more of the outsiders felt distinctly discriminated against as ruralites.[57] One study conducted in 1994–95 finds 79 percent who complained of a lack of guarantee for their rights.[58] Certainly, there is much in the literature pointing out the sense of unfairness and discrimination experienced by floaters in Chinese cities.[59] One graphic example is the following:

> When she first came to Beijing from a remote mountain district in Jiangsu and saw such a vast world, she became excited, baffled. Then she had a wish she never felt before, tearing at her heart, as she experienced ice cream and discos for the first time. Later she wondered, "Who can say these good things inherently belong just to city people?" She thought it was unfair.[60]

And in an investigation in Guangzhou in the early 1990s, a mere 18 percent felt they had adapted very well to the city,[61] as against the findings from other developing countries, where migrants to major cities adjusted well.[62] Among the Guangzhou respondents 54 percent reported that they would not want to abide in the city, even if it were possible, while just 34 percent said they would like to do so.[63] In the Pearl River

Delta, in 1994, a large survey found that only 15.5 percent of those surveyed expected to stay on for the long term, while 72 percent did not.[64] In 1995, even most of the wealthy inhabitants of Beijing's Zhejiang Village knew local residents only as their customers and did not want them for friends since, they felt, the latter looked down on them.[65]

Three factors that emerged from several studies help explain the differences between China and other places. First, given the effect of the *hukou* barrier on the lives of urban peasants, only 55 percent of nearly 200 peasants interviewed in four cities in 1992 felt that they had any future in the city.[66] Second, in the same study only those with high incomes felt very satisfied;[67] and, given the types of employment open to migrants as laid out in the last chapter, this number was just a small percentage.[68] And third, in Beijing in 1992 those from the most developed areas—who were also those with more of a community around them and making better incomes—felt far more contented than did those from the inland (87 percent of the former thought that peasants could adapt to big city life, but only 62 percent of inlanders felt this way, though some portion of the latter had state-connected jobs).[69]

And one more important differentiating factor emerges from the 1992 study of Beijing migrants: when informants compared their lives not just with those they had had at home, but also with those of Beijing natives, only slightly over one-third were glad to be living better lives than those they had left behind, while more than half compared their plight with the situation of the official local population and therefore found their own lives unsatisfactory.[70]

These findings reinforce several of the points made earlier: for instance, the discontents that sprang from the restrictions created by the household registration system; the differentiation among Chinese floaters with regard to places of origin, and the attendant levels of skill and income among them; and the advantages experienced by those who were part of a community. Combined with the material on job-seeking, we can conclude that up through the mid-1990s transients' grievances and relatively short stays were more the result of the institutional barrier of the *hukou*—whether directly or indirectly—and the concomitant marginal status under which even the wealthy among them labored—than from difficulties in getting work.

The urban *hukou* had declined very significantly in its utility for conducting daily life by the early 1990s.[71] Yet some migrants with cash still considered it worthwhile to purchase it, as we have seen in chapter 3.[72] Others made do without it by relying on what amounted to enclaves of co-provincials, labeled "villages" by the Chinese,[73] where they already had constituted as much as twice the number of official citizens by the late 1980s.[74] But many others still struggled in the absence of the *hukou*, and in their lack of sufficient resources to buy one.

Thus, we need to conceive of the search for modes of everyday survival as a multifaceted one: some relied on methods fading into disuse, some on schemes newly invented, some on strategies at best only marginally satisfactory. Most crucially, migrants' ability to solve their everyday issues varied with the nature of their connections. We begin our account of their temporary solutions to city survival with the villages, a mode of living without urban citizenship.

VILLAGES

When migrants first appeared in the cities, many settled in a murky world of suburban rentals, where land was more open, housing available, daily living costs lower, and management more lax.[75] These regions offered the outsiders a chance to set up facilities for commerce and business in used articles, handicrafts, manufacture, and processing; there they could sleep, conduct business, and store their carts and tools and raw materials, in rentals generally starting at around 50 yuan in 1990.[76] There the peasant interlopers made common cause with local peasants-turned-landlord, and a mutual deal was struck.[77] Native homeowners sectioned off a portion of their own dwellings to rent to the newcomers; abandoned their older home to rentals, constructing a finer one for themselves; or else built an inferior shack to house migrant tenants.[78] In these situations, it was to the advantage of both to accommodate one another: the residents got wealthy while the transients enjoyed a relatively cheap and protected abode. Meanwhile, everyone skirted regulations, the migrants failing to register and the landlords saving tax money they should have been paying.[79]

By the end of 1993, outsiders who were part of migrant communities or "villages" were "buying or building houses in Beijing and acquiring properties in the hopes of settling down and striking root in the city."[80] This was especially true in the Zhejiang Village in Fengtai district, Beijing, where peasants took to buying old, broken-down dwellings for use as combined living and working quarters. Some transients had even bought real estate there by mid-1993.[81] Even more flagrantly, in 1992, the local authorities (illegally, since without higher-level consent) in the Zhejiang Village region actually permitted wealthier, share-pooling residents to construct some forty buildings in large courtyards on village land and had signed leases with them.[82]

In Guangzhou and Shenzhen as well in the early 1990s the practice of throwing up structures and shantytowns had taken root, even as an observer categorized it as "illicit."[83] In Shanghai's Pudong district in 1994, at least 933 "illegal structures" had been erected by—or rented or lent by locals to—alien workers.[84] And so with the reform era, China's cities came to appear more and more similar to those elsewhere in the third world, as slumlike spaces reappeared for the first time in post-1949 China;[85] a specialist in Chinese urban studies remarks on the total absence of such areas—and of pavement dwellers—in 1980, before the migration had begun.[86]

It was not the poverty found among shantytown dwellers elsewhere[87] that placed Chinese floaters in these out-of-the-way sites.[88] Indeed, many of the members of the Zhejiang Village had annual incomes of more than 10,000 yuan in the mid-1990s, and yet they continued to live there.[89] As the sociologist Li Qiang asserted in 1993, "Even those with money live in shacks and save all their money. These same people may own a three-story house in the rural area."[90] The concentrated location just outside the municipality for many thousands of them was instead a form of segregation that reflected—and also reproduced—the state-imposed isolation of the city-sojourning, rural-registered from the proper urbanites. And it forced upon the former a substitute form of urban subsistence as it deprived them of citizenship.

Outskirts Outside the State

In these suburban areas incoming peasants—to varying extents in different communities—fashioned worlds of their own, where they made an accommodation outside the rules and restrictions thrown up by the registration system. The Chinese named these settlements after the provincial homelands of their dwellers. Though all the settlements were dubbed "villages," in fact, they existed in three different gradations by the mid-1990s. The most elementary in terms of structure and organization were ones that simply served as residential areas where people from the same province predominated. The second, more sophisticated form, entailed concentration of the inhabitants by profession, and those dwelling in them developed some economic cooperation as well as a degree of mutual aid in daily life.

Only in the third, most advanced, type did some leading residents arrange for the provision of community services and create informal, unofficial public welfare organizations. In Beijing, it was just the Zhejiang Village, to be discussed below, that qualified as the third kind of grouping by the mid-1990s.[91] This third, advanced form of occupational community was akin to what are called "ethnic enclaves"[92] elsewhere, especially if we take the term "ethnic" in its special, spatial Chinese sense.[93] These settlements are universally the product of chain migration, a system functional both in informing ruralites of the location of pockets of urban opportunity and in placing them in lodging and work upon arrival in town. As students of migration in other countries note, where newcomers have business acumen, they generally generate collective entrepreneurial ventures. A relatively complex division of labor within their trade also works to enhance the potential for the provision of community welfare.[94]

The very existence of these co-provincial villages openly challenged the state's capacity to overwhelm—indeed, to prohibit—the formation of unofficial, informal groups outside its aegis. For here just beyond the once tightly regimented urban areas, places where officialdom had for decades been able (with the exception of the period at the height of the Cultural Revolution) rather quickly to contain and suppress incipient nonstate organizations, were burgeoning an array of what amounted to contender, if nascent, ascriptive and corporate associations.

The people here were able to live so independently because the state did not—indeed could not—fit floating and often very transient migrants into the neighborhood associations that had customarily structured and kept up a steady surveillance over the "proper" urban residents' domestic existences. Neither were any of these itinerants on the outskirts members of any workplace *danwei*, the "units" that had long directed daily behavior at the office or the plant. City services were not supplied to their areas of congregation; nor were there any official associations that could absorb their energies or see to their social needs.

Left abandoned to scramble on their own, quite sizable concentrations of outsiders pooled their resources and carved out a means of subsistence over time. Thus a great paradox characterized floaters living in such collectivities. The state's registration system constrained them, excluded them from its privileges, and neglected them in its service network. And yet at the same time they were freed, if to a limited but growing extent, by their abandonment outside the pale of the state's organizations of administration and surveillance; they were also increasingly empowered by their own numbers.

There were two crucial differences in the Chinese case from the usual pattern elsewhere, in part a result of the *hukou* system and in part connected with the transition from socialism. One was that these people, though nationals, were barred by the *hukou* prohibition from acquiring city citizenship and so were denied any means of pressing their needs legally on urban and higher-level governments.[95] By way of contrast, in other polities in the developing world, where competitive party systems were present, native migrant squatters obtained the ballot and could sometimes bargain for city services and facilities in exchange for votes, at least around election time.[96]

The result of this lockout from the urban system for Chinese rural sojourners was that those with the wherewithal to do so were forced to form wholly alternate societies, nearly totally unconnected with the mainstream. As one researcher explains, "The population [of the Zhejiang Village in 1995] has no sense of belonging to Beijing society."[97] Of the respondents in a sample of 290 transients, 83 percent had not established any relations whatever with Beijing people as of 1992. Treated as foreigners, and seeing themselves that way too, some even felt they would benefit from setting up an ambassadorial organ to protect their interests![98]

The other important distinction was that, as we have seen, because of the continuing—if declining—presence of a powerful state-sponsored framework amid many fading socialist institutions, this mode of subsisting by living collectively was just one of three ways of existing found among urban outsiders. Though it offered more benefits and services than those available to unconnected stragglers, it proved inferior in this regard to the lot of the state-employed and bonded.

Co-provincial Colonies

By 1985, an "ethnic" cluster had clearly emerged in one district within the jurisdiction of Beijing City. The large number of hotel beds (24 percent of those in the city were there), open markets (about 20 percent of those in the whole city at that time), and business opportunities in the city's northwestern Haidian and Chaoyang districts had already drawn in groups of transients.[99] By the middle of the next decade, one source cites twenty-five compact communities in Beijing housing at least ten thousand out-of-towners each.[100] These included temporary colonies of Xinjiang Uighurs, along with natives of Hebei, Sichuan, Anhui, Tianjin, Henan, Jiangsu, Shandong, and, most conspicuously, Zhejiang.[101]

These areas each had their place in an informal hierarchy of social status: a Henanese informant on the streets of Beijing confided that he refused to live with his fellow provincials because of the low social status of their neighborhood.[102] For the spot the Henan natives, largely from

Gushi county, occupied, the Erlizhuang neighborhood in Haidian's Dong-sheng, was colloquially dubbed "garbage village," since most of the inhabitants lived off gathering and buying scrap material and junk. Within the site, a filthy market for old goods formed the foundation for the livelihood of over two thousand peasants, a mart barely distinguishable from the rubbish heap that constituted both the inhabitants' mine and their refuse.[103]

There were reports of migrant colonies in many cities besides the capital, including Shanghai, Guangzhou, Tianjin, Chengdu, and even Urumqi, to name a few.[104] People from Jiangsu's Nantong congregated as long-term residents along particular streets in Xinjiang's Changji district, in Heilongjiang's Daqing, and in Shanghai.[105] In Urumqi, close to the train station, there was located a *mangliu* (blind wanderers') village, allegedly made up of some twenty-seven thousand outsiders from the inland, formed into five natural villages as of late 1989.[106]

In the vicinity of Zhongshan University in Fenghecun on Guangzhou's outskirts a whole village of ten thousand peasants had rented more than two thousand rooms from the locals and outnumbered them in a ratio of three to one by the early 1990s.[107] In that city's Sanyuanli district, Xinjiang people lived together in a hotel, eating lamb and carrying knives, according to local lore.[108] Squatter settlements graced several other areas around the city.[109] Scrap collectors settled in Huizhou city's Huicheng district; close to the Guangzhou zoo, cotton fluffers stayed in plastic shacks. In border areas along the city's streets, by the mountains, near the fields, and along the villages, outsiders opened shops, repaired shoes, did odd jobs, and collected scraps.[110] Guangzhou's natives disdained these areas for their decrepit appearance and sickening hygiene; but transients set up their own temporary day-care centers, schools, and markets there.[111]

By the late 1980s in Shanghai, too, migrants had gradually moved to the border streets and suburbs of the cities, finding the city center saturated.[112] One suburb became a center for food-processing factories; a 1990 government investigation uncovered as many as thirty subterranean such workshops, engaged in catering and baking for city residents.[113] In the early 1990s when a new development zone was established in the city's eastern Pudong section, colonies of fellow provincials quickly followed.[114]

The Zhejiang Village

But it was the Zhejiang Village that was by far the most massive and articulated; it was also the place that was best researched.[115] Its location was in Fengtai district's Dahongmen, eight kilometers south of the city. One journalist traced the first Zhejiang tailors in Fengtai to 1983,[116] though the later-famous Zhejiang Village only became fully constituted around 1986.[117] By late 1988, the ratio of outsiders to locals was already as high as 2.33:1.[118] The great majority—perhaps up to 80 percent[119]—of these transients were taken upon arrival by their co-county folk into the fold of the tailoring trade, assembling, manufacturing, and selling garments. The remainder were there to service the needs of the seamstresses and salespeople.

Over the years 1986 to 1990, the numbers of inhabitants sprang from twelve thousand to thirty thousand, and newcomers continued to increase at the rate of 50 percent per year after 1990.[120] Most sources agree that by the mid-1990s about one hundred thousand transients, mostly from Zhejiang's Wenzhou prefecture, had taken up residence in Beijing's five administrative villages, corresponding to twenty-six natural villages.[121] According to one report, the conglomeration was composed of four districts, with villagers residing in them according to native place.[122]

Dahongmen has been compared to an American Chinatown, but in fact it was even more a self-contained community, sealed off as it was from the main life of the city by government intention, with city authorities restricting its residents to specific boundaries. For years the official administration of the city left the enclave to its own dictates. The exception was the city's demands for fees for residency papers and for hygiene services (without the transients deriving any benefit therefrom), and its requisition of taxes on their business and on every sewing machine, among other charges.[123]

As the inhabitants built up a life of their own, their original need for outside assistance steadily decreased.[124] Instead of waiting vainly for the Beijing authorities to service their wants, by 1993, residents of the village had established their own restaurants (catering exclusively Zhejiang dishes), some hundred barbershops, repair shops, twenty clinics and hospitals, day-care centers, five kindergartens, and markets, along with some two thousand small shops, all doing business in their Zhejiang dialect.[125]

Entrepreneurs also arranged daily buses to and from the home counties, set up rudimentary toilets, and installed long-distance phone lines (figure 7). And in the large courtyards mentioned above that were constructed in 1992, water, electrical, sewerage, postal, educational, and recreational facilities came into being. Despite these efforts, in general sanitation infrastructure and educational institutions remained terribly

Figure 7. Open sewers and food stalls in the Zhejiang Village, Beijing.

Figure 8. Pedicabs: the only form of transport within the Zhejiang Village, Beijing.

deficient, and sewerage, electrical power, and postal services "could hardly meet the needs of the place."[126] Still, the residents of this community had found a way to sustain themselves with scarcely any backing from the bureaucracy.

By contrast, the region of Beijing peopled by peasants hailing from Anhui was less compact, though two-thirds of those living there came from just three counties of that province. As more and more Anhuinese arrived, by 1992, the place took on the visage of a true village, with trash scattered liberally, young children scampering about as if on open fields, indoor toilets lacking or broken down or ignored, and vegetables sprouting. Because of the paucity of living space and of people's incomes, residents shared household goods and tended one another if they should fall ill.[127]

There, as opposed to the Zhejiang Village, the much poorer level of the populace, plus the simplicity of its main profession—trash-picking, done one by one, which did nothing to train its operators in division of labor and cooperation—discouraged, or at least failed to motivate, people from working together to create and perform community services beyond the most basic mutual assistance. That area managed to boast as its only joint undertakings a few small retail shops and a very basic restaurant.[128] Still, the resource of community that the residents shared gave them a potential for organization that transients living in a less concentrated fashion elsewhere in city lacked. We now turn to see how these other people survived.

HOUSING, GRAIN, HEALTH CARE, SCHOOLING

As of the late 1980s, such characterizations of the floaters as this one were popular in the public mind:

> They live without any fixed abode,
> Travel without even leaving a trace.
> They conceal their identity, bury their names;
> Between city and country they scatter apace.[129]

Similarly:

> Their nature is to float a lot: "They come without a shadow, leave without a trace." They have to rely on the laws of the market and supply and demand and so they go where there is work. Thus, it's normal for them to float. They can't be choosy.[130]

But in fact, even at that time[131] and certainly by the early 1990s only a small proportion of these growing numbers was truly living in such a state, one that was fairly common in nineteenth-century Hankou, at that time known as *wu-lai,* or having nothing to rely upon.[132] Indeed, neither were most of these itinerant people scattered randomly throughout the metropolises nor were they living on the loose.[133] In the main (if we omit for the moment those hoveled in crannies in the open), those with an indoor bed to rest on were settled, even if ever so briefly, and found ways to accommodate most of their quotidian needs.

Housing

In some ways transients in large Chinese cities who were not part of a "village" or domiciled in state enterprises had problems of finding shelter that were quite similar to those of rural migrants in cities elsewhere in the world. The most salient common issues were inadequate housing supplies and the scarcity of vacant land.[134] Prohibitive governmental regulations about land use also kept transients from finding satisfactory housing, in China and in many other places.[135] And like other migrants around the world, most Chinese floaters faced an unstable and uncertain job market and thus a fluctuating income; thus, perceiving themselves as only temporarily in town, they often were unwilling to invest in urban real estate.[136]

In China the relevant rulings were particularly strict: they barred outsiders not just from occupying land,[137] but even from building or buying houses, unless they were Overseas Chinese.[138] And for decades, the massive proportion of floor space owned by either urban governments or work units had been off-limits even for rental by outside peasants.[139] But because of the ongoing transition from socialism that accompanied the movement of peasants into cities, the practical severity of these regulations lessened as transgressions against them increased with time.[140]

Besides the shantytowns or "villages," there was quite an array of other housing opportunities, if only applicants had an occupation. By the end of 1995, in Shanghai, a survey of 4,714 employed migrants reports that almost half were renting accommodations, one-quarter were in dormitories, and one-fifth in shelters on work sites.[141] For those not in rentals, job often determined abode, as in the following description of one street in the city of Suzhou as of mid-1989. It illustrates the extent to which for many, in a pattern quite reminiscent of pre-1949 days, work routine and rest shared the same paltry space (figure 9).[142]

> Workers live in their work units' temporary housing; businesspeople and the majority of those in the service trade—except for a minority

Figure 9. One-room living/working space in the Zhejiang Village, Beijing: bed for two doubles as a worktable.

> who sleep in the open in places such as car sheds or under the eaves—rent in private people's homes, and they use the room they rent for both work and for sojourning.[143]

Similarly, this account by a cadre from Tianjin's public security office highlights the mix of renting and staying on site that characterized outsiders with jobs in the cities in the 1990s (figure 10):

> Among casual laborers (*dagongzhe*), 60 to 70 percent live in work shacks; *baomu* (nursemaids) stay in their employers' homes; coal delivery men and sanitation workers dwell in dormitories of the units that hired them; businesspeople reside in rentals, especially in the city's outskirts; sellers in the markets sleep in the markets; barbers live in their shops; and shoe repair (and other repair) people live in rentals.[144]

My own discussions in 1992 in Guangzhou, Wuhan, Nanjing, and Tianjin with fifty-one randomly selected transients at work or looking for work on the streets, in the stalls, or in a state-owned factory largely confirmed these data. Not surprisingly, since I encountered them on the street or in a factory, none were residents of a village enclave. Of these, twenty-three were selling food or wholesaling garments. Sixteen of them were renting rooms, four staying with relatives, and one each was living

Figure 10. On-site living shacks for construction workers, Wuhan.

in a hostel, in a spouse's unit, or sleeping in the market. All five restaurant workers I met were living in their workplaces. At all five construction sites I visited builders camped in worksheds (where the sheds' construction materials ranged from brick in the case of a prosperous county enterprise to aluminum and bamboo for the makeshift shacks of builders on the move).

Five of seven craftspeople I spoke with put up at their work sites; one (a primitive cotton-ginning family) slept out in a tent if the weather was poor and directly on the ground of a hot summer night; and one rented a room. Of seven job seekers, one had a free rental with suburban peasants for whom he was doing odd jobs in exchange; two were with relatives, and two more had been squeezed temporarily into friends' or relatives' work units; one more was in a hostel; and one, a fifty-one-year-old nurse, had holed up for the duration at the train station.[145] Both sets of scrap collectors lived in rented rooms, as did a married couple pulling a pedicab. The factory workers slept in a factory dorm, with several of them to a room.

Put differently, there were six separate sorts of solution. Of the fifty-one newcomers, twenty-one were living in rentals; two were putting up in factory dorms (including the man who lived in his spouse's unit); eight were being hosted by family or friends; two were dwelling in hostels; another fifteen were housed in their shops or at other work sites; and the remaining three slept in the open (at what may have been a work site) or else in a public place. I present these data in table 14.

Of all these transients, for the most part well ensconced in more or less livable dwellings, it was only the sixth and last category—those sleeping outdoors or in a public place—and which included just three informants (one of whom had his family with him), which would fit the label of people who "have no place to live," those, that is, with no connections or other resources. These were the members of the "three withouts" group, mentioned in earlier chapters.

By the mid-1990s the numbers of such people (if, perhaps, not their proportion of the whole)—without jobs or a proper place to sleep—had multiplied. They could be discovered settled (but barely) in hidden back streets, or in tunnels, under trucks and buses in parking lots, in the waiting areas of railway stations, and under bridges.[146] When sheltered at all, this marginal, undomiciled group made do with the rudest of adaptations of scrap metal, cardboard, and wood[147]—improvisations that resonated with the solutions adopted by those homeless New Yorkers who in the same years had constructed an "architecture of despair . . . in 'no-tech' shanty settlements of rigged makeshift structures," perched in "the shadow places" under bridges and amid the garbage of vacant lots.[148]

This pitiful scene stretched before a foreign researcher in 1993:

> Shantytowns have sprung up, seemingly overnight, in back alleys and on empty lots. In one behind a busy street I found about 50 shelters, in which hundreds of people, men, women, and children, were living without electricity or running water. Dressed in rags, they had faces black with dirt and hair that stuck together in clumps. All were from Anhui Province, and had not found work, but eked out a living through begging or scavenging junk. . . . These people belong to the lowest class of migrant workers, some of whom will never find work. . . . Without employment contracts or residency registration cards, they settle in impromptu camps and lean-tos.[149]

Two Chinese journalists paint similarly chilling portraits of two such lean-tos that they happened upon in 1989. One is a description of a hut of a family from Anhui, then unemployed but once supported by the husband's temporary repair work in an automotive repair plant:

> A low, suffocating small house in the Shanghai outskirts: the room about ten square meters, the door so narrow and low that fat and tall people couldn't enter. The roof so near the ground makes you feel the air is scarce; for security the small window is tightly covered with newspaper. One small wooden bed with two old covers for a couple

Table 14. Housing Solutions of Street Informants by Job Category, Four
Cities, Mid-1992

Job Category	In Rental	In Spouse's Unit	At Relatives/ Friends	In Hostel	In the Open	At Work Site
Commmerce	16	1	4	1	1	0
Restaurant	0	0	0	0	0	5
Construction	0	0	0	0	0	5
Crafts	1	0	0	0	1	5
None	1	0	4	1	1	0
Scrap collecting	2	0	0	0	0	0
Transport	1	0	0	0	0	0
Factory	0	0	0	0	0	1

SOURCE: Author's interviews, May–June 1992, Guangzhou, Tianjin, Nanjing, and Wuhan.

and two kids. On the floor, a stove for cooking, an aluminum pot, four
bowls and nothing else by way of personal possessions.[150]

And here is the other rough structure they found, this one occupied by
two cotton fluffers:

Using broken bamboo and torn plastic, they built a shed. . . .
"Living in this dilapidated shack is not easy," they confided. "Recently, at dusk suddenly three fierce men came, claiming to be security, and charging that our building this shed violates the city's regulations, wanting to fine us 100 yuan or send us to the public security bureau. We pulled out our business license, and then they went away, crestfallen. Another time at night a great wind blew. We struggled with the wind all night to protect this shack; thereafter, too tired to work, we slept for two days. When city people look at it, they feel it's disgusting, but it's our home. All day, have to have someone watching it. When we go to a restaurant to eat, have to take turns; if the house is torn down, what will become of us?"[151]

These data depict the range of options that were available to those of
China's reform-era urban transients living outside the new urban villages. Despite the swelling incursion of markets, which provided a gamut
of possibilities, even money-earning outsiders were kept outside the regular housing market. If holding a job with a measure of security, they
got a bed in a crowded dorm; if part of an urban village, the average

inhabitant could expect to share a cramped, rented workroom with three or four fellow townspeople; and if privately employed, they usually found space at the work site or in a rental. But those without jobs, acquaintances, or possibilities stayed stuck in a scarcely sheltered realm, where rummaging and foraging threatened to become their permanent lot.

Grain

Just as floaters took up a range of settlement patterns in accord with whether they possessed linkages that could sustain them—or the absence of any—they also followed varying styles of obtaining basic sustenance, in particular, grain, over the course of the 1980s and early 1990s. Those properly attached to the state—whether through jobs in state enterprises or in construction teams subcontracting with state units—had the most secure and cheapest means of procuring their grain, especially in the days of rationing, before grain was cheaply available in open marketplaces. For the grain ration system, with tickets assigned just to urbanites, constituted one of the most stringent barriers against city residence for ruralites up until the appearance of open markets in the early and mid-1980s, as we saw in chapter 2.

Indeed, well into the 1980s ration tickets were still essential to obtaining grain, and it was illegal for outsiders in the city to purchase grain without them. In that period, the fortunate ruralites in urban areas with state-sector jobs could count on their work unit either to buy higher, negotiated-price (yijia) grain for them or else to pay them extra wages that would enable them to buy such grain on their own. Some—though not all—state firms and state-connected construction teams got a steady and sufficient supply of grain for their peasant contract workers by arranging for it with the city's grain bureau. Groups on their own, such as a construction team hailing from a single rural village, would organize transportation to bring grain from home at regular intervals, thereby supplying a whole little community of outsiders.[152]

Peasants coming without an affiliation had other choices before grain markets emerged, but these were of variable reliability and tended to be costly besides. Those who had the capability to do so carted their own food along with them on the road. But others were forced to spend their urban earnings on the high-priced grain available either on black markets or else directly from urbanites who happened to possess a surplus. In this case, the peasants had to pay a price which was as high as 40 to 50 cents (fen) per half-kilogram (jin) above that of rationed grain throughout the 1980s, an amount that could be a serious constraint for many.[153] Alternatively, those with skills or commodities to trade could exchange their services or produce for the precious ration coupons or, if they had the cash for it, illegally buy the coupons.[154]

A 1986 State Council ruling rendered it possible for the unregistered to buy grain legally at negotiated prices on open markets, as noted in chapter 2.[155] And yet the benefits of this ruling, though ultimately crucial for floaters as prices declined, did not emerge immediately. Research in the Shanghai suburbs in 1988 shows that over half of the transients there continued to get their grain from their family or friends; only one-third took advantage of the new ruling to buy grain—still high priced, at that time—on the market; and the remainder preferred to plant it in their new locations.[156]

Despite the ruling, some local governments clearly disapproved of any policy that brought more peasants into town and therefore probably discouraged its execution. For instance, in July 1986 the Hubei provincial government passed a regulation on controlling the use of labor outside the state plan. "Why have the numbers of such workers increased so rapidly," the document inquired disapprovingly? "One reason," it maintained, was that "a lot of peasants enter the cities and towns, supplied with their own grain, and settle down to work or do business."[157]

Thus, even as markets opened up, fixed arrangements with the state continued to provide the most stable means of obtaining affordable sustenance for some time. Meanwhile, those at work in nonstate construction teams, foreign firms, or the entrepreneurial sector either underfed themselves or were dealt the most minimal and miserable meals their employers could safely manage.[158]

Health Care

Since state funding for public health facilities, medications, and personnel continued into the reform era to be pegged to a planned level of urban populace per city, arrangements for the health care of unattached newcomers from the outside appeared to bureaucrats to be out of the question. Responsible authorities decried the implications for the settled population of ignoring the epidemics and contagious diseases allegedly carried in by the migrants:

> Contagious diseases that rarely occur in Beijing occur among the migrant population. So far, no one in Beijing who has been immunized has contracted measles, but during both 1994 and 1995 measles epidemics occurred among adults from among the migrant population at construction sites.[159]

Whatever their worries, the bureaucrats were too strapped for resources to do anything about them.

Consequently, chances for at least some modicum of health care were by far the best if a floater were able to land a position in a successful state-owned firm, something that generally happened only to inlanders. Someone attached to an officially operated work unit would be able to qualify at least for basic attention, even if the level of care varied with local regulations, the financial standing of the firm, and management decisions.

Some random examples illustrate the variation: in mid-1992, Tianjin Labor Bureau officials claimed that if workers were sick for less than three months, they would receive full pay, just as permanent workers would; if ill for longer than that, they would receive a one-time subsidy—with the amount depending on the length of time already in the firm—and then be dismissed; also, that workers could stay in the firm's clinic free of charge for up to three months.[160]

But in the Tianjin No. Three Silk Weaving Factory (which was under the jurisdiction of this bureau), all peasant workers were made to contribute 3 yuan per month for health insurance.[161] If the costs of their illness exceeded that, it was up to the patients to make up the difference. Having paid that money, they could expect treatment from the factory, but no wages on sick days. Seriously sick workers had to go home, with no wages. Still, factory leaders professed, they were granted life insurance and insurance for unexpected accidents, for which the factory set aside 30 yuan per six months of work.

In Wuhan's No. One Cotton Mill, the system was quite different: 19 percent of all workers' wages was reserved each month as insurance money, which would be returned to the transients upon departure, provided they completed the contracted working term. As of summer 1992 rural workers there received 60 to 70 percent of their pay when sick, as regular workers would, but the regulars were to continue receiving this amount through their lifetime (at least according to the regulations), as well as getting a pension, neither of which privileges accrued to temporary workers.[162] In Zhengzhou, peasant employees were not permitted to stay in the factory's hospitals.[163]

Though there are no statistics measuring the proportion of peasants in state firms that really did receive medical care and benefits, one study shows that in Guangdong province, 56 percent of the migrant factory workers had some form of medical or accident insurance in 1994.[164] And a Shanghai study in mid-1995 notes that construction workers were the most likely group among the floating population in that city to have health insurance, which must have been the result of their being under contract with a state enterprise.[165]

In cases where the firm did not help out—and for the vastly greater portion of the outside population not hired by state work units—migrant laborers were thrown onto their own devices, with the options, as always, depending on the nature of the ties that the transients could bring to bear. As several researchers note, outside the state sector, "the only welfare [was] that provided by the migrant workers themselves."[166]

The most reliable form of help existed for those with community connections, especially those who lived in Beijing's village of Zhejiang people. There, as noted above, migrant leaders had, albeit illicitly, created their own clinics and hospitals by the mid-1990s, where treatment was provided by fellow Zhejiangese.[167] Since the Beijing city government—unlike state authorities elsewhere in the developing world[168]—did not allow outside doctors to practice medicine as late as 1995, unlicensed providers, nurses, and former "barefoot doctors" from the villages of origin practiced illegally, using medicine purchased in their home of Wenzhou, while their makeshift clinics were periodically fined and their implements confiscated.[169]

In Beijing's Anhui Village, a community too poor to establish a clinic, residents were afraid to spend their limited funds on entering a hospital and so turned to nonprofessionals. Sometimes they even went back home for treatment.[170] Their children's rate of inoculation was, accordingly, far below that of Beijing children's, and was also lower than that of young-sters from Zhejiang.[171]

But those wholly on their own had to throw themselves on the mercy of the city, which, if they were fortunate, might help out. Officials from the Tianjin Public Health Bureau maintained that individuals with urgent illnesses or other emergencies were treated immediately, with the pay-ment collected later. If patients had no formal unit responsible for them—as was the case with most floaters—they would be expected to put forth the payment in time. Realistically, though, few had the funds to reim-burse the clinic, the officials acknowledged, and would probably never pay back the debt.[172]

Rumor held, however, that most without communities surrounding them were forced to try their luck with untrained traveling "doctors" who floated among migrant communities treating maladies, such as venereal disease, believed to be common to this segment of humanity.[173] And cases such as the following were probably common enough among those who fell ill and threw themselves on the mercy of official hospitals:

> If a little sick, they don't go to the hospital or take medicine. If they're very sick, they just go home. One was hit on the head and was bleeding. The hospital stopped the bleeding and then the worker was obliged to leave. [The researcher] had to pay the hospital before the attendant would stitch him up.[174]

And not just problems of treatment were at issue: nearly one-fifth of the workers in five foreign-invested factories in the Pearl River Delta (where benefits were notoriously lacking, as we have seen in chapter 6) had sustained medical difficulties (anemia or white blood cell abnormalities) as a direct result of their jobs.[175]

Schooling

Reinhard Bendix targets "the right and duty to receive an elementary education" as "perhaps the most universally approximated implementation of national citizenship," since it is a benefit over which the government itself has authority and it is an obligation that all parents with children in a certain age group are required by law to fulfill.[176] Indeed, China's Law on Compulsory Education does stipulate that all children aged seven to fifteen must enroll and receive education for nine years. For these reasons, the quite uneven availability of basic schooling—more often absent than present—for the floating folk from the country particularly underscored their lack of valid membership in the official urban community. In Beijing, for instance, where 100 percent of native five- to twelve-year-old children were enrolled in schools in 1995, only 40 percent of migrant ones were.[177]

In this regard, China was not completely exceptional. Local governments in France in the late 1970s were able to persuade the central government to impose limits on the numbers of immigrant children permitted to attend public primary schools.[178] And in the United States, it required a Supreme Court decision (*Plyler v. Doe*, 1982) to override a state law passed in Texas in 1975 that had the intent to deny state money for the education of undocumented migrants.[179] This right was again under threat a decade or so later. But in these other cases it was genuine outsiders, not nationals—as Chinese peasants are in China—who were prevented from attending school.[180]

Moreover, the right to schooling is often present elsewhere when other rights for migrants—or at least their exercise—are lacking. This was the case in Taiwan in the 1960s, when migrants were either disinclined or unable to avail themselves of services other than schooling in the cities.[181] For the Chinatown Chinese discriminated against in American cities, education was historically one of the few bridges open to affiliation with and eventual acceptance by the larger society.[182] And though blacks migrating northward in the segregated, early twentieth-century United States were forced to attend separate and decidedly inferior schools, there was no prohibition against their becoming educated.[183] In the Soviet Union, though peasants officially had no right to legal residence in cities until 1974, younger people moved to cities well before that, expressly to obtain schooling unavailable in their homes in the countryside.[184]

In various Latin American societies, too, rural native newcomers have long been welcome in urban public schools: indeed, one of the chief attractions Lima of the 1960s held for peasants was its schools, which they were free to attend;[185] similarly, in Mexico City of that era, "almost all migrants . . . enter school when they arrive."[186] In Rio de Janeiro, as elsewhere in Latin America, migrants either found urban patrons to sponsor individual children into the regular classrooms or, by using petitions from immigrants' residents' associations, successfully pressured the government for schools of their own.[187]

But in formerly planned-economy China, despite the press of market relations, funding for education, like that for health care, continued into the 1990s to be available officially just for licensed city residents, leaving behind—at least legally—the two to three million school-age children of the floating population (as of mid-1995).[188] As late as 1995, there was no national policy or any regulations on educating the offspring of the floating population. A few local governments had set up unstable, unaccredited makeshift schools, whose quality varied greatly—hardly a case, even, of "separate but equal." But the central government had provided no funding for the migrants.[189]

In the words of a cadre in the Beijing Municipal Bureau of Education in early 1996:

> Beijing is very short on money for education. Looking after the present 1.5 million middle and primary school students in the city already strains resources, and there are 300,000 school-age children among the migrant population. Middle and primary schools in the city have already taken in more than 30,000 migrant children. Though the

> parents of some have paid, the amount of money paid is far from
> enough to educate these students . . . formerly these were the respon-
> sibility of the receiving area, but nowadays Beijing can't possibly solve
> the education problems of 300,000 migrant children.[190]

Since the domiciles of the offspring of the floating population were registered in the countryside for years, there was no sense of legal obligation
to teach them in the cities.[191] Without a residency permit, schooling was
legally unavailable up through the mid-1990s.

Over the same period, official agencies not only failed to provide for
the education of the transient young, but also forbade the urban immigrants who lived in clusters to establish their own schools beyond the
level of day-care centers and kindergartens[192]—perhaps as a disincentive
to migrants who might bring children in tow from the country. In two
districts of Guangzhou where migrants had cobbled together some forty
"shack schools," the local authorities soon ordered them shut down.[193]

One district administration in Beijing that was populated by Henan
natives would not let its transients open any sort of school at all as late
as 1995.[194] In defiance of local regulations, however, in 1992 the newly
established large courtyards of the Zhejiang Village set up educational
facilities of their own.[195] These intercommunity differences must explain
the fact that, citywide by 1995, only 35 percent of Zhejiang school-age
youngsters in Beijing were not in school, whereas over 81 percent of
those from Henan were not receiving an education.[196] In mid-1995, however, a nursery run by junior high school graduates in the Zhejiang
Village and staffed by hometown teachers was not even permitted to
register.[197]

Given these official barriers, most migrants in Beijing outside the
Zhejiang Village (as well as those in other big cities) who had brought
their children to town with them faced three options.[198] If somehow
affiliated with a bureaucrat, presumably on contract in a work unit, they
could try to get an official patron to slip their young into the schools in
their borrowed neighborhoods;[199] they could pay high fees (plus a bribe)
for their children's education in an urban school;[200] or they could forgo
urban instruction altogether.[201]

Lacking cadre backers or a community, the less-well-paid migrants or
those only intermittently employed could not afford the costs of school,
and the youngsters of those floating about with no fixed address would
not be found in the city classroom.[202] Not surprisingly, in one study of
nearly 300 migrants in late 1991 Beijing, it was the children of the
entrepreneurs who were most likely to have found a place in the educa-

tional system.[203] So the offspring of many were left at home in the countryside, where the costs of education were comparatively minimal. Or small children brought into town were sometimes enlisted to help their parents by begging, or by serving as their apprentices, especially among the poorest transients.[204] As for the older youths, rural adolescents often dropped out of school at home—sometimes after only a few years— to make their fortunes in town.[205]

Among my fifty-one migrant informants mentioned above, only nine discussed the issue of education. Seven of those, including two earning over 20,000 yuan per year in the garment and wholesale silk trades, had either sent their children home when they reached school age or left them behind in the first place.[206] For these wealthier migrants, their lack of a *hukou* and of an on-site community option, not costs, disposed them to educate their children in the villages. The one exception I encountered to this bleak picture as of 1992 was a special school established by the branch of Wuhan's Individual Entrepreneurs' Association, the quasi-official organ that governed that city's famous small commodities market on Hanzheng Street on behalf of the city. There sojourning youngsters could attend school for less than 100 yuan a semester.[207]

Thus, again the same threefold distinction that explained differences among types of migrants in handling the issues of daily life appears in other realms. On the whole, migrants with a bond to a state agency or to one of its officials had the upper edge as second-class citizens; and those who were part of a vibrant community or who had some assets also fared tolerably well in their own ways. The offspring of those who were unattached or without any cash to spare, however, were usually destined to mature without being taught.

But apart from their coping strategies—often on an individual basis— devised to satisfy daily needs that the state was determined not to meet— what forms of social organization characterized the migrant community? To begin with, under the P.R.C. into the 1990s popular organizations with even the remotest of political coloration were banned even for official urban residents, and so unofficial groupings labored under a heavy veil of risk. Thus, to the extent that migrants congregated, any association among them was fluid, secretive, and illicit; and always conducted along native-place lines.[208]

ORGANIZATION AND LEADERSHIP

In a 1994 survey of migrants in Beijing and Shanghai, only 9.4 percent responded that they belonged to a "spontaneous" (*zifa*) grouping of some type.[209] Yet an infinite number of quite informal associations, based on lines of blood and place of origin, succored those among the floating population who had access to them.[210] If nothing else, these groupings served as refuges when transients encountered trouble. For their purpose was to provide mutual assistance in daily life and in work.[211]

Cliques (bang) of migrants from the same native place and working at the same kind of job thus became networks for self-protection, mutual care, and joint action against outsiders, when necessary. But their scale remained very small, their degree of organization elementary and loose. For such bodies lacked fixed structure or any definition of internal relations. Moreover, unless members of such a group knew someone able to provide job opportunities, their mobility was endemic, their work life quite unstable.[212]

This feebleness of secondary associations was partly a reflection of the hazards that transient, scattered migrant workers encounter the world around.[213] But, more important, its chief source was the specific restraints against migrants' affiliation imposed by the Chinese government, restrictions not generally found in other societies. Indeed, despite the obstacles, in other places associations among outsiders in cities gave them the means to launch themselves into urban society.[214] In reform-era China, by contrast, the administrations of large cities refused to register or legally to incorporate—whether as part of a state organ or as an independent entity—any potentially sophisticated association among the sojourners.[215] Not only that; individual migrants usually could not even become formal members of an urban organ in Beijing, up through the mid-1990s.[216]

Regardless of this official denial, some enterprising transients went on building collective connections, to promote the coordination, if not the defense, of their interests. Indeed, if we consider the several chief occupations in which transients in the cities engaged, we find that in each of them at least some of the practitioners participated in group activity of one sort or another.

A most intricately orchestrated effort was one several wealthy traders from Rui'an City, Zhejiang, mounted in Beijing after the mid-1980s. Their aim was to create a trade association among well-known fellow entrepreneurs from home holding sizable assets and running a steady business. They hoped at a minimum to consolidate the economic power of Rui'an businesspeople in Beijing, protect their legal interests, and exchange market information. But ultimately they hoped to use the full weight of their combined capital to enter the city's mainstream market as a force powerful enough to face the city's own entrepreneurs in any potential conflict.[217]

The story is a decade-long string of disappointments. For the Beijing city government persistently rebuffed their efforts, in spite of their having won the strong backing of Rui'an's liaison office in Beijing and the support of their hometown government, plus that of both the Rui'an and Beijing Communist Parties' United Front Departments and both cities' industrial and commercial federations.[218]

The circuitous path these pioneers traveled in trying to win permission was multipronged in spite of repeated setbacks along the way. It began with the creation of a "preparatory group," which, though acquiring legal approval, did not manage to thrust the movement further. Another avenue of approach was to set up Beijing branch offices of two professional associations already in operation in Rui'an; yet another was to form a Rui'an *tongxianghui*, composed of influential Rui'an locals who had successfully been doing business or who had been part of the Rui'an cultural and intellectual circles in Beijing for at least three years.

They proceeded to hold evening parties to which they invited city district police and taxation officials, whom they requested to lecture, and with whom they promised to cooperate in controlling their errant fellows. There was also a plan for a joint defense committee that was to cooperate with the local public security in handling merchants from Rui'an who were behaving illegally.[219]

One last maneuver entailed a number of Rui'an individual businesspeople entering district-level industrial and commercial federations in Beijing as individual members and then composing a special group of Rui'an merchants within the federation.[220] Though none of these steps had led to the final, very minimal but essential goal of registration for their association as late as 1995, the ingenuity of the ringleaders and the multiplicity of entry points against which they pressed were impressive. Probably the aims, if not all the imaginative tactics, of this group were representative. For of the 9.4 percent of migrants professing to belong to some kind of organization in 1994, 33.9 percent were businesspeople. Their groups worked to divide up turf and coordinate prices.[221]

Bosses dominated the teams among construction and other manual laborers and operated through a core of close lieutenants plus a second ring of activists, surrounded by a flexible body of frequently shifting followers.[222] The bachelors who usually made up such teams often belonged to small-scale loyalty gangs, sometimes headed by an influential senior figure. These youths swore brotherhood oaths and passed their scant free hours in one another's company.[223] Scuffles were commonplace among such gangs, but they were over territory and held no larger political appeals.[224]

Nursemaids formed *baomu* associations for pursuing their needs (discussed in chapter 6); beggars and trash collectors organized bands.[225] Outsider beggars battled over sites with local ones.[226] And sometimes competition and economic interest split up a provincially homogeneous urban settlement by county or hometown, and again economically based conflicts were common.[227] There were tales of jealousy and battles among the subregional groups, setting up their own tiny fiefdoms, often using extortion against competitors, and milking their turf for its meager yield, as this vignette suggests:

> Many places in Guangzhou are carved out and occupied by gangs who set up separatist regimes; blackmailing each other becomes a way of life. If someone in such an area collects wine bottles, trash paper, and so on, the occupants levy a tax upon it.[228]

There were also rings that made their way within an underclass and reportedly dangerous underworld of "black" and secret societies.[229] These shady groups thrived as protection rackets, using extortion to collect monthly "security money" and dealing in crime, prostitution, and narcotics.[230]

Besides these occupationally based bodies, there was also a Christian organization composed of several thousand Zhejiang businesspeople in Beijing; though allegedly limited to religious affairs, it became a conduit through which business deals with locals were arranged.[231] All of these organizational forms and formats were clearly preliminary foundations for aggregating and asserting individual and group welfare and economic rights. Moreover they persisted in their actions even as both the top political elite and local urban administrations struggled to limit their significance.

What sort of leadership held these various groups together? Researchers' findings on the groups are mixed. Since there was "no legal organizational leadership" among the migrants,[232] some write of a total "absence of authority and administrative management" in the villages.[233] Still others speak of community elites with "authority, power, and a certain degree of control," plus prestige among the residents, at least in the Zhejiang Village. This dominance, they claim, made for a sort of self-administration within the village. But it lacked the clinching legitimation of the state and so was forced to exist parallel to but not as a part of it.[234]

Reportage literature and hearsay focus on the seamiest, most authoritarian, aspects of local rule. They assert that bosses held sway in areas such as the Zhejiang Village, ruling in factionalized, well-structured cliques. One source refers to "tribes," tightly controlled internally;[235] another describes "small independent kingdoms," led by the chiefs of "black societies," and dominated in the Zhejiang Village by a "Wenzhou clique," whose members gained their wealth through illicit activities.[236] This kind of account resonates with a report from a bureaucrat in Guangzhou, who refers to local villains or bullies running the shack settlements of his city.[237]

But other Chinese scholars who are deeply familiar with such areas uncover a realm of internally recognized and law-abiding authority in them. These researchers adjudge that the ability to adjust disputes among their confreres, experience, fairness, and wealth are some of the main qualities that conferred such leadership. Most important, however, are seniority within the village (as measured by length of time living there) and the abilities to provide employment opportunities and to manage crises for their fellows.[238]

Here we see the persisting effect of the state on power formation at the grass roots, even in communities largely beyond its reach. For these latter, decisive, skills were ultimately a function of these elites' having developed informal connections with local official organs, especially the police station, and with relevant departments in their rural home counties—but not with the central-level politicians who could have made major decisions on their fate and place within Chinese urban society. Because of their lack of a genuine, formal political imprimatur, these leaders could sometimes handle the transients' daily needs but exercised no administrative powers that stretched beyond their own people.[239]

Thus, the clout that had been nurtured among migrants by the mid-1990s was quite a circumscribed one, very much internal to the migrant communities themselves. That limitation was demonstrated in transients' powerlessness to stave off the Beijing City's demolition of many of the buildings of the Zhejiang Village in November 1995.[240] But even as this move triumphed physically (and temporarily), the autonomous and internally consolidated business dealings and networks among the village's commercial leaders built up over the previous years persisted nonetheless.[241] So once again we see the creation of lifestyles, solutions, and association outside and parallel to the state.

. . .

The floating population is generally depicted as an undifferentiated mass of people, one at a loss because of its deprivation of all of the perquisites and permissions the state bestowed on the urban citizenry. This stereotype is misleading in several ways. In particular, significant disparities within this population made for a great deal of difference in the conditions of a migrant's daily life. As in the case of their departure from the countryside, or in their insertion into urban labor markets, among their everyday lives once in the city we can starkly distinguish three broad modes of existence among these people. One urban lifestyle was protected by affiliation with the official framework or with its individual deputies; another was enclosed within the relative (and variable) safety of native-place enclaves; and only the third mode was drawn from itinerants who were forsaken, by dint of lacking any sort of useful bond at all.

We have examined these distinctions when it came to the housing arrangements, chances for getting grain and medical attention (and for getting sick), and educational opportunities enjoyed (or not enjoyed) by the members of these three gross sets of migrants. Some of those who were linked by place of origin (especially parts of Zhejiang), though deprived of even a minimum of the state-conferred benefits offered to the second-class citizens laboring in state firms, developed their own, sometimes quite sizable, villages in the cities, furnished with at least rudimentary city services, facilities, and infrastructure.

In all these dimensions of dailiness, possession of any of the resources pertinent to a time of transition from a planned, bureaucratically managed political economy to a market-based one could smooth the shocks of placement into a very unfriendly milieu. These resources were, respectively, cash (useful in the new, marketizing environment); connections to cadres (a legacy of the weight of the old, statist system); and membership in outsider communities (whose very institutional ambiguity was an emblem of a society in motion, undergoing change).[242]

In the transitional era when China was forsaking its socialist pattern, by the very act of sanctioning markets, its leadership was also involuntarily relinquishing its monopoly on the bestowal of the trappings of urban citizenship, insofar as these amounted to a share in the distribution of public goods and a right to membership in a community. The state was also thereby abandoning (if similarly unintentionally and surely unwillingly) its stranglehold over forms of association outside its own aegis. In short, because of their exclusion by the state institution of the *hukou*, combined with the workings of incipient markets, peasants in the cities—just by their presence alone—were participating in writing new rules of urban life.

These outsiders might not prefer to be the long-term recipients of just the unauthorized badge of belonging offered by the Zhejiang Village or rest content forever with the quality of the public goods they were dealt there. Still, for the interim, in their daily praxis these "villagers" were forging an alternative, nonauthoritative, ersatz form of urbanhood for themselves—one that for many was materially poorer than that of state-paid temporary workers, but better than that of vagabonds.

Theirs was a brand of citizenship that the government would eventually have to acknowledge, beyond the leadership's repetitive and ultimately useless coercive campaigns for driving migrants out of their settlements. Far more than migrants in other forms of polity, sojourners living in autonomous villages posed a most palpable challenge to a state with authoritarian pretensions, a state that had for years anchored its authority in its monopoly of supplying all needs, and controlling all activities, in the city.[243]

Conclusion: Floating to Where?

Citizenship and the Logic of the Market
in a Time of Systemic Transition

At the close of the century China shared with much of the world one particularly critical issue: how to handle the question of the citizenship of massive numbers of migrants pushing into its major cities. Everywhere the dilemma was stark: such transients are surely highly desirable for fueling a country's engine of economic growth. At the same time they inevitably seemed to many to threaten to diminish the pot of perquisites available to current members of the societies so invaded, while their cultural distinctiveness challenged whatever ethnic homogeneity these societies boasted.[1] Sojourning laborers were ever welcome to work, in short, but were seldom considered suitable candidates for citizenship.

This already tricky situation was even more complicated in China's case. For the first time in several decades, markets were appearing in the cities just as migrants were suddenly turning up there en masse, at the end of a reign of state socialism. The fallout from systemic transition—entailing both the novelty of market-supporting institutions but also the residues of the institutions of state socialism—interacted with the coming of outsiders, with multifold effects—for the newcomers, for the settled resident population, and for the state itself. And the combination meant uncertainty for all.

Accordingly, as for China at this point, T. H. Marshall's formulation about the evolution of citizenship is uncommonly open-ended. Marshall specifies,

> There is no universal principle that determines what those rights and
> duties [of citizenship] shall be, but societies in which citizenship is a
> developing institution create an image of an ideal citizenship against
> which achievement can be measured and toward which aspiration can
> be directed.[2]

277

Thus in China the sudden mixture of a multitude of peasant migrants with established urbanites in cities in the transition to a market economy offers researchers an important opportunity: the chance to speculate about how markets affect citizenship, in a context where markets are nascent and—precisely because of the incursion of markets—where the state's former capacity to determine definitively both the allocation of the goods of daily life and the roster of membership in the urban community is clearly waning. With what logic do markets affect this process? And what is the content of citizenship—the privileges of membership—under these circumstances; just who qualifies to receive them? These are the issues that this book addresses.

In many ways the contours of the subject parallel those present in the decline of the welfare state in the West. For in both cases populaces had to adapt to a new and less friendly regime: the welfare state, like state socialism, allayed the influence of the market, affording protection from market forces and substituting an alternate principle of distribution. And in both instances citizens accustomed to a set of rights resented the arrival of intruders just when they themselves were being made to confront the brunt of capitalism.

The reactions of the beneficiaries of the fading regimes to the demise of both institutions, socialism and the welfare state—and the chilly reception these beneficiaries accorded those they perceived as interlopers— suggest that capitalism, rather than promoting citizenship, may be antagonistic and detrimental to it, especially when it appears on the heels of a system of governmentally granted benefits.[3] Because of resistance and discrimination from the settled citizens, an influx of capitalism may actually delay newcomers' acquisition of membership rights—expressly because of interference from the lingering weight of those prior institutions and the expectations they created—rather than "liquidating traditional institutions" and thereby furthering the birth or expansion of citizenship, as Bryan S. Turner asserts.[4]

So in China's case, three older institutions—policies promulgated by officialdom, the cumbersome and well-entrenched bureaucracy, and the urban rationing regime—that had worked together to shore up citizenship remained in the reform era to contort the substance of that concept. And yet the migrants in the cities themselves—along with markets—had a major influence on the unfolding of policy, on the style of administration, and on the behavior of the managers, even as their presence and praxis contributed to refashioning the modes of distribution in the city. This reciprocally interactive relationship was apparent especially in the ways migrant workers created their own labor markets and in how some of them used markets to scrape together services central to survival in the cities, in the process depriving the state of its old ability to dispose of the work force and to distribute to the city populace exactly as it chose.

The mutually transforming relationship also emerged as once-peasants migrating into the cities were fitted—but also fitted themselves—into one of three forms of subsisting there. Some were included within state-sponsored regimens affording a second-tier citizenship; others fell back on their fellows from home, forging what could be labeled "ethnic enclaves," offering varying degrees of succor; and still others were left to roam the cities randomly in search of work and sustenance without any support.

Thus another major effect of markets on citizenship was their contribution to the formation of a virtual layering of types of citizens in cities— true citizens, second-class citizens, ersatz citizens (outside the state), and noncitizens—each of whom fared quite differently in the transition era. This new stratification of peasants living in cities replaced an earlier one, in which all peasants, in the city or country, were simply "second-class citizens" (*erdeng gongmin*).[5] Which outcome obtained for any given transients had much to do with their place of origin.

But the outcome had even more to do with migrants' previous peasanthood than it did for farmers who left the rural areas in other developing countries. Given the power of the *hukou* system, just the mere fact of being "peasants" in a Chinese city had a much more significant effect in overriding their own endowments than it did for ruralites in municipalities in most of the third world. For instance, a study of cities in Indonesia, Colombia, South Korea, and Iran in the mid-1970s found that,

> Occupational differences between migrants and natives reflect the background disadvantages of migrants rather than the impact of migration per se. . . . No obvious structural feature [inhibited] migrants from participating fully . . . relative to their skill level after a short settling-in period.[6]

Another investigator examining urban areas in Indonesia and the Philippines in the mid-1980s discovered that "occupational mobility is first a function of an individual's attributes."[7]

Also in support of my point are the words of a researcher in India who maintains that "existing socio-economic inequalities in the milieu of departure [especially land ownership and caste] are perpetuated and further sharpened by differential incorporation on arrival [in the city]."[8]

Thus, not all Indian farmers are barred from social incorporation in cities. And writing of Latin America, Bryan Roberts argues that the socioeconomic status of the family, as the chief determinant of its offspring's economic attainment (which in turn shapes the offspring's status in the cities), is more important than birth in the urban or rural areas.[9] These comparative findings illustrate the importance of context in assessing the effects of internal migration on citizenship. In particular they help me highlight the extent to which China's prior institutions, especially the *hukou*, could deter migration from the countryside from launching the mover on any linear path toward citizenship.

On a more positive note, perhaps the gaps in urban life in China that socialist arrangements had left vacant—such as the lack of a service sector—made for openings there that outsiders could move into and enlarge more easily than elsewhere. But the strategies they adopted in this process were similar enough to those of sojourning workers in other contexts to lead me to conclude that migrants, though frequently victims of discrimination, are really more than that. They are also sculptors of new spaces, generally beyond the reach of the state.[10] And as they create the spaces, they cannot but affect the state itself, especially when the state is undergoing a transition from one economic regime to another.

In the case of China, relevant political changes in the works did not appear to be moving in a direction beneficial to the migrants. Before the reform era, workers in state-owned enterprises obtained a variable but, at a minimum, basic package of welfare benefits, in addition to job security and relatively positive working conditions. But as underentitled and unentitled migrants who could do the same work became available in cities, and as market principles overran socialist mores, transients—and, if to a lesser extent, urban workers, as well—progressively had to take on the role of virtual drudges.

And as foreign investors increasingly inserted themselves into the economy as bosses in place of state managers and mistreated their employees, it began to look as if at least the local state had become, like the central one in India, the handmaiden of capital in "a common front against the fragmented and defenseless proletariat."[11] For a tacit alliance developed between local officials wishing to attract and hold onto foreign investment and the overseas entrepreneurs operating on their soil.[12] As two Chinese reporters interviewing in Guangdong province relayed the typical words of one of these officials, "Everyone knows the boss's pocket is fearsome, so no one wants to offend him. In labor-capital disputes, we management personnel often stand on the boss's side, very rarely say an impartial word for the migrant workers."[13]

Moreover, since the top leadership of the country refused through the 1990s to grant sojourning peasants the rights to associate in support of their interests or to become students in the regular schools (and even, up to 1996, to have any schools of their own), they denied them even the most fundamental tools just for "set[ting] the stage" for an entry into the polity, according to Reinhard Bendix.[14] The denial of rights and access, in conjunction with the absence of any meaningful elections at all in the cities, plus the refusal of the franchise to farmers there, meant that unlike in many third-world cities no entity within the state—and no party in opposition, for, of course, there were none in China at this time—would be motivated to seek their support.[15]

So, while state leaders and their bureaucrats were at once enticed by the rents they could capture from itinerants and also prodded by events outrunning their intentions to bend procedures, in order to stay atop the masses of migrants moving in their midst, they in no sense bowed to their entreaties. What does my analysis portend for the future form of citizenship for floating farmers in the metropolises?

To answer this query, should we look to structure or to agency? That is, is the future civic status of China's rural migrants to be explained by possible shifts in the structure that limited them through the 1980s and 1990s—shifts in which the leadership and its administrators would alter the rules of distribution and inclusion and admit peasants into the same regime of benefits that urbanites enjoy? Or should we instead turn to the floaters as agents and ask about the likely effectiveness of steps they might themselves take in the hope of improving their place in the city?

To begin with the structural, top-down answer, as the final words are being written in this book, the political leadership and its bureaucracy did seem willing to proceed over time—and in very tiny steps—to authorize gradual incorporation of a select group of migrants, but only into small towns in the rural areas. In late July 1997 the Ministry of Public Security, in cooperation with departments of planning, finance and economics, and construction, authorized the selection of 450 pilot county-level towns where economic and social development was relatively advanced, where there was a financial surplus, and where infrastructural facilities were adequate. There peasants who were pursuing legal, stable occupations or who had a steady source of livelihood and a secure, legal dwelling place, and who had already been resident for two years, were granted an urban *hukou*, complete with the right to send their children to school at subsidized rates and with eligibility for basic health and welfare benefits.[16]

Despite a promise to extend the experiment if successful, this study suggests several reasons for caution. In the first place, the mix of bureaucratic units charged with its execution were ones driven by disparate aims (as chapter 3 showed), which was sure to complicate coordination. Moreover, the list included some of the most recalcitrant among the bureaucracies. Its authorship by the public security ministry was particularly inauspicious.

In particular, Luo Gan, then vice chairman of the Central Committee for the Comprehensive Management of Public Security and secretary-general of the State Council, who announced the decision, had ominously warned the participants at a mid-1995 meeting on the reform of household registration that this issue was "directly related to the economic development and social stability of China."[17] And finally, among the list of reforms in this realm repeatedly announced beginning in 1984, some were quite similar in intent to this one.[18] But none had led to genuine first-class treatment for the peasants who partook of them.

What about the migrants as agents? Bryan S. Turner holds that "the critical factor in the emergence of citizenship is violence, that is, the overt and conscious struggle of social groups to achieve social participation."[19] And indeed there have been voices in China that do expect violence from the floating population, as this quotation from the sensationalist 1994 volume *Di sanzhi yanjing kan Zhongguo* (Seeing China through a third eye) evinces:

> The Chinese government can't find a solution at present to the *liumin* (roaming people) problem. It can't be stopped up or swept out; and the education and management of peasants who depart from the countryside to work are completely left on their own. The only measure that remains is for [the *liumin*] to create an explosive social movement; [then we could] mobilize the military police to suppress it . . . when this kind of disturbance erupts, they will shout some purely political or economic slogans.[20]

Even a scholar sympathetic to the migrants asserts that "if the government doesn't guide this [problem of mobile surplus rural labor], it will lead to large-scale social turmoil."[21]

But are there any symptoms that such turmoil is in the works, or that, should it occur, the leadership would be inclined to respond in a positive fashion, granting the rights demanded? True, some migrants did display a concern with rights and injustice—if mainly economic rights—almost as soon as they had made their way into the municipalities. One of the earlier manifestations was their feeling of unfairness over the blatant inequality they were forced to confront there. Journalists picked up the anger this engendered, much of it directed against the permanent population of the city. As an example:

> The peasants and semipeasants who enter the city feel comparatively deprived by the tightly locked city walls. Peasants coming in want to enjoy this fat meat with city people. When in the countryside, they feel that everyone is poor, so [their poverty] can be tolerated. But differences in wealth become obvious after entering the city. They feel, "The more you city people look down on me, the more I oppose you."[22]

Here is another, especially plaintive one:

> In the city, some people basically don't consider us to be people. They treat us as a thing. . . . We all appeal: the whole society shouldn't discriminate against peasant workers! Don't look down on country people![23]

With time, floaters demanded legal protection against the treatment they were receiving on the job, by remonstrating at public security stations and by calling in the press for the authorities to "please support our rights and interests (*qing weihu women quanyi*)."[24] Already in 1989 two roving journalists quoted peasant informants who also demonstrated an awareness of rights:

> We can't understand why some [construction] teams were paid nothing . . . they give us a receipt to stall us for some two or three years. Some never pay up. It makes peasant workers pour out endless grievances. We weren't paid for our rice as peasants, now we're not paid for our work. Why does this always fall on peasants' heads? Where have the state's banknotes gone?[25]

Another, elevating her misfortune to the level of the law, had an equally sorrowful tone:

> "They say everyone is equal before the law," complained a glass seller bullied and beaten up by thugs sent by a native competitor in Lanzhou, then given little solace by the local police. "Why can't we outside peasant workers be equal too?" she seemed to be howling.[26]

A few years later and on a somewhat larger scale, some 20 vegetable mongers from Zhejiang actually penned a protest to the city government in Beijing charging that "the market management people cheat outsiders" in assigning stall space.[27] Whether they received any reply is not documented.

By 1994, according to a survey undertaken among transient factory hands in the Pearl River Delta, at least 10 percent and sometimes as many as 61 percent of the workers in the firms there expressed each of these demands: for a guarantee of basic livelihood; for higher wages; for improved livelihood conditions; for better working conditions; and for equality of various sorts.[28] And, remarkably, in an early 1995 survey of leavers in 318 villages, as many as 79 percent of the respondents admitted that they felt that they lacked any guarantee of their rights and interests (quanyi).[29]

In response to these feelings, organized agitation had already begun to appear by the mid-1980s, with the emergence of unauthorized unions and illicit strikes. But unlike in Latin American cities, where, according to Roberts, "social movements are the most visible signs of the struggle to define and redefine citizenship," as protests initially growing out of neighborhood issues often expanded into citywide movements, in China localized efforts to redress wrongs foundered in the shallows.[30]

One of the first news releases described "thousands of peasants" from suburban factories protesting at party headquarters in Tianjin in mid-1985 against the city's refusal to grant them the cost-of-living raises provided regular urban residents. The protesters persisted for several days until police broke up their demonstration, detaining at least several hundred of them. According to the Agence France-Presse that publicized the incident, this was the third such demonstration around that time.[31]

By 1986, work stoppages and strikes were frequent among the temporary workers of the Shenzhen Special Economic Zone, home of a multitude of foreign-funded firms.[32] Incomplete statistics from Fujian's Xiamen, also an outpost for overseas capitalists, showed that the fifty strikes there in 1991 ballooned into a figure nine times as large within just two years.[33] The years 1992 and 1993 went on to witness more than a hundred strikes per year.[34]

Issues of treatment, hours, contract violation, and unsafe working conditions often figured in the resistance, though by far the majority of grievances—as many as 86 percent—in at least one city where statistics on this were recorded, were about pay.[35] In particular, workers attacked management for delaying or deducting from their wages.[36] There were also reports that many of the strikes specifically had revenge as a motive, surely evidence of feelings of rights that were wronged.[37]

Many of the actions occurred at foreign-funded plants, where foreign bosses must have generated more antagonism, especially given their often inhumane treatment of employees, along with workers' greater sense of freedom in expressing their outrage in such places. Besides, there were reportedly elements of anti-imperialism in such demonstrations.[38] In 1991, foreign-invested firms accounted for just 33 percent of the total number of enterprises in Shenzhen but were the sites for 68.6 percent of the total labor disputes.[39] Apparently some significant numbers of migrants were willing to brave the odds in the face of frightening official intransigence: 90 percent of the hundred strikes in foreign firms reported nationally in 1993 occurred in enterprises where trade unions did not play the role of mediators.[40] In some instances, it was the mobilization by outside labor activists that stirred up the migrants' bitterness.[41]

But not all of this organizational activity was activated by outsiders. There were also scattered stories of the workers themselves agitating for the right to form their own unions. For only the official All-China Federation of Trade Unions was recognized by the government, and its cadres were much more likely to suppress rather than to support signs of worker discontent;[42] any other association of workers was automatically labeled illegal.[43] In one case employees in a joint-venture hotel in Shanghai attempted to set up their own organization in summer 1993;[44] workers at a South Korean shoe company marched on the Tianjin labor bureau that autumn, demanding the right to establish a union for themselves.[45] In addition, some bold members of the floating temporary workers went ahead without permission and set up unregistered unions of their own. These organs sprang up mainly at joint-venture plants.[46]

When, in a rare exception, half of the four thousand migrant workers at a Zhuhai-based Hong Kong disk factory struck for three days with the support of official trade unionists, it was probably union assistance that convinced government officials to mediate, resulting in their meeting the workers' demands.[47] When we consider other cases of worker protest that found voice in the printed media, in almost all of them attempts at relief met with varying degrees of repression or rejection.

A typical example occurred when rampaging construction laborers outside Shenzhen wrecked a Communist Party headquarters in 1995. Their riot was brought to a halt with machine-gun fire by the local police, leading to the death of ten protesters.[48] At a Hong Kong subsidiary toy company in Shenzhen, three thousand female strikers out for better pay and working conditions finally forced an agreement for higher salaries. But the management denied every claim the workers made and threatened to relocate to the inland, where wages would be lower.[49] In another instance, after mediation, workers received less than half the pay raise requested, and their activists were dismissed from their jobs.[50]

Yet another time, when six hundred joint-venture workers in Shenzhen struck with the goal of getting the pay increase and improvement in working conditions that had been promised them, factory authorities refused to accede to the mediation efforts of local labor departments; some striking workers were beaten up and held in custody by security personnel. The upshot was a stand-off.[51] And a strike at a wholesale market for light industrial items in Fengtai district, Beijing, protesting over the "excessive taxation and unjustified fines" assessed by the local office of industry and commerce, and drawing in more than five hundred small traders, as in similar cases in the rural areas, found no adequate response.[52]

According to Anita Chan, factory management intransigence was bolstered by private security guards wielding electric batons and handcuffs, a very common presence on factory grounds in the 1990s. Though strikes among migrant workers involving the overall participation of as many as two hundred thousand workers had occurred by 1996, these tended to be relatively disorganized, spontaneous, one-shot events, unsupported by nearby laborers at other plants, and fairly easily squelched.[53] So, given the stance of the authorities, transients' awareness of injustice, even if not always baldly repressed, rarely got much redress.

Attempting a more peaceful approach, some peasants in Beijing intercepted the limousine of party chief and President Jiang Zemin in late 1996, in order to appeal for his help. In response, the city's public security bureau and central bodyguard bureau, along with the armed police, snapped into action, devising a detailed security plan to prevent any such "extreme act" from recurring.[54] Thus, through the mid-1990s increasingly frequent strikes and petitions among peasant workers in the cities, along with other products of the mounting consciousness of rights among them, relentlessly surged forward. Yet these initiatives were clearly no match for the regime; they were quickly shackled by its vigilant representatives executing its vigorous controls.

So if the outlook for peasant migrants' incorporation into urban society as citizens is essentially pessimistic whether we turn upward toward structure or downward toward agents, is the issue then settled? I contend that it is not. Granted, absent a radical transformation of the entire Chinese polity, the overwhelming majority of peasant migrants are not apt to become assimilated into urban society through an interpenetration of social networks of the type captured by the concept of "structural assimilation," whereby immigrants participate extensively in primary groups of the core society.[55]

Far more likely for the longer term is that that minority of once-ruralites who do remain in town over time will not all take their place socially in the city as second-class citizens; and they will not all become members of an underclass, as certain ethnic groups in the larger cities of Northern Europe and the United States are prone to do.[56] Yes, it may be accurate to assert (as some Chinese scholars do) for Anhui trash-pickers—at the bottom of the social heap in Beijing—that "occupationally they have very, very few opportunities to rise up or to see their fate basically change."[57]

But a more appropriate image of the floating population in the cities as a whole for the future is as a conglomeration, a mélange of collectivities. This heterogeneous mass will be arrayed not as in Bombay, according to race, religion, language, and caste,[58] nor as in the United States according to color, religion, income, culture, or proximity to the dominant ethnic group.[59] For Chinese floaters are by and large not divided up from proper urbanites by such markers. Instead its members will be distinguished in their fate in near-future China in terms of their relationship to institutions from the past: either by their ties to state officials and their positions in state-owned units; or by the social rank of their place of origin in the countryside, along with their own personal status among those in the city who left that place.

And yet another process is equally important in predicting how peasant migrants will fit into the pattern of social stratification in the cities in the coming years. The reform movement itself, the joint product of leadership choices and the unfolding of market forces, is rapidly draining the content of urban citizenship, as the privileges it once held diminish one by one.[60] No longer does membership mean what it once did. For no longer is the state holding itself responsible for allocating public goods even to its native urban dwellers. We can see this in the case of both job provision and state-bestowed welfare benefits.

The research of Wang Feng shows that the percentages of permanent, regular urbanites in Shanghai who found their jobs through the introduction of friends and relatives doubled for those hired over the period 1985 to 1995 from what they had been before (from 13.2 to 26.7 percent). Also over that time the percentage of those assigned to their jobs by local labor departments dropped by 36 percent (from 28 percent down to 18 percent); and the percentage who found jobs on their own went from 9 to 19 percent.[61] Among some 5,800 rural migrants in the city in October

1995, many more—47 percent—had been introduced to their places of work by relatives and friends, while 35 percent said they had found their jobs by themselves. But still, the trend indicated that urbanites were becoming more like migrants in their search for work.

The picture was similar in terms of benefits. Though only 10 percent of the migrants surveyed reported being in receipt of medical benefits, and fewer than 5 percent had any sort of pension, for city people the situation was clearly becoming worse with time. Where more than 80 percent of those hired before 1985 boasted medical insurance and over 90 percent had pensions, the percentage of those hired after 1985 with medical benefits dropped to 47 percent and of those with pensions, to 60 percent.[62]

This movement is contemporaneous with a decline in employment in the state- and collectively owned sectors in the urban areas (down from 78 percent in 1978 to 65 percent in 1995, and from 25 percent in 1985 to 18 percent in 1995, respectively), along with a rise in jobs in the private economy;[63] and with a marked increase in both the numbers and the proportions of posts in the service sector and in the informal sector generally, at the expense of those in the industrial sector.[64] Since the transients were for the most part working outside the state firms and mainly in the service and larger informal sectors, here again we find a growing convergence of sorts in the job situations of migrants and urbanites. All of these changes mean that Chinese urban society itself is undergoing a profound metamorphosis.[65]

But the market—first with its demand for the labor and services that the sojourners supplied in cities, later with its provision for them of the wherewithal for everyday existence, and finally with its opportunities for some few of them to amass wealth in the city—was not just revolutionizing urban society in ways that seemed to thrust outsiders in a direction not so different from that in which insiders were also traveling; it could also be a beneficent force in terms of their own daily lives. For it opened out a growing space for their daily activities as the state backed off in retreat. Overall, the market offered the floating population the opportunity to act as both the harbinger and the mirror of coming market society in China.

Still, left to itself, the market could not supply a full-fledged or permanent solution to the problem of citizenship for the transients. For as long as the state's repressive force dominated, there was no automatic pathway that could lead them as a group away from their confinement within parallel communities in the metropolises. Instead, institutional legacies, backed up by lingering coercive, authoritarian power at the top, forged a long-term tension between economic and political development.

As late as a decade and a half after state-authorized freedom of geographical mobility had moved millions of cultivators away from their fields, the agents and the agencies of the state had not yet caught up with their own rhetoric of law and rights; the only significant, behavioral transformation that had taken place among their ranks was their switch from behavior that just responded to bureaucratic commands toward action that created and traded in commodities and cash, including making commodities of the peasants themselves.

And yet, as the state's denials circumscribed the migrants' chances to satisfy their "rights and interests," the transients' own lives within their own urban markets were providing many of them with the tools of city existence, and tutoring them in urban-rooted protests for these interests. Moreover, because of the limited, purely socioeconomic, form that urban citizenship had taken for proper city residents in authoritarian China in the second half of the twentieth century—belongingness and a right to officially distributed goods, but no political rights—by that token just the mere presence of migrants subsisting in town made them semicitizens of the city.

Thus, the migrants—in conjunction with markets—were forging proto-citizens of themselves against the design of the state. For as the rules of the socioeconomy were altering about them, the migrants were also altering the rules. But the drama's final act was still in flux as the decade of the 1990s came to a close, dependent yet on decisions from the state. And this was a state much of whose leadership clung in desperation to sticky institutions, unwilling or unable to fulfill the promise of its own new, market-fostered discourse.

Given this obstinacy, plus the continuing clout in the capital to back it up, what may ultimately press the political elite to drop the official barriers against peasants' full and legitimate assimilation into the formal urban world? It will be more the specters of rebellion and upheaval or nightmares of an overwhelming of the structural foundations of the cities than it will be these actual events themselves.

Specters and nightmares owe their force to the confusion caused when migrants entered the cities along with markets. Their joint arrival encouraged the construction of awful images, as urbanites and politicians succumbed to the seduction of a metaphor linking migrants with markets, with everyone conflating the reality of the migrants with all the ills that markets were perceived as delivering. In the event, the mixture of migrants with markets, or of citizenship with capitalism, became a highly problematic one at best.

Notes

ZGXWS   Zhongguo xinwenshe (Chinese news agency [Beijing and Hong Kong])

ZM   *Zheng Ming* (Contend [Hong Kong])

ZRGGG   *Zhonghua renmin gongheguo guowuyuan gongbao* (Bulletin of the State Council of the Chinese People's Republic [Beijing])

CHAPTER 1

1. I use the term "peasant" quite intentionally (but also interchangeably with "farmer" or "ruralite") in this volume. I do so because in designating Chinese people living in or newly from the countryside, these people themselves and Chinese urbanites both use the Chinese word *nongmin* to convey a meaning that is similar in its inexactness and pejorative bias to the English word "peasant."

2. This sense of a mounting influx had an empirical basis: in the early 1980s several million peasants left the rural areas for the cities; by 1994 Ministry of Public Security statistics showed that the figure had shot up to a full 50 million (Ba jia, *Nongcun laodongli jingji*, A-03, 1; Zhang, "The Mobile Population," 23). See the appendix to this chapter for more detail.

3. I use this term, or sometimes "floaters," just for a shorthand version, and not because I agree with its implications of aimlessness.

4. I use the word "markets" to stand for the forces of supply and demand, which rely on profits and revenue generation as the motivators.

5. I am, admittedly loosely, equating "capitalism"—as an alternative to the command-driven economy of "socialism"—with the revival of the market mechanism and the concomitant driving force of profits in contemporary China.

6. Marshall, *Citizenship and Social Class*, 29; Turner, *Citizenship and Capitalism*, 23, 138; Lipset, "Some Social Requisites of Democracy"; Lipset, *Political Man*, 41; and Moore, *Social Origins*.

7. The migrants with whom I am concerned are those peasants dubbed the "floating population," people who have moved, usually just temporarily, from rural areas into the large cities of China, in order to better their incomes and their lot in life. I address the situation of just these sojourners, rather than considering all farmers moving anywhere in China in the post-Mao period because the interchange between the peasants who entered the major metropolises and the institutions of the state—between this excluded group and the full-blown "urban system" of the socialist state—was most direct and intense. See the appendix to this chapter for more on the definitions of these groups.

8. Walder, *Communist Neo-Traditionalism*.

9. Kornai, *The Socialist System*, 315.

10. See Lu and Perry, eds., *Danwei*.

11. *NMRB*, November 23, 1988, 3. For exceptions, see this chapter's appendix, note 13.

12. By "the state," I refer to the institution of citizenship, as delineated by the *hukou*, with its implications for distribution and belonging, and which relies on commands as motivator. I also consider the top leadership, relevant state policies, and the occupants of the various agencies of the official bureaucracy, to be components of "the state." This is similar to the usage of "state" in Skocpol, "Bringing the State."

13. Ding, "Xianxing huji guanli zhidu," 103.

14. *NMRB*, May 11, 1989, and November 23, 1988, 3.

15. Under the communes, set up in the late 1950s but dismantled with the onset of economic reform by 1982, peasants in their rural homes got a share of farm production, mutual assistance in labor, and, in most localities, rudimentary schooling and medical care. In most of rural China after the early 1980s, households were on their own or paid for these benefits.

16. Eckstein, "Civic Inclusion," 346.

17. Gong, "Zhongguo xianxing."

18. Dutton, editor's introduction, 8.

19. Brubaker, *Citizenship and Nationhood*, 24; on 180 he lists as crucial elements of citizenship "not only political rights but the unconditional right to enter and reside in the country, complete access to the labor market, and eligibility for the full range of welfare benefits."

20. Saiget, "Beijing Exiles," 33.

21. Solinger, "Human Rights Issues."

22. For Western Europe, see Rath, "Voting Rights," 128, where he states that "in most European countries, foreign residents do not have the right to vote or to run for office in local, regional or national elections"; Dutton, editor's introduction, 8, notes that in China the right to vote is denied those residing in a locale in which they are not permanent residents.

23. Brubaker, *Citizenship and Nationhood*, 21.

24. Thanks to Bin Wong and Kenneth Pomeranz for alerting me to this point.

25. Solinger, "The Floating Population in the Cities." On third-world cities, see Speare, Liu, and Tsay, *Urbanization and Development;* Goldscheider, "The Adjustment of Migrants"; Costello, Leinbach, and Ulack, *Mobility and Employment;* Chandra, *Social Participation;* Perlman, *Myth of Marginality;* Portes and Walton, *Urban Latin America;* Cornelius, *Politics and the Migrant Poor;* Lomnitz, *Networks and Marginality;* and Lloyd, *Slums of Hope?*

26. On the United States, see Feagin and Feagin, *Racial and Ethnic Relations,* Fainstein and Fainstein, "Urban Regimes and Black Citizenship," Massey and Denton, *American Apartheid,* and Harris, *The Harder We Run;* on South Africa, Seidman, *Workers' Movements in Brazil and South Africa,* and Wilson and Ramphele, *The South African Challenge.* Indeed, Chinese internal migrants had much in common with *indocumentos* in the United States, since for them as well the state's definition of their illegal status was

often combined with its denial to them of social welfare resources. See Rodriguez and Nunez, "An Exploration of Factors," 151–52.

27. Solinger, "Human Rights Issues."

28. Feagin and Feagin, *Ethnic and Racial Relations*, 15; Chan, "Post-Mao China," 145–47.

29. Turner, "Contemporary Problems," 2.

30. Soysal, *Limits of Citizenship*, 119; Meehan, *Citizenship and the European Community*, 22; Brubaker, *Citizenship and Nationhood*, 21; Layton-Henry, "The Challenge," 12.

31. Marshall, *Citizenship and Social Class*; Meehan, *Citizenship and the European Community*, 2.

32. Brubaker, introduction, 20; García, "Cities and Citizenship," 7; Turner, "Contemporary Problems," 9; and Barbalet, *Citizenship*, 17, 20.

33. For instance, see Barbalet, *Citizenship*, 2; Meehan, *Citizenship and the European Community*, 18; Heater, *Citizenship*, 246; and Freeman, "Migration," 53.

34. Meehan, *Citizenship and the European Community*, 17; Marshall, *Sociology at the Crossroads*, 87.

35. García, "Cities and Citizenship," 8, 9; Hollifield, *Immigrants, Markets, and States*, 18.

36. Turner, "Contemporary Problems," 9; Soysal, *Limits of Citizenship*, 12, 137; Barbalet, *Citizenship*, 72, 77; García, "Cities and Citizenship," 7–8; Hollifield, *Immigrants, Markets, and States*, 18.

37. Barbalet, *Citizenship*, 2; Meehan, *Citizenship and the European Community*, 20.

38. Soysal, *Limits of Citizenship*, 12. See also Cornelius, Martin, and Hollifield, "Ambivalent Quest"; and Hollifield, *Immigrants, Markets, and States*.

39. *Constitution of the People's Republic of China*, 31. The constitution was adopted on December 4, 1982, by the Fifth National People's Congress, fifth session.

40. On the role of the market in pre-1980 China, see Solinger, *Chinese Business*; chapter 2 of the present volume addresses the state's position on migration before the reform era.

41. Solinger, "China's Urban Transients."

42. Wang, "Invisible Walls," 18, referring to peasants purchasing the *hukou* in small towns. This is not always the case in the larger cities, however. Sometimes the purchased *hukou* can help, for instance, in enrolling one's children in an urban school.

43. My approach here resonates with that used in the volume Migdal, Kohli, and Shue, eds., *State Power and Social Forces*.

44. On this point, see Freeman, "Migration," 52, 62; Esping-Andersen, *Three Worlds*, 3; and Turner, *Citizenship and Capitalism*.

45. As Turner, *Citizenship and Capitalism*, 8–9, notes, the very institu-

tion of citizenship "generates political conflicts by raising expectations about entitlements."

46. See Calavita, "U.S. Immigration," 65, where she links the anxiety caused by economic uncertainty to hostility toward immigrants. Also, Gerber, "Cutting Out Shylock"; and Solberg, *Immigration and Nationalism*. They link negative native perceptions of an immigrant group to the confrontation locals are undergoing with expanding commercial capitalism and urbanization, respectively.

47. Gourevitch, *Politics in Hard Times*; Freeman, "Migration"; Cornelius, Martin, and Hollifield, "Ambivalent Quest," 33–34; Brubaker, introduction, 20; García, "Cities and Citizenship," 8, 15; Layton-Henry, "The Challenge," 12; Faist and Häussermann, "Immigration, Social Citizenship," 82, 97; Soysal, *Limits of Citizenship*, 134; and Messina, "The Not So Silent Revolution." See Ferge, "Social Citizenship" for a description of this mood in Eastern Europe with the end of socialism there.

48. See Almond, "Capitalism and Democracy," 468–69, who cites such authors as Joseph Schumpeter, Barrington Moore, Peter Berger, Robert A. Dahl, Karl Deutsch, Seymour Martin Lipset, and Daniel Lerner as attesting that there is a positive correlation between capitalism and democracy.

CHAPTER 1 APPENDIX

49. Goldstein and Goldstein, "Population Mobility," 91–97. Despite this official distinction, I use floater and migrant interchangeably in this study, in accord with common English parlance. For an incisive and thorough discussion of the methodological issues touched upon here, see Scharping, "Studying Migration."

50. Wu, "Guanyu liudong renkou," 44.

51. Sometimes Chinese documents and studies distinguish between "permanent migrants" who have managed to have their *hukou* altered and "temporary migrants" who have not. The 1990 census tabulated long-term temporary migrants (who remained more than a year within their current place of residence) but not short-term temporary migrants (present in a given city for less than a year). Thanks to Wang Feng for suggesting I include this material.

52. Layton-Henry, "The Challenge," 5, states that "in most European countries the official definition of an immigrant is of a person who moves to a country and resides there for longer than a specified period which is often quite short, usually from three to six months." Since I will be discussing only the floating population and not what the Chinese consider "migrants" (*qianyizhe*), except where explicit comparisons are being made between floaters and migrants, I will use the terms interchangeably.

53. Wu, "Guanyu liudong renkou," 44.

54. Ibid., 44–45.

55. Author's interview on May 13, 1992.

56. Banister, "One Billion," 16.

57. Wu, "Guanyu liudong renkou," 43.

58. According to Bauer et al., "Gender Inequality," 335, in 1987, 18 percent of the Chinese population possessed the urban *hukou*. The "urban" (or, as also termed, the nonagricultural) population into the 1990s (even after the termination of grain rationing) was a concept based on whether individuals were entitled to grain rationed by the state at low, subsidized prices or whether they depended on the rural commune (before 1982) or themselves (after the dissolution of the communes) for grain.

59. Potter and Potter, *China's Peasants*, 307–10; Cohen, "Cultural and Political Inventions," 159. Chan, *Cities with Invisible Walls*, 47, suggests that in the 1980s the numbers who had their registration converted in these ways, several million per year, were still quite a minuscule proportion of those who would have wished to be converted.

60. Li and Hu, *Liudong renkou*, 30.

61. Wu, "Guanyu liudong renkou," 43.

62. See Ostrom, *Governing the Commons*, 29–33, for a discussion of this concept.

63. Li and Hu, *Liudong renkou*, 3.

64. For example, Zhang, "Dui woguo liudong renkou," 3, states that a frequent estimate for the floating population was at that time 40 million; by August 14, 1988, 8, *RMRB* cited a figure of 50 million, an increase of 25 percent in just over two years.

65. For Fuzhou, FBIS, December 22, 1989, 21 (translated from *RMRB*, December 2, 1989), states that they accounted for one-fourth of that city's permanent population in late 1989; Vogel, *One Step Ahead*, 218, says that they constituted one-third of the population of Guangzhou by 1987; in Beijing, in 1988, the resident population was 10 million, and the official count of the floating population was 1.2 million (XH, November 2, 1988); and in Wuhan in 1990, according to the local labor bureau, there were 750,000 peasants (a number equal to 22 percent of the 3.4 million permanent residents). In Harbin, the figure was about one-tenth, according to demographers interviewed at the Heilongjiang Provincial Social Science Federation, July 18, 1991. The ratio of floaters to permanent resident population has also been given as one to three in Guangzhou, one to five in Beijing, and one to 3.7 in Shanghai, as of the end of 1989 (FBIS, January 19, 1990, 11; and Gu, "Renkou qianyi," 45). In Shanghai, there were reported to be 1.83 million, in Beijing, 1.15 million, and in Guangzhou, 1.1 million as of the late 1980s (*WWP*, April 18, 1990, 4, in FBIS, April 27, 1990, 39). These figures pertain to anyone present for any reason in cities without registered residence and therefore include persons who do not fit our definition of floaters. At the same time, large numbers of floaters fail to register their presence in the city, again complicating the count.

66. Li, "Surplus Rural Laborers," 12 (manuscript version), citing the research of the Wuhan University demographer Gu Shengzu.

67. Liang, "Zhongguo dalu liudong renkou," 39; and Nongyebu, "Jingji fazhanzhong," 43. Yang, "Temporary Residents," 103, cites *RMRB*, July 9, 1995, as claiming 80 million floating people nationwide. But a State Council researcher noted that probably only about 50 million of these were rural to urban migrants and that just 30 million of them crossed provincial borders (FBIS, August 12, 1994, 24).

68. Banister, "China: Internal and Regional Migration," 77.

69. Mallee, "Agricultural Labour," 2.

70. Xie, "Chengshi liudong renkou," 73–75.

71. Author's interview at the Guangzhou Urban Planning Automation Center, May 11, 1992.

72. This study is published in "Zhongguo 1986 nian 74 chengzhen," 6.

73. Gao, "Qianyi liudong renkou."

74. Li and Hu, *Liudong renkou*, 118, cite 70 million plus; Zhang in "Woguo liudong renkou," 13, mentions "nearly 70 million" as of 1990. In late summer 1993, FBIS, August 24, 1993, 50, quoting a Hong Kong journal, *Tangtai* (Trends), and August 24, 1993, 12, quoting the Chinese *GMRB*, respectively, spoke of a "vagrant population" of 160 million; and over 80 million "migratory laborers."

75. Chan, "Financing Local Government," ch. 3, 12.

76. Li and Hu, *Liudong renkou*, 15.

77. *WWP*, April 18, 1990, 4, translated in FBIS, April 29, 1990, 39. Chapter 5 treats this topic further.

78. *CD*, June 27, 1992, 3.

79. Wu and Xin, "Dadishang," 2, claim that nationally there were more than 200 million surplus laborers in the cities and the countryside as of the late 1980s. Of this total, they estimate that some 50 to 70 million entered the ranks of the floating population. Other researchers come up with different figures: Tian and Zhang, "Renkou qianyi liudong," believe that there are 220 million surplus laborers in the countryside alone, whereas Zhang, "Woguo liudong renkou," 14, surmises that there were 160 million surplus agricultural workers in 1990. But the *Gongren ribao* (Workers' daily), May 3, 1991, 3, referred to a rural surplus labor force of only 100 million. According to *WWP*, April 18, 1990, 4, arable land decreased from 1.5 billion *mu* (one *mu* is equal to one-sixth of an acre) in 1952 to 1.4 billion by the late 1980s, while rural labor forces shot up from 173.17 million in the earlier year to 323.08 by the later one.

80. ZGXWS, February 19, 1997, translated in *SWB*, FE/2848 (February 20, 1997), G/10.

81. Li and Hu, *Liudong renkou*, 11–12. According to the accounts of the different cities covered in this volume, 75 percent of those in Wuhan hold the rural *hukou* and 73 percent are from Hubei province, of which Wuhan is the capital (ibid., 167); in Chengdu, 84.5 percent come from Sichuan province, but only 58 percent are rural people (ibid., 219); and in both north central Taiyuan and East China's Hangzhou the peasant proportion approximated

that in Central China's Wuhan (74.4 percent in the former and 71.64 in the latter [ibid., 241 and 265, respectively]).

82. Nongyebu, "Jingji fazhanzhong," 43.

83. Zhang, Zhao, and Chen, "1994: Nongcun laodongli," 27.

84. Nongyebu, "Jingji fazhanzhong," 43.

85. Zhang, Zhao, and Chen, "1994: Nongcun laodongli," 27.

86. Ibid.; Nongyebu, "Jingji fazhanzhong," 43.

87. Xinhua, April 29, 1995, in FBIS, May 1, 1995, 85.

88. Wang and Zuo, "Rural Migrants in Shanghai," 4.

89. Guangdong wailai, "Zai liudongzhong," 113. Thanks to Shaoguang Wang for bringing this article to my attention.

90. Zhang, Zhao, and Chen, "1994: Nongcun laodongli," 27.

91. Li and Hu, *Liudong renkou*, 13. More material on this, and on marital status appears in chapter 7.

92. This is according to Wang and Jiang, "Baiwan 'yimin,'" 28, and is probably an impressionistic more than a scholarly figure. Rutkowski, "The China's Floating Population," 42, finds that men accounted for only 58.24 percent of the floaters in Guangzhou, in the same region. Li and Hu, *Liudong renkou*, 193, however, come up with a figure of 67.76 percent for men in Guangzhou as of late 1989, early 1990.

93. Ba jia, *Nongcun laodongli jingji*, A-03, 3.

94. Li and Hu, *Liudong renkou*, 14.

95. Nongyebu, "Jingji fazhanzhong," 45. Another study, this one in 318 villages in 29 provinces, carried out a year later, reports that 9.77 percent had been to senior high or above, while 54 percent had been to junior high; these figures were, respectively, higher than those among the total rural population by 2.57 and 17.4 percentage points (Zhang, Zhao, and Chen, "1994: Nongcun laodongli," 27).

96. Zhang, Zhao, and Chen, "1994: Nongcun laodongli," 27.

97. Chapman and Prothero, "Themes in Circulation," 598, 602. Goldstein and Goldstein, "Population Mobility," 41, refer to the Chinese floaters as "rural-to-urban circulators," following this usage.

CHAPTER 2

1. Feagin, *Racial and Ethnic Relations*, 20, defines this term.

2. According to Meehan, *Citizenship and the European Community*, 18, "A subject may be of the same nationality as a citizen and the lives of the two are regulated by laws passed by the same political authority, but, unlike the citizen, the subject has no rights to participate."

3. Marx, of course, held out the elimination of the distinction between city and countryside as one of the chief goals of the future Communist society. See Meisner, "Utopian Socialist Themes," 33–34; and Marx and Engels, "Manifesto," 28.

4. Mote, "Transformation of Nanking," 102, 103, 114, and 117; Rozman,

Urban Networks, 55–56, 89; Cohen, "Cultural and Political Inventions," 156–57; Whyte, "The Rural-Urban Gap," 4; and Whyte, "The Social Roots."

5. Barth, introduction; Mandel, "Ethnicity and Identity," 71–72; and Honig, *Creating Chinese Ethnicity,* 9, 36.

6. Cheng and Selden, "The City," 19.

7. Davis, "Urban Job Mobility," 101; and Kirkby, *Urbanisation in China,* 27.

8. On Marx's concept of the industrial reserve army, see Howard and King, *The Political Economy of Marx,* 98; see Hollifield, *Immigrants, Markets, and States,* 75–76, 215–16, on using international migrants for this purpose.

9. Hechter, *Internal Colonialism,* 8–9, 30–34; Feagin and Feagin, *Racial and Ethnic Relations,* 26.

10. Wong, *China Transformed,* ch. 4; and Lee and Wong, "Population Movements."

11. Wong, *China Transformed;* Rowe, HANKOW: *Commerce and Society,* 235–36, states that Chinese citizens under the Qing (as under earlier rules) were required to register in a given locality. But the purpose was not to deter geographic movement, but to enable the state to keep track of the population. Dutton, *Policing and Punishment,* 40–67, also discusses the household register, tracing its origins back to the Zhou dynasty and before. Its chief purpose of social control, Dutton finds, reflects the earlier dynasties' goal of administering corvée labor, collecting taxes, and conscripting soldiers (and later distributing aid), rather than limiting movement; also see Gong, "Zhongguo xianxing."

12. On provisioning, see Etienne-Will, Wong, and Lee, *Nourish the People.*

13. Lee, "Migration and Expansion," 22.

14. Mote, "Transformation of Nanking," 103; Rozman, *Urban Networks,* 89; Skinner, "Mobility Strategies," 35; Skinner, "Chinese Peasants and the Closed Community"; and Lary, "Hidden Migrations," 57.

15. Lee, "Migration and Expansion," 21, 26, 31, 34; Lee and Wong, "Population Movements," 54. Ho, *Studies on the Population of China,* chs. 7 and 10, document these more disaster-driven movements.

16. Rowe, HANKOW: *Community and Conflict,* 37, 43, 217; Rowe, HANKOW: *Commerce and Society,* 215–22.

17. Lee and Wong, "Population Movements," claim that this occurred for the first time only around 1900.

18. Mote, "Transformation of Nanking," 103; and Lee, "Migration and Expansion," 34.

19. Here I am simplifying greatly, for some dynasties, notably the Han, Tang, and Qing, had considerably more ambitious projects than others.

20. An exception here would be the Manchus' restriction against immigration into their homeland after they became the rulers of China in 1644.

This prohibition was increasingly contravened after about 1850, however. See Shi, "Heilongjiang diqu."

21. Mote, "Transformation of Nanking," 117.

22. Rowe, HANKOW: Community and Conflict, 46; Rozman, Urban Networks, 84–85.

23. According to Rowe, HANKOW: Commerce and Society, 236–37, only taxpaying landowners in the county for 20 years or descendants of such an owner could change their registration, after submitting a substantial monetary contribution.

24. This statement was not universally true, but it describes a strong tendency. See Rozman, Urban Networks, 88, and Rowe, HANKOW: Commerce and Society, 220–22.

25. Skinner, "Mobility Strategies," and Skinner, "Urban Social Structure," 539–40.

26. Lee, "Migration and Expansion," 34, 35.

27. Ibid., 35; and Skinner, "Urban Social Structure," 542.

28. Hershatter, The Workers of Tianjin; Lang, Chinese Family; Honig, Sisters and Strangers; Honig, Creating Chinese Ethnicity; and Perry, Shanghai on Strike.

29. Wakeman, Shanghai Police, 85.

30. Hershatter, The Workers of Tianjin, especially ch. 3.

31. Wakeman and Yeh, introduction, 8.

32. Honig, Sisters and Strangers, Hershatter, The Workers of Tianjin, and Perry, Shanghai on Strike. Honig, Creating Chinese Ethnicity, explores the notion of a hierarchy among native places. See also Goodman, Native Place, 14.

33. Goodman, Native Place, 63.

34. Kirkby, Urbanisation in China, 34.

35. On this, see Lary, "Hidden Migrations"; and Yang, "Temporary Residents."

36. Dutton, Policing and Punishment, 196, 206; Lewis and Rowland, Population Redistribution, 21–22; Hoffmann, Peasant Metropolis, 52; and Matthews, The Passport Society, chs. 2 and 3; ch. 1 traces the Russian tradition back to Peter the Great.

37. Hoffmann, Peasant Metropolis, 53; Mitchell, "Work Authority in Industry," 692; Grandstaff, Interregional Migration, 58; and Fitzpatrick, Stalin's Peasants, 96–100, 165.

38. Stuart and Gregory, "A Model of Soviet"; and Lewis and Rowland, Population Redistribution, 18; on 27, they even characterize population movement in the Soviet Union as "predominantly free," a statement that could certainly not be made about China.

39. Fitzpatrick, Stalin's Peasants, 97.

40. Lewis and Rowland, Population Redistribution, 14–15; Grandstaff, Interregional Migration, 3–4.

41. Dutton, *Policing and Punishment*, 189, 203, 198, 195; Grandstaff, *Interregional Migration*, 86.

42. Ofer, "Economizing on Urbanization," 289.

43. Fallenbuchi, "Internal Migration," 305–27; Hawrylyshyn, "Yugoslavian Development"; and Konrad and Szelenyi, "Social Conflicts."

44. Underurbanization is a term coined by Konrad and Szelenyi, "Social Conflicts," 206. According to ibid., 223–24, Hawrylyshyn, "Yugoslavian Development," 329, and Ofer, "Economizing on Urbanization," 295, commuting was the usual solution chosen by ruralites who had managed to secure urban employment throughout these countries.

45. Mitchell, "Work Authority in Industry," 689; Fitzpatrick, *Stalin's Peasants*, 93–96, 165; and Lewis and Rowland, *Population Redistribution*, 15, 21–27.

46. Dutton, *Policing and Punishment*, 202, 213; Lewis and Rowland, *Population Redistribution*, 23–25.

47. Lewis and Rowland, *Population Redistribution*, 23, 25, 27. Erlanger, "Russia to Replace," alleges that "many thousands managed to live illegally" in the cities.

48. Cheng and Selden, "The City," 25.

49. Kraus, *Class Conflict*; Potter and Potter, *China's Peasants*, 296–310, use the term "status group" to describe the difference between urbanites and ruralites in pre-1978 China.

50. Gong, "Zhongguo xianxing," 32.

51. Zhongguo nongcun laodongli, "Zhongguo nongcun laodongli jiuye."

52. Honig, *Creating Chinese Ethnicity*, 132, 4–5, and 9–10.

53. Potter and Potter, *China's Peasants*, 297. The order was the Directive on Establishing a System for Registration of Permanent Households, published in Guowuyuan fazhiju, *Zhongguo renmin gongheguo fagui huibian*, 1:197–200, and translated in Zhang, "Basic Facts," 103–6.

54. Gong, "Zhongguo xianxing," 34.

55. "Huji yanjiu" ketizu, "Xianxing huji guanli zhidu," 85.

56. Gong, "Zhongguo xianxing," 32. See also Ding, "Huji guanli," 28.

57. See Rossabi, *China and Inner Asia*, ch. 10; Schwarz, "Chinese Migration"; and Dreyer, "Go West," on the regime's efforts to move native Chinese out to the frontier areas dominated by minority peoples.

58. Chan, "Rural-Urban Migration"; and Chan, *Cities with Invisible Walls*.

59. "Huji yanjiu" ketizu, "Xianxing huji guanli zhidu," 83–84.

60. Keeping peasants on the land was in disregard of both the Common Program, created as an interim state constitution in 1949, and of the first posttakeover formal constitution of 1954. These documents decreed that there would be freedom of migration. See Cheng and Selden, "The City," 3. The next (1975) and subsequent constitutions, however, omitted this freedom. See "Huji yanjiu" ketizu, "Xianxing huji guanli zhidu," 83.

61. Zhang, "Basic Facts," 74.

62. Emerson, "The Labor Force," 242; Christiansen, "The Legacy," 419; and Mallee, "China's Household Registration," 4.

63. White, *Policies of Chaos*, 90; White, *Careers in Shanghai*, 150; Friedman, Pickowicz, and Selden, *Chinese Village*, 202; Emerson, "Employment," 420; Emerson, "Urban School-Leavers," 7–8; Banister, *China's Changing Population*, 331; and Kirkby, *Urbanisation in China*, 36–37.

64. Chan, *Cities with Invisible Walls*, 145. On other third-world cities, see Davis, "The Urbanization," 18; and Browning, "Migrant Selectivity," 311.

65. Zhang, "Luelun woguo," 37, maintains that population controls on urban residence were necessary because "we have to feed the urban population." Walder, "The Remaking," 28, and Potter and Potter, *China's Peasants*, 467, both explain the inability of the urban economy, as early as the 1950s, to employ on a formal permanent basis all of those who potentially would have wished to enter the urban labor force. See also Cheng, "Internal Migration," 56.

66. "Huji yanjiu" ketizu, "Xianxing huji guanli zhidu," 86; and Ding, "Xianxing huji guanli zhidu," 18.

67. Cheng, "Internal Migration," 50; Wang, "Renkou qianyi liudong," 44; and Chan, "Rural-Urban Migration."

68. Banister, *China's Changing Population*, 327; Cheng and Selden, "The City," 3; and Zhang, "Luelun woguo," 35–36.

69. Shanghai shi, *Shanghai liudong renkou*, 59.

70. Zhang, "Luelun woguo," 36.

71. Unless otherwise indicated, the following draws upon ibid.; Emerson, "Employment," 421; and Cheng and Selden, "The City," 10–12.

72. *Survey of China Mainland Press* (Hong Kong) 554 (1953): 24–25, from *RMRB*, April 17, 1953; an editorial commenting on the directive is in *RMRB*, April 20, 1953, translated in *Survey of China Mainland Press* 555 (1953): 23–24.

73. *RMRB*, March 15, 1954.

74. Bernstein, *Up to the Mountains*, 34.

75. Emerson, "The Labor Force," 242.

76. Friedman, Pickowicz, and Selden, *Chinese Village*, 193, 202.

77. Mu, "Zhongguo nongye shengyu laodong," 10.

78. Guowuyuan fazhiju, *Zhongguo renmin gongheguo fagui huibian*, 4: 225–26; and ibid., 5:100–102, respectively.

79. Kirkby, *Urbanisation in China*, 27; Howe, *Employment and Economic Growth*, 27, 70–71, 788–79.

80. Emerson, "Urban School-Leavers," 7; Zhang, "Luelun woguo," 36.

81. Walder, *Communist Neo-Traditionalism*, 36; see also Potter, "The Position of Peasants," 467. Emerson, "Employment," 418, states that, according to official figures, urban population grew from 71.6 to 99.5 million between 1953 and 1957.

82. Guowuyuan fazhiju, *Zhongguo renmin gongheguo fagui huibian,* 6: 481–83; and *RMRB,* December 14, 1957.

83. Cheng and Selden, "The City," 22. Kirkby, *Urbanisation in China,* 25. See also Perry and Li, *Proletarian Power,* 100.

84. Perry and Li, *Proletarian Power,* ch. 4.

85. Emerson, "Employment," 421; Emerson, "The Labor Force," 251–53; Howe, *Wage Patterns,* 107–8; Howe, *Employment and Economic Growth,* 135; Walder, *Communist Neo-Traditionalism,* 48–51; and Blecher, "Peasant Labour."

86. Guowuyuan fazhiju, *Zhongguo renmin gongheguo fagui huibian,* 6: 229–32. See also Zhang, "Luelun woguo," 36–37, and Kirkby, *Urbanisation in China,* 24. These organs are the detention centers (*shourongsuo*), still at work in China's cities as of the mid-1990s.

87. White, "Workers' Politics," 108; and Emerson, "Urban School-Leavers," 10. Within two months the State Council deemed it necessary to introduce supplementary measures in light of failure to comply. See Guowuyuan fazhiju, *Zhongguo renmin gongheguo fagui huibian,* 7:194–95.

88. These were the Regulations on Household Registration in the People's Republic of China, in Guowuyuan fazhiju, *Zhongguo renmin gongheguo fagui huibian,* 7:204–16, and translated in Zhang, "Basic Facts," 87–92.

89. In Zhang, "Basic Facts," 96–97.

90. Cheng, "Internal Migration," 51.

91. See Banister, *China's Changing Population,* 331; Cheng and Selden, "The City," 23–24; and Kirkby, *Urbanisation in China,* 17.

92. Taylor, "Rural Employment Trends," 742. Banister, *China's Changing Population,* 330, however, counts only 19 million. Walder, *Communist Neo-Traditionalism,* 36, says that employment in industry increased from 7.5 to 23 million just in the one year 1957–58.

93. Korzec, "Contract Labor," 120.

94. Kirkby, *Urbanisation in China,* 49; Cheng and Selden, "The City," 24–25.

95. Bernstein, *Up to the Mountains,* 35–36.

96. Walder, *Communist Neo-Traditionalism,* 36.

97. For relevant documents, see Lu, "The Origins," 68.

98. Emerson, "Employment," 422. Emerson, "The Labor Force," 242, cites Deng Xiaoping as having admitted to "more than 20 million" thrown out of cities between 1959 and 1961.

99. Kirkby, *Urbanisation in China,* 27, 49.

100. Walder, "The Remaking," 19; Cheng and Selden, "The City," 25–26; Lu, "The Origins," 69; Banister, *China's Changing Population,* 333; and Wang, "The Breakdown," 5–6; on 6, Wang says that "after 1961, the type of hukou became a document of entitlement."

101. Walder, "The Remaking," 5, 14. Walder, *Communist Neo-Traditionalism,* 51–54, details four types of temporary workers laboring in state firms as of the late 1970s and the treatment accorded each.

102. Evidence that this was under way is a set of State Council provisional regulations on state enterprises utilizing temporary staff and workers, of October 14, 1962, in Guowuyuan fazhiju, *Zhongguo renmin gongheguo fagui huibian*, 13:220–23. See Korzec, "Contract Labor," 127; and Bernstein, *Up to the Mountains*, 42.

103. According to "Huji yanjiu" ketizu, "Xianxing huji guanli zhidu," 83, in August 1964, the State Council passed a draft regulation authored by the Ministry of Public Security strictly limiting peasants entering cities and towns.

104. Korzec, "Contract Labor," 127.

105. Emerson, "Urban School-Leavers," 10; Kirkby, *Urbanisation in China*, 28; and Korzec, "Contract Labor," 121.

106. On Jiang's sympathy, see Perry and Li, *Proletarian Power*, 101.

107. Ibid., 100.

108. Emerson, "The Labor Force," 253, attributes this decision to Zhou Enlai and says that it was taken "by 1970"; Korzec, "Contract Labor," 121, says that the State Council made the ruling in November 1971. Perry and Li, *Proletarian Power*, 116, state that this was done in response to pressures workers raised during the Cultural Revolution.

109. Bernstein, *Up to the Mountains;* see 42; and Kirkby, *Urbanisation in China*, 28.

110. Zhou, "Urbanization Problems," 24.

111. Lardy, *Agriculture*, 196. Walder, *Communist Neo-Traditionalism*, 48, states that 13 million temporaries were working in state industrial enterprises as of 1980, of whom 9 million were legally rural residents.

112. Korzec, "Contract Labor," 127; "Huji yanjiu" ketizu, "Xianxing huji guanli zhidu," 83, refers to a November 1977 State Council order against peasants entering cities and towns.

113. Zhang, "Luelun woguo," 36, and Cheng and Selden, "The City," 14. White, *Policies of Chaos*, 90, however, avers that early registration was mainly aimed at capturing refugees from the land reform movement.

114. Cheng and Selden, "The City," 21.

115. Dutton, *Policing and Punishment*, 207; and Cheng and Selden, "The City," 11.

116. Cheng and Selden, "The City," 14; Zhang, "Luelun woguo," 36.

117. See note 53.

118. Guowuyuan fazhiju, *Zhongguo renmin gongheguo fagui huibian*, 2:566–74; at the same time the State Council also passed its order on the unified purchase and sale of grain in the countryside, in ibid., 575–85.

119. Guowuyuan fazhiju, *Zhongguo renmin gongheguo fagui huibian*, 2:411–17.

120. See note 88.

121. Section 15 calls for registering one's presence in the city after three days; Section 16 calls for acquiring formal legal extension of the registration if one remains more than three months.

122. Noted in Cheng and Selden, "The City," 21.

123. Potter and Potter, *China's Peasants*, 301.

124. "Huji yanjiu" ketizu, "Xianxing huji guanli zhidu," 82.

125. Solinger, *Chinese Business*, ch. 2; Banister, *China's Changing Population*, 330.

126. See note 118.

127. Wang, "The Breakdown," 5–6; Cheng and Selden, "The City," 20, 24, 25; and Kirkby, *Urbanisation in China*, 26, 27, 155. Chan, *Cities with Invisible Walls*, 76, states that food grain shortages in the early 1960s motivated the restraints on urban population size.

128. Cheng and Selden, "The City," 14.

129. Li and Hu, *Liudong renkou*, 15.

130. Chan, *Cities with Invisible Walls*, ch. 4, makes the same argument.

131. Taylor, "Rural Unemployment Trends."

132. According to Taylor and Banister, "China: The Problem," iii, open underemployment rose from less than 10 percent of the rural agricultural work force in 1978 to 36 percent by 1987; and Mallee, "Agricultural Labour."

133. See, for instance, Park and Rozelle, "Promoting Economic Development."

134. Yan, "The Movement of Labor," 528.

135. Li and Hu, *Liudong renkou*, 15.

136. As much as 75 percent of realized foreign direct investment in Guangdong province came from Hong Kong as of the early 1990s, according to Goodman, "The PLA and Regionalism," 5. This investment would not have appeared had it not been for the preferential policies granted the province (Vogel, *One Step Ahead*, 85–86); in 1992, 33 percent of foreign direct investment nationwide went to Guangdong province (*JETRO China Newsletter*, 22). After the central government conferred similar policies on Shanghai's Pudong region in April 1990, migrants flooded that area; possibly as many as a million descended there at New Year 1993 (Benkan jije, "Mingongchao," 7). Fan, "Economic Opportunities," demonstrates the connection between Guangdong as a magnet locale for migrants and the high level of foreign investment there.

137. Lardy, *Economic Growth*; and Yang, "Reforms, Resources."

138. Guo, "Dangqian nongcun laodongli," 21.

139. Dutton, editor's introduction, 15; and Kirkby, *Urbanisation in China*, 32.

140. Wei, "Urban Policy," elucidates upon this.

141. Oksenberg and Tong, "The Evolution"; and Wang, "The Rise of the Regions."

142. See Zhang, "Dui woguo liudong renkou," 4.

143. Banister, "China's Population," 235.

144. Banister, "Migration of Surplus Laborers."

145. Beijing renmin zhengfu, "Guanyu ba da chengshi," 22.

146. See Hu and Li, "Labor Market Reforms," 49.

147. See Xue, "Guanyu chengzhen laodong jiuye," cited in Sabin, "New Bosses," 948.

148. Sabin, "New Bosses," 948; Young, *Private Business.*

149. Feng and Jiang, "A Comparative Study," 73.

150. Wuhan shi, *Chengshi wailai,* 106.

151. Cui, "Woguo chengshi," 46.

152. See Zhang, "Dui woguo liudong renkou," 4.

153. Beijing renmin zhengfu, "Guanyu ba da chengshi," 23.

154. The scheme required workers to pay about 3 percent of their monthly salary into a pension fund. See *CD,* January 3, 1993, 1, reprinted in FBIS, January 4, 1993, 52.

155. "Huji yanjiu" ketizu, "Xianxing huji guanli zhidu," 87; and Taylor and Banister, "China: The Problem," 26, both state that peasants began to go to the cities in the early 1980s.

156. Emerson, "Urban School-Leavers," 8. The document is entitled State Council Notice on Strict Control over Rural Labor Entering Cities to Work and Agricultural Population Becoming Nonagricultural Population, dated December 31, 1981, published in ZRGGG 27 (374) (February 10, 1982): 885–87.

157. During the years 1979 to 1981 a policy entitled "economic readjustment" was in force. See Solinger, *From Lathes to Looms.*

158. Hu Yinkang, "The Reform of Household Registration Regulations and the Needs of Economic Development," *SHKX* 6 (1985): 37, cited in Banister, "Urban-Rural Population Projections," 9.

159. Solinger, "Research Note." Other cities were much slower with this. Tianjin, for example, only produced similar regulations a year and a half later (*Wenhui bao* [Cultural news (Shanghai)], October 22, 1984, 2, cited in Banister, "Urban-Rural Population Projections," 21).

160. *RMRB,* June 12, 1984, 2; and discussed in Zhu et al., "Nongcun renkou," 49; and Fang, "Mainland China's Rural Surplus Labor," 67.

161. *ZRGGG* 26 (447) (November 10, 1984): 919–20.

162. Fang, "Mainland China's Rural Surplus Labor," says 593,000 peasants had settled in towns nationwide within only two months of the issuance of this notice. Zhu et al., "Nongcun renkou," 49, allege that between 1984 and 1988 5 million entered the towns in accord with its stipulations. But Li Yingming, "Trends, Problems and Solutions: Future Problems of China's Population," Weilai yu Fazhan (Future and development) 3 (1987), 54, says the State Planning Commission gave a figure of 30 million by the end of 1985 (cited in Banister and Taylor, "China: Surplus Labor," 11).

163. Zhu et al., "Nongcun renkou," 51.

164. Kojima, *Urbanization and Urban Problems,* 20–21; Wakabayashi, "Migration," 509; Selden, *The Political Economy,* 182; and Oi, "Reform and Urban Bias."

165. The document, in *RMRB,* September 8, 1985, 4, and translated in FBIS, September 12, 1985, K12–14, is discussed in Banister and Taylor, "China: Surplus Labor," 14, and in "Huji yanjiu" ketizu, "Xianxing huji

guanli zhidu," 88. This new card was to be distinguished from the "temporary domicile card" (*zhanzhu zheng*), which was meant for anyone planning to stay at least three months for unstated reasons, not necessarily for work.

166. Taylor and Banister, "China: The Problem," 27; Tian, "Gaige he kaifang," 17.

167. Li and Hu, *Liudong renkou*, 26.

168. FBIS, June 18, 1993, 27. See Ordinance of the People's Republic of China on the Trial Implementation of the Resident Identity Card (dated April 6, 1984), ZRGGG 8 (429) (May 5, 1984): 246–47. XH, April 2, 1989, however, states that "China's five-year plan of issuing identity cards to all its citizens over the age of sixteen began more than three years ago."

169. FBIS, December 15, 1989, 31. See Circular of the Public Security Ministry of the People's Republic of China on Implementing the Use and Inspection System of the Residents' Identification Card Throughout the Country, ZRGGG 17 (598) (October 11, 1989): 653–57.

170. Thompson, "Afloat," 27.

171. Liu, "Economic Reform," 395.

172. Provisional Regulations on the Management of Temporary Labor in State-Owned Enterprises (October 5, 1989), ZRGGG 19 (600) (October 23, 1989): 714–16; and Provisions on Employing Contract Workers from Among the Peasants by State-Owned Enterprises, ZRGGG 28 (667) (October 18, 1991): 1001–16.

173. Author's interview, Wuhan Labor Bureau, September 19, 1990.

174. "Huji yanjiu" ketizu, "Xianxing huji guanli zhidu," 87, states that from 1978 to 1987, there are records of 10,165,000 such people, though there are no statistics for the years 1979 and 1981. This means that nationwide, an average of 1,270,000 peasants were hired legally in state firms per year. Also, Taylor, "Rural Employment Trends," 743, maintains that between 1978 and 1986 more than ten million peasants were recruited for urban jobs.

175. Korzec, "Contract Labor," 125–26.

176. Zhang, "Basic Facts," 74–75.

177. Wuhan shi, *Chengshi wailai*, 32–33. Here Yao claims that the cost is 500 yuan a year in Beijing and even more in Shanghai. But it is not clear whether he is referring to the costs of admitting a floater or a permanent migrant.

178. Ibid., 21.

179. Quoted in FBIS, November 24, 1992, 17, in a translation of a XH release of a few days before.

180. FBIS, October 7, 1994, 41, from *El País* (Madrid), October 6, 1994, 53.

181. FBIS, November 29, 1994, 43, from *Ching Pao* (Intelligence paper [Hong Kong]) 208 (November 5, 1994): 38–40.

182. FBIS, May 20, 1994, 32, from XH, May 19, 1994.

183. FBIS, February 6, 1995, 52–53, from XH of that date. Almost two years later, however, Chen, who at that point was a state councillor with

responsibility for key agricultural issues, conceded that "while regarding rural areas as a main outlet for the resettlement of surplus labor, we should also allow rural workers to . . . take jobs in industrial or other sectors of large and medium-sized cities. . . . The issue of whether rural surplus workers take up jobs in other parts of the country is not one of can you allow it or not, but one of whether or not you accept reality" (*NMRB*, October 29, 1995, 1, in *SWB*, FE/2770/S1/4 [November 15, 1996]).

184. FBIS, March 8, 1995, 13, from XH, March 7, 1995.

185. These are quotations from Luo Gan and Wu Bangguo, respectively, as translated in FBIS, July 11, 1995, 18, and FBIS, July 20, 1995, 12, from XH, July 9 and July 11, 1995, respectively.

CHAPTER 3

1. Wank, "Bureaucratic Patronage"; and Solinger, "Urban Entrepreneurs."

2. Polanyi, *The Great Transformation*, 41–42.

3. Mallee, "China's Household Registration," 20.

4. Cornelius, *Politics and the Migrant Poor*, 31; and Hollifield, *Immigration, Markets, and States*, 82. See also Cornelius, Martin, and Hollifield, eds., *Controlling Immigration*.

5. Using the word "foreign" is not far-fetched: one definition is of belonging to or characteristic of some place other than the one under consideration; another is of not being within the jurisdiction of a political unit. The Chinese term for laborers not native to the city, *wailai laodongli*, describes workers who have "come from outside," but *wailai* also means "foreign."

6. Brennan and Buchanan, *The Reason of Rules*; Knight, *Institutions and Social Conflict*; Koelble, "The New Institutionalism"; March and Olsen, *Rediscovering Institutions*; Powell and DiMaggio, introduction; North, *Institutions*; Jepperson, "Institutions"; Powell, "Expanding the Scope."

7. March and Olsen, *Rediscovering Institutions*, 24.

8. Jepperson, "Institutions," 152.

9. Knight, *Institutions and Social Conflict*, 170.

10. See ibid., 27, 183, 192; Brennan and Buchanan, *The Reason of Rules*, 12; North, *Institutions*, 68; and O'Donnell and Schmitter, *Transitions from Authoritarian Rule*, 6.

11. On this process, the best reference is Naughton, *Growing Out of the Plan*.

12. Knight, *Institutions and Social Conflict*, 189.

13. Thanks to Xinyuan Dai for helping me reach this formulation.

14. *CD*, May 17, 1994, 4, in FBIS, May 17, 1994, 30.

15. Quoted in Xiang, "How to Create," 35.

16. Solinger, "Research Note," 98–103, for my translation of an early set of urban regulations.

17. For instance, Wuhan shi, *Chengshi wailai*, 112, a regulation from

Guangdong on the use of outside labor from 1982; and ibid., 186–87, on rulings from Guangdong and Guangzhou from 1985 and 1986 on permits, fees, wages, and taxes entailed in the use of outside construction labor. There is also a directive from Hubei dated July 1986 on strictly controlling the use of out-of-plan labor in ibid., 233.

18. On the notion of peasants' advocates, see Bernstein, "Incorporating Group Interests."

19. The negligible impact is noted explicitly in Gilley, "Irresistible Force," 22. Many of the articles in Chinese academic journals supporting the floating population are written by scholars affiliated with this ministry. For just one example, there is Zhang, Zhao, and Chen, "1994: Nongcun laodongli." The newspaper *NMRB* (Peasants' daily) also takes a pro-migration stance.

20. Wuhan shi, *Chengshi wailai*, 112, 51, 30.

21. It was also responsible for sanitation workers, construction workers, those in shops, and those doing transport and packaging and family services. But its main job concerned factory labor (my interview, Wuhan Labor Bureau, September 19, 1990).

22. Author's interviews, Tianjin, June 16, 1992, and Wuhan, September 19, 1990, with city labor bureaus.

23. Author's interviews at the Wuhan Labor Bureau, September 19, 1990, and May 23, 1992; and Wuhan shi, *Chengshi wailai*, 175; also, Li and Hu, *Liudong renkou*, 179. The latter source claims that Wuhan overran its 1990 target by more than five times, as 460,000, not 90,000, outsiders entered the city to labor and do business.

24. Information from my interviews in Wuhan and Tianjin with local municipal construction commissions, May 25 and June 17, 1992, respectively.

25. There were two types of contract in use in the construction trade, one (*shuangbao*) that covered both the materials and the "project" (the workers and their labor); the other (*danbao*) regulated only the project.

26. Author's interviews, Wuhan and Tianjin, May 25 and June 17, 1992; the last point is consistent with Korzec, "Contract Labor," 125 n.18.

27. Author's interviews, Wuhan, May 27, 1992, and Tianjin, June 22, 1992.

28. See Nevitt, "Private Business Associations." The Individual Entrepreneurs' Association (IEA) is a *xiehui*, a government-controlled nongovernmental organization.

29. Author's interview, Tianjin, June 22, 1992.

30. Yuan et al., *Luoren*, 104.

31. Shanghai shi, *Shanghai liudong renkou*, 39, 77.

32. Clarke and Feinerman, "Antagonistic Contradictions," 143; and Zhang, "Luelun woguo," 36.

33. Author's interview, June 20, 1992; also information from the parallel office in Wuhan, September 14, 1990.

34. In FBIS, February 12, 1996, 23.

35. Yuan et al., *Luoren*, 112.

36. Author's interview, Tianjin Tax Bureau, June 22, 1992.

37. Author's interview, Wuhan, May 29, 1992, with Public Health Bureau.

38. Author's interview, Tianjin Housing Bureau, June 19, 1992.

39. Author's interview, Tianjin Housing Bureau, June 19, 1992.

40. Author's interview, Harbin Social Science Academy, July 19, 1991.

41. Byrd, *The Market Mechanism*, 115, states that improving economic results was by the mid-1980s already listed as more important than expanding production in a survey of more than 350 factory directors.

42. Author's interviews, Tianjin Textile Bureau, Labor Bureau, and No. Three Silk Weaving Mill, June 11, 16, and 18, 1992, respectively.

43. Freeman, "Migration," 56.

44. In Solinger, *Chinese Business*, ch. 4, I show how competition between state-owned trade organs and the remnants of private sectoral business led the state sector to quash nonstate circulation before 1978.

45. Author's interview, Wuhan Commerce Commission, May 26, 1992. In Tianjin people from the Commerce Commission also complained that their city's management was too strict, since having more outsider merchants would be an asset (my interview, Tianjin, June 23, 1992).

46. Author's interview, June 18, 1992, with Tianjin Grain Business Management Office.

47. Author's interview in Hong Kong, June 27, 1991, with a social scientist, formerly a resident of Beijing.

48. Author's interview with Tianjin Industrial and Commercial Administration (ICA) Individual Entrepreneurs' Office, June 22, 1992.

49. Cornelius, Martin, and Hollifield, "Ambivalent Quest," 13.

50. Sanderatne, "The Informal Sector," 73.

51. Gilley, "Irresistible Force," 19.

52. Liu, " 'Laomang' xiliuji," 102.

53. FBIS, January 19, 1995, 27, from *FZRB*, December 5, 1994, 3.

54. Rowe, HANKOW: *Community and Conflict*, 229–30.

55. See Honig, *Creating Chinese Ethnicity*, 48–49.

56. Wakeman, *Shanghai Police*, 87.

57. *CD*, April 19, 1990, for Beijing; FBIS, May 30, 1990, 67, from Agence France-Presse, May 29, 1990, for Tianjin.

58. For just one description, see Ge and Qu, *Zhongguo mingongchao*, 167.

59. On Guangzhou, *NFRB*, August 24, 1989, 2, and Huang and Ning, "Dao Guangzhou," 5, and my interview, Guangzhou Urban Automated Planning Center, May 11, 1992; on Beijing, XH, October 13, 1989, and FBIS, May 16, 1995, 61, from *CD*, May 15, 1995, 4.

60. Beja and Bonnin, "The Destruction." A half year before this razing, city public security authorities warned that it would occur (*CD*, May 15, 1995, 4, in FBIS, May 16, 1995, 61). For a thorough account, see Li Zhang, "Strangers in the City: Space, Identity, and the State Among China's 'Float-

ing Population' " (Ph.D. diss., Department of Anthropology, Cornell University, 1998).

61. Information from my student Li Zhang.

62. Shao, "Dongyao gongyouzhi," 50.

63. Kuhn and Kaye, "Bursting," 28.

64. Wang, Wu, and Jiang, "Cong xue."

65. Wuhan shi, *Chengshi wailai*, 37, 69, 70, 134, 184, 244.

66. Du, "Beijing chengli," 30.

67. Author's interview, Tianjin Tax Bureau, June 22, 1992.

68. Author's interview, Wuhan Construction Commission, May 25, 1992.

69. Author's interview, Tianjin Urban Transportation Bureau, June 26, 1992.

70. Author's interview, Wuhan Family Planning Commission, September 14, 1990.

71. Comments by Thomas Heberer, at the conference China's Provinces in Reform, Second Workshop, Zhejiang University, Hangzhou, China, October 20–24, 1996.

72. Wong, "Central-Local Relations"; and Park et al., "Distributional Consequences."

73. Quoted from the newspaper *Dagongbao* (Impartial daily [Hong Kong]), in Gilley, "Irresistible Force," 19.

74. Wu, "Houniao renkou," 42.

75. FBIS, June 20, 1994, 38, from *SCMP*, June 20, 1994, 7.

76. Cheng, "Problems of Urbanization," 75; and Yang and Goldstein, "Population Movement in Zhejiang," 514.

77. Liao and Liao, "Guangdongsheng renkou."

78. Wenzhou, though a wealthy area, had high levels of migration by skilled, not manual, labor (see chapter 5). Its leadership also recognized the value of exporting labor for, among other reasons, keeping its own planned birth figures within quota. See Miao, "Qianxi wenzhou," 17.

79. Li, "Beijing di yayunhou," ZM 158 (1990): 19.

80. FBIS, June 20, 1994, 37, from *SCMP*, June 20, 1994, 7.

81. Ge and Qu, *Zhongguo mingongchao*, 167.

82. Ibid., 169.

83. Ibid., 172, quoting the deputy department head of the party's Rural Policy Research Office in the province. See also chapter 2, note 138.

84. FBIS, March 14, 1995, 11, from *EE*, March 14, 1995, 8.

85. Xiong Qingquan, party chief of Hunan, is quoted in XH, March 30, 1993, translated in FBIS, March 30, 1993, 53.

86. ZGXWS, March 12, 1994, in FBIS, March 24, 1994, 18.

87. FBIS, June 21, 1991, 36, from *CD*, June 14, 1991, 3.

88. *SCMP*, December 14, 1994, 9, in FBIS, December 14, 1994, 10.

89. FBIS, April 7, 1992, 28, from Hong Kong *Liaowang* (overseas edition) 12 (1992): 5–6.

90. FBIS March 9, 1990, 40, from Hainan Provincial Radio, February 9, 1990; and FBIS, February 22, 1994, 27, from ZGXWS (Beijing), February 19, 1994.

91. Ge and Qu, *Zhongguo mingongchao*, 175.

92. See note 86.

93. The urban level sets taxes on sales and profits made by all city enterprises, collectives, and private businesses in the city. See Wong, Heady, and Woo, *Fiscal Management*, 105.

94. Hendrischke, "Tianjin," 13.

95. Though at the Tianjin No. Three Silk Weaving Mill, the rate was 15 percent (my interview, June 18, 1992).

96. Author's interviews, Wuhan No. One Cotton Mill, May 23, 1992; and the Tianjin City Textile and Labor Bureaus, June 11 and 16, 1992, respectively.

97. JPRS-CAR-92-054 (July 24, 1992), 25–26, from *Zhongguo tongji xinxi bao* (Chinese statistical news gazette), June 1, 1992, 1.

98. Author's interviews, Wuhan No. One Cotton Mill, May 23, 1992; Tianjin Textile Bureau, June 11, 1992.

99. Author's interviews at ICA Individual Entrepreneurs' Offices in Wuhan, May 27, 1992; and in Tianjin, June 22, 1992.

100. Author's interview, May 24, 1992.

101. Author's interview, Wuhan, May 24, 1992.

102. Author's interview, Wuhan ICA Open Markets Office, May 27, 1992. Both a butcher on the street and the vice chairman of the Hanzheng Street IEA quoted a rate of 6 percent in my interviews, May 24, 1992.

103. I don't know how high that tax was, but, certainly, above Wuhan's rate of 0.0 percent (my interview, Tianjin ICA Open Markets Office, June 22, 1992).

104. Author's interviews, vice chairman, Hanzheng Street IEA, May 24, 1992; and Laodong Jie Residents' Committee, May 30, 1992, Wuhan.

105. Author's interviews, public security researcher, June 12, 1992; and Tianjin ICA Individual Entrepreneurs' Office, June 22, 1992.

106. Author's interview, Zhongshan University, May 12, 1992.

107. Ge and Qu, *Zhongguo mingongchao*, 85.

108. Author's interviews, Tianjin Textile Bureau, June 11, 1992; Tianjin No. Three Silk Weaving Mill, June 18, 1992; Tianjin ICA Individual Entrepreneurs' Office, June 22, 1992; and Wuhan shi, *Chengshi wailai*, 33.

109. Woon, "Rural Migrants," 22–23.

110. *NFRB*, October 15, 1989.

111. Ge and Qu, *Zhongguo mingongchao*, 170.

112. Wuhan shi, *Chengshi wailai*, 156.

113. Beja and Bonnin, "The Destruction," 22, 23. Also, conversation with Li Zhang, December 9, 1996.

114. Li and Hu, *Liudong renkou*, 255.

115. Author's interview, June 19, 1992.

116. Author's interview with official from theTianjin ICA Open Markets Office, June 22, 1992.

117. Author's interview, Wuhan ICA, May 27, 1992.

118. Author's interview, Tianjin Tax Bureau, June 22, 1992.

119. Yuan et al., *Luoren*, 105.

120. Zhu, "Mangliu Zhongguo," 353.

121. *TJRB*, March 7, 1989, 2.

122. Author's interview, June 8, 1992, researcher from the Tianjin Population Information Center.

123. FBIS, March 27, 1995, 33, from *Kyodo*, March 25, 1995.

124. On this, see FBIS, April 11, 1989, 46, on the one in Beijing, and February 26, 1993, 70, on the one in Tianjin; also *TJRB*, December 4, 1989, 2; Zhu, "Mangliu Zhongguo"; and Yuan et al., *Luoren*, 25.

125. Author's interviews, relevant bureaus, Tianjin, June 16, 17, 22, and 15, 1992, respectively. As Thomas Bernstein suggested privately, another probable reason for not letting the outsiders organize was that it might have led them to advance claims.

126. FBIS, October 17, 1994, 80, from ZGXWS (Beijing), October 14, 1994.

127. See chapter 2, note 88.

128. To give one example, Wuhan shi, *Chengshi wailai*, 286, notes that in Wuhan the public security bureau passed procedures for implementation in 1982 and 1985 based on the NPC ruling.

129. Author's interview, Zhongshan University, May 12, 1992.

130. FBIS, October 27, 1994, 35, from XH, October 27, 1994. According to my interview, public security researcher, Tianjin, June 12, 1992, the rules in that city were yet again a bit different.

131. As in Baoding; see Wuhan shi, *Chengshi wailai*, 204.

132. Author's interview, vice chairman, Hanzheng Street IEA, May 24, 1992.

133. On Western Europe, specifically, France, Britain, and Germany, see Castles and Kosack, *Immigrant Workers*, 100. As in China, the residence permits are issued by the police and the labor permits by the labor market authorities.

134. The following material comes from my interviews with Wuhan Labor Bureau, May 23, 1992; Wuhan Construction Commission, May 25, 1992; Wuhan ICA Individual Entrepreneurs' Office, May 27, 1992; Tianjin Labor Bureau, June 16, 1992; Wuhan Labor Bureau, September 19, 1990; and Wuhan shi, *Chengshi wailai*, 164–65 and 247–48. It differs a bit from the national procedures described in chapter 6, which cites Li and Hu, *Liudong renkou*, 335.

135. Officials from the Tianjin ICA Individual Entrepreneurs' Office, in my interview on June 22, 1992, stated that businesspeople needed to exchange their business license from home for a Tianjin temporary business license.

136. Wuhan shi, *Chengshi wailai*, 203.

137. According to Yuan et al., *Luoren*, 59–60, married female migrants from Rui'an City, Zhejiang, who lived in Beijing in the early 1990s were compelled to return home to Rui'an four times a year to be examined for pregnancy.

138. As spelled out by the Tianjin Family Planning Commission, June 20, 1992, and the Wuhan Family Planning Commission, September 14, 1990.

139. According to Xiang, "How to Create," 8, 10, in the early and mid-1980s, migrating farmers still by and large followed state regulations, at least in the area he studied.

140. Gilley, "Irresistible Force," 20. The same figures are in Zhang, Zhao, and Chen, "1994: Nongcun laodongli," 28.

141. Xiang, "How to Create," 16.

142. Wong, "China's Urban Migration."

143. Haikou Radio, February 9, 1990, translated in FBIS, March 9, 1990, 40; on Harbin, see Wuhan shi, *Chengshi wailai*, 94; for Wuhan, ibid., 130, and my interview, Wuhan Policy Research Office, September 14, 1990; also, Huang and Chen, "Wuhan shiqu liudong renkou," 267. On Hangzhou, Li and Hu, *Liudong renkou*, 267.

144. Author's interviews, Tianjin public security official, June 10, 1992, and with a researcher for the public security, Tianjin, June 12, 1992.

145. Author's interview with reasearcher, Tianjin Social Science Academy, June 23, 1992.

146. Author's interview, Zhongshan University, May 12, 1992.

147. FBIS, February 22, 1994, 59, from ZGXWS, February 19, 1994, and FBIS, March 29, 1994, 47, from *WWP*, March 21, 1994, A5.

148. FBIS, April 8, 1991, 73, from XH, April 6, 1991.

149. FBIS, February 18, 1992, 59, from ZGXWS, February 15, 1992.

150. FBIS, May 16, 1995, 61, from *CD*, May 15, 1995, 4.

151. *BJRB*, June 20, 1995, 1, in FBIS, July 6, 1995, 71–72.

152. XH, December 1, 1994, in FBIS, December 5, 1994, 73.

153. Wang, "Communities of 'Provincials,' " 18.

154. Yuan et al., *Luoren*, 122. Of course, fees on peasants or peddlers providing services in the cities were nothing new in socialist China. On this, see Solinger, *Chinese Business*, ch. 4. Perry and Li, *Proletarian Power*, 106, note it as one of the charges such people brought forth during the Cultural Revolution decades ago.

155. Ge and Qu, *Zhongguo mingongchao*, 94.

156. Ibid., 84.

157. Author's interview with the scrap collectors, May 20, 1992, Nanjing. Officers in Wuhan took the same approach, according to my interview with a pedicab driver, May 28, 1992, Wuhan. A fine of 50 yuan for failure to register is nationally regulated, according to an official from the Tianjin public security bureau's *hukou* management office, in an interview, June 10, 1992.

158. Ge and Qu, *Zhongguo mingongchao*, 84–85.

159. According to Wuhan shi, *Chengshi wailai,* 128, as the market became the measure, and wages became linked to economic results, this practice became more common.

160. Wuhan shi, *Chengshi wailai,* 72.

161. Zhang, "Basic Facts," 96–97.

162. Wuhan shi, *Chengshi wailai,* 33.

163. Hu and Li, "Labor Market Reforms," 35.

164. Wuhan shi, *Chengshi wailai,* 70, 71.

165. Wong, "China's Urban Migration."

166. For instance, FBIS, March 21, 1990, 42, from *WWP,* March 9, 1990, 17; *Hong Kong Standard,* March 4, 1992, A5, reprinted in FBIS, March 4, 1992, 41; and FBIS, February 23, 1994, 45, from Haikou Radio, February 21, 1994.

167. Chan, *Cities with Invisible Walls,* 118–22.

168. "Huji yanjiu" ketizu, "Xianxing huji guanli zhidu," 85, mentions Shanghai's 1987 price of 40,000 yuan for the city district, 20,000 for the outlying city districts, and 10,000 for the suburbs, and Guangzhou's price of 10,000. Wakabayashi, "Migration," 519, also cites the figure of 40,000, though in her piece that is the charge for enterprises and offices for hiring a person to work. Wuhan proposed an "urban fee for increasing *capacity*" (*chengshi zengrongfei*) of 12,000 yuan for the city and 8,000 for the suburbs (Huang and Chen, "Wuhan shiqu 'liu wu,' " 19).

169. Ding, "Xianxing huji guanli zhidu," 19. As the *NMRB* noted in mid-1989, "People go on a 'black road' to get an urban *hukou;* those with power use power, those with money buy it; those with neither write, [and] run back and forth" (May 11, 1989). Thanks to Tom Bernstein for this reference. Kuhn and Kaye, "Bursting," 28, state that "local officials have lined their pockets to the tune of about 25 million yuan with the sale of nearly three million household registrations to date," citing a report in the *China Business Times.*

170. Li, "Population Mobility," 41; Chan, *Cities with Invisible Walls,* 119–22.

171. Chan, "Financing Local Government," ch. 3, 12.

172. Published in *Zhonghua renmin gongheguo gongan falu chuanshu,* 689 and 715–16, respectively. Thanks to Scot Tanner for this reference.

173. *CD,* October 5, 1992, 28.

174. Cao, "Lanpi lanyin hukou."

175. FBIS, January 25, 1994, 39, from *Dagongbao,* January 16, 1994, 2. This Hong Kong paper is an unofficial organ of the Chinese Communist Party.

176. Cao, "Lanpi lanyin hukou," 38.

177. FBIS, March 29, 1994, 47, from *WWP,* March 21, A5; and March 4, 1994, 22, from *CD,* March 3, 1994, 3; and Kuhn and Kaye, "Bursting," 28. Apparently, one could only remain a "preparatory citizen" (*yubei shimin*) according to this policy if one's investment and employment efforts actually

worked out. This is reported in *SJRB*, May 24, 1994, and cited in Kipnis, "Chinese Household Registration," 9.

178. Salins, "Take a Ticket," 15. Salins uses this term to refer to those with high levels of skill or education.

179. See *CF* 2, no. 12 (1994): 1, 8. The fee was 50,000 for residence in the suburbs and 30,000 in the outlying areas. Also, employers were told to pay a fee of 10,000 yuan for each peasant employed.

180. *SJRB*, November 6, 1994, cited in Kipnis, "Chinese Household Registration," 9–10.

181. Tse, "A Study of Job-Related Attitudes," 20; author's interview, Wuhan Number One Cotton Mill, May 23, 1992 (1 percent could become regular workers after four years); on Guangzhou, FBIS, August 8, 1994, 64, from XH, August 3, 1994 (there, young workers needed to distinguish themselves in ten respects); and in Xinhui, Guangdong, 20 of the best migrant workers, or 0.02 percent of the total, were to be awarded permanent residence in accord with their contributions and observance of local laws (FBIS, May 3, 1995, 34, from *CD*, May 3).

182. Reported in *ZM* 173 (1992): 96.

183. See FBIS, January 31, 1993, 43 (from XH, January 18, 1994).

184. The 1989 notice demanded that leaders in the sending areas forbid peasants to leave home and ordered those in receiving places to mobilize them to leave (Wuhan shi, *Chengshi wailai*, 224–25).

185. FBIS, December 7, 1994, 22, translated from XH, December 3, 1994.

186. Wuhan shi, *Chengshi wailai*, contains numerous regulations from many cities through the 1980s, including from Guilin, Baoding, Guangzhou, Xian, Xiamen, Harbin, Guiyang, Yichang, and Shenyang, as well as some from various provinces, including Guangdong and Hubei.

187. For instance, Wuhan shi, *Chengshi wailai*, 112, a regulation from Guangdong on the use of outside labor from 1982; and ibid., 186–87, on rulings from Guangdong and Guangzhou from 1985 and 1986 on permits, fees, wages, and taxes entailed in the use of outside construction labor. There is also a directive from Hubei dated July 1986 on strictly controlling the use of out-of-plan labor in ibid., 233.

188. Author's interview, Wuhan Family Planning Commission, September 14, 1990.

189. Author's interview with official from the municipal public security bureau's household registration management office, Tianjin, June 10, 1992, including not just hiring practices, but also rentals, living conditions, and birth control. For Beijing, see FBIS, February 18, 1992, 59, from ZGXWS, February 15, 1992.

190. As recounted by a researcher from the city's public security bureau (my interviews, June 12, 1992) and its women's federation (June 15, 1992).

191. FBIS, April 19, 1995, 15, from XH, April 19, 1995.

192. ZGXWS (Beijing), April 18, 1996, in FBIS, April 22, 1996, 43.

193. FBIS, April 12, 1994, 58, from *BYT*, February 25, 1994, 9–11.

194. *Shichangbao*, December 18, 1993, reprinted in *RMRB*, translated in FBIS, January 24, 1994, 58–59.

195. *Liaowang* 3 (1995): 22–23, in FBIS, February 24, 1995, 37.

196. FBIS, January 4, 1995, 21, from Beijing Central People's Radio Network, December 24, 1994.

197. Huang, "How to Ensure the Orderly Flow," *Liaowang* 13 (1996): 30–31, in FBIS, June 5, 1996, 30.

198. XH, February 8, 1996, in FBIS, February 8, 1996, 37.

199. Hollifield, *Immigrants, Markets, and States*, 82. Judging from Hollifield's words, it seems these protocols were more effective than were efforts at absolute suspension of worker immigration.

200. Author's interview, Zhongshan University, May 12, 1992; see also FBIS, December 24, 1991, 38, from XH, December 17, 1991; and FBIS, April 7, 1992, 30, from *Liaowang* (overseas edition) 12 (1992): 5–6.

201. *Jingji ribao* (Economic daily), December 20, 1994, 1, in FBIS, March 16, 1995, 34.

202. Benkan jije, "Mingongchao," 7.

203. XH, April 2, 1989. ZRGGG 17 (598) (October 11, 1989): 653–57, lists the numerous occasions on which the card must be presented and its many functions. There is an early version of the regulation in ibid., 429 (May 10, 1984): 246–48.

204. Ding, "Xianxing huji guanli zhidu," 100.

205. Mentioned in chapter 2, first introduced on a small scale in the mid-1980s.

206. FBIS, January 19, 1995, 27, from *FZRB*, December 5, 1994, 3. The regulations that instituted the card were first announced at the twelfth meeting of the Standing Committee of the Sixth National People's Congress in September 1985, requiring all citizens over the age of 16 to apply for a card. This is discussed in Wong, "China's Urban Migration." The citation given there is Guowuyuan fazhiju, *Zhongguo renmin gongheguo fagui huibian*, January–December 1985 (Beijing: Falu chubanshe [Legal publishing], 1986), 35–38.

207. *RMRB*, January 31, 1994.

208. Quoted in *RMRB*, January 31, 1994, translated in FBIS, February 14, 1994, 61.

209. Ibid. CASS's Han Jun also was quoted in the *Wall Street Journal*, April 26, 1994, as saying that the "ultimate target was to get rid of the whole system of division." According to XH, January 31, 1994, translated in FBIS, January 31, 1994, 41, the Ministry of Public Security, in conjunction with those of construction and agriculture, and the State Commission for Restructuring the Economy had begun surveys to consider the reform of the *hukou* system, aimed at its gradual elimination, as of early 1994.

210. Matthews, *The Passport Society*, 81–85.

211. FBIS, January 31, 1994, 41.

212. *RMRB*, January 31, 1994.

213. *Wall Street Journal,* April 26, 1994. This emphasis also appeared in FBIS, November 30, 1994, 17, from *MP,* October 27, 1994, B1.

214. *Wall Street Journal,* April 26, 1994. On all the issues, Han Jun, the chief champion for change at CASS, took a far more liberal position. See *CD,* May 17, 1994, 30. The last of these proposals was accepted in mid-1998.

215. See *SWB,* FE/2691 (August 15, 1996), G/6, from ZGTXS, August 11, 1996. See also *FEER,* July 18, 1996, 26.

216. Quoted in FBIS, January 19, 1995, 27, from *FZRB,* December 5, 1994, 3.

217. For instance, Vice Premier Wu Bangguo voiced it at a meeting in early 1996. See Huang, "How to Ensure the Orderly Flow," 30.

218. For one citation, see *Liaowang* 30 (1995): 4–5, in FBIS, August 8, 1995, 14.

219. Conversations with, and the work of, my student Thu-huong Nguyen-Vo helped me reach this formulation.

CHAPTER 4

1. Pieke, "Bureaucracy, Friends, and Money," 512–13.

2. Han, "Cheng-xiang geli," 10.

3. *SCMP,* May 22, 1995, 8, in FBIS, May 22, 1995, 25.

4. *BJRB,* March 7, 1995, 1, in FBIS, May 1, 1995, 31.

5. Ding and Stockman, "On Floating Population," unpaged.

6. Yuan et al., *Luoren,* 123.

7. Solinger, "China's Urban Transients."

8. Ferge, "Social Citizenship," 111, reviews how the transition from socialism in Eastern Europe undermined what she called "the existential security" of the population there.

9. Huang, *Inflation and Investment Control in China,* 305–6, for a discussion of inflation control as a public good.

10. Casella and Frey, "Federalism and Clubs," 642; see also Atkinson and Stiglitz, *Lectures on Public Economics,* 483–94; Hardin, *Collective Action,* 17; and Olson, *The Logic of Collective Action,* 14.

11. Other, crucial services that were much more readily excludable, such as medical care, schooling, housing, and pensions, remained strictly off-limits for peasant migrants (unless employed in a state firm), as we see in chapter 7.

12. Cohen, *The New Helots,* 186–87; on the United States, see Simon and Alexander, *The Ambivalent Welcome;* Calavita, "U.S. Immigration," 63; Rossi, *Down and Out,* 17; Keyssar, *Out of Work,* 138; on Western Europe, Castells, "Immigrant Workers and Class Struggles," 370; Hollifield, *Immigrants, Markets, and States,* 70; Ireland, *The Policy Challenge,* 261; Brubaker, *Citizenship and Nationhood,* 76; Cornelius, Martin, and Hollifield, "Ambivalent Quest," 5, 34; Castles and Kosack, *Immigrant Workers,* 107; and, on the third world, Lipton, *Why Poor People Stay Poor,* 219.

13. Rowe, HANKOW: *Community and Conflict,* 231; emphasis added.

14. Calavita, "U.S. Immigration," 62–65.

15. García y Griego, "The Rights of Undocumented Mexicans," 74.

16. Simon, *The Economic Consequences,* and Hollifield, *Immigrants, Markets, and States,* both take the assumption for granted. For some media examples of the presence of this creed in the United States, see Rohter, "Revisiting Immigration," 4; Mydans, "Californians Trying to Bar Service," A10; and Verhovek, "Stop Benefits for Aliens?" A1, A12.

17. Wong, Heady, and Woo, *Fiscal Management,* 32.

18. Simon, *The Economic Consequences,* 208, 106–9, and 208–9.

19. Hollifield, *Immigrants, Markets, and States,* 85.

20. Ding and Stockman, "On Floating Population."

21. On the *favelados,* squatting peasants in the cities of Brazil who took this role, see Perlman, *Myth of Marginality,* 259.

22. Du, "Beijing chengli," 60.

23. "The Impact of the 'Floating Population' and Surplus Labor," *Daxuesheng* (University student) 5 (1990): 36–38, translated in JPRS-CAR-90-054 (1990), 44.

24. Wang and Hu, "Zhongshi tiaojie," 72.

25. Ge and Qu, *Zhongguo mingongchao,* 34.

26. Ibid., 126.

27. Liu, "Liudong di 'shimin,' " 32.

28. Xie, "Chengshi liudong renkou," 75.

29. Li and Hu, *Liudong renkou,* 357.

30. JPRS-CAR-90-054 (August 17, 1990), 44.

31. Wong, "Financing Local Government," 19; my interview with Tianjin Grain Commission, June 18, 1992. On the U.S. conflict, see *New York Times,* December 4, 1994, 20.

32. Zhai, "Adroitly Guide the 'Tide of Laborers,' " 50; Zhang, "Guanyu chengshi liudong," 54.

33. Wang and Han, "Speed of Recent Urbanization," 83; Goldstein and Goldstein, "Town and City," 31; and Li and Hu, *Liudong renkou,* 68.

34. See also Chan, *Cities with Invisible Walls,* 58 ff.; and Ma, "Changes in the Pattern," 208.

35. Liu, "Eryuan shehui," 35.

36. See chapter 2, notes 42–44.

37. Kirkby, *Urbanisation in China,* 156, 164–71.

38. Tian, "Gaige he kaifang," 15.

39. Liu, "Eryuan shehui," 35.

40. Beijingshi renmin zhengfu, "Guanyu ba da chengshi," 23.

41. For discussions of urban subsidization before and on the eve of the reform era, see Lardy, "Consumption and Living Standards," 853–55; and Lardy, *Agriculture,* 163–65 and 192–99.

42. Li and Hu, *Liudong renkou,* 63.

43. Dutton, *Policing and Punishment,* 195–207.

44. Wu, "Guanyu liudong renkou," 43.

45. Author's interviews, Tianjin Bureaus of Grain and Finance, June 18 and June 22, 1992, respectively.

46. Chai, "Liudong renkou," 10.

47. As Christine Wong points out, "In the process of reform, price subsidies typically grow in importance as government progressively reduces the scope of its price-setting authority . . . but still wishes to cushion the impact of market forces on personal consumption" ("Economic Reform," 92).

48. Li and Hu, *Liudong renkou*, 291.

49. Author's interview, Tianjin, June 22, 1992, with bureaucrats from the city finance bureau.

50. Ge and Qu, *Zhongguo mingongchao*, 177.

51. Author's interview, June 22, 1992.

52. Li and Hu, *Liudong renkou*, 46–47.

53. Wong, "Central-Local Relations," 705.

54. *CD*, April 18, 1992, 3, in FBIS, April 20, 1992, 52; and *CD*, December 11, 1992, 1, in FBIS, December 11, 1992, 45.

55. Casella and Frey, "Federalism and Clubs," 642; Flatters, Henderson, and Mieszkowski, "Public Goods," 108; and Hardin, *Collective Action*, 17.

56. Gurr, *Why Men Rebel*, 124.

57. For a range of views on this, see Skeldon, *Population Mobility*, 162; Jones, Introduction; Todaro, *Internal Migration*, 2; Portes and Bach, *Latin Journey*, 15–20; Borjas, *Friends or Strangers*, 81, 90; and Piore, *Birds of Passage*, 86–87.

58. Chen, Xu, and Zhang, "Investigation and Analysis," 37; Han, *Kua shiji*, 311.

59. Sun, "Floating Population in Shanghai," 11.

60. Li and Hu, *Liudong renkou*, 32–33.

61. Wang, "Pros and Cons," 66.

62. Sun, "Floating Population in Shanghai," 11; and XH, April 30, 1996, in FBIS, April 30, 1996, 54.

63. Ding and Stockman, "On Floating Population."

64. *CD*, December 20, 1993, 1.

65. Whyte, "The Changing Role."

66. *EE*, April 8–9, 1995, 6, in FBIS, April 10, 1995, 46.

67. ZGXWS, June 23, 1995, in FBIS, June 28, 1995, 81.

68. Ibid., July 31, 1996, in *SWB*, FE/2680 S1/3 (August 2, 1996).

69. Li and Hu, *Liudong renkou*, 330.

70. Li, "Tidal Wave," pt. 2, 4.

71. Borjas, *Friends or Strangers*, 118, 122–23, 135, finds that changing economic conditions in the United States have made for a poor fit between the type of immigrants our policies attract and the skill and educational levels in the source countries from which immigrants come.

72. De Wenden, "The Absence of Rights," 33, writes of Western Europe that "in periods of recession, governments have to be seen to be protecting

their labor markets." Mandel, "Ethnicity and Identity," 61, notes that after the recessions of 1967 and 1973, West Germany refused to admit foreign labor into the country.

73. Piore, *Birds of Passage*, 87, 102; and Massey, "The Settlement Process," 671, identifies these phases for migrants from Mexico coming to the United States.

74. *Liaowang* 48 (1995), in FBIS, February 12, 1996, 20; also see Cai, "Recent Trends," 11.

75. Ge and Qu, *Zhongguo mingongchao*, 177; Wuhan shi, *Chengshi wailai* contains numerous regulations from various localities in this period ordering the dismissal of migrants to accommodate the local unemployed; also see FBIS, February 7, 1990, 32, from *MP*, January 29, 1990, 10, for an example from Guangdong.

76. Author's interview, June 16, 1992; see chapter 3, note 97, on Tianjin's reduction of its unemployment rate in 1991.

77. FBIS, January 31, 1994, 29, from Hong Kong ZGTXS, January 23, 1994.

78. Kernen, "Surviving Reform in Shenyang," 11. Cao, "A Good Trend," claims that even in mid-1997, "Since the providing of new job opportunities to the tens of millions of unemployed urban workers has now become a number one issue for the city governments, an immediate effective method has been to reduce the tide of countryside laborers and to give the unemployed city workers priority over all others."

79. Rural Development Research Institute, "Increasing Peasants' Incomes," S1/2.

80. See chapter 7 on these "villages."

81. Light and Bonacich, *Immigrant Entrepreneurs*; "ethnic enclaves" is a term used by Portes and Rumbaut, *Immigrant America*, 21.

82. Chen, *Chinatown No More*, 102, contends that even in the present "most Chinese workers can get jobs only in ethnic-enclave businesses in which wages are low and only simple English is necessary," so that they "do not take jobs from native American workers."

83. By the end of 1990, the individual and private economic sectors had absorbed 22.6 million laborers, according to *RMRB*, November 20, 1991, 5, translated in FBIS, December 9, 1991, 42.

84. For one author among many making this point, see Jones, introduction, 10. On the situation in contemporary China, see Liu and Wang, "Guanyu Beijingshi."

85. According to *RMRB*, March 23, 1995, 9, in FBIS, June 16, 1995, 35, peasant workers amounted to just 5 percent of the total number of staff and workers in state enterprises (since presumably none were staff, their proportion of the work force would be higher); this figure was increasing at an annual average rate of 9 percent at that point. But the *EE* declared that they accounted for as much as 30 percent of Shanghai's work force then (April 8–9, 1995, 6, in FBIS, April 10, 1995, 46).

86. This analysis draws on Borjas, *Friends or Strangers*, 81–91.

87. This argument is made forcefully in Simon, *The Economic Consequences*. It also appears, among many other places, in Keyssar, *Out of Work*, 89–90.

88. Simon, *The Economic Consequences*, 339.

89. See chapter 6.

90. Skeldon, *Population Mobility*, 162.

91. For instance, Kernen, "Surviving Reform in Shenyang," 8–11.

92. Information from China National Information Center, cited in *New York Times*, October 19, 1992, A4.

93. FBIS, October 6, 1992, 50, from *CD Business Weekly Supplement*, October 4–11, 1992, 2.

94. XH, April 3, 1993, reported in FBIS, April 5, 1993, 41–42.

95. FBIS, September 7, 1994, from XH, September 7, 1994. These figures surely grossly understate the reality. See Sabin, "New Bosses."

96. FBIS, April 26, 1994, 41–42, from Hong Kong ZGTXS, April 22, 1994. These figures include new firms in the rural, town-and-village sector.

97. FBIS, June 2, 1994, 46, from Hong Kong ZGTXS, May 19, 1994.

98. Han, *Kua shiji*, 311.

99. See *CF* 8 (1994): 8. The "green card" was a nickname people in Beijing used (with reference to the card immigrants to the United States must use once they have become permanent residents, but before they are naturalized citizens). Here it referred to the "city construction and appearance fee" outsiders were asked to pay to the Beijing municipal government in late 1994. See chapter 3, note 178.

100. Zhang, "The Mobile Population," 24.

101. Xiang, "How to Create," 23–24. Li Zhang suggested that Zhejiang Village residents obtained the rights to these services and supplies by negotiating with the local government, presumably for a price (conversation, December 9, 1995).

102. Chan, "Financing Local Government," ch. 3, 35.

103. Economy, "Reforms and Resources," 5, 9, 12, 16.

104. ZGXWS, February 14, 1995, in FBIS, February 15, 1995, 48.

105. Li and Hu, *Liudong renkou*, 64. There is material on China, and especially Beijing City's water problems in Smil, *China's Environmental Crisis*, 42–43 and 48–49.

106. *Inside Mainland China*, July 1990, 26.

107. Wang, *Xuexi shi nian guihua*, 226.

108. FBIS, August 8, 1994, 55.

109. JPRS-CAR-92-056, 65, from ZGXWS, June 8, 1992; XH, January 21, 1988.

110. Beijingshi renmin zhengfu, "Guangyu ba da chengshi," 26.

111. XH, July 21, 1996, in FBIS, July 23, 1996, 34.

112. Li, "Tidal Wave," pt. 2, 8.

113. Li and Hu, *Liudong renkou*, 152.

114. Shanghai shi, *Shanghai liudong renkou*, 251.

115. The figure of 3.3 million (of which about 2.5 million are staying for a longer term) is given in Xiang, "Shanghai wailai liudong renkou," 85. The same figure for the date December 10, 1993, is in Jiao, "Problems of Managing Floating Populations," 60.

116. Li and Hu, *Liudong renkou*, 140.

117. Li, "Tidal Wave," pt. 1, 12.

118. Gao, "On the Sharp End," 13.

119. Sun, "Floating Population in Shanghai," 14.

120. Ikels, *The Return of the God of Wealth*, 61.

121. Wang and Zuo, "Rural Migrants in Shanghai," 9.

122. Li and Hu, *Liudong renkou*, 140; Economy, "Reforms and Resources," 25.

123. *Harbin yuebao* (Harbin monthly) 3 (May 26, 1987): 4, 7.

124. Cao, "Yangtze Diversion," 40.

125. Tyler, "China Proposes Huge Aqueduct," A1, A7.

126. ZGXWS, February 14, 1995, in FBIS, February 15, 1995, 48.

127. Gao, "On the Sharp End," 13.

128. Zhou, "Guangzhou 'wailai sangong,' " 50. The survey analyzed in Wang and Zuo, "Rural Migrants in Shanghai," 9, found that only 18 percent of the sample households had their own kitchens.

129. Shao, "Dongyao gongyouzhi," 48.

130. XH Overseas, January 21, 1988.

131. Li and Hu, *Liudong renkou*, 181.

132. Ibid., 204.

133. An example: a hydropower station, begun in 1988, was completed only at the end of 1994, which was to supply 1.2 million kilowatts of energy to Hubei, Hunan, Henan, and Jiangxi provinces, at a cost of 3.6 billion yuan. See also XH, November 26, 1994, translated in FBIS, November 28, 1994, 72. Another is the 20-year, $10-billion Three Gorges Dam project, which was projected to produce 17,000 megawatts of electricity. See Tyler, "China Proposes Huge Aqueduct."

134. Author's interview with social scientist in Harbin, July 18, 1991; with official researchers at the Wuhan Policy Research Office, September 14, 1990; and with scholars at the Wuhan Social Science Academy, September 17, 1990. According to Liu, "Tantan woshi," 55, in 1985 there were as many as 3,293 people to each bus stop in Harbin.

135. Ding and Stockman, "On Floating Population."

136. *NMRB*, March 30, 1995, 4, in FBIS, May 26, 1995, 66.

137. Zhang, "The Mobile Population," 23.

138. Shanghai shi, *Shanghai liudong renkou*, 259.

139. Li and Hu, *Liudong renkou*, 280.

140. Tan, *Zhongguo renkou*, 151.

141. Gao, "Qianyi liudong renkou," 62.

142. Li and Hu, *Liudong renkou*, 228, 175.

143. Quoted from *Dazhong ribao* (Masses' daily), September 6, 1979, in Kirkby, *Urbanisation in China*, 155–56.

144. Li and Hu, *Liudong renkou*, 46; and Kojima, *Urbanization and Urban Problems*, 77–78.

145. Li and Hu, *Liudong renkou*, 63.

146. Kojima, *Urbanization and Urban Problems*, 78.

147. Yuan et al., *Luoren*, 39.

148. Luo et al., "Quanmian renshi," 30. The same point is made in Gao, "Qianyi liudong renkou," 61.

149. Author's interview with the Tianjin Public Utilities Bureau, June 26, 1992.

150. Shanghai shi, *Shanghai liudong renkou*, 259.

151. Zhang, Zhao, and Chen, "1994: Nongcun laodongli," 29.

152. Author's interview, June 26, 1992.

153. A jin is equivalent to one-half a kilogram.

154. Beijingshi renmin zhengfu, "Guanyu ba da chengshi," 21. According to Li and Hu, *Liudong renkou*, 47, in 1990 Beijing supplied 240 million kilograms of grain, and the same amount of vegetables and meat annually, for the floating population. On 140, they note that for each extra person the city must annually supply 183 kilograms of grain and the same amount of vegetables.

155. Zhang, "Zunzhong 'waidiren,' " 25.

156. Wakabayashi, "Migration," 519.

157. Author's interview, May 12, 1992.

158. Zhou, "Zhujiang sanjiaozhou," 2.

159. Li and Hu, *Liudong renkou*, 181, for Wuhan; 228 for Chengdu; 274 for Hangzhou; and 291 for Zhengzhou.

160. Kuhn and Kaye, "Bursting," 27.

161. Xu, "Da chengshi liudong renkou," 59; and Luo et al., "Quanmian renshi," 31.

162. For construction workers, see Yuan et al., *Luoren*, 34, 39; on scrap collectors, my street interviews, Nanjing, May 20, 1992.

163. Castles and Kosack, *Immigrant Workers*, 328; Cohen, *The New Helots*, 137.

164. On December 30, 1990, XH reported (translated in FBIS, January 3, 1991, 58) that urban residents were then purchasing 60–70 percent of their vegetables and nonstaple food from free markets. According to ZGTXS, September 12, 1994, in FBIS, September 22, 1993, 42, on that day, "28 provinces and some 2,000 counties lifted restrictions on purchasing and marketing prices for grain and oil; and prices for over 90 percent of consumer goods are determined by market demand and supply."

165. Author's interview with the city finance bureau, June 22, 1992.

166. According to Wong, "Central-Local Relations," 704–5, the central government allocated a fixed "price subsidy" to each province to cover the gap between the quota procurement price of grain and its urban retail price

for a specified quota of urban population. If the consumption of subsidized grain surpassed the quota amount, the province had to bear the cost of the subsidy to procure extra supplies. The local government was also responsible for the costs of handling, transporting, storing, and processing urban food grain. My interviews indicated that provinces were passing these costs down to the cities by the early 1990s (Guangzhou Urban Planning Automation Center, May 11, 1992, and Tianjin Grain and Finance Bureaus, June 18 and 22, 1992, respectively).

167. Cheng, "Da chengshi liudong renkou," 19.

168. Li and Hu, *Liudong renkou*, 274.

169. Ibid., 177.

170. Author's interview, Population Institute, Chinese Academy of Social Sciences (hereafter CASS), September 12, 1990.

171. The material that follows comes from my interview at the Guangzhou Urban Planning Automation Center, May 11, 1992.

172. According to *RMRB*, March 29, 1995, 10, in FBIS, May 10,1995, 53, by January 1, 1993, the whole country had lifted restrictions on market prices for grain and oil and ceased the circulation of grain coupons. Cheng and Tsang, "The Changing Grain Marketing System," say on 1101 that that was not the case until the end of 1993.

173. FBIS, April 20, 1993, 52, from *CD*, April 18, 1992, 3.

174. FBIS, May 10, 1995, 53, translated from *RMRB*, May 29, 1995, 10. Inexplicably, another source states that in 1992 state subsidies for grain and edible oil sales were cut by 10.9 billion yuan. This is in FBIS, August 13, 1993, 37, from *CD*, August 13, 1993, 3.

175. This is from FBIS, September 28, 1992, 39, from XH. Ration coupons for grain were reintroduced in many cities in late 1994 and early 1995 to control inflation, but most residents continued to rely on open markets. See FBIS, April 7, 1995, 53, from *Window* (Hong Kong), April 7, 1995, 18–19.

176. Luoyi Ningge'er, *Di sanzhi yanjing*, 64.

177. *MP*, January 13, 1995, A2, in FBIS, January 17, 1995, 37.

178. *MP*, March 6, C2, in FBIS, March 15, 1996, 31.

179. Yuan, Zhang, and Wang, "Self-Organize," 2.

180. Ding and Stockman, "On Floating Population."

181. Tyler, "Crime (and Punishment)."

182. Li and Hu, *Liudong renkou*, 49; *CD*, May 17, 1994, 4; and Bi and Xu (from the Research Office of the Beijing Public Security Bureau), "Factors in the Social Environment," 25–26.

183. Xiang, "Shanghai wailai liudong renkou," 85, notes that 43 percent of the migrant law-breakers in Shanghai in 1992 were criminals to begin with and were involved in 44 percent of the major crimes; and *RMRB*, March 29, 1996, 10, in FBIS, May 12, 1995, 18; Xiang, "How to Create," 28.

184. Guangdong wailai, "Zai liudongzhong," 20.

185. Author's interview with a criminologist, June 23, 1992.

186. Friman, "GAIJINHANZAI," for a similar reliance on flawed data to associate immigrants in Japan with drug offenses.

187. Beijingshi renmin zhengfu, "Guanyu ba da chengshi," 21.

188. Wu, "Job Hot Line," 60.

189. ZGXWS, January 25, 1994, translated in FBIS, January 26, 1994, 70.

190. Li, "Population Flows," 20.

191. ZGXWS, June 2, 1994, in FBIS, June 3, 1994, 20.

192. Bi and Xu, "Factors in the Social Environment," 25.

193. Ibid., and ZGXWS, June 2, 1994, in FBIS, June 3, 1994, 20.

194. Author's interview, Tianjin, June 23, 1992.

195. ZGXWS, June 2, 1994, in FBIS, June 3, 1994, 20.

196. NMRB, March 30, 1995, 4, translated in FBIS, May 26, 1995, 64.

197. Perry, *Shanghai on Strike*; Honig, *Sisters and Strangers*; Honig, "Migrant Culture"; and Wakeman and Yeh, Introduction.

198. Chai, "Liudong renkou," 8; Li and Hu, *Liudong renkou*, 53; NFRB, June 13, 1988, 2; SCMP (Sunday Spectrum), June 27, 1993, 1, 2, in FBIS, June 28, 1993, 20; Tyler, "China's Migrants"; Kaye, "Conflicts of Interest," 26; Shanghai shi, *Shanghai liudong renkou*, 79; Liaoning Provincial Radio Service, July 18, 1990, in FBIS, July 26, 1990, 46; and Xiang, "Shanghai wailai liudong renkou," 86.

199. Luoyi Ningge'er, *Di sanzhi yanjing*, 67.

200. Thompson, "Afloat," 27; Johnson, "Bright Lights," 47; *Hong Kong Standard*, September 20, 1993, 1,3, in FBIS, September 20, 1993, 25; FBIS, February 14, 1995, 22.

201. Kuhn and Kaye, "Bursting," 27.

202. Huang, Liu, and Peng, "Laizi Changshashi"; Zhu, "The Sale of Women," 4–5; and Shao, "Dongyao gongyouzhi," 49.

203. CD, August 12, 1988, 1, in FBIS, August 15, 1988, 30.

204. Sha, "An Analysis," 10.

205. Wang, "The Public Order Situation," 23.

206. Beijing renmin zhengfu, "Guanyu ba da chengshi," 21.

207. Jiao, "Problems of Managing Floating Populations," 60. This was already the case in Shanghai by 1988. See Shanghai shi, *Shanghai liudong renkou*, 78.

208. FBIS, January 24, 1994, 60; and Li and Hu, *Liudong renkou*, 177.

209. NFRB, March 31, 1988, 2.

210. Li and Hu, *Liudong renkou*, 161.

211. Ibid., 51.

212. Ibid., 52; and ZGXWS, June 2, 1994.

213. Shanghai shi, *Shanghai liudong renkou*, 92.

214. Li and Hu, *Liudong renkou*, 160.

215. Glazer and Moynihan, *Beyond the Melting Pot*, 21, on foreigners flooding American cities and charged with urban ills; Solberg, *Immigration and Nationalism*, 93, 116, on blaming outsiders for unfamiliar social tensions in Chile and Argentina at the close of the nineteenth century; Calavita, "U.S.

Immigration," 63, on the same approach toward Mexicans in the United States; and Castles and Kosack, *Immigrant Workers,* 343–44, 372, for Western Europe.

216. *MP,* October 6, 1991, in FBIS, October 6, 1991, 19; FBIS, June 1, 1994, 33; Wuhan shi, *Chengshi wailai,* 58; and Shanghai shi, *Shanghai liudong renkou,* 73, 139.

217. Ge and Qu, *Zhongguo mingongchao,* 115.

218. Castles and Kosack, *Immigrant Workers,* 342, 371–72, 452.

219. Ge and Qu, *Zhongguo mingongchao,* 94.

220. Ibid., 103.

221. Ibid., 31.

222. Ibid., 107; and *NFRB,* June 13, 1988, 2.

223. Min, "A Village," 4.

224. Yuan et al., *Luoren,* 97.

225. *CF* 3, no. 2 (1995): 6.

226. *CF* 4, no. 7 (1996): 4.

227. Yuan et al., *Luoren,* 97.

228. Ibid., 110.

229. Zhang, Zhao, and Chen, "1994: Nongcun laodongli," 28.

230. XH, February 8, 1994, in FBIS, February 18, 1994, 23.

231. One account claims that among the already detained *mangliu* in Wuhan, 80 percent had been involved in criminal behavior (Li and Hu, *Liudong renkou,* 177). Shanghai shi, *Shanghai liudong renkou,* 79, states that in 1988 vagrants and beggars were picked up 13,480 times in Shanghai, and that the increase of crime was closely related to the growing numbers of such elements.

232. Henansheng nongcun shehui, "Guanyu nongcun renkou waichu," 46.

233. Li and Hu, *Liudong renkou,* 54.

234. Ibid., 8, 55.

235. Shanghai shi, *Shanghai liudong renkou,* 39, 77.

236. Cited in Roberts and Wei, "Floating Population," 31.

237. For comparative material on the prevalence among workers in the informal economy of bribery, trading in false documents, and contravention of official rules on registration, see de Soto, *The Other Path;* Chickering and Salahdine, eds., *The Silent Revolution;* Portes, Castells, and Benton, eds., *The Informal Economy;* de Wenden, "The Absence of Rights," 28; West and Moore, "Undocumented Workers," 7; Dewind, Seidl, and Shenk, "Contract Labor"; "U.S. Arrests of Illegal Immigrants in '90 Continued an Upward Trend," *Los Angeles Times,* November 19, 1991, A29; Sontag, "Reshaping New York City's Golden Door," *New York Times,* June 13, 1993; Kilborn, "Law Fails to Stem Abuse"; and Suro, "Boom in Fake Identification Cards."

238. Chickering, Introduction, 13.

239. De Soto, *The Other Path,* 154.

240. For instance, a XH report, in FBIS, October 5, 1992, 27–29. Another

half decade later, an official from the Ministry of Construction still termed the "practice of selling urban dwelling permits to farmers" "common" (*CD*, July 16, 1992, 1, in FBIS, July 17, 1992, 15).

241. According to informal conversations in two Chinese cities in the summer of 1992, the black-market price of a Beijing *hukou* could run at least as high as 20,000 yuan.

242. Xu, "Cong renkou liudong kan," 40.

243. Ge and Qu, *Zhongguo mingongchao*, 47.

244. Li and Hu, *Liudong renkou*, 47, 251–52, 333; Wuhan shi, *Chengshi wailai*, 128.

245. According to the 1958 Household Registration Regulations discussed in chapter 2, temporary registration had to be made after three days and could be extended up to three months. See Zhang, "Basic Facts," 33–34. For a reference to the rules in practice since the mid-1980s, see Li and Hu, *Liudong renkou*, 177.

246. The following responses were all elicited in the same week in my interviews on this topic: "If you don't register, it's not illegal, it's [just] being not in accord with regulations" (September 14, 1990, at the Wuhan Policy Research Office); "Not getting a license is illegal; a lot of the floating population engage in this illegal activity" (September 17, 1990, Wuhan Social Science Academy); and "For full legality, you need a certificate from the home government, an urban job and a temporary residence certificate; without this, one is technically illegal. The majority don't go through this process. Legality and illegality are in a gray area" (Sociology Institute, CASS, September 12, 1990).

247. Li and Hu, *Liudong renkou*, 182.

248. According to *CD*, August 4, 1995, 2, in FBIS, August 7, 1995, 22, "about 55 percent of the 80 million transient laborers and business people have applied for the permit." Zhang, Zhao, and Chen, "1994: Nongcun laodongli," 28, state that 31 percent of those in their 1994–95 sample of peasant itinerants complied with procedures in their place of departure, and just 21 percent did so at the destination; only 13.4 percent applied for and obtained temporary household registration in the place of in-migration.

249. Zhu, "Chengshizhong di nongmin," 6. But some years later, Xiang Biao quotes a resident of the Zhejiang Village as saying that "no one seems to bother [about the regulations] anymore." See Xiang, "How to Create," 13. Zhang, "The Mobile Population," 23, however, notes that the number doing business without a proper license was just "more than 40 percent."

250. Beijingshi renmin zhengfu, "Guanyu ba da chengshi," 21. The same figure for Shanghai for 1988 is in Shanghai shi, *Shanghai liudong renkou*, 56.

251. Sanderatne, "The Informal Sector," 95.

252. Chickering and Salahdine, *The Silent Revolution*, 190–91; and de Soto, *The Other Path*, 12.

253. Beja and Bonnin, "The Destruction," 25.

254. Author's interviews, Zhongshan University, May 12, 1992, and

Tianjin Bureau of Civil Affairs, June 25, 1992. On the link between migrants' feeling of permanence and investing in housing in cities, see Nelson, "Sojourners versus New Urbanites," 721.

255. Li and Hu, *Liudong renkou,* 54, 229, 257; Yuan et al., *Luoren,* 82, 98, 105, 96, 100.

256. Xiang, "How to Create," 4.

257. Beja and Bonnin, "The Destruction," 25.

258. For other accounts of attacks on tax collectors, see Beijing renmin zhengfu, "Guanyu ba da chengshi," 22; Peng, "Chinese Taxation," 37.

259. Beja and Bonnin, "The Destruction," 25. According to Min, "A Village," 4, "the overwhelming majority of the productive households in the Zhejiang Village fail to pay" taxes.

260. Xiang, "How to Create," 26.

261. Yuan et al., *Luoren,* 358.

262. Author's interview, social science researcher, Harbin, July 4, 1991. Similarly, controls were looser in all cities' outskirts than in the center, so there were fewer registrants in those areas (my interview, Population Research Institute, Zhongshan University, May 12, 1992).

263. Xiang "How to Create," 29, states that a November 1994 survey of floaters in Beijing found that in the heart of the Zhejiang Village, 91 percent of the more than 3,700 employers were doing business without a license.

264. Xu, "Cong renkou liudong kan," 38, is one place among many that discusses the nonregistrants as "the out-of-control population" (*shikong renkou*) that neither place's household management departments can manage (referring to the place of origin and the place of destination).

265. Yuan et al., *Luoren,* 104: "The floaters don't understand or don't observe market management regulations that only do them harm and no good."

266. *Tianjin ribao* (Tianjin daily), December 4, 1989, 2.

267. Yuan et al., *Luoren,* 108–9.

268. A similar argument is made in Zhou, *How the Farmers Changed China,* ch. 6.

269. Chengdushi, "Chengdushi liudong renkou," 4.

270. Author's interview, Tianjin Tax Bureau, June 23, 1992.

271. Li and Hu, *Liudong renkou,* 174. According to Huang and Chen, "Wuhan shiqu liudong renkou," 688, the annual tax income from the city's free markets was 14.27 million yuan around 1987.

272. Sun, "Floating Population in Shanghai," 12.

273. Cheng, "Da chengshi liudong renkou," 19; Li and Hu, *Liudong renkou,* 173.

274. Li and Hu, *Liudong renkou,* 158.

275. Ibid., 269.

276. JPRS-CAR-900-054, 45.

277. Tian and Zhang, "Renkou qianyi liudong," 69.

278. Li and Hu, *Liudong renkou,* 171.

279. Ibid., 173.

280. Shi, "Beijing's Privately-Owned Small Businesses," 161.

281. Shanghai shi, *Shanghai liudong renkou*, 224.

282. Cockcroft, *Outlaws in the Promised Land*, 130.

283. Li and Hu, *Liudong renkou*, 288–89.

284. Ibid., 223, 225, 269, 289.

285. Ibid., 223, 269.

286. A few sample authors on this point are Burawoy, "The Functions and Reproduction"; Sassen-Koob, "Immigrant and Minority Workers"; and Sassen-Koob, *The Mobility of Labor and Capital*.

287. Li and Hu, *Liudong renkou*, 347.

288. This point of view is offered in Cui, "Woguo chengshi," 46.

289. Author's interview, Tianjin Commerce Commission, June 23, 1992; Li and Hu, *Liudong renkou*, 133; my interview with Wuhan Commerce Commission, May 26, 1992; Zhang, "Guanyu chengshi liudong renkou," 53; and Xie, "Chengshi liudong renkou," 74.

CHAPTER 5

1. See Mines, "Network Migration," 140.

2. See Huntington and Nelson, *No Easy Choice*, 99–100.

3. Connell et al., *Migration from Rural Areas*, 2, 7–8, 10, 17, 30, 200. Similarly, Lee, *Why People Intend to Move*, 31. See also Mazumdar, "Rural-Urban Migration," 1107–10, 1124.

4. Wood, "Equilibrium and Historical-Structural Perspectives," 300.

5. Todaro, *Internal Migration*, 35–36.

6. Jackson, *Migration*, 38.

7. Wood, "Equilibrium and Historical-Structural Perspectives," 305.

8. Jackson, *Migration*, 24–25.

9. Wood, "Equilibrium and Historical-Structural Perspectives," 302.

10. Portes and Bach, *Latin Journey*, 3–7.

11. Wood, "Equilibrium and Historical-Structural Perspectives," 307.

12. Portes and Rumbaut, *Immigrant America*, 230 and 232.

13. Portes and Bach, *Latin Journey*, 3.

14. García y Griego, "The Rights of Undocumented Mexicans," 61.

15. Wood, "Equilibrium and Historical-Structural Perspectives," 302.

16. Skeldon, *Population Mobility*, 144.

17. Mines, "Network Migration," 140–41; Portes and Bach, *Latin Journey*, 10.

18. Nongcun shengyu laodongli, "28ge xian," 22.

19. Honig, *Sisters and Strangers*, and Hershatter, *The Workers of Tianjin*.

20. Wu, "The Wave of Peasants"; research by Croll and Huang using data from 1994 shows that by that time, "in all villages [whether or not labor was surplus or land sufficient], farmers have concluded that agriculture is an

unprofitable, unattractive and even redundant economic activity"(Croll and Huang, "Migration For and Against Agriculture," 129).

21. White, *Against the Grain*, discusses how a high birthrate was sanctioned and at times even encouraged by the government.

22. Lee and Wang, "Malthusian Mythology," 149.

23. Davis, *Long Lives*.

24. Thomas Scharping cautions against taking this too literally because of concealed land holdings (private communication).

25. Emerson, "The Labor Force," 225.

26. Zhang, "Woguo liudong renkou," 14, 15. Other sources vary slightly; for instance, Tian and Zhang, "Renkou qianyi liudong," 16, offer a figure of 1.33 for 1988.

27. *RMRB*, January 7, 1994, 4. But Scott Rozelle points out (private communication) that the ditty is quite inaccurate.

28. *SCMP*, June 18, 1995, 6, in FBIS, June 19, 1995, 41.

29. Thomas Rawski urges caution in accepting "any statistics that come out in this area" (private communication).

30. *RMRB*, November 17, 1987, states that of a rural labor force of 44,180,000 in Sichuan, 23,040,000 were surplus.

31. Taylor, "Rural Employment Trends," 760; Yan, "The Movement of Labor," 528–29; Banister and Taylor, "China: Surplus Labor," 5–8; Feng and Jiang, "A Comparative Study"; and Banister, "Migration of Surplus Laborers."

32. Gu, "Zhongguo nongcun shengyu laodongli?" 79.

33. Han, *Kua shiji*, 311.

34. Ge and Qu, *Zhongguo mingongchao*, 77, 89, 90, 91, 118, 121.

35. Author's interview, Nanjing, May 19, 1992.

36. *NMRB*, October 29, 1995, 1, in *SWB*, FE/2770/S1/1 (November 15, 1996); Xu and Ye, "Inevitable Trend"; and Chen, "A Study." Kirkby reports that over the years 1957 to 1982, the proportion of all cultivated land considered to be under basic mechanization rose from 2 to 42 percent (Kirkby, *Urbanisation in China*, 183).

37. Ge and Qu, *Zhongguo mingongchao*, 133, 134, 136.

38. Author's interview, Nanjing, May 20, 1992.

39. Author's interview, Tianjin, June 27, 1992.

40. Halpern, "Creating Socialist Economies."

41. Taylor and Banister, "China: The Problem," 41.

42. Chai, "Consumption and Living Standards," 740.

43. Roberts, "China's 'Tidal Wave,' " 10 (ms. version), quoting Justin Yifu Lin, "Rural Reforms and Agricultural Growth in China," *American Economic Review* 82, no. 1 (1992): 34–51. See also Oi, "Reform and Urban Bias," on these issues.

44. There is much uncertainty about how to calculate these figures, given factors such as the state subsidization of basic necessities in cities (and its

gradual decline over time); the increasing mobility of rural residents; and the changing composition of rural households as a result of the increased mobility. This set of official statistics is flawed but offers a rough approximation of overall patterns.

45. *RMRB*, December 28, 1995, 1–4.

46. Quoted by XH, August 23, 1991, and translated in FBIS, August 26, 1991, 65. Ge and Qu, *Zhongguo mingongchao*, 60, find that it took five *mu* to produce an annual income of 100 yuan in 1989. If both are right, regional differences must explain the difference.

47. Liu, "Economic Reform," 396.

48. Li and Hu, *Liudong renkou*, 27.

49. Ministry of Agriculture, "Problems and Strategic Changes," 49.

50. The research of Thomas Bernstein makes this point. See also Park et al., "Distributional Consequences."

51. Li and Hu, *Liudong renkou*, 28; and Shirk, *The Political Logic*, 110.

52. See Rozelle, Li, and Brandt, "Land Tenure."

53. Chen, "Policy Measures," 22.

54. Ge and Qu, *Zhongguo mingongchao*, 51, 128.

55. Croll and Huang, "Migration For and Against Agriculture," 141–42.

56. Khan, Griffin, Riskin, and Zhao, "Household Income," 1029, 1037–38. But Scott Rozelle notes (private communication) that urban residents in effect paid high indirect taxes, since their consumer goods were more expensive.

57. Park et al., "Distributional Consequences."

58. Ge and Qu, *Zhongguo mingongchao*, 48–49.

59. Bernstein and Solinger, "The Peasant Question."

60. *CD*, August 24, 1994, 2, in FBIS, August 24, 1994, 27. See also Rozelle, "Stagnation Without Equity."

61. FBIS, March 26, 1992, 27; FBIS, March 10, 1995, 27, from XH, March 9, 1995; FBIS, March 13, 1995, 84, from XH, March 11, 1995; and FBIS, March 20, 1995, 63, from XH, March 12, 1995.

62. Zweig, "The People," 165–66.

63. Author's interview, Tianjin Number Three Silk Weaving Mill, June 18, 1992.

64. Author's interview, Wuhan, May 31, 1992.

65. Author's interview, Nanjing, May 20, 1992.

66. See *SCMP*, June 18, 1995, 6, in FBIS, June 19, 1995, 41 (12 percent); Ba jia, *Nongcun laodongli jingji*, B-01, 2 (12.5 percent of rural labor forces were normally living and working outside); Nongyebu, "Jingji fazhanzhong," 43 (14 percent of rural labor forces had left, crossing an administrative border); and Nongcun shengyu laodongli, "28ge xian," 20 (13.3 percent of total labor forces had left the county).

67. Lloyd, *Slums of Hope?* 23, makes the point that in most third-world countries, an urban sojourn may deprive peasants of their right to own land in the village they left.

68. Mallee, "Rural Household Dynamics," makes the very interesting case for the decision to migrate as a household-based one, and as a function of family size and of stage in the mother's life cycle, not as a simple choice by an autonomous individual.

69. *CD*, June 28, 1993, 4, and *RMRB*, January 7, 1994, 4, in FBIS, January 24, 1994, 59; Yuan and Tang, "Xinjiang liudong renkou"; and Wang and Jiang, "Baiwan 'yimin,' " 29.

70. Ba jia, *Nongcun laodongli jingji*, D-01, 5.

71. Zhu, "Mingongchao," 33.

72. Population data taken from Guojia tongjiju bian, *Zhongguo tongji nianjian 1993*, 83.

73. Rural workers in cities were dismissed, but with opportunities also more contracted in the villages than earlier, peasants may have been more disposed to leave than they had been before.

74. Thomas Scharping points out (private communication) that this list includes places where high person-to-land ratios signify high labor inputs, multicropping, and high yields rather than labor surplus.

75. Connell et al., *Migration from Rural Areas*, 15. On contemporary China, see Croll and Huang, "Migration For and Against Agriculture," 134.

76. The leadership also hoped that building small towns in the countryside could absorb labor off the land. But, as Du and Wang recognize in "Jiangsusheng," 64, towns' ability to accommodate workers was to a great extent determined by the degree of development of their township enterprises. See also Xu, "Shanqu nongcun renkou," 29. The successful towns in the Wenzhou area are almost all on the coastal plains, where communications are eased by waterways. See Liu, "The 'Wenzhou Model,' " 701.

77. Feng and Jiang, "A Comparative Study," 68–69; Taylor, "Rural Employment Trends," 759–60; and Rozelle, "Stagnation Without Equity."

78. Liu, "Nongcun laodongli," 60.

79. FBIS, April 5, 1993, 42, from ZGTXS (Hong Kong), April 1, 1993. The same figure was still being cited in early 1995 (FBIS, March 20, 1995, 63, quoting XH, March 12, 1995).

80. Putterman, *Continuity and Change*, 79.

81. Parish, Zhe, and Li, "Nonfarm Work," 699.

82. Parris, "Local Initiative," 243; and Liu, "The 'Wenzhou Model,' " 696. The seminal article on this is Skinner, "Urban Social Structure."

83. Skinner, "Mobility Strategies," 355.

84. Chen, "Labor Export," 23; Liu, "Liudong di 'shimin,' " 31.

85. Nongcun shengyu laodongli, "28ge xian," 20. The study does not indicate the period of time over which they had gone.

86. Of course, as Thomas Bernstein notes (private communication), regional categories are very crude: the east as well as the west contains pockets of severe poverty. See FBIS, April 5, 1993, 42; and Rozelle, "Stagnation Without Equity," relate the gap to the uneven growth of TVEs among regions. See also ZGTXS, April 1, 1993, in FBIS, April 5, 1993, 42.

87. *EE*, March 25–26, 7, in FBIS, March 27, 1995, 3. Yang, "Mingong liudong," 27, has a slightly different index: for 1983, 100 in the west, 126 in the center, 144 in the east; and for 1992, 100 in the west, 115 in the center, and 166 in the east.

88. According to Deng, "Shilun woguo," 36, in 1985, agricultural productivity in the nine western provinces was a mere 57.8 percent of that in the developed areas, and only 74.5 percent of that in the central provinces.

89. According to *CD*, March 11, 1993, 4, citing the newspaper *Wenhuibao* (Cultural paper [Shanghai]), in 1991 the disparity of annual per capita rural output value between East and Central China was 1,858 yuan. See also Croll and Huang, "Migration For and Against Agriculture."

90. *CD*, June 27, 1992, 3; Taylor, "Rural Employment Trends," 756; and Feng and Jiang, "A Comparative Study," 69. Chen, "Labor Export," 23, notes that a lack of capital for rural industrialization is a basic constraint on the transfer of labor out of agriculture; and Zhongguo nongcun laodongli, "Zhongguo nongcun laodongli," 14, states that each job in a TVE requires 8,000 to 12,000 yuan, including both direct and indirect investment.

91. In 1995, a per capita annual income of 530 yuan was considered the poverty line (FBIS, May 31, 1996, 39).

92. Chen, "The Pattern," 23.

93. Cited in Oi, "China's Polity," 14.

94. XH, February 8, 1994, in FBIS, February 18, 1994, 23.

95. Cited in Oi, "China's Polity," 14; see also Rozelle, "Stagnation Without Equity," which uses figures from the State Statistical Bureau giving the same result.

96. Oi, "Rural China Takes Off."

97. FBIS, April 29, 1993, 11, from Hong Kong's *Hsin Pao* (News), April 20, 1993, 22.

98. According to Zhongguo tongjiju nongcun, *Zhongguo nongcun tongji*, 347, the average per capita income in Sichuan province as a whole was 590.21 yuan in 1991. Odgaard, "Entrepreneurs," 91, gives the rural net income per person in Renshou as 287 yuan in 1987, when 463 yuan was the average nationally in the countryside.

99. For a thorough recounting of this riot, see Bernstein, "In Quest of Voice," 70–77.

100. Connell et al., *Migration from Rural Areas*, 15.

101. The pull of the state's positive policies got stronger as the leadership increasingly legitimized private entrepreneurship and markets beginning in the early 1980s. On this see Solinger, *Chinese Business*; and Young, *Private Business*.

102. Fang et al., "Xibu fazhan."

103. Zhongguo renmin daxue, "Dui Miyunxian renkou."

104. See Xu, "Shanqu nongcun renkou."

105. Chen, "Labor Export."

106. Roberts, "China's 'Tidal Wave,'" 25, quoting Zhang Chunyun,

"Economic Reform and Population Mobility in Poor Areas of China" (ms., Beijing University, 1991).

107. FBIS, June 7, 1996, 60, from Zhang Haiwen, "Rational Options for Adjusting the Industrial Structure of Western China's Township Enterprises," *Kaifa yanjiu* (Development research) 3 (1995).

108. Portes and Rumbach, *Immigrant America*, 10, 12; and Connell et al., *Migration from Rural Areas*, 18, 28, 59, 65, and 67.

109. Connell et al., *Migration from Rural Areas*, 82. Kam Wing Chan notes (private communication) that this may vary by type of region and by stage in the migration process.

110. Zhang, Zhao, and Chen, "1994: Nongcun laodongli," 30.

111. FBIS, May 31, 1996, 39, from *CD*, May 31, 1996, 2, and FBIS, June 7, 1996, 61.

112. Connell et al., *Migration from Rural Areas*, 15.

113. Elizabeth Perry makes the interesting conjecture (private communication) that the villages might have been chosen for the survey expressly because of transport convenience for the surveyors. However, we might reasonably conclude that transport was equally prohibitive for potential native leavers living in nonselected villages.

114. Zhang, Zhao, and Chen, "1994: Nongcun laodongli," 26.

115. Cai, "Recent Trends," 11.

116. According to Du, "Improving Access," 29, in one poor township in the Ningxia Hui Autonomous Region in the early 1990s, the average rural household loan was just 100 yuan. If financial need just for daily living was intense, few reserves would be left for use in moving away.

117. Wang Chunguang of the Social Development Institute of the State Planning Commission, quoted in *Liaowang* 48 (1995): 20–23, in FBIS, February 12, 1996, 20.

118. Ge and Qu, *Zhongguo mingongchao*, 113.

119. Zhu, "Chengshizhong di nongmin," 12, 15.

120. "Zhongguo pinkun diqu," 59.

121. Liu, "Economic Reform," 400.

122. Zhang, Zhao, and Chen, "1994: Nongcun laodongli," 29.

123. Nongcun shengyu laodongli, "28ge xian," 20.

124. Ibid., 21, 28.

125. Wuhan shi, *Chengshi wailai*, 115; my interview, Wuhan Social Science Academy, September 17, 1990.

126. Zhang, Zhao, and Chen, "1994: Nongcun laodongli," 28, say 62 percent were introduced to their first employer by familiar people; Nongyebu, "Jingji fazhanzhong," 43–44, says 71 percent.

127. This percentage is a function of the type of job involved; for instance, Shi, "Beijingshi getihu," 38, reports that research by the Beijing Municipality Bureau of Labor found that over 90 percent of the hired labor in private firms got their jobs by relying on friends and relatives; only 1 percent were introduced by labor departments (thanks to Thomas Heberer for this reference).

For other types of work, see Zhang, Zhao, and Chen, "1994: Nongcun lao-dongli," 28, which cites 7 percent; Nongcun shengyu laodongli, "28ge xian," 22, states that in 1993, the 191 professional introduction organizations at the county, township, and market town levels in the 28 counties investigated were responsible for arranging jobs for only 8.2 percent of those who went out; and Nongyebu, "Jingji fazhanzhong," 44, also reports that organized units (village collectives or professional organizations) accounted for 8.5 percent of the placements.

128. Greenhalgh, "Networks and Their Nodes," 535, states that in migration into the cities of Taiwan, 75 percent of the introductions were made by kin and friends. Connell et al., *Migration from Rural Areas*, 28, reporting on a study of five urban centers on three continents, say 80 percent of the migrants interviewed found their jobs through friends and relatives.

129. Mines, "Network Migration," 141; and Skeldon, *Population Mobility*, 141, 144.

130. Benkan jije, "Mingongchao," 7.

131. Author's interview, May 17, 1992.

132. Chan and Unger, "Immigrants," 24–25. Author's interviews, Tianjin Textile Bureau, June 11, 1992, and Tianjin Labor Bureau, June 16, 1992.

133. Author's interview, May 23, 1992.

134. Author's interview, May 25, 1992.

135. For instance, see Portes and Bach, *Latin Journey*, 10; and Goldstein, "Temporary Migration," 13.

136. Liu, "Economic Reform," 403.

137. Zhang, Zhang, and Shen, "Shanghai liudong renkou," 57; and Shanghai shi, *Shanghai liudong renkou*, 121.

138. Decree no. 87 of the State Council of the People's Republic of China: Provisions on Employing Contract Workers from Among Peasants by State-Owned Enterprises, ZRGGG 28 (October 18, 1991): 1002.

139. Wuhan shi, *Chengshi wailai*, 137. There are also arrangements between Guizhou province and Dongguan, Guangdong, as reported in Wang and Jiang, "Baiwan 'yimin,' " 27, and Ge and Qu, *Zhongguo mingongchao*, 139–40; and between Mao's old base in Jinggangshan, Jiangxi, and the special economic zone of Shenzhen, in ibid., 145.

140. *Jingji ribao* (Economic daily), December 11, 1993, 1, translated in JPRS-CAR-94-011 (February 15, 1994), 27.

141. Circular of the State Council on a Report of the Ministry of Labor on the Employment Situation and Proposals about Future Work, ZRGGG 18 (August 6, 1992): 703, 687–90, dated May 13, 1992. A related report is in FBIS, April 7, 1992, from Hong Kong, Liaowang Overseas, 12 (March 23, 1992, 5–6), 30.

142. Author's interview, Wuhan Labor Bureau, September 19, 1990.

143. Author's interview, Tianjin Construction Commission, June 17, 1992.

144. Author's interview with the researchers, Population Institute, Guangdong Academy of Social Science (hereafter GASS), May 13, 1992.

145. In exchange for its services, as of 1992 the women's federation was collecting registration fees of 3 yuan each from each potential maid and the same amount from the employer; after the maid had found a situation, each side paid another 5 yuan.

146. Author's interview with the federation branch in Tianjin, June 15, 1992.

147. For the earlier period, when Mao urged rural areas to develop the "five small industries," see Sigurdson, "Rural Industry"; and Sigurdson, *Rural Industrialization*. For the current version, see Korzec, "Contract Labor," 128.

148. Chan and Unger, "Immigrants," 24–25.

149. Author's interviews, Guangzhou, May 13, 1992; Wuhan, May 23, 1992; and Tianjin, June 18, 1992.

150. Ge and Qu, *Zhongguo mingongchao*, 173.

151. Zhongguo renmin daxue, "Dui Miyunxian renkou," 39.

152. Shi, *Zhongguo renkou qianyi shigao*, 466.

153. Wu, "Houniao renkou," 39.

154. Oshima, "The Present Condition," 206. There are many, many other cases reported, such as FBIS, April 7, 1992, 30; FBIS, February 22, 1994, 56; and FBIS, May 8, 1995, 83; Ge and Qu, *Zhongguo mingongchao*, 172; and *CD*, June 27, 1992, 3.

155. Beja and Bonnin, "The Destruction," 23.

156. Ba and Ma, "Taojinzhe," 53; on Jiangxi, specifically, FBIS, December 11, 1992, 51.

157. FBIS, April 12, 1994, 57, from *BYT*, February 25, 1994, 9–11.

158. "China on the Move," *Economist*, July 6, 1996, 34.

159. FBIS, January 3, 1994, 43, from XH.

160. *CD*, June 27, 1992, 3; and Wang and Jiang, "Baiwan 'yimin,' " 27.

161. Solinger, "Urban Reform."

162. Author's interview with rural workers on such a contract, Nanjing, May 17, 1992.

163. Wuhan shi, *Chengshi wailai*, 145.

164. Author's interview, May 23, 1992.

165. Author's interview, May 16, 1992.

166. Author's interview, Tianjin Construction Commission, June 17, 1992. This kind of arrangement is discussed in Yuan et al., *Luoren*, 33.

167. Author's interview with researchers, Guangzhou, May 13, 1992.

168. Author's interview, May 19, 1992.

169. Author's interview with the sister of such an agent from mountainous Yingcheng county in Hubei's west, working in Wuhan's outskirts, May 28, 1992.

170. Author's interviews, Nanjing, May 17, 1992.

171. Huang, Liu, and Peng, "Laizi Changshashi"; Wang, Wu, and Jiang, "Cong xue"; *TJRB*, December 4, 1989, 2, and FBIS, February 26, 1993, 70.

172. Wuhan shi, *Chengshi wailai*, 115; Zhang, Zhao, and Chen, "1994: Nongcun laodongli," 28, report that of the 2,986 rural laborers they investigated who crossed an administrative border to get work, fewer than 3 percent got their first job through labor markets (62 percent were introduced by familiar people and 24 percent found work on their own; besides this 3 percent, no other figures were given).

173. Wang, Wu, and Jiang, "Cong xue," 3; the team from Yingcheng county mentioned just above did take on extras this way. Also, a privately operated restaurant in Tianjin hired workers at a labor market, after an interview of 10 to 30 minutes (my interview, Tianjin, June 19, 1992).

174. Ge and Qu, *Zhongguo mingongchao*, 130; also, Wang and Jiang, "Baiwan 'yimin,' " 29.

175. Author's interviews at the station, May 17, 1992.

176. Gao, "On Their Own," 28.

177. Author's interview, May 13, 1992.

178. Author's interview, June 15, 1992.

179. Granovetter, *Getting a Job*, shows how interpersonal relations always affect job searches and placement. But surely formal procedures and qualifications have larger parts in advanced market economies than in transitional, initially urbanizing ones. For an analytical treatment of this subject in the Chinese countryside of the 1990s, see Parish, Zhe, and Li, "Nonfarm Work."

180. In one 1993 study of migrant workers in the Pearl River Delta, 27 percent of the interviewees refused to answer, but of the remaining 73 percent who did, only 9 percent claimed to send no money home. See Ba jia, *Nongcun laodongli jingji*, A-02, 6.

181. Mines, "Network Migration," 140–41.

182. Wood, "Equilibrium and Historical-Structural Perspectives," 301, refers to this as the "neoclassical" model of migration, which sees migrants as "agents of change."

183. Alba, "Urban Aspects of Labor Migration," 229–30.

184. Jones, Introduction, 9.

185. Alba, "Urban Aspects of Labor Migration," 232.

186. Taylor, "Rural Employment Trends," 760. Benkan jije, "Min-gong-chao," 9. Mallee, "Agricultural Labour," takes up this issue.

187. Nelson, "Sojourners versus New Urbanites"; Gallin, "Rural to Urban Migration in Taiwan," 277, gives a Chinese example from Taiwan.

188. On South Africa, see Spandau, "Residence and Work Place."

189. Cohen, "Family Management," 365–66.

190. The directive was published in ZRGGG 26 (447) (November 10, 1984): 919–20.

191. Zhu, "Nongcun renkou chengshihua," 61, written in June 1989, states that 79.2 percent kept the family dwelling, allowing friends or family to live there or holding it empty, while 47.8 percent handed their land over

to family members, relatives, and friends. Taylor and Banister, "China: The Problem," 23, state that as of early 1988, 99 percent of the peasants holding urban jobs kept the land contracted to their households (their "responsibility fields") in the family.

192. Zhu, "Nongcun renkou chengshihua," 61.

193. Nongcun shengyu laodongli, "28ge xian," 27.

194. Pan, "Nongcun liudong renkou," 91.

195. Author's interview, June 10, 1992; Zhu, "Chengshizhong di nongmin," 14.

196. Zhang and Yang, "Mingongchao," 45.

197. Zhou, "Guangzhou 'wailai sangong,' " 50.

198. Zhu, "Chengshizhong di nongmin," 40.

199. Taylor and Banister, "China: The Problem," 23.

200. Yang, "The Nature," 8. Of course, in addition, Chinese tradition dictates that single men go back to their home communities to marry. See Gallin and Gallin, "The Integration of Village Migrants," 345.

201. *RMRB*, November 17, 1987, 2.

202. Roberts and Wei, "Floating Population," 28.

203. Zhang and Yang, "Mingongchao," 45; JPRS-CAR-94-025 (April 19, 1994), 38; FBIS, February 1, 1994, 39; Wang and Jiang, "Baiwan 'yimin,' " 31; Chen, "Labor Export," 22; Lu and Wang, "Cong nongcun jianzhudui," 34; and Gilley, "Provincial Prodigals."

204. Author's interview, May 28, 1992.

205. Ge and Qu, *Zhongguo mingongchao*, 60–67.

206. Li and Hu, *Liudong renkou*, 345.

207. Ge and Qu, *Zhongguo mingongchao*, 161.

208. Gu, "Dushi 'mangliu,' " 9; Chen, "China: Maid Service" (thanks to David Strand for supplying this article); and Xu, "Nongcun shengyu laoli," 48.

209. Liu, "Economic Reform," 407.

210. Connell et al., *Migration from Rural Areas*, 201.

211. Taylor and Banister, "China: The Problem," 42; Chen, "Labor Export," 22; and Wood, "Equilibrium and Historical-Structural Perspectives," 299–301.

212. Connell et al., *Migration from Rural Areas*, 82; Jones, Introduction, 9; and Mazumdar, "Rural-Urban Migration," 1097.

213. Wu, "Houniao renkou," 41.

214. Wood, "Equilibrium and Historical-Structural Perspectives," 303–4.

215. Xu and Ye, "Inevitable Trend," 21.

216. Wang and Jiang, "Baiwan 'yimin,' " 31.

217. FBIS, May 8, 1995, 83.

218. Xu, "Shanqu nongcun renkou," 28. But another source says that the province earned about six billion from its 2.5 million out-of-province migrant workers in 1994. This is Gilley, "Provincial Prodigals," 22.

219. FBIS, March 21, 1994, 58, from XH; and Liu, "Nongcun laodongli,"

62. Figures on provincial gross domestic product come from *Zhongguo tongji nianjian 1995*, tables 2–11, as reported in *Provincial China* 1 (1996): 37. Sichuan's gross domestic product for 1993 was 209.6 billion yuan. As Thomas Scharping points out (private communication), different tabulators might count different sorts of migrants; and some might count only earners while others include their dependents.

220. Xu, "Shanqu nongcun renkou," 28.

221. Thomas Bernstein makes these points (private communication).

222. Gilley, "Irresistible Force," 20.

223. Ba jia, *Nongcun laodongli jingji*, A-02, 6.

224. Zhou, "Guangzhou 'wailai sangong,' " 50, found that in Guangdong, casual laborers whose business was poor could only afford to pay their rent and buy their food, with nothing left to remit.

225. Author's interviews, May 17, May 18, May 20, 1992, in Nanjing; and May 24, May 28, and May 31, 1992, in Wuhan.

226. Xu, "Shanqu nongcun renkou," 29; Gilley, "Irresistible Force," 18; and Huang, "Why China Will Not Collapse," 66–67, all make such claims.

227. From *Provincial China* 1 (1996): 49 and 37, respectively. The data for these conclusions come from the *Chinese Statistical Yearbook for 1995* (tables 9–16 and 2–11, respectively).

228. As Carl Riskin points out (private communication), even if remittances did not stem relative decline in these places, they may have prevented greater inequality.

CHAPTER 6

1. Piore, "Notes for a Theory," 126. Piore is the chief theorist of this model.

2. I use the term "exploitation" in a Marxist sense, to refer to the employment of workers at rates of pay below the true value of their productive effort, and without humane or even adequate working conditions or welfare benefits.

3. Bian emphasizes the extent to which *guanxi* (connections) always supplemented administrative forms of recruitment, even in the days of strict state planning, but notes greater reliance on *guanxi* in job searches as market reforms relaxed bureaucratic controls (Bian, "Guanxi and the Allocation," 973). See also Bian, *Work and Inequality*.

4. Chan, *Cities with Invisible Walls*, 77.

5. Sabin, "New Bosses."

6. One general treatment of these themes is White, *Riding the Tiger*.

7. Potter, "Riding the Tiger."

8. On this, see Zhao and Nichols, "Management Control of Labour."

9. Solinger, "The Chinese Work Unit."

10. Goldstein, "Are We There Yet?" 60.

11. There are parallels here with treatment of workers in state-owned firms in Latin American cities, as described by Roberts, in *The Making of Urban Citizens*, 115. But the benefits appear to be only for urbanites.

12. According to analysis of a survey of rural migrant workers in Shanghai at the end of 1993, workers in state-owned firms were more than three times as likely to stay in the city more than one year as those working in manual labor, construction, handicrafts, and the private sector, who were even less likely to have a long stay [*sic*] (Roberts and Wei, "Floating Population," 29).

13. Faist, "States, Markets, and Immigrant Minorities."

14. Chan, *Cities with Invisible Walls*, 52–59, 74–79.

15. Hu and Li, "Labor Market Reforms," 49; Ye, "Suzhoushi wailai," 57; Liu and Wang, "Guanyu Beijingshi 'zhaogong nan,' " 36; and FBIS, July 25, 1991, 53. At the Wuhan Number One Cotton Mill, I was told on May 23, 1992, that "the factory would prefer city labor, but city people don't want to do it."

16. Rofel, "Eating Out of One Big Pot," 93.

17. In fact, however, studies show that about 50 percent of the floaters had been at least to junior high. Nongyebu, "Jingji fazhanzhong," 44, cites 45 percent, whereas among the rural labor forces only 33 percent had this much schooling at that time; Nongcun shengyu laodongli, "28ge xian," 27, cites 54 percent having been to junior high, and illiterates and semiliterates accounting for under 4 percent of the migrants.

18. For instance, Castles and Kosack, *Immigrant Workers*, 112; Lomnitz, *Networks and Marginality*, 209; and Piore, *Birds of Passage*, 18.

19. Christiansen, "The Legacy," 423.

20. Piore, *Birds of Passage*, 103–4.

21. Gao, "On the Sharp End," 12.

22. For instance, Ireland, *The Policy Challenge*, 11, states that "recruitment patterns and the influence of family and kin networks have had more to do with which specific industrial sectors immigrant workers have entered than any previous experience."

23. Honig, *Creating Chinese Ethnicity;* and Goodman, *Native Place*, 4–6.

24. As Zhu, "Chengshizhong di nongmin," 11, explains, "The economic and cultural elements of one's home area are decisive."

25. Shi, "Beijingshi getihu," 37 (thanks to Thomas Heberer).

26. Goodman, *Native Place*, 14, 29. According to Yuan et al., *Luoren*, 51, those from Wenzhou county, Zhejiang, where there is an ancient tradition of commercial activity, had the highest incomes and the most stable work.

27. On the ability of native private entrepreneurs to form ties with urban officialdom—indeed, on the necessity for them to do so—see Bruun, *Business and Bureaucracy*, 87, 92, 133; Bruun, "Political Hierarchy"; Young, *Private Business*, 126; and Wank, "Bureaucratic Patronage." But a tiny handful of the successful Zhejiang merchants had managed to establish some official ties by the mid-1990s; see Yuan et al., *Luoren*, 57–62.

28. Gao, "On the Sharp End," 12; and Lee, "Production Politics." Yuan et al., *Luoren*, also emphasize the importance of mutual support.

29. Ba jia, *Nongcun laodongli jingji*, A-01, 8.

30. Personal communication from Han Jun of the Rural Development Institute, CASS, March 3, 1995; Guangdong wailai, "Zai liudongzhong," 116 (thanks to Shaoguang Wang for bringing this article to my attention); and Scharping and Schulze, "Economic, Labor and Income," 11; Wang and Zuo, "Rural Migrants in Shanghai," 4–5, say that three-quarters of those who reported that they had come to town to work (meaning they may already have had a job prospect before coming) began to work immediately upon arriving. Yuan et al., *Luoren*, 25, state that "very few first enter the city and then look for work."

31. Zhu, "Chengshizhong di nongmin," 11. This point was made by Gerber, "Cutting Out Shylock," 208: "ethnic job segregation implies that commercial relations between[immigrant] Jews and native-born Americans were not competitive ones."

32. Goodman, *Native Place*, 31.

33. Author's interviews at the Wuhan ICA Individual Entrepreneurs' Office, May 27, 1992, and at the Tianjin ICA Open Markets Office, June 22, 1992, respectively.

34. Yuan et al., *Luoren*, 124–25, report in a 1994 survey that sojourners in Beijing and Shanghai felt that it was harder to get work in that year than it had been in the year before.

35. Skinner, "Urban Social Structure"; and Skinner, "Mobility Strategies," 327–64.

36. Yuan et al., *Luoren*, 9, 125, 100.

37. Zhu, "Chengshizhong di nongmin," 11. A public security researcher in Tianjin, interviewed on June 12, 1992, named several other Anhui counties (Huai'an, Gu'an, Huaibei) as the home place for those in his city.

38. Scholars interviewed in Harbin (July 4, 1991), Guangzhou (May 11, 1992), and Tianjin (June 22, 1992) agreed. See also Zhou, "Guangzhou 'wailai sangong,' " 50. According to Zhu, "Chengshizhong di nongmin," 11, Huangyan county, Zhejiang, specialized in shoemaking.

39. Zhu, "Chengshizhong di nongmin," 11. She also alludes to Jiangsu's Zhangjiagang in this regard. The public security researcher in Tianjin, interviewed on June 12, 1992, added Fujian to Wenzhou as the home of those who make and market clothing in Tianjin.

40. Except where otherwise noted, the material on professions comes from the same sources as in the previous several footnotes.

41. Liu, "Economic Reform," 398–99.

42. Pan, "Nongcun liudong renkou," 24.

43. Author's interview, June 25, 1992.

44. Benkan jije, "Mingongchao," 8.

45. Harris and Todaro, "Migration, Unemployment, and Development."

46. Piore, "Notes for a Theory," 126.

47. Kannappan, "Urban Employment," 699–73; Edwards, "Social Relations," 4; Portes and Bach, *Latin Journey*, 16–18; Hondagneu-Sotelo, *Gendered Transitions*, 27–28; Bonacich, "A Theory of Ethnic Antagonism"; Tannen, "Labor Markets in Northeast Brazil"; Telles, "Urban Labor Market Segmentation"; Castells and Portes, "World Underneath," 12; Sassen-Koob, "Immigrant and Minority Workers," 17; Skeldon, *Population Mobility*, 162; Portes, "Modes of Structural Incorporation," 297; Jackson, *Migration*, 78; Morrison, "Functions and Dynamics," 65.

48. Telles, "Urban Labor Market Segmentation," 231.

49. Yuan et al., *Luoren*, 100.

50. Kannappan, "Urban Employment," 713, 721.

51. De Soto, *The Other Path*, 146, emphasizes discrimination by income in Peru's labor market, with mistreatment and difficult access for the poor, but not necessarily for peasant outsiders as a status group.

52. Ba jia, *Nongcun laodongli jingji*, A-02, 10. Christiansen, "The Legacy," 424, concurs: "Clientelism has restrained the introduction of market forces."

53. Yuan et al., *Luoren*, 25, say that "those entering blindly have to rely on low-cost job information channels and illegal labor markets."

54. Kannappan's "Urban Employment" suggests such an approach but no systematic explanation for the variation he observes.

55. The numbers of young women serving as prostitutes, masseuses, and "night club escorts"—apparently often tricked or even kidnaped into the trade—may have been as sizable as those in these other, more openly and frequently discussed occupations, but there is far less detailed information available to date about the structure of their trade. See Hershatter, "Chinese Sex Workers," 4; also, *CF* 4, no. 7 (1996): 4; Li, "200 Million Mouths," 12; Ge and Qu, *Zhongguo mingongchao*, 63–67.

56. According to a survey of Beijing cited in XH, April 19, 1995, in FBIS, April 19, 1995, 15, about 70 percent of its 3.295 million transients were there for employment or trade; an October 1995 survey in Shanghai found that 74 percent of the migrants were economic-type (Wang and Zuo, "Rural Migrants in Shanghai," 7). Other purposes included study, errands for their offices, tourism, visits to a doctor or to friends and relatives, and other family affairs.

57. XH, October 27, 1995, in FBIS, October 27, 1994, 35; *CD*, January 21, 1995, 3, in FBIS, January 23, 1995, 74; and *EE*, April 8–9, 6, in FBIS, April 10, 1995, 46.

58. *EE*, March 14, 1995, 8, in FBIS, March 14, 1995, 11.

59. Nongcun shengyu laodongli, "28ge xian," 20.

60. Reported in Gilley, "Irresistible Force," 19.

61. Han, "Income, Consumption, and Employment," 40.

62. Li, "Zhujiang sanjiaozhou," 37.

63. Gilley, "Sisters Act," 20.

64. Zhang, Zhao, and Chen, "1994: Nongcun laodongli," 27; Nongyebu, "Jingji fazhanzhong," 44; and Hou, "Meitian 140 wan," 44.

65. Han, "Income, Consumption, and Employment," 40; and Wang and Zuo, "Rural Migrants in Shanghai," 7.

66. Li and Hu, *Liudong renkou,* 332.

67. Yuan et al., *Luoren,* 30.

68. Liang, "Lun chengshi liudong renkou"; and Li and Hu, *Liudong renkou,* 333 and 251.

69. Wang and Feng, "Jingji tizhi gaigezhong," 10; and Wuhan shi, *Chengshi wailai,* 130, states that "the labor department has no effective means of control, so there is some outside labor outside of control, especially in construction work."

70. According to Li and Hu, *Liudong renkou,* 333, the legal, state-set profit rate for this sector was only 2.5 percent of output value (in contrast to rates of 74.9 percent for the petroleum industry or even 29.03 percent in electronics and 9.5 percent in building materials), as of 1990.

71. De Soto, *The Other Path,* focuses on excessive regulations and red tape, and the high cost of doing business legally, as the conditions that made for irregularities in Peru's informal labor market.

72. Ibid., 329.

73. Cited in Mallee, "China's Household Registration," 12, and Chan, *Cities with Invisible Walls,* 131.

74. Chan, *Cities with Invisible Walls,* 131. On Beijing in 1986, see Du, "Beijing shiqu," 13.

75. *NFRB,* March 23, 1988, 2.

76. Li and Hu, *Liudong renkou,* 157. The statistic refers to the numbers of "those who built recent construction projects." See also Shanghai shi, *Shanghai liudong renkou,* 137. For Chengdu and Wuhan, see Li and Hu, *Liudong renkou,* 223 and 329, respectively.

77. Wang, Shi, and Song, "Beijing's Mobile Population," 45.

78. Shanghai shi, *Shanghai liudong renkou,* 135.

79. Author's interview with the scholar Ma Shuluan in Nanjing, May 15, 1992, and at Nanjing University's sociology department, May 21, 1992.

80. Author's interviews with the Wuhan Construction Commission and Labor Bureau, May 25 and May 23, 1992, respectively.

81. Author's interview with the head of the construction manangement office of the Wuhan Construction Commission, May 25, 1992. The system is also referred to in Wuhan shi, *Chengshi wailai,* 289–91.

82. Li and Hu, *Liudong renkou,* 335. The procedures differ a bit from those described in chapter 3 on the basis of my interviews in Wuhan and Tianjin.

83. Ibid., 334 and 335; see also Korzec, "Contract Labor," 125. Also, my interview with the Wuhan Labor Bureau, September 19, 1990.

84. Ge and Qu, *Zhongguo mingongchao*, 75.

85. Author's interview, Tianjin, June 10, 1992; Christiansen, "The Legacy," 422.

86. Author's interview, Tianjin Construction Commission, June 17, 1992; at that time, Tianjin was drawing about 20 percent of these workers from its own suburbs and counties and the rest from Henan, Hebei, and even from as far away as Sichuan.

87. Korzec, "Contract Labor," 125; and my interview with a county-managed team from Hubei, May 25, 1992.

88. Author's interview with officials from the commission, June 17, 1992.

89. Yuan et al., *Luoren*, 49–50.

90. Author's interview at Population Research Institute, Zhongshan University, May 12, 1992. One example of the arrangements well-connected bosses could make for their gangs (before the late 1980s, when access to state-subsidized grain still required coupons) was to buy grain coupons on the black market (my interview with researchers, Harbin, July 18, 1991).

91. Kirkby, *Urbanisation in China*, 30.

92. Wuhan shi, *Chengshi wailai*, 128, 145.

93. Author's interview with scholars, Harbin, July 22, 1991.

94. Author's interview, Nanjing University, May 21, 1992.

95. Lomnitz, *Networks and Marginality*, 13. Yuan et al., *Luoren*, 30–31, 36.

96. See FBIS, February 25, 1994, 47 (from a letter to *RMRB*, February 15, 1994, 2); and Yuan et al., *Luoren*, 46. Temporary workers interviewed in Nanjing, May 18, 1992, confirmed this style of work of their foreman.

97. FBIS, June 14, 1996, 18, from *RM*, May 21, 1996, 11.

98. Author's interview with a researcher from the Tianjin Public Security Bureau, June 10, 1992. I spoke with the boss of a Subei team (from Gaoyou City) operating in this fashion in Nanjing, May 19, 1992. Most of his workers came from Subei, but a few, from Anhui, were mostly relatives of his Subei neighbors.

99. Author's interviews, Guangzhou Urban Planning Automation Center, May 11, 1992, and Wuhan Labor Bureau, May 23, 1992.

100. Unpleasant encounters at work sites, Nanjing, May 19, 1992; Wuhan, August 10, 1994. Yuan et al., *Luoren*, 47, concur.

101. Author's interview with Harbin scholars, July 2, 1991.

102. Author's interview at Zhongshan University's Population Research Institute, May 12, 1992.

103. Wank, "Bureaucratic Patronage," 159.

104. The relationships between local official teams and the townships and counties to which they were connected are laid out in Yuan et al., *Luoren*, 31–32.

105. Korzec, "Contract Labor," 125.

106. FBIS, October 27, 1993, 26; also, my interview, sociology department, Nanjing University, May 21, 1992.

107. Author's interview with team leaders from Daye county, Hubei, May 25, 1992.

108. Author's interview, Population Research Institute, Zhongshan University, May 12, 1992.

109. Yuan et al., *Luoren*, 31, 32.

110. Li and Hu, *Liudong renkou*, 331,

111. In an interview in Wuhan with a technical engineering firm from Shenzhen on May 25, 1992, I learned that the firm employed four types of workers, the first three as permanent employees of this state firm, the last as temporary, local workers. Their respective daily wages were as follows: drainage workers: 20–30 yuan; electrical workers: 20–30 yuan; renovation workers: 300–500 yuan; and ordinary excavation workers: 10–15 yuan.

112. Li and Hu, *Liudong renkou*, 331.

113. Ibid., 251.

114. Author's interview, May 25, 1992.

115. See, for example, the official *CD*, May 14, 1992, which cites a twenty-six-year-old from Subei (northern Jiangsu) who, to earn extra money, often worked more than twelve hours per day. A team whose foreman I interviewed in Nanjing on May 19, 1992, worked anywhere from seven up to twelve hours a day.

116. Shanghai shi, *Shanghai liudong renkou*, 138.

117. Ibid.

118. Shanghai shi, *Shanghai liudong renkou*, 135, states that 28.6 percent had a primary school education, and 56 percent had been to junior high; Li and Hu, *Liudong renkou*, 334, state that of peasant construction workers in Wuhan, 23.26 percent had a primary school education, while 55.9 percent had been to junior high.

119. Shanghai shi, *Shanghai liudong renkou*, 135; Wuhan shi, *Chengshi wailai*, 281.

120. Yuan et al., *Luoren*, 31.

121. Li and Hu, *Liudong renkou*, 333.

122. Author's interview with social science researcher, Harbin, July 22, 1991.

123. Li and Hu, *Liudong renkou*, 251; and Cheng, "Da chengshi liudong renkou," 19.

124. Li and Hu, *Liudong renkou*, 251, 334; Wuhan shi, *Chengshi wailai*, 281.

125. Li and Hu, *Liudong renkou*, 334.

126. Such haphazard management must only exaggerate the irregularities that are normally the mark of the construction trade in any environment. See Marie, "From the Campaign Against Illegal Migration," 122.

127. Benkan jije, "Mingongchao," 8.

128. Author's interview, Nanjing, May 17, 1992.

129. Yuan et al., *Luoren*, 35.

130. The following account comes from these articles and books: Wang,

Wu, and Jiang, "Cong xue," 2; Shanghai shi, *Shanghai liudong renkou*, 136–38 and 222; Ge and Qu, *Zhongguo mingongchao;* and from my interviews with a social science researcher in Harbin, July 22, 1991, with a researcher at the Guangzhou Urban Planning Automation Center, May 11, 1992, with construction workers at their worksheds in Guangzhou, May 13, 1992, at a labor exchange in Nanjing, May 17, 1992, with the Daye county, Hubei, construction team, May 25, 1992, and with the Tianjin Construction Commission, June 17, 1992.

131. Yuan et al., *Luoren*, 37, 39.

132. Shanghai shi, *Shanghai liudong renkou*, 138.

133. Yuan et al., *Luoren*, 38.

134. In Harbin, for instance, those construction workers who waited out the winter might take to peddling food in the cold months and scouting out employment for the spring (my interview with social science researcher, July 22, 1991).

135. See Sassen-Koob, "New York City's Informal Economy," 65.

136. As Anita Chan astutely points out, much of what was billed as "foreign"-funded investment actually came from China's "compatriots" in Hong Kong and Taiwan, especially in firms along the southeastern coast, where many abuses were reported. See her piece in O'Leary, *Adjusting to Capitalism*. Work in the smaller township and village firms usually run by rural administrations closely resembled that in overseas-owned operations.

137. In many of Guangzhou's firms they already made up more than 25 percent of the work force in 1989 (Li and Hu, *Liudong renkou*, 34); a 1994 study of peasants working in cities in Henan found that a full 30 percent of them were employed in state-owned firms (Li, "Zhujiang sanjiaozhou," 44). In the Pearl River Delta's Dongguan City, though, only 1.3 percent were at work in state firms in 1992 (Guangdong wailai, "Zai liudongzhong," 117).

138. Author's interview, Tianjin Labor Bureau, June 16, 1992.

139. Author's interview with Tianjin Textile Bureau, June 11, 1992; and Wuhan shi, *Chengshi wailai*, 139.

140. Li and Hu, *Liudong renkou*, 269.

141. CD, July 24, 1991, 6.

142. FBIS, June 7, 1994, 48, from XH of that date.

143. Author's interview, May 23, 1992.

144. Li and Hu, *Liudong renkou*, 339–40. When five factories advertised for technical trainees in 1985, fewer than half the number requested signed up. In 1989, the city's recruitment target was 2,585 people, but in the first two months after advertising, only 200 showed up. By the late 1980s, an average of over 1,800 people were requesting transfers out of textiles each year.

145. Sun, "Floating Population in Shanghai," 11. Li, "200 Million Mouths," 4–7, states that over 90 percent of Shanghai's textile factories were shut down by 1994 under pressure from rising costs and competitive pres-

sures, leading to the loss of about 250,000 jobs in two years. Others were forced to withhold wages. See also XH, April 30, 1996, in FBIS, April 30, 1996, 54, which gives somewhat smaller numbers.

146. Li and Hu, *Liudong renkou,* 342.

147. Author's interview, Tianjin Textile Bureau, June 11, 1992. Also see Honig, *Sisters and Strangers,* ch. 2; and Solinger, *From Lathes to Looms,* ch. 2.

148. See Li and Hu, *Liudong renkou,* 223.

149. Li and Hu, *Liudong renkou,* 342; Rofel, "Eating Out of One Big Pot," 93. Author's interviews, Wuhan Labor Bureau, May 23, 1992; Wuhan Number One Cotton Mill, May 23, 1992; Tianjin Textile Bureau, June 11, 1992.

150. On the 1930s forerunner of the guarantor system, see Honig, *Sisters and Strangers,* 83, 90.

151. Provisional Regulations on the Management of Temporary Labor in Enterprises Owned by the Whole People; and Decree no. 87 of the State Council of the People's Republic of China: Provisions on Employing Peasant Contract Workers by State-Owned Enterprises. According to the second document, peasants hired on a temporary basis in state firms were officially to be treated rather similarly to permanent, urban contract workers. On the contract system to which these regulations refer, see Korzec, "Contract Labor," 129–30; White, "The Politics of Economic Reform"; and Davis, "Unequal Chances."

152. In the words of a sociologist at GASS, May 11, 1992, "We [in the state sector] have regulations to give basic guarantees on welfare, and the government investigates to check up. There are the trade unions, the individual workers' association, and the women's federation."

153. Variability of benefits for outside, contract, labor obtained in the prereform period (before 1980) as well. See Walder, *Communist Neo-Traditionalism,* 54. In the reform period, the amount of benefits a firm was able to provide was a function of its profits (Wuhan Labor Bureau, May 23, 1992, and Tianjin Labor Bureau, June 16, 1992).

154. Even in the cases where overall treatment was definitely wanting, as in the official *CD* (July 24, 1991, 6) description of the situation of rural women employed in Hubei textile firms who were "excluded from favorable treatment," much outside labor in state firms still received contracts ensuring a certain term of employment as of the early 1990s. Author's interviews, Wuhan Labor Bureau, May 23, 1992; Wuhan Number One Cotton Mill, May 23, 1992; Tianjin Textile Bureau, June 11, 1992; Tianjin Number Three Silk Weaving Mill, June 18, 1992; and Li and Hu, *Liudong renkou,* on Zhengzhou, 342.

155. There were cases to the contrary. For instance, according to XH, June 27, 1989 (translated in FBIS, July 19, 1989, 40), enterprises in Nanjing were recruiting peasants from northern Jiangsu and putting them to work immediately without any training at all. But in my interviews in Tianjin and

Wuhan I was given a number of examples of training (Tianjin, June 11 and 18, 1992; and Wuhan, May 11, 1992).

156. These working conditions appeared to apply generally, according to my interviews (for instance, the Tianjin Textile Bureau officials, June 11, 1992, alleged that their peasant workers worked eight-hour days, six days a week, the same as the regular labor), and lack of mention of this issue in the documentary material I surveyed.

157. Not all firms employing migrant workers housed them (Li and Hu, *Liudong renkou,* 269), but some housed at least a portion of them. Rather than supply individual apartments or at least a room like those for permanent workers (and their families), factories at best housed transient workers in collective dormitories that placed anywhere from three to twenty workers together in one room. Those whom the factory could not accommodate had to find their own housing, and a few factories helped with the rental costs (ibid., 344). Author's interviews with factory and labor and textile bureau officials, Wuhan and Tianjin, May and June 1992, respectively.

158. The individual enterprise made its own decision on medical assistance, in spite of the 1991 national State Council regulations.

159. Author's interviews at state-owned textile mills, Wuhan and Tianjin, May–June 1992. An average wage in industrial state-owned firms for staff and workers in 1992 was about 250 yuan per month, according to Guojia tongjiju bian, *Zhongguo tongji nianjian 1993,* 130. But in addition, urban workers still received substantially more benefits and subsidies than rural ones did.

160. Han, "Income, Consumption, and Employment"; and Guangdong wailai, "Zai liudongzhong," 114. In general, survey reports of average wages range widely, depending upon the region, the job, and gender. Moreover, most migrant workers (outside state factories) could not count on working every month of the year or every day of the week. On the whole, it seems that the average range was as reported here.

161. Bian, "Guanxi and the Allocation," 179–88, on the labor insurance, welfare benefits, and subsidies granted state-sector (and some collective-sector) workers in the mid- and late 1980s.

162. *RMRB,* July 17, 1993 (thanks to Thomas Heberer for showing me this article).

163. Author's interview, June 16, 1992.

164. Li and Hu, *Liudong renkou,* 346.

165. According to an official Chinese statistic, in the early part of 1996 there were 230,000 foreign-funded enterprises in China, employing 12 million workers, of which women accounted for more than half. (XH, March 12, 1996, in FBIS, March 13, 1996, 19). The conditions described below also obtained in most in collective enterprises owned and managed by rural administrative units, and in private-sectoral firms.

166. For details, see, among other writings, Hershatter, *The Workers of Tianjin;* Honig, *Sisters and Strangers;* and Lang, *Chinese Family.*

167. On this, see Pearson, *Joint Ventures.*

168. One excellent example is Ge and Qu, *Zhongguo mingongchao,* especially 146–56. Guangzhou's *NFRB* and the Shanghai journal *Shehui* also contain such stories.

169. Solinger, "The Danwei."

170. Ge and Qu, *Zhongguo mingongchao,* contains a number of stories of this sort.

171. See note 136 above.

172. Agence France-Presse, February 20, 1994, translated in FBIS, February 22, 1994, 53, and *Liaowang* 5 (1994): 26–29, translated in FBIS, March 3, 1994, 33, for Xiamen. The figures were not much different in Shantou and Zhuhai, according to the Beijing report. For Shandong, see FBIS, June 29, 1994, 53, from Jinan's *Dazhong ribao,* June 19, 1994, 6.

173. FBIS, October 28, 1993, 46, from XH of the same date.

174. *CD,* February 21, 1994, 1, reprinted in FBIS, February 22, 1994, 50.

175. *NFRB,* December 14, 1988, 2.

176. "The Impact of the 'Floating Population' and Surplus Labor," *Daxuesheng* (University student) 5 (1990): 36–38, translated in JPRS-CAR-90-054 (August 17, 1990), 43.

177. A report by the Guangdong federation of trade unions states that 37 percent of the workers in foreign firms in that province had been threatened with the loss of their jobs for complaining (in FBIS, January 13, 1994, 57, from *MP,* January 8, 1994, A9).

178. Brauchli and Kahn, "Toil and Trouble."

179. See FBIS, June 29, 1994, 53, from Jinan's *Dazhong ribao,* June 19, 1994, 6. There is reference there to state stipulations that the basic wages of staff and workers in foreign-funded firms should be at least 20 percent higher than that of workers in state-owned firms in the same trades in the same localities.

180. XH, February 23, 1994, translated in FBIS, same date, 41, says that a study of such firms in Guangdong province conducted by the provincial trade union federation found that in more than two-thirds of the firms, workers were paid less than the yearly local average; see also FBIS, March 13, 1996, from XH, March 12, 1996.

181. Wang and Jiang, "Baiwan 'yimin,' " 30.

182. *CD,* January 31, 1993, 6, reprinted in FBIS, February 3, 1993, 44, and *NFRB,* July 16, 1990, 1.

183. Ge and Qu, *Zhongguo mingongchao,* reports thus.

184. FBIS, September 21, 1993, 49, from *FZRB,* August 25, 1993, 1, 4.

185. *NFRB,* July 16, 1990, 1. There are many reports of deductions and unreturned deposits, such as Jiang, "Gonghui," 17; FBIS, February 2, 1994, 52 (from ZGTXS [Hong Kong]); and *SWB,* FE/3016 G/6 (September 5, 1997) from ZGXWS.

186. Yuan et al., *Luoren,* 117.

187. Brauchli and Kahn, "Toil and Trouble," state that the fees amount

to 350 yuan, and that they were told by workers that individuals who failed to register could be sent to a labor camp, where they would be forced to work without pay. As time went on, state firms too became guilty of this sort of infraction (XH, January 26, 1996, in FBIS, February 7, 1996, 41).

188. FBIS, April 5, 1994, 43 (from *Tangtai* [Contemporary (Hong Kong)] 36 [March 15, 1994]: 38–39). Brauchli and Kahn, "Toil and Trouble," survey a factory where workers were housed in a walled-off section of the factory floor, thirty to a room. *CD*, July 24, 1991, notes that joint ventures are "not responsible for rural employees' housing and other welfare needs."

189. "The Impact of the 'Floating Population' and Surplus Labor," *Daxuesheng*, translated in JPRS-CAR-90-054 (1990), 44; and Wang and Jiang, "Baiwan 'yimin,'" 30, for the present; Honig, *Sisters and Strangers*, 146, for pre-1949.

190. Jing, "Dongwan huozai," 25.

191. On workweeks, for a few citations of many, see ibid.; FBIS, August 23, 1988, 40–41; Jiang, "Gonghui," 18; Wang and Jiang, "Baiwan 'yimin'"; *NFRB*, July 16, 1990, 1; and FBIS, February 2, 1994, 52 (from Hong Kong's ZGTXS).

192. Rutkowski, "The China's Floating Population," 19–20. It is very likely that those firms providing pensions and other security benefits were the ones owned by Westerners, employing the educated, urban workers seconded away from state-sectoral firms. Enterprises employing the floating population, where a given worker's time on the payroll was generally brief and intermittent, were far less apt to provide these.

193. Jiang, "Gonghui," 17; Wang and Jiang, "Baiwan 'yimin,'" 30; FBIS, November 9, 1992, 47–48 (from ZGTXS); FBIS, February 22, 1994, 53, from Agence France-Presse (Hong Kong), February 20, 1994. Brauchli and Kahn, "Toil and Trouble," A8, report that some firms retained a doctor, but by no means all did.

194. FBIS, April 1, 1994, 88 (from *SCMP*, March 31, 1994, 2); see also Jing, "Dongwan huozai"; FBIS, July 25, 1991, 53, and January 10, 1994, 31 (from *CD*); and *Liaowang* 4 (1994): 40, in FBIS, February 4, 1994, 17–18.

195. FBIS, February 22, 1994, 53.

196. FBIS, January 13, 1994, 57–58.

197. The term "self-exploitation" is often encountered in writing on the private informal sector in other economies. Hill Gates defines it as "working for less than the market rate for labor," in Gates, "Owner, Worker," 144.

198. See FBIS, June 10, 1994, 55; November 9, 1992, 47; February 10, 1994, 41; February 4, 1994, 17; Jiang, "Gonghui," 18; FBIS, March 3, 1994, 38; February 22, 1994, 50 (from *CD*, February 21, 1994, 1); and March 3, 1994, 38.

199. Author's interview, Gulao neighborhood household labor introduction station (*jiawu laodong jieshaosuo*), Nanjing, May 17, 1992.

200. Author's interview, women's federation official, Tianjin, June 15, 1992.

201. Ibid.

202. According to FBIS, April 11, 1989, 46, a market for maids became active and sizable in 1984; Huang, Liu, and Peng, "Laizi Changshashi," describes one set up at first by the Tianjin women's federation that, lacking effective supervision, fell under the domination of criminal elements.

203. Wang and Feng, "Jingji tizhi gaigezhong," 10. Around 1985, according to statistics provided by the public security, there were already 50,000 *baomu* in the city (Zhu, "Mangliu Zhongguo"). But Li and Tang, "Beijing chengzhen," 22, writing in early 1988, states that in the past several years, at most there were 30,000 *baomu* in the capital.

204. Zhu, "Chengshizhong di nongmin," 10.

205. Author's interview, Wuhan Social Science Academy, September 17, 1990.

206. Chan, *Cities with Invisible Walls*, 126.

207. As of the mid-1980s, over half the women in the capital were members of a loosely constituted Anhui *bang* (clique), and most of them were natives of its Wuwei county (Zhu, "Mangliu Zhongguo"). Most of the maids in Nanjing were also from Anhui, according to my interview at a maids' labor exchange station, May 17, 1992.

208. Author's interview with a residents' committee, Wuhan, May 30, 1992, and with the Wuhan Social Science Academy and the Wuhan Policy Research Office, September 17 and 14, respectively, 1990. FBIS, October 27, 1994, 35, from XH, same date, states that 80 percent of the housekeepers in Beijing were from outside the city.

209. In Nanjing in 1992, I encountered street-level labor introduction stations; in Wuhan, I interviewed at a residents' committee, which was managing a labor exchange jointly with its superior, street-level's labor service company; and in Tianjin, the women's federation had set up a Tianjin City Family Service Introduction office, modeled after Beijing's March 8 Family Labor Service Company, created by the Beijing City Women's Federation.

210. Author's interviews, Wuhan, May 30, and Tianjin, June 15, 1992.

211. The Tianjin exchange also held monthly meetings for the women and organized social activities.

212. Author's interviews, Nanjing University sociology department, May 21, 1992, at a residents' committee, Wuhan, May 30, 1992, and with an official from the Tianjin women's federation, June 15, 1992.

213. *Baomu* groups were noted as being the only organized groups among the floating population in my interview at the Wuhan Social Science Academy, September 17, 1990; and at my interviews in Wuhan, May 30, 1992, and Tianjin, June 15, 1992; see also the talk by Hu Xiaobo.

214. In the early 1990s, in Nanjing the hourly pay was 25 yuan, in Beijing and Shanghai hourly wages went up to 40 yuan, and the women were more inclined to take Sunday off (my interviews, Harbin, July 7, 1990). Harbin itself does not use outside maids but relies on the family or on local women

(according to my interview on July 18, 1990; and in Nanjing, with the scholar Ma Shuluan, May 15, 1992).

215. Yuan et al., *Luoren*, 101–2.

216. The official from the Tianjin women's federation whom I interviewed alleged that a maid hired in a spontaneous market might land a salary as high as 200 yuan a month in that city's unofficial markets (June 15, 1992).

217. Huang, Liu, and Peng, "Laizi Changshashi," 16; my interview at labor exchange, Nanjing, May 17, 1992; and FBIS, April 11, 1989, 46.

218. Chen, "China: Maid Service."

219. Author's interviews, GASS, May 10 and 11, 1992, and Tianjin, with a women's federation official, June 15, 1992.

220. Yuan et al., *Luoren*, 25, 53, 57, 59, and 111.

221. On the activities of merchants from Rui'an, Zhejiang, resident in Beijing in the 1990s, see ibid., 53–59.

222. See Wang, Shi, and Song, "Beijing's Mobile Population," 46; also, *CD*, January 21, 1995, 3, in FBIS, January 23, 1995, 74; in "Beijingshi getihu," 36, Shi says that in one Beijing district, 70 percent of the proprietors and 75 percent of the hired laborers were outsiders.

223. See Yuan et al., *Luoren*, 53, 56, for examples.

224. Bruun, *Business and Bureaucracy*, 133. See de Soto, *The Other Path* on the difficulties of access for the poor—but not necessarily for all migrants— in Peru's labor market.

225. Wank, "Bureaucratic Patronage," 160, 164, 178; Bruun, *Business and Bureaucracy*, 87, 92; and Bruun, "Political Hierarchy," 192, 200.

226. Yuan et al., *Luoren*, 58, 62.

227. Bruun, *Business and Bureaucracy*, 85, 92.

228. Xiang, "How to Create," 20–21, contrasts the hard path for outsiders trying to be private entrepreneurs in Beijing with the easier one for those native to the city.

229. Author's interview at Beijing open market, August 6, 1994.

230. Xiang, "How to Create," 13.

231. Information from You Ji, Hong Kong, June 27, 1991; Xiang, "How to Create."

232. Zhu, "Chengshizhong di nongmin," 15; and Zhao, "Some Special Phenomena of Income Distribution During Transformation of Economic System in China," *Jingji yanjiu* (Economic research) 1 (1992): 53–63 (translated in JPRS-CAR-92-043 [June 22, 1992], 13), states that among private firms in large cities, only one-fifth of the entrepreneurs earn more than 1,000 a year.

233. Wang and Zuo, "Rural Migrants in Shanghai," 4.

234. Wuhan shi, *Chengshi wailai*, 114, 115.

235. Zhou, "Guangzhou 'wailai sangong,'" 50.

236. Author's interview with representative from the Tianjin Commercial Commission, June 23, 1992; on Wuhan, see Zhongguo shehui kexueyuan, *Zhongguo renkou nianjian 1987*, 684.

237. Goldstein and Goldstein, "Population Mobility," 33.

238. Goldstein and Goldstein, "Town and City," 30; Li and Hu, *Liudong renkou*, 249; and Shanghai shi, *Shanghai liudong renkou*, 106, 64. On where they lived, see my interview, Tianjin Housing Bureau, June 19, 1992, and personal observation and interviews in the open markets of Tianjin, Nanjing, and Wuhan, May–June 1992.

239. Yuan et al., *Luoren*, 77, with reference to dealers in aquatic products from Yixian, Hebei.

240. Author's interview with social scientists, Harbin, July 4, 1991.

241. See Ge and Qu, *Zhongguo mingongchao*, describing the "three fears" of small peddlers. For background on the treatment of small traders between 1949 and 1980, see Solinger, *Chinese Business*.

242. Communication from Li Zhang; Shi, "Beijingshi getihu," 37.

243. Yuan et al., *Luoren*, 82.

244. Author's interview with cadre from the Tianjin Commercial Commission, June 23, 1992.

245. Fang et al., "Xibu fazhan"; Goldstein and Goldstein, "Population Mobility," 34.

246. Author's street interview, Hexi district, Tianjin, June 27, 1992, and Tianjin, May 1992.

247. Author's interview with Harbin social science researcher, July 22, 1991.

248. Zhou, "Guangzhou 'wailai sangong,' " 50, 54.

249. As one social scientist in Harbin commented, "If they repair shoes for three seasons (six months each), they can go home and build a two-story house" (my interview, July 4, 1991). In Wuhan social scientists maintained that a shoe repairer could make 3,000 to 5,000 yuan a day (my interview at the Wuhan Social Science Academy, May 22, 1992); in Tianjin a market official claimed their net income to be 600 to 700 a month (June 22, 1992). The two estimates would jibe if the average cobbler worked half the year.

250. *CD*, July 30, 1991, 6.

251. Ge and Qu, *Zhongguo mingongchao*, 97.

252. Ibid., 98.

253. On *tongxianghui*, the seminal work in Chinese is Ho, *Zhongguo huiguan*. Also see Golas, "Early Ch'ing Guilds"; Goodman, *Native Place*; Skinner, "Urban Social Structure"; Rowe, *HANKOW: Commerce and Society*; and Rowe, *HANKOW: Community and Conflict*.

254. Li and Tang, "Beijing chengzhen," 21.

255. Author's interview with the vice chairman of the semiofficial Hanzheng Street IEA, May 24, 1992.

256. Liu, "Liudong di 'shimin,' " 31; Min, "A Village," 4; and Beja and Bonnin, "The Destruction," 22.

257. By way of comparison, in the catering trade only 75 percent of the employees were outsiders; in other services, 60 percent, and in repairs,

only 44 percent. Li and Tang, "Beijing chengzhen," 21, 22. Li and Hu, *Liudong renkou*, 41, have the same figure of over 90 percent for employees, for 1989.

258. Li and Hu, *Liudong renkou*, 358.

259. Zhu, "Chengshizhong di nongmin," 22, writes of a Zhejiang Village of tailors of 20,000 in early 1992; but later that year, Nickerson, "Migrant Workers," claims, Zhejiang Village housed 200,000–300,000 people. An official from the Tianjin ICA Open Markets Office in a June 22, 1992, interview said that over 6,000 people from the south were processing clothing in that city.

260. Yuan et al., *Luoren*, 75.

261. On this process, see Xiang, "How to Create." For a discussion of these villages, see chapter 7.

262. Li and Hu, *Liudong renkou*, 358; my interview, August 5, 1994.

263. Author's interview, August 7, 1994.

264. Author's interviews, August 5, 1994; Min, "A Village"; Wang, "Communities of 'Provincials,' " 18; and Piante and Zhu, "Life and Death," 13; Xiang, "How to Create," 15.

265. Gates, "Owner, Worker," 153, 160.

266. Zhu, "Chengshizhong di nongmin," 22; and Liu, "Liudong di 'shimin,' " 31.

267. Xiang, "How to Create," 16.

268. Min, "A Village"; my interview, August 5, 1994. Xiang, "How to Create," 15, states that there were interest rates charged among relatives, but that they ran in the range of only 2 to 3 percent.

269. Johnson, "Bright Lights," 47; according to Beja and Bonnin, "The Destruction," drawing on market research, their share of the market in several products was in the range of 40 to 50 percent; but for leather jackets, it was up to 70 to 80 percent and as high as 90 percent for buttons and zippers.

270. Li and Hu, *Liudong renkou*, 356, state that 30 percent of the migrants rent from city residents and 70 percent from local peasants.

271. Nickerson, "Migrant Workers."

272. Nickerson, "Migrant Workers," gives a figure of 600 yuan a month. But many of the workers did not receive their pay until the end of the year, and the amount they got depended on how much of their output was actually sold. *SCMP*, March 13, 1994, 8–12, reprinted in FBIS, March 15, 1994, 43, states that peasants in cottage industries earned about half the pay of state employees. In an interview, August 5, 1994, I was told that employees' earnings were about 5,000–6,000 yuan per year. Also, my interview, February 14, 1994; Li and Hu, *Liudong renkou*, 358.

273. Kuhn and Kaye, "Bursting," 27.

274. Beja and Bonnin, "The Destruction," 22.

275. Xiang, "How to Create," 8–9.

276. Li and Hu, *Liudong renkou*, 358.

277. Min, "A Village."

278. Wang and Hu, "Zhongshi tiaojie," 72; Liu, *Zhongguo di qigai qunluo*, 213; my interviews with Guangzhou Urban Planning Automation Center, May 11, 1992, and with scholars at Wuhan Social Science Academy, May 22, 1992; and Li and Hu, *Liudong renkou*, 54.

279. Li and Hu, *Liudong renkou*, 54: "In Guangzhou, together they account for 3 to 4 percent of the total floating population." But on 22 they cite a percentage of 1 to 10, and say that in a number of major cities, such as Beijing, Shanghai, Guangzhou, Wuhan, Chengdu, and Zhengzhou, the numbers were rising as of 1989.

280. Zhang, Zhao, and Chen, "1994: Nongcun laodongli," 30; Ba jia, *Nongcun laodongli jingji*, A-01, 7, says 10 percent come "blindly"; and A-02–8 cites 14.7 percent.

281. Compare Gu, "Dushi 'mangliu,' " 8; Chai, "Liudong renkou," 9; and Tang and Chen, "Qiangxing jiju," 19.

282. Zeng, "Dadushi," 24; Liu, *Zhongguo di qigai qunluo*, 197–98; and Li and Hu, *Liudong renkou*, 54, respectively.

283. Li, "Under Neon Lights," 5.

284. Gu, "Dushi 'mangliu,' " 8; *CD*, July 30, 1991, 6, mentions the similar, if indeterminate figure of "tens of yuan per day." See Liu, *Zhongguo di qigai qunluo*, 211, for the lower figure.

285. Feng and Li, "Liulang qitao"; Liu, *Zhongguo di qigai qunluo*, 214–15.

286. Gao, "On the Sharp End," 13, terms them "the lowest class of migrant workers."

287. Magritte, "Trashpickers' Urban Wasteland," 8.

288. Ibid.

289. Yuan et al., *Luoren*, 9, 11, 125.

290. Schak, *A Chinese Beggars' Den*, 10–24, 66, 146–69, on the Qing and Taipei; and Wakeman, *Shanghai Police*, Honig, *Creating Chinese Ethnicity*, 66, and Perry, *Shanghai on Strike*, 5, on Republican Shanghai. Schak found it impossible to get information on the leaders' outside ties to politicians in 1970s Taipei.

291. Chai, "Liudong renkou," 9; *CD*, July 30, 1991, 6; Zeng, "Dadushi," 24; Liu, *Zhongguo di qigai qunluo*, 198, 205–10; FBIS, October 17, 1994, 80 (from ZGXWS); and my interview, June 10, 1992, with a cadre from Tianjin's public security office.

292. Kaye, "Conflicts of Interest," 26.

293. Shao, "Dongyao gongyouzhi," 49–50.

294. Zeng, "Dadushi," 25, says that "those not in a *bang* were excluded and get low incomes."

295. Huang, "Liudongzhong," 21, writes of a father collecting junk with his twelve-year-old son, who did this job in lieu of school.

296. Author's interview on the street, Nanjing, May 20, 1992.

297. Yuan et al., *Luoren*, 121: "Even Zhejiang people with a high income

felt they had to rely on themselves to protect their interests and just went to fellow villagers when they needed help."

298. A prime example is the effort of city bureaucrats to push out private entrepreneurs periodically, usually at times of major events, such as the international women's conference in 1995 or the Asian Games of 1990. A crackdown may also happen suddenly and without any warning, even to a community as a whole, as it did to garment workers from Zhejiang in Beijing in autumn 1995. See Beja and Bonnin, "The Destruction"; and Zhang, "Strangers in the City."

CHAPTER 7

1. Zhang, "Basic Facts," 8.

2. For instance, see *The Independent* in cooperation with *Yomiuri shimbun* (Tokyo), November 13, 1994, 7A; *NMRB*, March 30, 1995, 4, in FBIS, May 26, 1995, 64.

3. This process is superbly detailed in Xiang, "How to Create."

4. Ibid., 9, quotes a resident of Beijing's Zhejiang Village as saying, "I was walking out of certain protection [in 1982] in leaving him [a director of a state supply and marketing cooperative]." But ibid., 24, states that the "new structure," the Zhejiang Village, "provides certain protection to migrants, who can realize many social demands outside the state system."

5. Ibid., 9, quotes a member of the Zhejiang Village, who, as he came to depend more and more on market relations and less on the assistance of a state official, remarked, "I didn't worry. We had quite a tidy sum of money with us . . . the most important thing was to get enough money"; as one migrant laborer in Beijing in summer 1994 observed, "If you're without a *hukou*, money is the biggest issue; with money, you can buy a house, go to school, *hukou* or not" (my interview, Beijing migrant labor market, August 7, 1994). See also Zhang and Yang, "Mingongchao," 45.

6. The issue of ties with state officials is a complex one. The members of the nucleus of what later became Zhejiang's famous Zhejiang Village got their start by cooperating with and being befriended by cadres, at a time when they dared not step outside the stringent regulations of officialdom. At a later stage they were able to throw off that support and forge ahead by cooperating among themselves, but they were ultimately vulnerable without state protection. Moreover, joint partnerships with local administrators helped to create and legitimate elites within the village and fostered large-scale undertakings. See Xiang, "How to Create," 8–10, 18, 20, 27, 17, 33.

7. See Portes and Stepick, *City on the Edge*, 8.

8. Wang, "Communities of 'Provincials,' " 20.

9. Wang and Zuo, "Rural Migrants in Shanghai," 15; Chan, "Post-Mao China," 146–47.

10. Han, "It's Imperative," 10; and Ba jia, *Nongcun laodongli jingji*, A-02, 11.

11. Taeuber, "Migrants and Cities," 363.

12. Mazumdar, "Rural-Urban Migration," 1116–17.

13. See Li and Hu, *Liudong renkou*, 167 (Wuhan); 128 (Beijing); and 154 (Shanghai); on 193, they report Guangzhou's migrant population as 67.76 percent male; and on 265, Hangzhou's as 66 percent male (as chapter 6 pointed out, this major center of the textile trade recruited only women from the countryside).

14. Zhou, "Guangzhou 'wailai sangong,' " 47.

15. Li, "Understanding," 27.

16. Wang and Zuo, "Rural Migrants in Shanghai," 2.

17. Ba jia, *Nongcun laodongli jingji*, A-03, 3.

18. Gilley, "Sisters Act," 20.

19. Li and Hu, *Liudong renkou*, 167.

20. Tang, "Changzhu liudong renkou," 39–40, applies this line of reasoning but does not explore it empirically with any rigor. Wang and Zuo, "Rural Migrants in Shanghai," 7, also note that "most females were working in service and sales as small vendors" in Shanghai in 1995.

21. According to *NFRB*, December 19, 1988, 2, in the Pearl River Delta, where foreign firms concentrate, there were then a million outside workers, 70 to 80 percent of them female.

22. Demographers at GASS, May 11, 1992, explained that young women were preferred in textiles and electronics because they were more *lingchao* (careful, clever). This occupational prejudice is an old one; it is also cited in Honig, *Sisters and Strangers*.

23. In Beijing in 1987, of the nonresident workers hired by private entrepreneurs, 60 percent were female (Li and Tang, "Beijing chengzhen," 22).

24. Li and Hu, *Liudong renkou*, 51.

25. Zhu, "The Sale of Women," 4–5. This article maintains that from 1986 to 1994, 48,000 women were abducted across the country and sold in just six counties in Xuzhou city, Jiangsu. It also notes that the price of women rose from 200 to 300 yuan a few years earlier to as much as 4,000 by 1994.

26. Tang, "Changzhu liudong renkou," 39; also Roberts and Wei, "Floating Population," 5, 28.

27. Yang, "The Nature." The respective percentages were 50 percent for men and only 32.8 percent for women.

28. Suggestion by a sociologist at GASS, May 13, 1992.

29. Guangdong wailai, "Zai liudongzhong," 112. Roberts and Wei, "Floating Population," 12, state that "many women stop migrating after marriage."

30. Zhou, "Guangzhou 'wailai sangong,' " 48.

31. Roberts and Wei, "Floating Population," 11.

32. Wang and Zuo, "Rural Migrants in Shanghai," 4.

33. Yuan et al., *Luoren*, 102. And yet, according to JPRS-CAR-92-004 [*sic*] (January 25, 1993), 32, a translation of Yang Jinxing, "The Impact of China's Population Flow Between Urban and Rural Areas on Population Con-

trol," from *RKYJJ*, 5 (1992), a 1988 survey of Shanghai reports 4,744 women of childbearing age among the floating population, 2,706 of them married; but of these, 68.2 percent were living separately from their husbands.

34. Nongcun shengyu laodongli, "28ge xian," 28. According to my interview with an official from the Tianjin Public Security Bureau, June 10, 1992, the only occupation in which workers tended to be married was commerce, since businesspeople made enough money to bring their families and children.

35. Hondagneu-Sotelo, *Gendered Transitions*, 20, 26, notes that in the late nineteenth century Mexican migrants were mainly men but that, with the maturation of social networks over the next century, women and entire families made up a significant component of the migrant population.

36. Researcher Han Jun of the Rural Development Institute, CASS, in a letter dated March 3, 1995, states, "According to surveys, about 5 percent of the floating population can't find jobs"; a Guangdong survey of 1992 learned that under 10 percent did not find work within a week of arriving in the city (Guangdong wailai, "Zai liudongzhong," 116); Guangdong province Public Security Bureau statistics for the end of 1994 come up with the same figure (Ba jia, *Nongcun laodongli jingji*, A-02, 9); 1994–95 research using a nation-wide sample of 318 villages reports that only 0.75 percent never found work (Zhang, Zhao, and Chen, "1994: Nongcun laodongli," 28); a Shanghai sample survey of out-of-town workers in late 1995 shows that of the 34.8 percent of the total sample who had a job lined up before arriving, 74 percent began working right away, and that of those 65.2 percent of the total who "came to look for a job," 50.6 percent (or 33 percent of the total sample) could find work within less than a month (Wang and Zuo, "Rural Migrants in Shanghai," 4–5).

37. Author's interviews, August 7, 1994.

38. Nongcun shengyu laodongli, "28ge xian," 28.

39. Ba jia, *Nongcun laodongli jingji*, A-02, 10, finds that more than 50 percent of the migrants in Guangdong province stayed away from home less than two years. Zhang, Zhao, and Chen, "1994: Nongcun laodongli," 28, find that 42 percent had been away from home continuously for two years with stable employment.

40. Nongyebu, "Jingji fazhanzhong," 43, says 40 percent of the migrant labor investigated in an early 1994 study in 75 villages in 11 provinces was seasonal; in another study in the same year, in 28 counties in 15 provinces, however, seasonal labor accounts for only 20.7 percent of the total (Nongcun shengyu laodongli, "28ge xian," 27).

41. Li, "Understanding," 30.

42. Nongyebu, "Jingji fazhanzhong," 47.

43. For the mid-1980s, Liu and Chang, "Chengshi liudong renkou," 46, give 51.7 percent for Shanghai in 1986 and 51.6 percent for Beijing in 1985; Piante and Zhu, "Life and Death," 12, say that 55 percent of the migrants in Beijing had been there for more than six months in 1995.

44. Han, "It's Imperative," 11.

45. Gao, "Qianyi liudong renkou," 61–62. Many, but by no means all, returned home at the rural busy season and at Chinese New Year's.

46. Bonilla, "Rio's Favelas," 81.

47. Perlman, *Myth of Marginality*, 182; also Huntington and Nelson, *No Easy Choice*, 109; and Nelson, *Migrants*, 57, 61.

48. Nelson, *Access to Power*, 107.

49. Nelson, *Migrants*, 48, 51; Cornelius, *Politics and the Migrant Poor*, 72.

50. Portes and Bach, *Latin Journey*, 285–86.

51. Yang, "The Nature," 6. This was also found in Lu, "Shandong 4 chengzhen," 63. This latter source notes in a 1986 survey that the satisfaction was highest among those with the lowest cultural level, and that the more educated the migrants, the less satisfied they were.

52. Zhu, "Chengshizhong di nongmin," 17.

53. Author's interview with Gu Shangfei, New York, February 14, 1994.

54. Cornelius, *Politics and the Migrant Poor*, 24; similarly, Perlman, *Myth of Marginality*, 182, finds that more than 80 percent of the migrants in Rio de Janeiro did not want to return to the places they left.

55. Costello, Leinbach, and Ulack, *Mobility and Employment*, 12; in Kanpur City in India, only 18 percent gave an emphatic no about settling permanently there (Chandra, *Social Participation*, 81).

56. Yang, "The Nature," 6, 8.

57. Yuan et al., *Luoren*, 121, based on a 1994 survey of 1,200 outsiders in Beijing and Shanghai report that 16 percent felt severe discrimination and 52 percent felt some; see also Li, "Tidal Wave," pt. 1, 11; and Yuan, Zhang, and Wang, "Self-Organize," 2.

58. Zhang, Zhao, and Chen, "1994: Nongcun laodongli," 28.

59. Wuhan shi, *Chengshi wailai*, 139.

60. Du, "Beijing chengli," 25.

61. Zhou, "Guangdong 'wailai sangong,' " 52.

62. Speare, Liu, and Tsay, *Urbanization and Development*, 169.

63. Zhou, "Guangdong 'wailai sangong,' " 52. Wang and Zuo, "Rural Migrants in Shanghai," 14, state that the same proportion, "about a third," expressed an intention to stay in Shanghai, if possible, in late 1995; in Beijing at this time only slightly more, 40 percent, hoped for a long-term stay, according to Yuan et al., *Luoren*, 2.

64. Ba jia, *Nongcun laodongli jingji*, A-02, 7. One thousand questionnaires were distributed to 149 factories.

65. Yuan et al., *Luoren*, 65, 68–69, 123–24.

66. Yang, "The Nature," 8.

67. Ibid., 6; and Yuan et al., *Luoren*, 75, concur. The interviews in the latter source indicate that those who had expanded their businesses felt very satisfied with their urban lives.

68. Wang and Zuo, "Rural Migrants in Shanghai," 14, also note that

potential for upward mobility, as expressed in occupation and education, disposed migrants to stay in the city.

69. Zhu, "Chengshizhong di nongmin," 38.

70. Ibid., 36.

71. Kuhn and Kaye, "Bursting," 27–28; Thompson, "Afloat," 26–27.

72. Wang, "Invisible Walls," 18, however, perhaps exaggerating somewhat, terms the purchased *hukou* a worthless piece of paper.

73. Zhu, "Chengshizhong di nongmin," 22, states that in Beijing by 1992 there were more than ten such concentrated areas.

74. Zhang, "Guanyu Beijingshi," 23, says that there were 2.3 times as many people from Zhejiang as there were Beijingers in this section of the city; Li and Hu, *Liudong renkou,*, 218–19, note that even in far inland Chengdu, in one area of the city one and a half times the native population were people from elsewhere in 1989. One study finds that the ratio of locals to outsiders in Beijing's Anhui Village by 1995 was actually one to nine (Yuan et al., *Luoren,* 77).

75. Xie, "Chengshi liudong renkou," 74.

76. Li and Hu, *Liudong renkou,* 56. The study lists the names of the relevant areas in Beijing, Guangzhou, Tianjin, Wuhan, Harbin, and Shenyang.

77. Ibid., 112.

78. Author's interviews, Harbin, July 19, 1991; GASS, May 10, 1992; Department of Sociology, Nanjing University, May 21, 1992; and talk with Gu Shangfei, a Chinese social scientist, New York, February 14, 1994; Tang and Chen, "Qiangxing jiju," 19; and Vogel, *One Step Ahead,* 218.

79. Tang and Chen, "Qiangxing jiju," 21; and Li and Hu, *Liudong renkou,* 57; *NFRB*, March 30, 1990, 2.

80. JPRS-CAR-93-091 (December 29, 1993), 45; Xu and Li, "China's Open Door Policy."

81. FBIS, July 14, 1993, 53.

82. Xiang, "How to Create," 16, 22, 34; Beja and Bonnin, "The Destruction," 22.

83. Wong, "China's Urban Migration."

84. Wang, "The Public Order Situation," 24.

85. Rowe, *HANKOW: Community and Conflict,* 230, states that in 1865 the city of Wuhan contained a "vast population of squatters." Hershatter, *The Workers of Tianjin,* ch. 3, describes the rampant slum conditions that obtained in early twentieth-century Tianjin.

86. Ma, "Urban Housing Supply," 256.

87. On the income barrier elsewhere, see Portes and Walton, *Urban Latin America,* 27, 38, 49, 54, 56; Rossi, *Down and Out,* 41 (on the U.S. homeless, for whom low incomes preclude obtaining suitable housing); Lees, *Exiles of Erin,* 5; Bonilla, "Rio's Favelas," 74; Castles and Kosack, *Immigrant Workers,* 57; and Lloyd, *Slums of Hope?* 26.

88. See especially Tang and Chen, "Qiangxing jiju," 19–21.

89. Wang, "Communities of 'Provincials,' " 17.

90. Lecture, Columbia University on November 10, 1993.

91. Yuan et al., *Luoren*, 103.

92. Portes and Rumbaut, *Immigrant America*, 21. Examples of the many studies of migrant enclave communities in quite diverse times and places are Gunes-Ayata, "Migrants and Natives," 239; Lees, *Exiles of Erin*; Crissman, "The Segmentary Structure"; Portes and Rumbaut, *Immigrant America*, 21; Portes and Walton, *Urban Latin America*; Keyssar, *Out of Work*, 78; and Rosenzweig, *Eight Hours*, 31. Portes and Bach, *Latin Journey*, 27, speak of "economic enclaves."

93. As in Honig, *Creating Chinese Ethnicity*.

94. Yuan et al., *Luoren*, 103, 113–14.

95. Ibid., 26.

96. Gunes-Ayata, "Migrants and Natives," 234–48 (Turkey); Cornelius, "Urbanization," 1132–33, and Cornelius, *Politics and the Migrant Poor*, 59–63 and 159–60 (Mexico); Gallin and Gallin, "The Integration of Village Migrants into Urban Society," 170 (Taiwan); Lloyd, *Slums of Hope?* 32 (third world); and Roberts, *The Making of Urban Citizens*, 174 (Latin America).

97. Wang, "Communities of 'Provincials,' " 18.

98. Zhu, "Chengshizhong di nongmin," 23, 30, 36–42.

99. Du, "Beijing shiqu," 13.

100. Zhang, "The Mobile Population," 23.

101. *EE*, August 20–21, 1994, 8; Liu, "Liudong di 'shimin,' " 31; *CD*, June 18, 1992, 3.

102. Author's interview, Beijing, August 7, 1994.

103. JPRS-CAR-091-93 (December 29, 1993), 45; Zhu, "Chengshizhong di nongmin," 22. Zhu finds it to be the home of 2,400 people in late 1991, four times the number of Beijing locals living there.

104. Wang, "Communities of 'Provincials,' " 17; Quan, "Beware!" 24; and Sun, "Floating Population in Shanghai," 13.

105. Wu, "Houniao renkou," 41.

106. Yuan and Tang, "Xinjiang liudong renkou," 51.

107. Zhu, "Cong zhua."

108. Author's interview, Guangzhou Urban Planning Automation Center, May 11, 1992.

109. *NFRB*, August 24, 1989, 2.

110. *NFRB*, March 30, 1990, 2.

111. Wong, "China's Urban Migration."

112. Shanghai shi, *Shanghai liudong renkou*, 63.

113. Zhou, *How the Farmers Changed China*, ch. 6.

114. Sun, "Floating Population in Shanghai," 13.

115. My sources on Dahongmen include Zhu, "Chengshizhong di nongmin," 20–22; FBIS, November 16, 1992, 38 (from *SCMP*, November 16,

1992, 10); JPRS-CAR-93-091 (December 29, 1993), 45; Johnson, "Bright Lights"; my interviews with Gu Shangfei, New York, February 14, 1994, and Beijng, August 5, 1994; Ming, "Wo kandao"; Magritte, "Trashpickers' Urban Wasteland"; Min, "A Village"; Wang, "Communities of 'Provincials' "; Beja and Bonnin, "The Destruction"; Piante and Zhu, "Life and Death"; and Xiang, "How to Create."

116. Liu, "Liudong di 'shimin,' " 31.

117. Xiang, "How to Create," 13.

118. Zhang, "Guanyu Beijingshi," 23–24. Within another seven years, the ratio had changed to 8:1 in parts of the area, according to Beja and Bonnin, "The Destruction," 22.

119. This is the estimate of Gu Shangfei.

120. Xiang, "How to Create," 16.

121. JPRS-CAR-93-091 (December 29, 1993); Xiang, "How to Create," 4, explains that, according to the calculation of a government department, of the 100,000 or so resident in this area in late 1994, 14,000 were native Beijingers, and 96,000 were from the outside. Among the migrants, over 50,000 were businesspeople and their families, 75 percent of them from Yueqing county in Wenzhou prefecture, and 20 percent came from its Yongjia county. Other prefectures in Zhejiang account for 5 percent. The remaining 40,000 came from Hebei, Anhui, and Hubei provinces.

122. Piante and Zhu, "Life and Death," 14. The districts were named Dengcun, Macun, Shicun, and Houcun.

123. Magritte, "Trashpickers' Urban Wasteland."

124. Xiang, "How to Create."

125. Ming, "Wo kandao," 25; Zhu, "Chengshizhong di nongmin," 22; JPRS-CAR-93-091 (December 29, 1993), 45; Min, "A Village," 4.

126. Xiang, "How to Create," 29; also Zhu, "Chengshizhong di nongmin," 22; and my interview with Gu Shangfei, February 14, 1994.

127. Yuan et al., *Luoren*, 75–85.

128. Ibid., 19, 103, 111, 114, 115.

129. "Tamen ju wu ding suo, xing wu ding zong; yin xing maiming, chengxiang liucuan"; from Huang and Chen, "Wuhan shiqu," 689.

130. Hao, Kang, and Wang, "Haerbinshi ziliu renkou," 83.

131. On the variety of housing situations in the late 1980s, see Zhang, "Guanyu chengshi liudong renkou," 52–53. Li and Hu, *Liudong renkou*, give breakdowns for Beijing (128–29), Shanghai (152), Wuhan (168), Guangzhou (192), Chengdu (218) as of 1989. However, though this volume is the outcome of one governmental study, the categories employed by the researchers in each city are totally noncomparable. The main problem is the collapsing together of different categories in different cities. There are also reports for the mid-1980s for Beijing in Wang and Feng, "Jingji tizhe gaigezhong," 5; Luo et al., "Quanmin renshi"; and for Shanghai in Zheng et al., "Shanghai shiqu," 2–3. Li and Hu, *Liudong renkou*, 129, note that compared with the situation in 1985, a smaller percentage of the sojourning population was

composed of hotel dwellers by the late 1980s: 27 percent as against 40 percent in the earlier year. Meanwhile, the proportion living on construction sites had increased further, from 1985's 21 percent up to 29.8 percent. Beijing as of 1990 is reported in Wang, Shi, and Song, "Beijing's Mobile Population."

132. Rowe, HANKOW: *Community and Conflict*, 217.

133. Zhu, "Chengshizhong di nongmin," 22, states that two living patterns obtained among the floating population: scattered and concentrated.

134. Kirkby, in *Urbanisation in China*, 165 and 177; Lees, *Exiles of Erin*, 55; Perlman, *Myth of Marginality*, 7, 12; Rossi, *Down and Out*, 185; Stuart and Gregory, "A Model of Soviet," 86; and Cornelius, *Politics and the Migrant Poor*, 27.

135. Perlman, *Myth of Marginality*, 13; Portes and Walton, *Urban Latin America*, 54, 58; and de Soto, *The Other Path*, 11.

136. Nelson, "Sojourners versus New Urbanites," 745; Vargas, *Proletarians of the North*, 127; Butterworth, "A Study," 102, 111. According to Zhu, "Chengshizhong di nongmin," 20, only 5 percent of her sample of nearly 300 respondents in Beijing in late 1991 considered that they had come to the city to live permanently (rather than stay a while just to earn money). Thus, she concluded, they did not care about enjoying life, nor did they have the inclination to make the quality of their lives in the city comfortable.

137. Author's interview, Tianjin Housing Bureau, June 19, 1992; and with Gu Shangfei, New York, February 14, 1994; and Xu and Li, "China's Open Door Policy," 56.

138. Although Xu and Li, "China's Open Door Policy," 56, note exceptions in the towns of the Pearl River Delta as of 1989.

139. As of 1982, the state owned 82.3 percent of floor space in cities nationwide (28.7 percent by city housing bureaus and 53.69 percent by enterprises or other work units) (Kirkby, *Urbanisation in China*, 166). Lee, "The Urban Housing Problem," 397, puts a date of 1981 on this data. In Tianjin in 1992, 60 percent of the housing was city-owned and 32 percent unit-owned, according to the city's Housing Bureau (my interview, June 19, 1992).

140. Author's interview, Tianjin Housing Bureau, June 19, 1992.

141. Wang and Zuo, "Rural Migrants in Shanghai," 9.

142. Lang, *Chinese Family*, 84; Hershatter, *The Workers of Tianjin*, ch. 3.

143. Ye, "Suzhoushi wailai," 56.

144. Author's interview, Tianjin, June 10, 1994.

145. Xu and Li, "China's Open Door Policy," 56, contend that most new arrivals stayed with family or friends. In my data, only just over half did so; the others found other accommodations.

146. Li, "Under Neon Lights," 3. See also ZGXWS, March 15, 1995, in FBIS, March 16, 1995, 64 (4,000 to 5,000 were sleeping in Guangzhou's streets during the Spring Festival that year); and Li, "Tidal Wave," pt. 1, 12, 14 (on shacks in Beijing holding more than 500 people in just 300 square meters or offering just one toilet for more than 6,000 people).

147. Gao, "On the Sharp End," 13.

148. Brown, "The Architecture"; and Morgan, "In the Shadow."

149. Gao, "On the Sharp End," 13.

150. Ge and Qu, *Zhongguo mingongchao*, 46.

151. Ibid., 86–88.

152. Author's interviews with Wuhan Grain Bureau, May 26, 1992, with Wuhan Number One Cotton Mill, May 23, 1992, and with Tianjin Grain Bureau, June 18, 1992.

153. Author's interview, Tianjin Grain Bureau, June 18, 1992. In the early 1980s, the income of the average floater was only about 1 yuan per day, although by 1985 it had climbed up to 3 to 4 yuan per day (my interview, Tianjin Finance Bureau, June 22, 1992). By the early 1990s, it was probably in the range of 10 yuan a day (personal interviews). Hao, Kang, and Wang, "Haerbinshi ziliu renkou," 84, portray grain costs as a genuine hardship among those with unstable incomes. See Ding, "Nongmin hetonggong," 18, on the difficulties the policy caused for those in factories that did not provide grain or wage supplements for the purchase of grain; also, see Li and Hu, *Liudong renkou*, 343.

154. Author's interviews, Harbin, July 7, 1991; Tianjin Grain Bureau, June 18, 1992; Wuhan Social Science Academy, September 17, 1990.

155. Taylor and Banister, "China: The Problem," 27.

156. Zhu, "Nongcun renkou chengshihua," 61.

157. Wuhan shi, *Chengshi wailai*, 233.

158. For one description of the fare of the construction team workers, which was quite typical, see Yuan et al., *Luoren*, 34–35. This volume describes meals of steamed buns and cabbage most of the time. Most material cited on foreign-firm workers in chapter 6 comments on their miserable diets. Scrap-pickers interviewed on the streets deprived themselves (my interview, Nanjing, May 20, 1992).

159. *Liaowang* 48 (1995): 20–23, in FBIS, February 12, 1996, 23.

160. Author's interview, June 16, 1992.

161. Author's interview, June 18, 1992.

162. Author's interview, May 23, 1992.

163. Li and Hu, *Liudong renkou*, 344.

164. FBIS, February 22, 1994, 53, from Agence France-Presse, February 20, 1994.

165. Wang and Zuo, "Rural Migrants in Shanghai," 9.

166. Gao, "On Their Own," 28; this point comes up repeatedly in Yuan et al., *Luoren*. See, for instance, 85, 94, 103.

167. Author's interview with Gu Shangfei, New York, February 14, 1994; and JPRS-CAR-93-091 (December 29, 1993) from *RKYJJ* 4 (1993), 45; Xiang, "How to Create," 16; Min, "A Village," 4.

168. In other parts of the third world, granted, the superior medical facilities in cities served just the rich (Roberts, *The Making of Urban Citizens*, 158). But certainly it was not illegal for the poor to create their own if they could.

169. Yuan et al., *Luoren*, 16–18, 24.

170. Ibid., 103–4.

171. Ibid., 95–96.

172. Author's interview, Tianjin Public Health Bureau, June 9, 1992.

173. *ZM* 151 (May 1990): 26–27.

174. Zhou, "Guangdong 'wailai sangong,' " 50.

175. Gao, "On Their Own," 6.

176. Bendix, *Nation-Building*, 102, 87.

177. Yuan et al., *Luoren*, 1.

178. Schain, "Patterns of Policy-Making in France," 5.

179. García y Griego, "The Rights of Undocumented Mexicans."

180. Nickerson, "Migrant Workers," 38. In my June 22, 1992, interview, an official from theTianjin ICA Open Markets Office held that children were not permitted to go to school without a *hukou*.

181. Gallin, "Rural to Urban Migration in Taiwan," 281.

182. Chen, *Chinatown No More*, 24.

183. National Museum, "Black Migration," 10.

184. Stuart and Gregory, "A Model of Soviet," 88–90.

185. Andrews and Phillips, "The Squatters of Lima," 212.

186. Butterworth, "A Study," 109.

187. Perlman, *Myth of Marginality*, 33.

188. This figure was reported by XH, June 6, 1996, in FBIS, same date, 22.

189. Zhao, "Floating Population and Compulsory Education." According to Zhou, "Children of Migrants," in 1996 the State Education Commission encouraged six cities to set up pilot programs for the education of migrants' children. And in mid-1996 the commission decreed that most school-age children of migrants could attend local schools as "temporary students," in exchange for enrollment fees, a practice that had already been in use for some years anyway (XH, June 6, 1996, in FBIS, same date, 22).

190. *Liaowang* 48 (1995), in FBIS, February 12, 1996, 22; Yang, "Come and Gone," 33.

191. Yang, *Beyond Beijing*, 138, states that the Chinese government's Decision on Reforming the Educational System of May 1985 turned over the job of providing basic education and the provision of nine-year compulsory education to the localities at the county, city, and township levels and made the job dependent upon funding from local revenue and other local resources.

192. The Zhejiang Village had established its first kindergarten as early as 1988 (Xiang, "How to Create," 16); by 1995, there was a nursery school and five kindergartens (Min, "A Village," 4); my interview with Gu Shangfei, New York, February 14, 1992. Wong, "China's Urban Migration," states that temporary dwellers organized makeshift schools in Guangzhou and Shenzhen in the early 1990s but does not indicate whether these were kindergartens or at a higher level.

193. Jian, "The Urban Floating Population," 3.

194. Ibid., 8.

195. Xiang, "How to Create," 34.

196. Yuan et al., *Louren*, 127.

197. Yuan et al., *Luoren*, 16.

198. According to ibid., 82, transients from Yixian, Hebei, a poor area southwest of Beijing, did not bring their children to the city.

199. Kirkby, *Urbanisation in China*, 31.

200. Amounts of the fees vary enormously. Beja and Bonnin, "The Destruction," 25, report that in 1995, fees could be as high as 5,000 yuan per year, in addition to a "substantial bribe." In my own interviews, I heard a range of 2,000 yuan a year for primary school in some Guangzhou schools in 1992 (interview, GASS, May 10, 1992) to only 150 yuan more per year than city residents paid in the outskirts of Wuhan in the same year (my interviews on the streets of the city, May 24 and May 28, 1992). According to an informant in Nanjing (my street interview, May 17, 1992), the fees there were somewhere between 200 and 400 yuan a year in 1992, but money had to be supplemented by *guanxi*. Piante and Zhu, "Life and Death," on the other hand, claim that there was just a surcharge of 70 yuan beyond the regular school fees in Beijing in the mid-1990s.

201. According to Yuan et al., *Luoren*, 95, 103, migrants from Anhui in Beijing sent their children home to study once they were seven years old. This was true of many other migrants as well (my street interviews, Wuhan, May 24, 1992).

202. Wong, "China's Urban Migration"; also, my interview at GASS, May 13, 1992.

203. Zhu, "Chengshizhong di nongmin," 20.

204. Author's interview, GASS, May 11, 1992; and Huang, "Liudongzhong."

205. FBIS, November 16, 1992, 38.

206. Author's interviews on Hanzheng Street, Wuhan, May 24, 1992.

207. Author's interview with the vice chairman of this association, May 24, 1992.

208. Guangdong wailai, "Zai liudongzhong"; and Lee, "Production Politics," 15:13.

209. Yuan et al., *Luoren*, 14.

210. Ba jia, *Nongcun laodongli jingji*, A-02, 11; Yuan et al., *Luoren*, 19, 128.

211. Ba jia, *Nongcun laodongli jingji*, A-02, 7.

212. Yuan et al., *Luoren*, 22, 81, 94, 115; Shi, "Beijingshi getihu," 37; and Zhou, "Guangzhou 'wailai sangong,'" 51.

213. Huntington and Nelson, *No Easy Choice*, 106–7; Piore, *Birds of Passage*, 110.

214. Cornelius, "Urbanization," 1133–34 (Mexico); Perlman, *Myth of Marginality*, 15, 33, 162–63 (Brazil); Lloyd, *Slums of Hope?* 198 (third world); Chandra, *Social Participation*, 77, 127 (India); Glazer and Moynihan,

Beyond the Melting Pot, 18 (the United States); Feagin, *Racial and Ethnic Relations,* 252 (Europeans in the United States) and 346 (Japanese in the United States); Roberts, *The Making of Urban Citizens,* 174, 181, 192 (Latin America); Harris, *The Harder,* 51, 67, 75 (blacks in the United States); and Hollifield, *Immigrants, Markets, and States,* 87 (postwar France and Germany).

215. Yuan et al., *Luoren,* 15.

216. Ibid., 120.

217. Ibid., 58–59, 71.

218. Ibid., 26, 54–55, 64.

219. Ibid., 57, 58.

220. Ibid., 54, 55, 57, 62, 64.

221. Ibid., 14, 15.

222. Ibid.

223. Ibid., 19; Ba jia, *Nongcun laodongli jingji,* A-03, 5.

224. Author's interview, social scientist, Harbin, July 25, 1991; Wang, Wu, and Jiang, "Cong xue," 2; and Zhang, "Zunzhong 'waidiren,' " 25.

225. According to Yuan et al., *Luoren,* 96, beggar cliques were especially prominent among the beggars from Anhui. Beggar and trash bands are also mentioned in Ba jia, *Nongcun laodongli jingji,* A-03, 5.

226. Liu, *Zhongguo di qigai qunluo,* 210.

227. Wang, "Communities of 'Provincials,' " 20–21.

228. Ba and Ma, "Taojinzhe," 54.

229. United Press International, March 2, 1993. Also on this point, the official *CD* of March 23, 1989, noted that "among the growing groups of the lumpenproletariat, an 'underground society' is taking shape" (quoted in Liu, "Economic Reform," 405); and Zhou, "Guangdong 'wailai sangong,' " 51.

230. Piante and Zhu, "Life and Death," 14; Zhou, "Guangdong 'wailai sangong,' " 51; Guangdong wailai, "Zai liudongzhong," 117; Ba jia, *Nongcun laodongli jingji,* A-02, 8, and A-03–3; Beja and Bonnin, "The Destruction," 22; and Kaye, "Conflicts of Interest," 26.

231. Yuan et al., *Luoren,* 24, 122–23.

232. Guangdong wailai, "Zai liudongzhong," 117.

233. Wang, "Communities of 'Provincials,' " 18.

234. Xiang, "How to Create," 16, 36; and Zhang, "Strangers in the City."

235. Tang and Chen, "Qiangxing jiju," 19.

236. Ming, "Wo kandao," 27.

237. Author's interview at Guangzhou Urban Planning Automation Center, May 11, 1992.

238. Yuan, Zhang, and Wang, "Self-Organize;" and Zhang, "Strangers in the City."

239. Zhou, "Guangdong 'wailai sangong,' " 51; Ba jia, *Nongcun laodongli jingji,* A-03, 5; Piante and Zhu, "Life and Death," 14; Xiang, "How to Create," 17, 27, 33; and Yuan et al., *Luoren,* 19–20, 26, 27, 61–62, and 127–28.

240. Beja and Bonnin, "The Destruction"; and see chapter 3's discussion. Zhang, "Strangers in the City," ch. 8, recounts the incident in detail.

241. Information from Li Zhang, and from Zhang, "Strangers in the City," ch. 9.

242. This formulation has some resonance with the analysis in Pieke, "Bureaucracy, Friends, and Money."

243. Although migrants living "informally" in Peru "creat[ed] a breach through which the rest of society was also deserting the formal sector," according to de Soto, *The Other Path*, 11–12, the Peruvian state had never sought such totalistic urban control in the first place—nor had it grounded its legitimacy in totalistic provision.

CONCLUSION

1. Faist and Häussermann, "Immigration, Social Citizenship," 83.

2. Marshall, *Sociology at the Crossroads*, 87.

3. Marshall is aware of the uncertain relationship between the principle of citizenship and that of the market. But he presumes that the former would help to neutralize the inequalities of the latter (Barbalet, "Citizenship, Class Inequality," 77); see also Roberts, "The Social Context," 44, and Turner, *Citizenship and Capitalism*, 12.

4. Turner, *Citizenship and Capitalism*, 23, 26.

5. See Liu, "Mangliu"; and Zhang, "Zunzhong 'waidiren,' " 25.

6. Goldscheider, "The Adjustment of Migrants," 242–43.

7. Costello, Leinbach, and Ulack, *Mobility and Employment*, 110.

8. Breman, *Footloose Labour*, 226.

9. Roberts, *The Making of Urban Citizens*, 137.

10. Lomnitz, *Networks and Marginality*, on Mexico.

11. Breman, *Footloose Labour*, 246.

12. Whyte, "The Changing Role," 13; Lee, "Production Politics," 15.14.

13. Ge and Qu, *Zhongguo mingongchao*, 156.

14. Bendix, *Nation-Building*, 79.

15. See chapter 7, note 96.

16. "Gradually Reform Small Towns' Household Management System," *Baokan wenzhai* (Periodicals digest) (Beijing), July 24, 1997, 1; *SWB* FE/2986 G/8 (August 1, 1997), from XH, July 30, 1997, and FE/2989 G3–4 (August 5, 1997), from XH, July 30, 1997; and AFP, August 16, 1997.

17. FBIS, July 11, 1995, 17–18, from XH, July 9, 1995.

18. See chapter 2 on the post-1984 policies toward peasant mobility.

19. Turner, *Citizenship and Capitalism*, 11, 26.

20. Luoyi Ningge'er, *Di sanzhi yanjing*, 64.

21. Gu, "Zhongguo nongcun shengyu laodongli," 86.

22. Tang and Chen, "Qiangxing jiju," 20.

23. Ge and Qu, *Zhongguo mingongchao*, 159–60.

24. *NFRB*, December 14, 1988, 2.

25. Ge and Qu, *Zhongguo mingongchao,* 76.

26. Ibid., 103.

27. Shi, "Beijingshi getihu," 37.

28. Ba jia, *Nongcun laodongli jingji,* A-02, 7.

29. Zhang, Zhao, and Chen, "1994: Nongcun laodongli," 28.

30. Roberts, "The Social Context," 181.

31. FBIS, June 20, 1985, R1, from AFP of the same date.

32. FBIS, August 23, 1988, 41, from Beijing Domestic Service, August 19, 1988. According to *MP,* January 30, 1991, 7, in FBIS, March 30, 1991, 67, at least one-fifth of the seventy-plus strikes in Shenzhen and Zhuhai in 1989 and 1990 were the result of mobilization by gangs of workers from the same native place.

33. FBIS, February 10, 1994, 41, from ZGTXS (Hong Kong), February 4, 1994.

34. Ibid.

35. The "defensive" nature of these strikes bears out the point made in Perry, *Shanghai on Strike,* 6off., that unskilled workers (in that study, in late nineteenth- and early twentieth-century Shanghai) tend to strike over purely economic grievances and do not raise political demands.

36. *FZRB,* August 25, 1993, 1, 4, translated in FBIS, September 21, 1993, 49, reports this about the city of Dongguan in the Pearl River Delta.

37. FBIS, March 31, 1994, 27, from *EE,* March 31, 1994, 9.

38. Jiang, "Gonghui," 16–20.

39. Lee, "Production Politics," 15.11.

40. *Liaowang* 5 (1994): 26–29, translated in FBIS, March 3, 1994, 40. Another report speaks of 250,000 disputes and strikes since 1988, mainly in joint ventures without trade unions. This is in FBIS, February 22, 1994, 50, from *CD,* February 21, 1994, 21.

41. *SCMP,* May 17, 1994, 1, 8, in FBIS, May 17, 1994, 19; and FBIS, May 24, 1994, 52–53, from *EE,* May 23, 1994.

42. According to a report from 1994, "Workers are discriminated against by official unionists." This was taken from an interview with a researcher at the Trade Union Education Centre in Hong Kong, who spoke on the basis of his own experience with these workers in China, and reported in *SCMP,* June 14, 1994, 5, reprinted in FBIS, June 14, 1994, 31. See also Lee, "Production Politics," 15.12.

43. Willy Wo-Lap Lam, "Party Circular Warns of Spread of Illegal Trade Unions," *SCMP,* June 4, 1996, 1, in FBIS, June 5, 1996, 20; Lee, "Production Politics," 15.14.

44. *SCMP,* July 9, 1993, reprinted in FBIS, July 9, 1993, 25,

45. AFP, September 28, 1993, in FBIS, September 28, 1993, 36.

46. According to the *SCMP,* June 14, 1994, 5, reprinted in FBIS, June 14, 1994, 31, though government and party officials' repression obstructed the formation of unions in Hong Kong– and Taiwan-funded factories, migrant

workers in joint ventures were more aggressive than those in the state-run firms.

47. FBIS, May 31, 1994, 70, from *SCMP*, May 30, 1994, 8.

48. As told in Peter Stein, "China Learns to Like Migrant Workers," *Wall Street Journal*, December 12, 1995, A16.

49. From *Hong Kong Standard*, June 22, 1995, 1, and June 27, 2, reprinted in FBIS, June 22, 1995, 68, and June 27, 1995, 82, respectively.

50. Lee, "Production Politics," 15.12.

51. *Sing Tao Jih Pao* (Singtao daily [Hong Kong]), March 27, A9, reprinted in FBIS, April 2, 1996, 63.

52. "Trouble at Zhejiang Village," *Fazhi wencui bao* (Legal culture news), March 31, 1994, translated in *China Perspectives* 2 (1995): 5–16; and Yuan et al., *Luoren*, 6–7.

53. Chan, "Briefing"; Chan, "Changing," 178.

54. *MP*, October 11, 1996, A10, in *SWB*, FE/2741 (October 12, 1996), G/15–G/16.

55. Portes and Bach, *Latin Journey*, 21; Gordon, *Assimilation*.

56. García, "Cities and Citizenship," 15; Feagin, *Racial and Ethnic Relations*, 40.

57. Yuan et al., *Luoren*, 115.

58. Patel and Turner, *Bombay*, xvi.

59. Glazer and Moynihan, *Beyond the Melting Pot*, 15.

60. Solinger, "China's Urban Transients."

61. Calculated from data in Wang, "Invisible Walls," table 2.

62. Ibid., 11–12.

63. West, "The Changing Effects of Economic Reform," 5.

64. According to ibid., 6, 62 percent of all urban private enterprises were in trade and the restaurant industry, while manufacturing firms accounted for only 17 percent in the mid-1990s. Also, in 1994, the number of workers in the service sector exceeded those in industry for the first time. See also Buckley, "Walls and Alleys."

65. On this theme, see also Davis, "Emergent Structures."

Bibliography

Abrami, Regina M. "Origins and Destinations: Locating the Floating Population." Manuscript. April 1992.

Alba, Francisco. "Urban Aspects of Labor Migration: A Review of Exit Countries." In *Third-World Cities: Problems, Policies and Prospects*, edited by John D. Kasarda and Allan M. Parnell, 220–34. Newbury Park, Calif.: Sage Publications, 1993.

Almond, Gabriel A. "Capitalism and Democracy." *PS: Political Science and Politics* (September 1991): 467–74.

Andrews, Frank M., and George W. Phillips. "The Squatters of Lima: Who They Are and What They Want." *Journal of the Developing Areas* 4, no. 2 (1970): 211–23.

Atkinson, Anthony B., and Joseph E. Stiglitz. *Lectures on Public Economics*. New York: McGraw-Hill, 1980.

Ba, Liang, and Ma Lun. "Taojinzhe di meng" [The dream of the gold panners]. *Tequ wenxue* [Special zone literature] 4 (1989): 48–66.

Ba jia "Nongxun laodongli liudong yanjiu" keti weituo nongyebu nongcun jingji yanjiu zhongxin ketizu bianji [Eight "rural labor force mobility research" tasks commissioned by the Ministry of Agriculture, Rural Economic Research Center Task Group, ed.] *Nongcun laodongli jingji yanjiu tongxun* [Bulletin of rural labor mobility studies]. N.p., 1995.

Banister, Judith. "China: Internal and Regional Migration Trends." In *Floating Population and Migration in China: The Impact of Economic Reforms*, edited by Thomas Scharping, 72–97. Hamburg: Institut für Asienkunde, 1997.

———. *China's Changing Population*. Stanford: Stanford University Press, 1987.

———. "China's Population Changes and the Economy." In *China's Economic Dilemmas in the 1990s: The Problems of Reforms, Modernization, and Interdependence*, 1:234–51. Joint Economic Committee, U.S. Congress. Washington, D.C.: U.S. Government Printing Office, 1991.

———. "One Billion and Counting." *Chinese Business Review* (May–June 1991): 14–18.

———. "The Migration of Surplus Laborers in China." Paper presented at the International Academic Conference on China's Internal Migration and Urbanization, Beijing, December 1989.

———. "Urban-Rural Population Projections for China." CIR Staff Paper no. 15. Washington, D.C.: Center for International Research, U.S. Bureau of the Census, March 1986.

Banister, Judith, and Jeffrey R. Taylor. "China: Surplus Labor and Migration." *Asia-Pacific Population Journal* 4, no. 4 (n.d.): 3–20.

Barbalet, J. M. "Citizenship, Class Inequality, and Resentment." In *Citizenship and Social Theory*, edited by Bryan S. Turner, 36–56. London: Sage Publications, 1993.

———. *Citizenship: Rights, Struggle, and Class Inequality.* Milton Keynes: Open University Press, 1988.

Barth, Fredrik. Introduction to *Ethnic Groups and Boundaries: The Social Origin of Cultural Difference*, edited by Fredrik Barth, 9–38. London: George Allen and Unwin, 1969.

Bauer, John, Wang Feng, Nancy E. Riley, and Zhao Xiaohua. "Gender Inequality in Urban China: Education and Employment." *Modern China* 18, no. 3 (July 1992): 333–70.

Beijingshi renmin zhengfu yanjiushi shehuichu [Beijing City People's Government Research Office, social section]. "Guanyu ba da chengshi liudong renkou wenti di zonghe baogao" [A comprehensive report on the question of the floating population in eight big cities]. *Shehuixue yanjiu* [Sociological research (Beijing)] 3 (1991): 20–24.

Beja, Jean Philippe, and Michel Bonnin. "The Destruction of the 'Village.' " *China Perspectives* 2 (1995): 21–25.

Bendix, Reinhard. *Nation-Building and Citizenship: Studies of Our Changing Social Order.* New York: John Wiley and Sons, 1964.

Benkan jije [Staff reporter]. "Mingongchao: fengqi yunyong you yinian" [Human labor tide rolls on with full force yet another year]. *Liaowang* 8 (1993): 4–10.

Bernstein, Thomas P. "Incorporating Group Interests into the Policy Process: The Case of Farmers During the Reform Era." Paper prepared for the conference The Non-Economic Impact of China's Economic Reforms, Harvard University, September 20–22, 1996.

———. "In Quest of Voice: China's Farmers and Prospects for Political Liberalization." Paper presented to the University Seminar on Modern China, Columbia University, February 10, 1994.

———. *Up to the Mountains and Down to the Villages: The Transfer of Youth from Urban to Rural China.* New Haven: Yale University Press, 1977.

Bernstein, Thomas P., and Dorothy J. Solinger. "The Peasant Question for the Future: Citizenship, Integration, and Political Institutions?" Paper prepared for the conference China and World Affairs in 2010, sponsored by the Institute for International Studies, Stanford University, April 25–26, 1996.

Bi Shuqi and Xu Song. "Factors in the Social Environment Contributing to

Increase in Crime Committed by Migrant Laborers." *Guangming ribao* [Bright daily (Beijing)], October 5, 1994, 5. Translated in Foreign Broadcast Information Service, November 3, 1994, 25–26.

Bian, Yanjie. "Guanxi and the Allocation of Urban Jobs in China." *China Quarterly* 140 (1994): 971–99.

———. *Work and Inequality in Urban China.* Albany: State University of New York Press, 1994.

Blake, Fred C. *Ethnic Groups and Social Change in a Chinese Market Town.* Honolulu: University Press of Hawaii, 1981.

Blecher, Marc. "Peasant Labour, for Urban Industry: Temporary Contract Labour, Urban-Rural Balance, and Class Relations in a Chinese County." *World Development* 11, no. 8 (1983): 731–45.

Bonacich, Edna. "A Theory of Ethnic Antagonism: The Split Labor Market." *American Sociological Review* 37 (October 1972): 547–59.

Bonilla, Frank. "Rio's Favelas: The Rural Slum Within the City." In *Peasants in Cities: Readings in the Anthropology of Urbanization,* edited by William Mangin, 72–84. Boston: Houghton Mifflin, 1970.

Borjas, George J. *Friends or Strangers: The Impact of Immigrants on the U.S. Economy.* New York: Basic Books, 1990.

Brauchli, Marchus W., and Joseph Kahn. "Toil and Trouble." *Wall Street Journal,* May 19, 1994.

Breman, Jan. *Footloose Labour: Working in India's Informal Economy.* Cambridge: Cambridge University Press, 1996.

Brennan, Geoffrey, and James M. Buchanan. *The Reason of Rules: Constitutional Political Economy.* Cambridge: Cambridge University Press, 1985.

Brown, Patricia Leigh. "The Architecture of Those Called Homeless." *New York Times,* March 28, 1993.

Browning, Harley. "Migrant Selectivity and the Growth of Large Cities in Developing Societies." In *Rapid Population Growth: Consequences and Policy Implications,* 273–314. Baltimore: National Academy of Sciences, Johns Hopkins University Press, 1971.

Brubaker, Rogers. *Citizenship and Nationhood in France and Germany.* Cambridge, Mass.: Harvard University Press, 1992.

———. Introduction to *Immigration and the Politics of Citizenship in Europe and North America,* edited by William Rogers Brubaker, 1–27. Lanham, Md.: University Press of America, 1989.

Bruun, Ole. *Business and Bureaucracy in a Chinese City: An Ethnography of Private Business Households in Contemporary China.* Research Monograph no. 43. Berkeley: Institute for East Asian Studies, University of California, 1993.

———. "Political Hierarchy and Private Entrepreneurship in a Chinese Neighborhood." In *The Waning of the Communist State: Economic Origins of Political Decline in China and Hungary,* edited by Andrew G. Walder, 184–212. Berkeley: University of California Press, 1995.

Buckley, Christopher. "Walls and Alleys, Changing Patterns of Urban Social Mobility Under Economic Reform." Paper prepared for the conference

Unintended Social Consequences of Chinese Economic Reform, Harvard School of Public Health and the Fairbank Center for East Asian Studies, Harvard University, May 23–25, 1997.

Burawoy, Michael. "The Functions and Reproduction of Migrant Labor: Comparative Material from Southern Africa and the United States." *American Journal of Sociology* 81, no. 5 (1976): 1050–87.

Butterworth, Douglas S. "A Study of the Urbanization Process among Mixtec Migrants from Tilantongo in Mexico City." In *Peasants in Cities: Readings in the Anthropology of Urbanization,* edited by William Mangin, 98–113. Boston: Houghton Mifflin, 1970.

Byrd, William A. *The Market Mechanism and Economic Reforms in China.* Armonk, N.Y.: M. E. Sharpe, 1991.

Cai, Fang. "Recent Trends of Migration and Population in Shandong." Paper presented at International Conference on Migration and Floating, Cologne, May 2–4, 1996. Published in *Floating Population and Migration in China: The Impact of Economic Reforms,* edited by Thomas Scharping, 216–35. Hamburg: Institut für Asienkunde, 1997.

Calavita, Kitty. "U.S. Immigration and Policy Responses: The Limits of Legislation." In *Controlling Immigration: A Global Perspective,* edited by Wayne A. Cornelius, Philip L. Martin, and James F. Hollifield, 55–82. Stanford: Stanford University Press, 1995.

Cao, Jingchun. "A Good Trend or a Reason for Worry?" *China Focus* 5, no. 8 (1997): 8.

———. "Lanpi lanyin hukou yinfa di sikao" [Some deliberations on the blue seal household registration permit]. *Renkou yu jingji* [Population and economy (Beijing)] 5 (1993): 38–42.

Cao, Min. "Yangtze Diversion Rolls Toward Launch Date." *China Daily* (Beijing), November 17, 1994, 1. Reprinted in Foreign Broadcast Information Service, November 17, 1994, 40.

Casella, Alessandra, and Bruno Frey. "Federalism and Clubs: Towards an Economic Theory of Overlapping Public Jurisdictions." *European Economic Review* 36 (1992): 39–46.

Castells, Manuel. "Immigrant Workers and Class Struggles in Advanced Capitalism: The Western European Experience." In *Peasants and Proletarians: The Struggles of Third-World Workers,* edited by Robin Cohen, Peter C. W. Gutkind, and Phyllis Brazier, 353–79. New York: Monthly Review Press, 1979.

Castells, Manuel, and Alejandro Portes. "World Underneath: The Origins, Dynamics, and Effects of the Informal Economy." In *The Informal Economy: Studies in Advanced and Less Developed Countries,* edited by Alejandro Portes, Manuel Castells, and Lauren A. Benton, 11–37. Baltimore: Johns Hopkins University Press, 1989.

Castles, Stephen, and Godula Kosack. *Immigrant Workers and Class Structure in Western Europe.* 2d ed. New York: Oxford University Press, 1985.

Chai, Joseph C. H. "Consumption and Living Standards in China." *China Quarterly* 131 (1992): 721–49.

Chai Junyong. "Liudong renkou—chengshi guanli di yi da kunrao" [The floating population—the puzzle in urban management]. *Shehui* [Society (Shanghai)] 10 (1990): 8–10.

Chan, Anita. "Briefing to the Australian/China Parliamentary Friendship Group." Canberra, September 12, 1996.

———. "The Changing Ruling Elite and Political Opposition in China." In *Political Oppositions in Industrialising Asia*, edited by Garry Rodan, 161–87. London: Routledge, 1996.

———. "Union Bargaining in the New Economic Sectors." In *Adjusting to Capitalism: China's Workers and the State*, edited by Greg O'Leary, 122–49. Armonk, N.Y.: M. E. Sharpe, 1998.

Chan, Anita, and Jonathan Unger. "Immigrants in the Promised Land." *Access China* 1 (March 1992): 24–25.

Chan, Kam Wing. "Urbanization and Urban Infrastructure Services in the PRC," in "Financing Local Government in the People's Republic of China." Draft report for the Ministry of Finance study of subprovincial fiscal relations, TA 2118-PRCP, edited by Christine Wong. November 1995.

———. *Cities with Invisible Walls: Reinterpreting Urbanization in Post-1949 China*. Hong Kong: Oxford University Press, 1994.

———. "Post-Mao China: A Two-Class Urban Society in the Making." *International Journal of Urban and Regional Research* 20, no. 1 (1996): 134–50.

———. "Rural-Urban Migration in China, 1950–1982: Estimates and Analysis." *Urban Geography* 9, no. 1 (1988): 53–84.

Chandra, Subhash. *Social Participation in Urban Neighbourhoods*. New Delhi: National Publishing House, 1977.

Chapman, Murray, and R. Mansell Prothero. "Themes in Circulation in the Third World." *International Migration Review* 17 (1983): 597–632.

Chen, Bing. "Policy Measures for Dealing with the Transfer of Rural Labor Forces." *Renkou xuekan* [Population bulletin (Changchun)] 2 (1990): 22–24.

Chen, Hsiang-shui. *Chinatown No More: Taiwan Immigrants in Contemporary New York*. Ithaca: Cornell University Press, 1992.

Chen, Jiyuan. "A Study on Transferring China's Surplus Agricultural Labor." *Nongye jingji wenti* [Agricultural economic issues (Beijing)] 1 (1988): 24–27. Translated in Joint Publications Research Service-CAR-88-029 (June 13, 1988).

Chen, Wu. "The Pattern of Dual-Stepped Continuous Transfer of Agricultural Surplus Labor." *Jingji yanjiu* [Economic research (Beijing)] 11 (1992): 52–55. Translated in Joint Publications Research Service-CAR-93-022, April 8, 1993.

Chen, Yao Hua. "China: Maid Service." *Third World Week*, April 7, 1989, 43–44.

Chen, Yi. "Labor Export and the Transfer of Rural Labor Forces to Other Districts—an Investigation of Baochang Chu, Haimen County, Nantong City, Jiangsu Province." *Renkou yanjiu* [Population research (Beijing)] 5 (1987): 20–25.

Chen, Yicai. "Liudong renkou dui shehui jingji fazhan di yingxiang" [The influence of the floating population on social economic development]. *Renkou xuekan* [Population bulletin (Changchun)] 2 (1988): 39–42.

Chen, Zhigang, Xu Zhenghui, and Zhang Ruiling. "Investigation and Analysis of the Unemployment Situation Among the Urban Workforce." *Zhongguo gaige* [Chinese reform (Beijing)] 2 (1995): 35–38. Translated in Foreign Broadcast Information Service, April 3, 1995, 37–38.

Cheng, Chaoze. "Internal Migration in Mainland China: The Impact of Government Policies." *Issues and Studies* (Taipei) 27, no. 8 (1991): 47–70.

Cheng, Ke. "Da chengshi liudong renkou wenti yu duice" [The problem of large cities' floating population and policy measures]. *Chengxiang jianshe* [Urban-rural construction (Beijing)] 5 (1988): 18–20.

Cheng, Tiejun, and Mark Selden. "The City, the Countryside and the Sinews of Population Control: The Origins and Social Consequences of China's Hukou System." Draft for presentation at the conference Construction of the Party-State and State Socialism in China, 1936–1965, Colorado Springs, June 1993.

———. "The Origins and Social Consequences of China's Hukou System." *China Quarterly* 139 (1994): 644–68.

Cheng, Xuan. "Problems of Urbanization Under China's Traditional Economic System." In *Chinese Urban Reform: What Model Now?* edited by R. Yin-wang Kwok, William L. Parish, and Anthony Gar-on Yeh with Xu Xueqiang, 65–77. Armonk, N.Y.: M. E. Sharpe, 1990.

Cheng, Yuk-shing, and Tsang Shu-ki. "The Changing Grain Marketing System in China." *China Quarterly* 140 (1994): 1080–1104.

Chengdushi chengshi kexue yanjiuhui [Chengdu City Urban Scientific Research Association]. "Chengdushi liudong renkou fenxi" [An analysis of Chengdu City's floating population]. *Renkou yu fazhan* [Population and law] 12 (1987): 1–6.

Chickering, A. Lawrence. Introduction to *The Silent Revolution: The Informal Sector in Five Asian and Near Eastern Countries*, edited by A. Lawrence Chickering and Mohamed Salahdine, 1–14. San Francisco: ICS Press, 1991.

Chickering, A. Lawrence, and Mohamed Salahdine, eds. *The Silent Revolution: The Informal Sector in Five Asian and Near Eastern Countries*. San Francisco: ICS Press, 1991.

China Daily (Beijing). Selected issues, 1988–96.

Christiansen, Flemming. "The Legacy of the Mock Dual Economy: Chinese Labour in Transition, 1978–1992." *Economy and Society* 22, no. 4 (1993): 411–36.

Clarke, Donald C., and James V. Feinerman. "Antagonistic Contradictions: Criminal Law and Human Rights in China," *China Quarterly* 141 (1995): 135–54.

Cockcroft, James D. *Outlaws in the Promised Land: Mexican Immigrant Workers and America's Future*. New York: Grove Press, 1986.

Cohen, Myron L. "Cultural and Political Inventions in Modern China: The Case of the Chinese 'Peasant.'" *Daedalus* 122, no. 2 (spring 1993): 151–70.

————. "Family Management and Family Division in Contemporary Rural China." *China Quarterly* 130 (1992): 357–77.

Cohen, Robin. *The New Helots: Migrants in the International Division of Labor.* Aldershot, England: Avebury, 1987.

Connell, John, Biplab Dasgupta, Roy Laishley, and Michael Lipton. *Migration from Rural Areas: The Evidence from Village Studies.* Delhi: Oxford University Press, 1976.

Constitution of the People's Republic of China. Beijing: Foreign Languages Press, 1982.

Cornelius, Wayne A. *Politics and the Migrant Poor in Mexico City.* Stanford: Stanford University Press, 1975.

————. "Urbanization and Political Demand Making: Political Participation Among the Migrant Poor in Latin American Cities." *American Political Science Review* 68 (1974): 1125–46.

Cornelius, Wayne A., Philip L. Martin, and James F. Hollifield. "The Ambivalent Quest for Immigration Control." In *Controlling Immigration: A Global Perspective,* edited by Wayne A. Cornelius, Philip L. Martin, and James F. Hollifield, 3–41. Stanford: Stanford University Press, 1995.

Costello, Michael A., Thomas R. Leinbach, and Richard Ulack. *Mobility and Employment in Urban Southeast Asia: Examples from Indonesia and the Philippines.* Boulder, Colo.: Westview Press, 1987.

Crane, George T. *The Political Economy of China's Special Economic Zones.* Armonk, N.Y.: M. E. Sharpe, 1990.

Crissman, Lawrence W. "The Segmentary Structure of Urban Overseas Chinese Communities." *Man* 2, no. 2 (1967): 187–204.

Croll, Elisabeth J., and Huang Ping. "Migration For and Against Agriculture in Eight Chinese Villages." *China Quarterly* 149 (1997): 128–46.

Cui, Lin. "Woguo chengshi disan chanye di fazhan he chengshi renkou wenti" [The development of the tertiary sector and the question of urban population]. *Renkou yu jingji* [Population and economy (Beijing)] 1 (1989): 43–47.

Davis, Deborah S. "Emergent Structures and Dynamics of the Urban Opportunity Structure." Paper presented at the conference China and World Affairs in 2010, Institute for International Studies, Stanford University, April 25–26, 1996.

————. *Long Lives.* 2d ed. Stanford: Stanford University Press, 1991.

————. "Unequal Chances, Unequal Outcomes: Pension Reform and Urban Inequality." *China Quarterly* 114 (1988): 223–42.

————. "Urban Job Mobility." In *Chinese Society on the Eve of Tiananmen: The Impact of Reform,* edited by Deborah Davis and Ezra F. Vogel, 85–108. Cambridge, Mass.: Council on East Asian Studies, Harvard University, 1990.

Davis, Kingsley. "The Urbanization of the Human Population." In *The City in Newly Developing Countries: Readings on Urbanism and Urbanization,* edited by Gerald Breese, 5–20. Englewood Cliffs, N.J.: Prentice-Hall, 1969.

De Soto, Hernando. *The Other Path: The Invisible Revolution in the Third World.* New York: Harper and Row, 1989.

De Wenden, Catherine Wihtol. "The Absence of Rights: The Position of Illegal Immigrants." In *The Political Rights of Migrant Workers in Western Europe,* edited by Zig Layton-Henry, 27–46. London: Sage Publications, 1990.

Deng, Yiming. "Shilun woguo bufada diqu nongye laodongli di zhuanyi" [A tentative discussion of the transfer of our country's undeveloped districts' agricultural labor power]. *Zhongguo renkou kexue* [Chinese population science (Beijing)] 3 (1988): 43–47.

Dewind, Josh, Tom Seidl, and Janet Shenk. "Contract Labor in U.S. Agriculture: The West Indian Cane Cutters in Florida." In *Peasants and Proletarians: The Struggles of Third-World Workers,* edited by Robin Cohen, Peter C. W. Gutkind, and Phyllis Brazier, 380–96. New York: Monthly Review Press, 1979.

Ding, Jianhua. "Nongmin hetonggong di qidai" [Peasant contract labor's wait]. *Shehui* [Society (Shanghai)] 11 (1989): 17–19.

Ding, Jinhong, and Norman Stockman. "On Floating Population and the Integration of the City Community—a Survey on Acceptance by the Shanghai Residents of the Floating Population." Paper presented at European Science Foundation Workshop on European Chinese and Chinese Domestic Migrants, Oxford, July 3–5, 1996.

Ding, Shuimu. "Huji guanli yu shehui kongzhi—xianxing huji guanli zhidu zaiyi" [Household registration management and social control—another opinion on the present household management system]. *Shehui* [Society (Shanghai)] 3 (1989): 26–29.

———. "Xianxing huji guanli zhidu chuyi" [A preliminary view of our present household registration management system]. *Shehui* [Society (Shanghai)] 1 (1987): 18–19.

———. "Xianxing huji zhidu di gongneng ji qi gaige zouxiang" [The functions of the present household system and the direction of its reform]. *Shehuixue yanjiu* [Sociological research (Beijing)] 6 (1992): 100–104.

Dreyer, June Teufel. "Go West, Young Han." *Pacific Affairs* 48, no. 3 (1975): 353–69.

Du, Weidong. "Beijing chengli di 'jipusairen' " ['Gypsy' in Beijing]. *Xin Guancha* [New observer] 7–11 (1988): 18–33, 60.

Du, Wenzhen, and Wang Chen. "Jiangsusheng xiao chengzhen liudong renkou" [Jiangsu province's small towns' floating population]. *Zhongguo renkou kexue* [Chinese population science (Beijing)] 4 (1989): 63–64.

Du, Wulu. "Beijing shiqu liudong renkou wenti tantao" [An inquiry into the question of the floating population in Beijing's urban district]. *Renkou yu jingji* [Population and economy (Beijing)] 1 (1986): 12–14.

Du, Xiaoshan. "Improving Access to Rural Credit for Poor Households: Experimenting with a Chinese-Style Grameen Bank." In "Promoting Economic Development in China's Poor Areas: A Collection of Research Policy Briefs," edited by Albert Park and Scott Rozelle, 27–33. Presented by members of the China Poverty Research Association at a discussion forum for Chinese Researchers and Policy Makers sponsored by the Ford Foundation, Beijing, October 26, 1994.

Duara, Prasenjit. *Culture, Power, and the State: Rural North China, 1900–1942.* Stanford: Stanford University Press, 1988.

Dutton, Michael R. Editor's introduction to "Basic Facts on the Household Registration System," by Zhang Qingwu. *Chinese Economic Studies* 22, no. 1 (1988): 3–21.

———. *Policing and Punishment in China: From Patriarchy to "The People."* New York: Cambridge University Press, 1992.

Eckstein, Harry. "Civic Inclusion and Its Discontents." In *Regarding Politics: Essays on Political Theory, Stability, and Change,* edited by Harry Eckstein, 343–77. Berkeley: University of California Press, 1991.

Economy, Elizabeth. "Reforms and Resources: The Implications for State Capacity in the PRC." *Project on Environmental Scarcities, State Capacity, and Civil Violence, a Joint Project of the University of Toronto and the American Academy of Arts and Sciences.* Cambridge, Mass.: American Academy of Arts and Sciences, Committee on International Security Studies, 1997.

Edwards, Richard C. "The Social Relations of Production in the Firm and Labor Market Structure." In *Labor Market Segmentation,* edited by Richard C. Edwards, Michael Reich, and David M. Gordon, 3–26. Lexington, Mass.: D. C. Heath, 1975.

Emerson, John Philip. "Employment in Mainland China: Problems and Prospects." In *An Economic Profile of Mainland China,* 2:407–69. Joint Economic Committee, U.S. Congress. Washington, D.C.: Government Printing Office, 1967.

———. "The Labor Force of China, 1957–80." In *China Under the Four Modernizations,* pt. 1, 224–67. Joint Economic Committee, U.S. Congress. Washington, D.C.: U.S. Government Printing Office, 1982.

———. "Urban School-Leavers and Unemployment in China." *China Quarterly* 93 (1983): 1–16.

Erlanger, Stephen. "Russia to Replace Residency Permit." *New York Times,* December 27, 1992.

Esping-Andersen, Gosta. *Three Worlds of Welfare Capitalism.* Cambridge, Mass.: Polity Press, 1990.

Etienne-Will, Pierre, and R. Bin Wong, with James Lee. *Nourish the People.* Ann Arbor: Center for Chinese Studies, 1991.

Fainstein, Norman, and Susan Fainstein. "Urban Regimes and Black Citizenship: The Economic and Social Impacts of Black Political Incorporation in U.S. Cities." *International Journal of Urban and Regional Research* 20, no. 1 (1996): 22–37.

Faist, Thomas. "States, Markets, and Immigrant Minorities: Second-Generation Turks in Germany and Mexican-Americans in the United States in the 1980s." *Comparative Politics* 26, no. 4 (1994): 439–60.

Faist, Thomas, and Hartmut Häussermann. "Immigration, Social Citizenship, and Housing in Germany." *International Journal of Urban and Regional Research* 20, no. 1 (1996): 83–98.

Fallenbuchi, Zbigniew M. "Internal Migration and Economic Development under Socialism: The Case of Poland." In *Internal Migration: A Comparative Perspective*, edited by Alan A. Brown and Egon Neuberger, 305–27. New York: Academic Press, 1977.

Fan, C. Cindy. "Economic Opportunities and Internal Migration: A Case Study of Guangdong Province, China." *Professional Geographer* 48, no. 1 (1996): 28–45.

Fan, Ping. "Constraints to Labor Mobility and Human Capital Development in Remote Areas." In "Promoting Economic Development in China's Poor Areas: A Collection of Research Policy Briefs," edited by Albert Park and Scott Rozelle, 34–37. Presented by members of the China Poverty Research Association at a discussion forum for Chinese Researchers and Policy Makers sponsored by the Ford Foundation, Beijing, October 26, 1994.

Fang, Ming, Sun Bingyao, Li Hanlin, Wang Qi, and Wang Ying. "Xibu fazhan yu liudongshi renkou qianyi moshi" [The development of China's west and the migration pattern of floating-style population: On an investigation of Dongsheng City, Inner Mongolia]. *Zhongguo renkou kexue* [Chinese population science (Beijing)] 5 (1988): 20–26.

Fang, Shan. "Mainland China's Rural Surplus Labor." *Issues and Studies* (Taipei) 22, no. 4 (1986): 51–68.

Feagin, Joe R. *Racial and Ethnic Relations.* Englewood Cliffs, N.J.: Prentice-Hall, 1978.

Feagin, Joe R., and Clairece Booher Feagin. *Racial and Ethnic Relations.* 4th ed. Englewood Cliffs, N.J.: Prentice Hall, 1993.

Fei, Xiaotong. *From the Soil: The Foundations of Chinese Society as Viewed by Fei Xiaotong.* Berkeley: University of California Press, 1992.

Feng, Lanrui, and Jiang Weiyu. "A Comparative Study of the Modes of Transference of Surplus Labor in China's Countryside." *Social Sciences in China* (Beijing) 9, no. 3 (1988): 64–77.

Feng, Zelin, and Li Tianxiang. "Liulang qitao xianxiang chensilu" [A record of meditations on the phenomenon of homeless, wandering beggars]. *Shehui* [Society (Shanghai)] 3 (1989): 13–14.

Ferge, Zsuzsa. "Social Citizenship in the New Democracies: The Difficulties in Reviving Citizens' Rights in Hungary." *International Journal of Urban and Regional Research* 20, no. 1 (1996): 99–115.

Fitzpatrick, Sheila. *Stalin's Peasants: Resistance and Survival in the Russian Village after Collectivization.* New York: Oxford University Press, 1994.

Flatters, Frank, Vernon Henderson, and Peter Mieszkowski. "Public Goods, Efficiency, and Regional Fiscal Equalization." *Journal of Public Economics* 3, no. 2 (1974): 99–112.

Foreign Broadcast Information Service. *Daily Report: China.* Springfield, Va., 1989–96.

Freeman, Gary P. "Migration and the Political Economy of the Welfare State." *Annals of the American Academy of Political and Social Science* 485 (1986): 51–63.

Friedman, Edward, Paul G. Pickowicz, and Mark Selden. *Chinese Village, Socialist State.* New Haven: Yale University Press, 1991.

Friman, H. Richard. "GAIJINHANZAI: Immigrants and Drugs in Contemporary Japan." *Asian Survey* 36, no. 10 (1996): 964–77.

Gallin, Bernard. "Rural to Urban Migration in Taiwan: Its Impact on Chinese Family and Kinship." In *Chinese Family Law and Social Change in Historical and Comparative Perspective,* edited by David C. Buxbaum, 261–82. Seattle: University of Washington Press, 1978.

Gallin, Bernard, and Rita S. Gallin. "The Integration of Village Migrants in Taipei." In *The Chinese City Between Two Worlds,* edited by Mark Elvin and G. William Skinner, 331–58. Stanford: Stanford University Press, 1974.

———. "The Integration of Village Migrants into Urban Society: The Case of Taipei, Taiwan." In *Internal Migration Systems in the Developing World with Special Reference to Latin America,* edited by Robert N. Thomas and John M. Hunter, 153–76. Boston: G. K. Hall, 1980.

Gao, Mobo C. F. "On Their Own: The Plight of Migrant Workers in South China." *China Rights Forum* (fall 1994): 4–7, 28.

———. "On the Sharp End of China's Economic Boom—Migrant Workers." *China Rights Forum* (spring 1994): 12–13, 27.

Gao, Qingxu. "Qianyi liudong renkou diaocha yanjiuzhong di rogan wenti" [Certain questions in a superficial discussion of investigation and research on the floating population]. *Renkou yu jingji* [Population and economy (Beijing)] 2 (1989): 58–62.

García, Soledad. "Cities and Citizenship." *International Journal of Urban and Regional Research* 20, no. 1 (1996): 7–21.

García y Griego, Manuel. "The Rights of Undocumented Mexicans in the United States After *Plyler v Doe:* A Sketch of Moral and Legal Issues." *Journal of Law and Education* 15, no. 1 (winter 1986): 57–82.

Gates, Hill. "Owner, Worker, Mother, Wife: Taibei and Chengdu Family Businesswomen." In *Putting Class in Its Place: Worker Identities in East Asia,* edited by Elizabeth J. Perry, 127–66. Berkeley: Institute of East Asian Studies, University of California, 1996.

Ge, Xiangxian, and Qu Weiying. *Zhongguo mingongchao: "Mangliu" zhenxianglu* [China's tide of labor: A record of the true facts about the "blind floaters"]. Beijing: Chinese International Broadcasting Publishing, 1990.

Gerber, David A. "Cutting Out Shylock: Elite Anti-Semitism and the Quest for Moral Order in the Mid-Nineteenth-Century American Marketplace." In *Anti-Semitism in American History,* edited by David A. Gerber, 210–32. Champaign: University of Illinois Press, 1986.

Gilley, Bruce. "Irrestible Force: Migrant Workers Are Part of the Solution, Not a Problem." *Far Eastern Economic Review* (Hong Kong), April 4, 1996.

———. "Provincial Prodigals: Some Migrant Workers Return Home as Entrepreneurs." *Far Eastern Economic Review* (Hong Kong), April 4, 1996.

———. "Sisters Act." *Far Eastern Economic Review* (Hong Kong), April 4, 1996.

Glazer, Nathan, and Daniel Patrick Moynihan. *Beyond the Melting Pot.* Cambridge, Mass.: MIT Press, 1963.

Golas, Peter J. "Early Ch'ing Guilds." In *The City in Late Imperial China*, edited by G. William Skinner, 555–80. Stanford: Stanford University Press, 1977.

Goldscheider, Calvin. "The Adjustment of Migrants in Large Cities of Less Developed Countries: Some Comparative Observations." In *Urban Migrants in Developing Nations: Patterns and Problems of Adjustment*, edited by Calvin Goldscheider, 233–53. Boulder, Colo.: Westview Press, 1983.

Goldstein, Alice. "Temporary Migration in Shanghai and Beijing." *Studies in Comparative International Development* 27 (1992): 39–56.

Goldstein, Carl. "Are We There Yet?" *Far Eastern Economic Review* (Hong Kong), July 7, 1994.

Goldstein, Sidney, and Alice Goldstein. "Population Mobility in the People's Republic of China." Papers of the East-West Population Institute no. 95. Honolulu, East-West Center, 1985.

———. "Town and City: New Directions in Chinese Urbanization." In *Chinese Urban Reform: What Model Now?* edited by R. Yin-wang Kwok, William L. Parish, and Anthony Gar-on Yeh with Xu Xueqiang, 17–44. Armonk, N.Y.: M. E. Sharpe, 1990.

Gong, Xikui. "Zhongguo xianxing huji zhidu toushi" [A perspective on China's present household register system]. *Shehui kexue* [Social science (Shanghai)] 2 (1989): 32–36.

Goodman, Bryna. *Native Place, City, and Nation: Regional Networks and Identities in Shanghai, 1853–1937.* Berkeley: University of California Press, 1995.

Goodman, David S. G. "The PLA and Regionalism: Guangdong Province." Manuscript. Asia Research Centre, Murdoch University, Western Australia, 1993.

Gordon, Milton M. *Assimilation in American Life: The Role of Race, Religion, and National Origins.* New York: Oxford University Press, 1964.

Gourevitch, Peter. *Politics in Hard Times: Comparative Responses to International Economic Crises.* Ithaca: Cornell University Press, 1986.

Grandstaff, Peter J. *Interregional Migration in the U.S.S.R.: Economic Aspects, 1959–1970.* Durham: Duke University Press, 1980.

Granovetter, Mark S. *Getting a Job: A Study of Contacts and Careers.* Cambridge, Mass.: Harvard University Press, 1974.

Greenhalgh, Susan. "Networks and Their Nodes: Urban Society on Taiwan." *China Quarterly* 99 (1984): 529–52.

Gu, Chu. "Dushi 'mangliu' mianmian guan" [A look at the face of big cities' "blind wanderers"]. *Shehui* [Society (Shanghai)] 1 (1990): 7–9.

Gu, Shengzu. "Renkou qianyi he liudong yanjiu" [Research on population migration and mobility]. *Wuhan Daxue Xuebao* [Wuhan University bulletin] 2 (1989): 44–49.

————. "Zhongguo nongcun shengyu laodongli xiang he chuqu?" [Where is China's rural surplus labor going?]. *Gaige* [Reform (Beijing)] 4 (1994): 79–87.

Guangdong wailai nongmingong lianhe ketizu [Guangdong outside peasant workers joint task group]. "Zai liudongzhong shixian jingying yimin—guangdongsheng wailai mingong diaoyan baogao" [In floating choose the select migrants—Guangdong province outside workers investigation report]. *Zhanlue yu guanli* [Strategy and management (Beijing)] 5 (1995): 112–20.

Gunes-Ayata, Ayse. "Migrants and Natives: Urban Bases of Social Conflict." In *Migrants, Workers, and the Social Order*, edited by Jeremy Eades, 234–48. London: Tavistock, 1987.

Guo, Zhengmo. "Dangqian nongcun laodongli 'mangliu' xianxiang di hongguan jingji beijing yu shudao celue" [The macroeconomic background of the present phenomenon of "blind wandering" of rural labor forces and tactics for clearing it up]. *Nongye wenti* [Agricultural issues (Beijing)] 7 (1989): 20–23.

Guojia tongjiju bian [State Statistical Bureau, ed.]. *Zhongguo tongji nianjian 1991* [Chinese statistical yearbook 1991]. Beijing: Zhongguo tongji chubanshe, 1991.

Guowuyuan fazhiju, Zhonghua renmin gongheguo fagui huibian bianji weiyuanhui, bian [State Council Legal System Bureau, editorial committee of the Compendium of Legal Documents of the People's Republic of China, eds.]. *Zhongguo renmin gongheguo fagui huibian* [Compendium of legal documents of the People's Republic of China]. Selected volumes. Beijing: Falu chubanshe, 1950–62.

Gurr, Ted Robert. *Why Men Rebel*. Princeton: Princeton University Press, 1970.

Haggard, Stephan, and Robert R. Kaufman. *The Political Economy of Democratic Transitions*. Princeton: Princeton University Press, 1995.

Halpern, Nina. "Creating Socialist Economies: Stalinist Political Economy and the Impact of Ideas." In *Ideas, Institutions, and Political Change*, edited by Judith Goldstein and Robert O. Keohane, 87–110. Cornell: Cornell University Press, 1993.

Han, Jun. "It's Imperative to Reform Household Registration." *Ban Yue Tan* [Biweekly chats (Beijing)], 11. Translated in Foreign Broadcast Information Service, August 5, 1994, 10.

————. "Cheng-xiang geli biran dapo—Zhongguo huji guanli zhidu gaige zaiji" [Urban-rural segregation must be broken—the time for reform of the Chinese household registration managment system is near at hand]. *Shidian* [Viewpoint] 6, no. 8 (1994): 6–11.

————. *Kua shiji de nanti—Zhongguo nongye laodongli zhuanyi* [A knotty problem straddling the century—China's rural labor forces' transfer]. Taiyuan: Shanxi jingji chubanshe [Shanxi economic publishing], 1994.

Han, Xiaoyun. "Income, Consumption, and Employment Characteristics—Part 3 of a Special Study of the Rural Migrant Workers." *Zhongguo nongcun jingji* [Chinese rural economy (Beijing)] 5 (1995): 40–44. Translated in Foreign Broadcast Information Service, September 7, 1995, 44–48.

Hao, Shouzhong, Kang Zizhen, and Wang Mingqin. "Haerbinshi ziliu renkou jihua shengyu guanli diaocha" [An investigation of the management of planned birth among the drifting population of Harbin City]. *Xueshu jiaoliu* [Academic exchange (Harbin)] 2 (1988): 79–85.

Harbin yuebao [Harbin monthly]. Selected issues, 1985–91.

Hardin, Russell. *Collective Action*. Baltimore: Johns Hopkins University Press, 1982.

Harris, John R., and Michael P. Todaro. "Migration, Unemployment, and Development: A Two-Sector Analysis." *American Economic Review* (Nashville) 60, no. 1 (March 1970): 126–42.

Harris, William H. *The Harder We Run: Black Workers Since the Civil War.* New York: Oxford University Press, 1982.

Hawrylyshyn, Oli. "Yugoslavian Development and Rural to Urban Migration: The Evidence of the 1961 Census." In *Internal Migration: A Comparative Perspective*, edited by Alan A. Brown and Egon Neuberger, 329–45. New York: Academic Press, 1977.

Heater, Derek. *Citizenship: The Civic Ideal in World History, Politics and Education*. London: Longman, 1990.

Hechter, Michael. *Internal Colonialism: The Celtic Fringe in British National Development, 1536–1966*. Berkeley: University of California Press, 1975.

Henansheng nongcun shehui jingji diaochadui [Henan province rural social-economic research team]. "Guanyu nongcun renkou waichu liudong qingkuang di diaocha" [An investigation of the situation of rural population flowing out]. *Renkou yu jingji* [Population and economy (Beijing)] 3 (1991): 42–46.

Hendrischke, Hans. "Tianjin: Quiet Achiever?" Paper prepared for the conference China's Provinces in Reform, 2d Workshop, Zhejiang University, Hangzhou, October 20–24, 1996.

Hershatter, Gail. "Chinese Sex Workers in the Reform Period." In *Putting Class in Its Place: Worker Identities in East Asia*, edited by Elizabeth J. Perry, 199–224. Berkeley: Institute of East Asian Studies, University of California, 1996.

———. *The Workers of Tianjin, 1900–1949*. Stanford: Stanford University Press, 1986.

Ho, Ping-ti. *Studies on the Population of China, 1368–1953*. Cambridge, Mass.: Harvard University Press, 1959.

———. *Zhongguo huiguan shi lun* [A historical study of Huikuan in China]. Taipei: Hsueh-sheng shu chu, 1966.

Hoffmann, David L. *Peasant Metropolis: Social Identities in Moscow: 1929–1941*. Ithaca: Cornell University Press, 1994.

Hollifield, James F. *Immigrants, Markets, and States: The Political Economy of Postwar Europe*. Cambridge, Mass.: Harvard University Press, 1992.

Hondagneu-Sotelo, Pierrette. *Gendered Transitions: Mexican Experiences of Immigration*. Berkeley: University of California Press, 1994.

Honig, Emily. *Creating Chinese Ethnicity: Subei People in Shanghai, 1850–1980.* New Haven: Yale University Press, 1992.

———. "Migrant Culture in Search of a Subei Identity." In *Shanghai Sojourners,* edited by Frederic Wakeman Jr. and Wen-hsin Yeh, 239–65. China Research Monograph no. 40. Berkeley: Institute of East Asian Studies, University of California, 1992.

———. "Regional Identity, Labor, and Ethnicity in Contemporary China." In *Putting Class in Its Place: Worker Identities in East Asia,* edited by Elizabeth J. Perry, 225–44. Berkeley: Institute of East Asian Studies, University of California, 1996.

———. *Sisters and Strangers: Women in the Shanghai Cotton Mills, 1919–1949.* Stanford: Stanford University Press, 1986.

Hou, Jianzhang. "Meitian 140 wan: beijing di liudong zhanzhu renkou" [Every day 1,400,000: Beijing's floating temporary population]. *Chengshi wenti* [Urban issues (Beijing)] 6 (1992): 40–44.

Howard, M. C., and J. E. King. *The Political Economy of Marx.* Harlow, England: Longman, 1975.

Howe, Christopher. *Employment and Economic Growth in Urban China, 1949–1957.* Cambridge: Cambridge University Press, 1971.

———. *Wage Patterns and Wage Policy in Modern China, 1919–1972.* Cambridge: Cambridge University Press, 1973.

Hu, Teh-wei, and Elizabeth Hon-Ming Li. "Labor Market Reforms in China." Paper presented at the Center for Chinese Studies, Spring Regional Seminar, University of California, Berkeley, April 11, 1992.

Hu, Xiaobo. Talk at the conference China and Constitutionalism: Cross-National Perspectives, sponsored by the Center for the Study of Human Rights, the Center for Chinese Legal Studies, and the East Asian Institute, Columbia University, April 30, 1993.

Huang, Bicheng, Liu Yong, and Peng Shaoci. "Laizi Changshashi laowu shichang di baogao" [A report from Changsha's labor market]. *Shehui* [Society (Shanghai)] 3 (1988): 15–17.

Huang, Haixia. "How to Ensure the Orderly Flow of the Rural Surplus Labor Force?—Interviewing Labor Minister Li Boyong." *Liaowang* [Observer] 13 (1996): 30–31. Translated in Foreign Broadcast Information Service, June 5, 1996, 29–32.

Huang, Hongyun, and Chen Xianshou. "Wuhan shiqu 'liu wu' qijian renkou qianyi zhuangkuang fenxi" [Analysis of population migration in Wuhan City during the period of the sixth Five-Year Plan]. *Zhongguo renkou kexue* [Chinese population science (Beijing)] 2 (1989): 14–19.

———. "Wuhan shiqu liudong renkou qingkuang diaocha baogao" [A report on an investigation of the situation of the floating population in Wuhan City]. In *Zhongguo renkou nianjian 1987* [Almanac of China's population], edited by Zhongguo shehui kexue yanjiuso [Chinese Social Science Academy], 684–90. Beijing, 1988.

Huang, Jinhong, and Ning Quancheng. "Dao Guangzhou 'zhao fanwan' di waidiren" [Outsiders going to Guangzhou to seek their rice bowl]. *Guangzhou wenyi* [Guangzhou literature and art] 7 (1987): 2–11.

Huang, Ruide. "Liudongzhong di xiayidai" [The next generation among the floaters]. *Nanfang chuang* [Southern window (Guangzhou)] 9 (1989): 20–21.

Huang, Yasheng. *Inflation and Investment Control in China: The Political Economy of Central-Local Relations During the Reform Era.* New York: Cambridge University Press, 1996.

———. "Why China Will Not Collapse." *Foreign Policy* 99 (1995): 54–68.

"Huji yanjiu" ketizu ["Household registration research" task group]. "Xianxing huji guanli zhidu yu jingji tizhi gaige" [The present household registration management system and economic system reform]. *Shanghai shehui kexueyuan xueshu jikan* [Shanghai Academy of Social Science Academic Quarterly] 3 (1989): 81–91.

Huntington, Samuel P., and Joan M. Nelson. *No Easy Choice: Political Participation in Developing Countries.* Cambridge, Mass.: Harvard University Press, 1976.

Ikels, Charlotte. *The Return of the God of Wealth: The Transition to a Market Economy in Urban China.* Stanford: Stanford University Press, 1996.

Ireland, Patrick R. *The Policy Challenge of Ethnic Diversity: Immigrant Politics in France and Switzerland.* Cambridge, Mass.: Harvard University Press, 1994.

Jackson, J. A. *Migration.* London: Longman, 1986.

Jepperson, Ronald L. "Institutions, Institutional Effects, and Institutionalism." In *The New Institutionalism in Organizational Analysis,* edited by Walter W. Powell and Paul J. DiMaggio, 143–63. Chicago: University of Chicago Press, 1991.

JETRO China Newsletter 105 (July–August 1993).

Jian, Xinhua. "The Urban Floating Population: Problems and Solutions." *Zhongguo renkoubao* [Chinese population news], July 8, 1996, 3. Translated in Foreign Broadcast Information Service, July 8, 1996.

Jiang, Kelin. "Gonghui: burong hushidi zhongyao jiaose—wushi niandai shanghai waishang qiye laozi guanxidi lishi kaocha ji qi qishi" [The prominent role of unions—Shanghai's foreign enterprises in the 1950s: A historical examination and illumination of the relation between labor and capital]. Prepared for presentation at the Luce Seminar on Shanghai Labor, May 8, 1993, Center for Chinese Studies, University of California, Berkeley.

Jiao, Qingle. "Problems of Managing Floating Populations." *Fazhi ribao* [Legal daily (Beijing)], July 21, 1993, 1. Translated in Joint Publications Research Service-CAR-94-048, 60.

Jing, Yi. "Dongwan huozai yunanzhe jiashu caifangji" [Records from visits to Dongwan fire disaster victims' family members]. *Zheng Ming* [Contend (Hong Kong)] 169 (1991): 22–27.

Johnson, Marguerite. "Bright Lights, Pink City." *Time,* February 21, 1994, 47.

Joint Publications Research Service. Selected issues, 1985–96.

Jones, Charisse. "New Welfare Law Sows Panic Among Immigrants." *New York Times,* August 26, 1996.

Jones, Richard C. Introduction to *Patterns of Undocumented Migration: Mexico and the United States,* edited by Richard C. Jones, 1–12. Totowa, N.J.: Rowman and Allanheld, 1984.

Kannappan, Subbiah. "Urban Employment and the Labor Market in Developing Nations." *Economic Development and Cultural Change* 33, no. 4 (July 1985): 699–73.

Kaye, Lincoln. "Conflicts of Interest." *Far Eastern Economic Review* (Hong Kong), August 4, 1994.

Kernen, Antoine. "Surviving Reform in Shenyang—New Poverty in Pioneer City." *China Rights Forum* (summer 1997): 8–11.

Keyssar, Alexander. *Out of Work: The First Century of Unemployment in Massachusetts.* Cambridge: Cambridge University Press, 1986.

Khan, Azizur Rahman, Keith Griffin, Carl Riskin, and Zhao Renwei. "Household Income and Its Distribution in China." *China Quarterly* 132 (1992): 1029–1061.

Kilborn, Peter. "Law Fails to Stem Abuse of Migrants, U.S. Panel Reports." *New York Times,* October 22, 1992.

Kipnis, Andrew. "Chinese Household Registration Law Reform." Manuscript. 1995.

Kirkby, R. J. R. *Urbanisation in China: Town and Country in a Developing Economy, 1949–2000 A.D.* London: Croom Helm, 1985.

Knight, Jack. *Institutions and Social Conflict.* Cambridge: Cambridge University Press, 1992.

Koelble, Thomas A. "The New Institutionalism in Political Science and Sociology." *Comparative Politics* 27, no. 2 (1995): 231–43.

Kojima, Reeitsu. *Urbanization and Urban Problems in China.* Tokyo: Institute of Developing Economies, 1987.

Konrad, Gyorgy, and Ivan Szelenyi. "Social Conflicts of Underurbanization." In *Urban and Social Economics in Market and Planned Economies: Policy, Planning, and Development,* edited by Alan A. Brown, Joseph A. Licari, and Egon Neuberger, 1:206–26. New York: Praeger, 1972.

Kornai, Janos. *The Socialist Service: The Political Economy of Communism.* Princeton: Princeton University Press, 1992.

Korzec, Michael. "Contract Labor, the 'Right to Work,' and New Labor Laws in the People's Republic of China." *Comparative Economic Studies* 30, no. 2 (1988): 117–49.

Kraus, Richard Curt. *Class Conflict in Chinese Socialism.* New York: Columbia University Press, 1981.

Kuhn, Anthony, and Lincoln Kaye. "Bursting at the Seams." *Far Eastern Economic Review* (Hong Kong), March 10, 1994.

Lang, Olga. *Chinese Family and Society.* New Haven: Yale University Press, 1946.

Laodongbu jiuyesi laodongbu xinxi zongxin [Employment Department and Information Center, Ministry of Labor]. "Guanyu 'Zhongguo nongcun laodongli jiuye yu liudong zhuangkuang diaocha' jieguo di fenxi (zhaiyao)" [Results of an analysis of "investigation of Chinese rural labor forces employment and mobility situation" (abstract)]. In Ba jia, ed.,

Nongcun laodongli jingji yanjiu tongxun [Bulletin of rural labor mobility studies], B-01–B-09. N.p., 1995.

Lardy, Nicholas R. *Agriculture in China's Modern Economic Development.* Cambridge: Cambridge University Press, 1983.

———. "Consumption and Living Standards in China, 1978–1983." *China Quarterly* 100 (1984): 849–65.

———. *Economic Growth and Distribution in China.* New York: Cambridge University Press, 1978.

Lary, Diana. "Hidden Migrations: Movement of Shandong People, 1949 to 1978." *Chinese Environment and Development* 7, nos. 1–2 (spring–summer 1996): 56–72.

Layton-Henry, Zig. "The Challenge of Political Rights." In *The Political Rights of Migrant Workers in Western Europe,* edited by Zig Layton-Henry, 1–26. London: Sage Publications, 1990.

———, ed. *The Political Rights of Migrant Workers in Western Europe.* London: Sage Publications, 1990.

Lee, Ching-kwan. "Production Politics and Labour Identities: Migrant Workers in South China." In *China Review 1995,* edited by Lo Chi Kin, Suzanne Pepper, and Tsui Kai Yuen, 15.1–15.28. Hong Kong: Chinese University Press, 1995.

Lee, James. "Migration and Expansion in Chinese History." In *Human Migration: Patterns and Policies,* edited by William H. McNeill and Ruth S. Adams, 20–47. Bloomington: Indiana University Press, 1978.

Lee, James, and R. Bin Wong. "Population Movements in Qing China and Their Linguistic Legacy." *Journal of Chinese Linguistics,* monograph series no. 3 (1991): 52–77.

Lee, James Z., and Wang Feng. "Malthusian Mythology and Chinese Reality: The Population History of One Quarter of Humanity, 1700–2000." Manuscript, 1997. Published as *One Quarter of Humanity: Malthusian Mythology and Chinese Reality.* Cambridge, Mass.: Harvard University Press, 1999.

Lee, Sun-Hee. *Why People Intend to Move: Individual and Community-Level Factors of Out-Migration in the Philippines.* Boulder, Colo.: Westview Press, 1985.

Lee, Yok-shiu F. "The Urban Housing Problem in China." *China Quarterly* 115 (1988): 387–407.

Lees, Lynn Hollen. *Exiles of Erin: Irish Migrants in Victorian London.* Ithaca: Cornell University Press, 1979.

Lewis, Robert A., and Richard H. Rowland. *Population Redistribution in the U.S.S.R: It's [sic] Impact on Society, 1897–1977.* New York: Praeger, 1979.

Li, Cheng. "200 Million Mouths Too Many." CL-10. Shanghai: Institute of Current World Affairs, 1994.

———. "Surplus Rural Laborers and Internal Migration in China: Current Status and Future Prospects." *Asian Survey* 36, no. 11 (1996): 1122–45.

———. "Tidal Wave of Migrant Laborers in China," pt. 1: " '94ers: Eastward Ho!" CL-9. Shanghai: Institute of Current World Affairs, 1994.

———. "Tidal Wave of Migrant Laborers in China," pt. 2: "200 Million

Mouths Too Many." CL-10. Shanghai: Institute of Current World Affairs, 1994.

—. "Under Neon Lights: Street People in Shanghai." CL-16. Shanghai: Institute of Current World Affairs, 1994.

Li, Mengbai, and Hu Xin, eds. *Liudong renkou dui da chengshi fazhan di yingxiang ji duice* [The influence of the floating population on big cities' development and countermeasures]. Beijing: Jingji ribao chubanshe [Economic daily publishing], 1991.

Li, Rongshi. "Understanding and Thoughts on the Mobile Population in China Today." *Renkou yanjiu* [Population research (Beijing)] 97 (1996): 10–14. Translated in Foreign Broadcast Information Service, May 30, 1996, 27–31.

Li, Roujian. "Zhujiang sanjiaozhou laodongli shichangzhong wailai longdongli di yanjiu" [A study of the nonnative work force in the labor market of the Pearl River]. *Renkou yu jingji* [Population and economy (Beijing)] 4 (1994): 34–38.

Li, Si-ming. "Population Mobility and Urban and Rural Development in Mainland China." *Issues and Studies* (Taipei) 31, no. 9 (1995): 37–54.

Li, Tan. "Population Flows into the Big Cities." *Beijing Review* 29 (1994): 15–19. Reprinted in Foreign Broadcast Information Service, July 20, 1994, 20–21.

Li, Xiaohua. "Beijing di yayunhou yizheng" [The legacy of the Asian Games in Beijing]. *Zheng Ming* [Contend (Hong Kong)] 158 (1990): 19.

Li, Yu, and Tang Bu. "Beijing chengzhen getihuzhong di liudong renkou" [The floating population among the Beijing urban individual proprietors]. *Shehuixue yanjiu* [Sociological research (Beijing)] 2 (1988): 21–23.

Liang, Qiushi. "Zhongguo dalu liudong renkou ji jiejue banfa" [The floating population on the Chinese mainland and the way to solve it]. *Minzhu Zhongguo* [Democratic China] 25 (1995): 39–42.

Liang, Ziming. "Lun chengshi liudong renkou di zuoyong he guanli" [On the use and management of the urban floating population]. *Yangcheng wanbao* [Sheep City evening news (Guangzhou)], March 16, 1988.

Liao, Shitong, and Liao Shitian. "Guangdongsheng renkou liudong qushi ji qi daoxiang" [The trend of population mobility and its direction in Guangdong province]. *Zhongguo renkou kexue* [Chinese population science (Beijing)] 6 (1989): 7–9, 25.

Light, Ivan, and Edna Bonacich. *Immigrant Entrepreneurs: Koreans in Los Angeles, 1965–1982.* Berkeley: University of California Press, 1988.

Lipset, Seymour Martin. *Political Man: The Social Bases of Politics.* New York: Doubleday, 1963.

—. "Some Social Requisites of Democracy: Economic Development and Political Legitimacy." *American Political Science Review* 53 (March 1959): 69–105.

Lipton, Michael. *Why Poor People Stay Poor: A Study of Urban Bias in World Development.* London: Temple Smith, 1972.

Liu, Alan P. L. "Economic Reform, Mobility Strategies, and National Integration in China." *Asian Survey* 31, no. 5 (1991): 393–408.

————. "The 'Wenzhou Model' of Development and China's Modernization." *Asian Survey* 32, no. 8 (1992): 696–711.

Liu, Bingyi. "Liudong di 'shimin'" [Floating "city people"]. *Qing Chun* [Youth] 6 (1989): 31–32.

Liu, Chunbin. "Eryuan shehui jiegou yu chengshihua (xu)" [Dual social structure and urbanization (continued)]. *Shehui* [Society (Shanghai)] 4 (1990): 34–35.

————. "Mangliu: Eryuan shehui jiegou: nongcun chengshihua" [Blind wanderers: Dual social structure and urbanization]. *Xiandai renbao* [Contemporaries' paper (Guangzhou)], April 25, 1989.

Liu, Dawei, and Wang Qiangzhi. "Guanyu Beijingshi 'zhao gong nan' wenti di diaocha baogao" [An investigation report on the problem of labor being hard to find in Beijing City]. *Shehui kexue yu shehui diaocha* [Social science and social investigation (Changchun)] 1 (1987): 34–40.

Liu, Dongming. "Tantan woshi renkou jixie zengzhang wenti" [Talking about the problem of our city's population's mechanical growth]. *Harbin yanjiu* 6 (1986): 54–56.

Liu, Hantai. *Zhongguo di qigai qunluo* [China's beggar community]. *Wenhui yuekan* [Encounter monthly (Shanghai)] 10 (1986): 197–234.

Liu, Jimin. "Nongcun laodongli zou xiang shichang di zhang'ai yu chulu" [Obstacles and outlet for rural labor heading for the market]. *Renkou yu jingji* [Population and economy (Beijing)] 6 (1995): 60–64, 39.

Liu, Jinglin, and Chang Shaorong. "Chengshi liudong renkou ji qi guanli" [The urban floating population and its management]. *Xuexi yu tansuo* [Study and exploration (Harbin)] 5 (1993): 46–49.

Liu, Xuejie. " 'Laomang' xiliuji" [The record of the Western journey of the blind]. *Luzhou* (Oasis) 6 (1989): 88–102.

Lloyd, Peter. *Slums of Hope? Shanty Towns of the Third World.* Manchester: Manchester University Press, 1979.

Lomnitz, Larissa Adler. *Networks and Marginality: Life in a Mexican Shantytown.* New York: Academic Press, 1977.

Lu, Feng. "The Origins and Formation of the Unit (*Danwei*) System." *Chinese Sociology and Anthropology* 25, no. 3 (1993).

Lu, Li, and Wang Xiuyin. "Cong nongcun jianzhudui jincheng kan woguo renkou chengzhenhua di yitiao tujing" [Looking at a road for our country's population urbanization from the perspective of rural construction teams entering the cities]. *Renkou yu jingji* [Population and economy (Beijing)] 6 (1984): 34–37.

Lu, Xiaobo, and Elizabeth J. Perry, eds. *Danwei: The Chinese Workunit in Historical and Comparative Perspective.* Armonk, N.Y.: M. E. Sharpe, 1997.

Lu, Yu. "Shandong 4 chengzhen qianru renkou qianyihou di bianhua" [Changes in migrants before and after migration in four cities and towns in Shandong]. *Zhongguo renkou kexue* [Chinese population science (Beijing)] 5 (1989): 62–64.

Luo, Maochu, Zhang Jian, Gao Qingxu, Liu Hongyi, and Liu Hongbin. "Quanmian renshi renkou liudong xianxiang, shenshen xuanze duicui—

Beijingshi liudong renkou diaocha" [Fully understand the phenomenon of population mobility, carefully select the object—an investigation of Beijing City's floating population]. *Renkou yanjiu* [Population research (Beijing)] 3 (1986): 2–7, 19.

Luoyi Ningge'er. *Di sanzhi yanjing kan Zhongguo* [Seeing China through a third eye]. Translated by Wang Shan. Taiyuan: Shanxi renmin chubanshe, 1994.

Ma, Laurence J. C. "Urban Housing Supply in the People's Republic of China." In *Urban Development in Modern China*, edited by Laurence J. C. Ma and Edward W. Hanten, 222–59. Boulder, Colo.: Westview Press, 1981.

Ma, Xia. "Changes in the Pattern of Migration in Urban China." In *Migration and Urbanization in China*, edited by Lincoln H. Day and Ma Xia, 193–216. Armonk, N.Y.: M. E. Sharpe, 1994.

Magritte, N. A. "Trashpickers' Urban Wasteland." *Eastern Express* (Hong Kong), August 20–21, 1994.

Mallee, Hein. "Agricultural Labour and Rural Population Mobility: Some Preliminary Observations." Paper presented at the International Conference on Flow of Rural Labour in China, Beijing, June 25–27, 1996.

———. "China's Household Registration System Under Reform." *Development and Change* 26 (1995): 1–29.

———. "Rural Household Dynamics and Spatial Mobility in China." Paper presented at International Conference on Floating and Migration in China, Cologne, May 2–4, 1996. Published in *Floating Population and Migration in China: The Impact of Economic Reforms*, edited by Thomas Scharping, 278–96. Hamburg: Institut für Asienkunde, 1997.

Mandel, Ruth. "Ethnicity and Identity Among Migrant Guestworkers in West Berlin." In *Conflict, Migration, and the Expression of Ethnicity*, edited by Nancie L. Gonzalez and Carolyn S. McCommon, 60–74. Boulder, Colo.: Westview Press, 1989.

March, James G., and Johan P. Olsen. *Rediscovering Institutions: The Organizational Basis of Politics*. New York: Free Press, 1989.

Marie, Claude-Valentin. "From the Campaign Against Illegal Migration to the Campaign Against Illegal Work." *Annals of the the American Academy of Political and Social Science* 534 (1994): 118–32.

Marshall, T. H. *Citizenship and Social Class and Other Essays*. Cambridge: Cambridge University Press, 1950.

———. *Sociology at the Crossroads and Other Essays*. London: Heinemann, 1963.

Matthews, Mervyn. *The Passport Society: Controlling Movement in Russia and the U.S.S.R.* Boulder, Colo.: Westview Press, 1993.

Marx, Karl, and Friedrich Engels. "Manifesto of the Communist Party." In *Marx and Engels: Basic Writings on Politics and Philosophy*, edited by Lewis S. Feuer. Garden City, N.Y.: Anchor Books, 1959.

Massey, Douglas S. "The Settlement Process Among Mexican Migrants to the United States." *American Sociological Review* 51, no. 5 (1986): 1372–1403.

Massey, Douglas S., and Nancy A. Denton. *American Apartheid: Segregation and the Making of the Underclass.* Cambridge, Mass.: Harvard University Press, 1993.

Mazumdar, Dipak. "Rural-Urban Migration in Developing Countries." In *Handbook of Regional and Urban Economies: Urban Economics,* edited by Edwin S. Mills, 2:1097–1128. Amsterdam: North-Holland, 1987.

Meehan, Elizabeth. *Citizenship and the European Community.* London: Sage Publications, 1993.

Meisner, Maurice. "Utopian Socialist Themes in Maoism: The Relationship Between Town and Countryside." In *Marxism, Maoism, and Utopianism: Eight Essays,* edited by Maurice Meisner, 28–75. Madison: University of Wisconsin Press, 1982.

Messina, Anthony M. "The Not So Silent Revolution: Postwar Migration to Western Europe." *World Politics* 49 (1996): 130–54.

Miao, Hongxun. "Qianxi Wenzhou liudong renkou yu jihua shengyu" [An elementary analysis of Wenzhou's floating population and planned birth]. *Renkou yu jingji* [Population and economy (Beijing)] 2 (1989): 17–19.

Migdal, Joel S., Atul Kohli, and Vivienne Shue, eds. *State Power and Social Forces: Domination and Transformation in the Third World.* New York: Cambridge University Press, 1994.

Min, Kangwu. "A Village in the Capital." *China Focus* 3, no. 8 (1995): 4.

Mines, Richard. "Network Migration and Mexican Rural Development: A Case Study." In *Patterns of Undocumented Migration: Mexico and the United States,* edited by Richard C. Jones, 136–58. Totowa, N.J.: Rowman and Allanheld, 1984.

Ming, Lei. "Wo kandao di Beijing 'zhejiangcun' " [The "Zhejiang Village" of Beijing that I have seen]. *Zheng Ming* [Contend (Hong Kong)] 2 (1994): 25–27.

Ministry of Agriculture, Rural Economic Research Center. "Problems and Strategic Changes in China's Rural Economic Development." *Jingji yanjiu* [Economic research (Beijing)] 1 (1994): 31–39. Translated in Foreign Broadcast Information Service, May 13, 1994, 48–56.

Mitchell, Katharyne. "Work Authority in Industry: The Happy Demise of the Ideal Type." *Comparative Studies in Society and History* 34, no. 4 (1992): 679–94.

Moore, Barrington, Jr. *Social Origins of Dictatorship and Democracy: Lord and Peasant in the Making of the Modern World.* Boston: Beacon Press, 1966.

Morgan, Thomas. "In the Shadow of Manhattan Skyscrapers, a Society of Shantytowns Grows." *New York Times,* October 20, 1991.

Morrison, Peter A. "The Functions and Dynamics of the Migration Process." In *Internal Migration: A Comparative Perspective,* edited by Alan A. Brown and Egon Neuberger, 61–72. New York: Academic Press, 1977.

Mote, F. W. "The Transformation of Nanking, 1350–1400." In *The City in Late Imperial China,* edited by G. William Skinner, 101–53. Stanford: Stanford University Press, 1977.

Mu, Guangzong. "Zhongguo nongye shengyu laodong di zhuanyi ji pingjia"

[An assessment of China's rural surplus labor transfer]. *Zhongguo renkou kexue* [Chinese population science (Beijing)] 5 (1989): 6–13.

Mufson, Steven. "China Uses Arrests, Threats to Silence Domestic Critics." *Washington Post*, December 28, 1995.

Mydans, Seth. "Californians Trying to Bar Service to Aliens." *New York Times*, May 22, 1994.

Nanfang ribao [Southern daily (Guangzhou)]. Selected issues, 1988–92.

National Museum of American History, Smithsonian Institution. "Black Migration and the American City." Washington, D.C., 1988.

Naughton, Barry. *Growing Out of the Plan: Chinese Economic Reform 1978–1993*. Cambridge: Cambridge University Press, 1995.

Nelson, Joan M. *Access to Power: Politics and the Urban Poor in Developing Nations*. Princeton: Princeton University Press, 1979.

———. *Migrants, Urban Poverty, and Instability in Developing Nations*. Occasional Papers in International Affairs no. 22. Cambridge, Mass.: Center for International Affairs, Harvard University, 1969.

———. "Sojourners versus New Urbanites: Causes and Consequences of Temporary versus Permanent Cityward Migration in Developing Countries." *Economic Development and Cultural Change* 24, no. 4 (1976): 721–57.

Nevitt, Christopher. "Private Business Associations in China: Evidence of Civil Society or Local State Power." *China Journal* 36 (1996): 25–43.

Nickerson, Dede. "Migrant Workers Said 'Flocking' to Beijing." *South China Morning Post* (Hong Kong), November 16, 1992.

"Nongcun shengyu laodongli zhuanyi yu laodongli shichang ketizu" [Research team on the transfer of surplus agricultural labor and the labor market]. "28ge xian (shi) nongcun laodongli kuaquyu liudong di diaocha yanjiu" [Survey and research on rural labor migration from 28 counties and cities]. *Zhongguo nongcun jingji* [Chinese rural economy (Beijing)] 4 (1995): 19–28.

Nongmin ribao [Peasants' daily (Beijing)]. Selected issues, 1987–89.

Nongyebu "'Mingongchao' di genzong diaocha yu yanjiu" ketizu [Research team on "'Labor tide' investigation and research" of the Ministry of Agriculture]. "Jingji fazhanzhong di nongcun laodongli liudong—dui dangqian nongcun laodongli waichu qingkuang di diaocha yu sikao" [Rural labor migration in economic development—investigation and thinking on the current situation of rural labor migration]. *Zhongguo nongcun jingji* [Chinese rural economy (Beijing)] 1 (1995): 43–50.

North, Douglass C. *Institutions, Institutional Change and Economic Performance*. New York: Cambridge University Press, 1990.

Odgaard, Ole. "Entrepreneurs and Elite Formation in Rural China" *Australian Journal of Chinese Affairs* 28 (1992): 89–108.

O'Donnell, Guillermo, and Philippe C. Schmitter. *Transitions from Authoritarian Rule: Tentative Conclusions about Uncertain Democracies*. Baltimore: Johns Hopkins University Press, 1986.

Ofer, Gur. "Economizing on Urbanization in Socialist Countries: Historical Necessity or Socialist Strategy." In *Internal Migration: A Comparative*

Perspective, edited by Alan A. Brown and Egon Neuberger, 277–303. New York: Academic Press, 1977.

Oi, Jean. "China's Polity in the Year 2010: The Challenges of Successful Rural Industrialization." Paper prepared for the Conference on China and World Affairs in 2010, Institute for International Studies, Stanford University, April 26–27, 1996.

———. "Reform and Urban Bias in China." *Journal of Development Studies* 29, no. 4 (1993): 129–48.

———. *Rural China Takes Off: The Political Foundation for Economic Reform.* Berkeley: University of California Press, 1999.

Oksenberg, Michel, and James Tong. "The Evolution of Central-Provincial Fiscal Relations in China, 1971–1984: The Formal System." *China Quarterly* 125 (1991): 1–32.

Olson, Mancur. *The Logic of Collective Action: Public Goods and the Theory of Groups.* Cambridge, Mass.: Harvard University Press, 1971.

Oshima, Kazutsugu. "The Present Condition of Inter-regional Movements of the Labor Force in Rural Jiangsu Province, China." *Developing Economies* (Tokyo) 28, no. 2 (1990): 202–20.

Ostrom, Elinor. *Governing the Commons: The Evolution of Institutions for Collective Action.* Cambridge: Cambridge University Press, 1990.

Pan, Li. "Nongcun liudong renkou di diyuan juji xiaoying he diyuan liansuo xiaoying" [The geographic concentration of rural labor population and its geographic chain effect]. *Shehui* [Society (Shanghai)] 6 (1991): 24–25.

Parish, William, Xiaoye Zhe, and Fang Li. "Nonfarm Work and Marketization of the Chinese Countryside." *China Quarterly* 143 (1995): 697–730.

Park, Albert, and Scott Rozelle, eds. "Promoting Economic Development in China's Poor Areas: A Collection of Research Policy Briefs." Presented by members of the China Poverty Research Association at a discussion forum for Chinese Researchers and Policy Makers sponsored by the Ford Foundation, Beijing, October 26, 1994.

Park, Albert, Scott Rozelle, Christine Wong, and Changqing Ren. "Distributional Consequences of Reforming Local Public Finance in China." *China Quarterly* 147 (1996): 751–78.

Parris, Kristen. "Local Initiative and National Reform: The Wenzhou Model of Development." *China Quarterly* 134 (1993): 242–63.

Pearson, Margaret. *Joint Ventures in the People's Republic of China: The Control of Foreign Direct Investment Under Socialism.* Princeton: Princeton University Press, 1991.

Peng, Jun. "Chinese Taxation—Vindicate Your Dignity." *Jingji ribao* [Economic daily], October 12, 1994, 3. Translated in Foreign Broadcast Information Service, October 28, 1994, 37.

Perlman, Janice E. *The Myth of Marginality: Urban Poverty and Politics in Rio de Janeiro.* Berkeley: University of California Press, 1976.

Perry, Elizabeth J. *Shanghai on Strike: The Politics of Chinese Labor.* Stanford: Stanford University Press, 1993.

Perry, Elizabeth J., and Li Xun. *Proletarian Power: Shanghai in the Cultural Revolution.* Boulder, Colo.: Westview Press, 1997.

Piante, Catherine, and Zhu Haibo. "Life and Death of 'Zhejiang Village': A Law unto Itself—Peking's 'Zhejiang Cun.' " *China Perspectives* 2 (1995): 12–15.

Pieke, Frank N. "Bureaucracy, Friends, and Money: The Growth of Capital Socialism in China." *Comparative Studies in Society and History* 37, no. 3 (1995): 494–518.

Piore, Michael J. *Birds of Passage: Migrant Labor and Industrial Societies.* Cambridge: Cambridge University Press, 1979.

———. "Notes for a Theory of Labor Market Stratification." In *Labor Market Segmentation,* edited by Richard C. Edwards, Michael Reich, and David M. Gordon, 125–50. Lexington, Mass.: D. C. Heath, 1975.

Polanyi, Karl. *The Great Transformation.* Boston: Beacon Press, 1957.

Portes, Alejandro. "Modes of Structural Incorporation and Present Theories of Labor Immigration." In *Global Trends in Migration,* edited by Mary M. Kritz, Charles B. Keely, and Silvano M. Tomasi, 279–97. New York: Center for Migration Studies, 1981.

Portes, Alejandro, and Robert L. Bach. *Latin Journey: Cuban and Mexican Immigrants in the United States.* Berkeley: University of California Press, 1985.

Portes, Alejandro, and Ruben G. Rumbaut. *Immigrant America: A Portrait.* Berkeley: University of California Press, 1990.

Portes, Alejandro, and Alex Stepick. *City on the Edge: The Transformation of Miami.* Berkeley: University of California Press, 1993.

Portes, Alejandro, and John Walton. *Urban Latin America: The Political Condition from Above and Below.* Austin: University of Texas Press, 1976.

Portes, Alejandro, Manuel Castells, and Lauren A. Benton, eds. *The Informal Economy: Studies in Advanced and Less Developed Countries.* Baltimore: Johns Hopkins University Press, 1989.

Potter, Pitman B. "Riding the Tiger: Legitimacy and Legal Culture in Post-Mao China." *China Quarterly* 138 (1994): 325–58.

Potter, Sulamith Heins. "The Position of Peasants in Modern China's Social Order." *Modern China* 9, no. 4 (1983): 465–99.

Potter, Sulamith Heins, and Jack M. Potter. *China's Peasants: The Anthropology of a Revolution.* Cambridge: Cambridge University Press, 1990.

Powell, Walter W. "Expanding the Scope of Institutional Analysis," In *The New Institutionalism in Organizational Analysis,* edited by Walter W. Powell and Paul J. DiMaggio, 183–203. Chicago: University of Chicago Press, 1991.

Powell, Walter W., and Paul J. DiMaggio. Introduction to *The New Institutionalism in Organizational Analysis,* edited by Walter W. Powell and Paul J. DiMaggio, 1–38. Chicago: University of Chicago Press, 1991.

Provincial China: A Research Newsletter (Sydney, Australia). Selected issues, 1996–97.

Putterman, Louis. *Continuity and Change in China's Rural Development: Collective and Reform Eras in Perspective.* New York: Oxford University Press, 1993.

Quan, Lixin. "Beware! Mafia-type Organized Crime—a General Crackdown on Organized Crime in Beijing in Recent Years." *Xuexi yu yanjiu* [Study and research] 24 (1994): 35–37. Translated in Foreign Broadcast Information Service, February 14, 1995, 22–25.

Rath, Jan. "Voting Rights." In *The Political Rights of Migrant Workers in Western Europe*, edited by Zig Layton-Henry, 127–57. London: Sage Publications, 1990.

Renmin ribao [People's daily (Beijing)]. Selected issues, 1954–96.

Roberts, Bryan R. *The Making of Urban Citizens: Cities of Peasants Revisited*. London: Arnold, 1995.

———. "Migration and Industrializing Economies: A Comparative Perspective." In *Why People Move: Comparative Perspectives on the Dynamics of Internal Migration*, edited by Jorge Balan, 17–42. Paris: UNESCO Press, 1981.

———. "The Social Context of Citizenship in Latin America." *International Journal of Urban and Regional Research* 20, no. 1 (1996): 38–65.

Roberts, Kenneth D. "China's 'Tidal Wave' of Migrant Labor: What Can We Learn from Mexican Undocumented Migration to the United States?" Manuscript. Georgetown, Tex., 1994. Published in *International Migration Review* 31, no. 2 (1997): 249–93.

Roberts, Kenneth D., and Wei Jinsheng. "The Floating Population of Shanghai in the mid-1990s." Manuscript. Georgetown, Tex., 1997.

Rodriguez, Nestor, and Rogelio T. Nuñez. "An Exploration of Factors that Contribute to Differentiation Between Chicanos and *Indocumentados*." In *Mexican Immigrants and Mexican Americans: An Evolving Relation*, edited by Harley L. Browning and Rodolfo O. de la Garza, 138–56. Austin: Center for Mexican American Studies Publications, 1986.

Rofel, Lisa. "Eating Out of One Big Pot: Silk Workers in Contemporary China." In *Workers' Expressions: Beyond Accommodation and Resistance*, edited by John Calagione, Doris Francis, and Daniel Nugent, 79–97. Albany: State University of New York Press, 1992.

Rohter, Larry. "Revisiting Immigration and the Open Door Policy." *New York Times*, September 19, 1993.

Rosenzweig, Roy. *Eight Hours for What We Will: Workers and Leisure in an Industrial City, 1870–1920*. Cambridge: Cambridge University Press, 1983.

Rossabi, Morris. *China and Inner Asia from 1368 to the Present Day*. London: Thames and Hudson, 1975.

Rossi, Peter H. *Down and Out in America: The Origins of Homelessness*. Chicago: University of Chicago Press, 1989.

Rowe, William T. *HANKOW: Commerce and Society in a Chinese City, 1796–1889*. Stanford: Stanford University Press, 1984.

———. *HANKOW: Community and Conflict in a Chinese City, 1796–1895*. Stanford: Stanford University Press, 1989.

Rozelle, Scott. "Stagnation Without Equity: Patterns of Growth and Inequality in China's Rural Economy." *China Journal* 35 (1996): 63–92.

Rozelle, Scott, Li Guo, and Loren Brandt. "Land Tenure, Property Rights, and Productivity in China's Agricultural Sector." In *Property Rights and Economic Reform in China*, edited by Andrew Walder and Jean Oi. Stanford: Stanford University Press, forthcoming.

Rozman, Gilbert. *Urban Netwoks in Ch'ing China and Tokugawa Japan*. Princeton: Princeton University Press, 1973.

Rural Development Research Institute, Chinese Academy of Social Sciences, and Office for Rural Social Economic Statistics, State Statistical Bureau. " 'Increasing Peasants' Incomes Is Top Priority in Rural Economic Development." *Zhongguo nongcun jingji* [Chinese rural economy (Beijing)] April 20, 1997. Translated in *Summary of World Broadcasts* FE/3020, 10 September 1997, S1/1-S1/4.

Rutkowski, Michal. "The China's Floating Population and the Labor Market Reforms [*sic*]." Preliminary draft. Washington, D.C.: World Bank, December 1991.

Sabin, Lora. "New Bosses in the Workers' State: The Growth of Non-State Sector Employment in China." *China Quarterly* 140 (1994): 944–70.

Saiget, Robert J. "Beijing Exiles the Floating Population." *Kyodo* (Tokyo), March 25, 1995. Reprinted in Foreign Broadcast Information Service, March 27, 1995, 33.

Salins, Peter D. "Take a Ticket." *The New Republic*, December 27, 1993, 13–15.

Sanderatne, Nimal. "The Informal Sector in Sri Lanka: Dynamism and Resilience." In *The Silent Revolution: The Informal Sector in Five Asian and Near Eastern Countries*, edited by A. Lawrence Chickering and Mohamed Salahdine, 71–103. San Francisco: ICS Press, 1991.

Sassen, Saskia. *The Mobility of Labor and Capital: A Study in International Investment and Labor Flow*. New York: Cambridge University Press, 1988.

Sassen-Koob, Saskia. "Immigrant and Minority Workers in the Organization of the Labor Process." *Journal of Ethnic Studies* 8, no. 1 (1980): 1–34.

———. "New York City's Informal Economy." In *The Informal Economy: Studies in Advanced and Less Developed Countries*, edited by Alejandro Portes, Manuel Castells, and Lauren A. Benton, 60–77. Baltimore: Johns Hopkins University Press, 1989.

Schain, Martin A. "Patterns of Policy-Making in France: The Case of Immigration." Paper prepared for presentation at the Annual Meeting of the American Political Science Association, Chicago, September 1992.

Schak, David C. *A Chinese Beggar's Den: Poverty and Mobility in an Underclass Community*. Pittsburgh: University of Pittsburgh Press, 1988.

Scharping, Thomas. "Studying Migration in Contemporary China: Models and Methods, Issues and Evidence." In *Floating Population and Migration in China: The Impact of Economic Reforms*, edited by Thomas Scharping, 9–55. Hamburg: Institut für Asienkunde, 1997.

Scharping, Thomas, and Walter Schulze. "Economic, Labor and Income Developments in the Pearl River Delta: A Migration Survey of Foshan and Shenzhen." Paper presented at International Conference on Migration and Floating in China, Cologne, May 3–5, 1996. Published as "Labour and

Income Developments in the Pearl River Delta: A Migration Survey of Foshan and Shenzhen," in *Floating Population and Migration in China: The Impact of Economic Reforms*, edited by Thomas Scharping, 166–200. Hamburg: Institut für Asienkunde, 1997.

Schwarz, Henry G. "Chinese Migration to North-West China and Inner Mongolia 1949–1959." *China Quarterly* 16 (1963): 62–74.

Seidman, Gay W. *Workers' Movements in Brazil and South Africa, 1970–1985*. Berkeley: University of California Press, 1994.

Selden, Mark. *The Political Economy of Chinese Development*. Armonk, N.Y.: M. E. Sharpe, 1993.

Sha, Song. "An Analysis of the Characteristics of Robbers who Come to Shanghai from Outside." *Shehui* [Society (Shanghai)] 10 (1990): 10–12.

Shanghai shi tongjiju bian [Shanghai City statistics bureau], ed. *Shanghai liudong renkou* [Shanghai's floating population]. Shanghai: Chinese Statistical Publishing House, 1989.

Shao, Jun. "Dongyao gongyouzhi genji di mangliu dajun" [The great army of migrants is shaking the roots of the public ownership system]. *Zhongguo zhi chun* [China's spring (New York)] 8 (1990): 48–50.

Shi, Fang. "Heilongjiang diqu renkou qianyishi gaishu" [A general narrative of the population migration history of the Heilongjiang region]. *Xueshu jiaoliu* [Academic exchange (Harbin)] 5 (1987): 75–82.

———. *Zhongguo renkou qianyi shigao* [A history of Chinese population migration]. Harbin: Heilongjiang People's Publishing, 1990.

Shi, Xianmin. "Beijingshi getihu di fazhan licheng ji leibie fenhua—Beijing xichengqu getihu yanjiu" [The categorization and development history of Beijing City's private entrepreneurs—Research on Beijing Xicheng district's private entrepreneurs]. *Zhongguo shehui kexue* [Chinese social science (Beijing)] 5 (1992): 19–38.

———. "Beijing's Privately-Owned Small Businesses: A Decade's Development." *Social Sciences in China* (Beijing) 14, no. 1 (spring 1993): 153–64.

Shirk, Susan. *The Political Logic of Economic Reform in China*. Berkeley: University of California Press, 1993.

Sigurdson, Jon. "Rural Industry and the Internal Transfer of Technology." In *Authority, Participation and Cultural Change in China*, edited by Stuart Schram, 199–232. Cambridge: Cambridge University Press, 1973.

———, ed. *Rural Industrialization in China*. Cambridge, Mass.: Council on East Asian Studies, Harvard University, 1977.

Simon, Julian L. *The Economic Consequences of Immigration*. Oxford: Basil Blackwell, 1989.

Simon, Rita J., and Susan H. Alexander. *The Ambivalent Welcome: Print Media, Public Opinion, and Immigration*. Westport, Conn.: Praeger, 1993.

Skeldon, Ronald. *Population Mobility in Developing Countries: A Reinterpretation*. London: Belhaven, 1990.

Skinner, G. William. "Chinese Peasants and the Closed Community: An Open and Shut Case." *Comparative Studies in Society and History* 13, no. 3 (1971): 270–81.

———. "Introduction: Urban Social Structure in Ch'ing China." In *The City in Late Imperial China*, edited by G. William Skinner, 521–53. Stanford: Stanford University Press, 1977.

———. "Mobility Strategies in Late Imperial China: A Regional Systems Analysis." In *Regional Analysis*, edited by Carol A. Smith, 1:327–64. New York: Academic Press, 1976.

Skocpol, Theda. "Bringing the State Back." In "Strategies of Analysis in Current Research," *Bringing the State Back In*, edited by Peter R. Evans, Dietrich Rueschemeyer, and Theda Skocpol, 3–37. Cambridge: Cambridge University Press, 1985.

Smil, Vaclav. *China's Environmental Crisis: An Inquiry into the Limits of National Development*. Armonk, N.Y.: M. E. Sharpe, 1993.

Solberg, Carl. *Immigration and Nationalism: Argentina and Chile, 1890–1914*. Austin: University of Texas Press, 1970.

Solinger, Dorothy J. *Chinese Business Under Socialism: The Politics of Domestic Commerce, 1949–1980*. Berkeley: University of California Press, 1984.

———. "The Chinese Work Unit and Transient Labor in the Transition from Socialism." *Modern China* 21, no. 2 (1995): 155–83.

———. "The Danwei Confronts the Floating Population." In *The Danwei: The Changing Chinese Workplace in Historical and Comparative Perspectives*, edited by Liu Xiaobo and Elizabeth J. Perry, 195–222. Armonk, N.Y.: M. E. Sharpe, 1997.

———. "The Floating Population in the Cities: Chances for Assimilation?" In *Urban Spaces in Contemporary China*, edited by Deborah S. Davis, Richard Kraus, Barry Naughton, and Elizabeth J. Perry, 113–48. New York: Cambridge University Press, 1995.

———. *From Lathes to Looms: China's Industrial Policy in Comparative Perspective, 1979–1982*. Stanford: Stanford University Press, 1991.

———. "Human Rights Issues in China's Internal Migration: Insights from Comparisons with Germany and Japan." In *The East Asian Challenge for Human Rights*, edited by Joanne R. Bauer and Daniel A. Bell. New York: Cambridge University Press, 1999.

———. "Research Note: 'Temporary Residence Certificate' Regulations in Wuhan, May 1983." *China Quarterly* 101 (1985): 98–103.

———. "Urban Entrepreneurs and the State: The Merger of State and Society." In *State and Society in Contemporary China: The Consequences of Reform*, edited by Arthur Lewis Rosenbaum, 121–41. Boulder, Colo.: Westview, 1992.

———. "Urban Reform and Relational Contracting in Post-Mao China: An Interpretation of the Transition from Plan to Market." *Studies in Comparative Communism* 22, nos. 2–3 (1989): 171–85.

Sontag, Deborah. "Reshaping New York City's Golden Door." *New York Times*, June 13, 1993.

South African Challenge: Report for the Second Carnegie Inquiry into Poverty and Development in Southern Africa. New York: W. W. Norton, 1989.

Soysal, Yasemin Nuhoglu. *Limits of Citizenship: Migrants and Postnational Membership in Europe.* Chicago: University of Chicago Press, 1994.

Spandau, Arnt. "Residence and Work Place in Dynamic Tension: A Study in the Dual Labor Market of a South African Plant." In *Internal Migration: A Comparative Perspective,* edited by Alan A. Brown and Egon Neuberger, 417–39. New York: Academic Press, 1977.

Speare, Alden, Jr., Paul K. C. Liu, and Ching-lung Tsay. *Urbanization and Development: The Rural-Urban Transition in Taiwan.* Boulder, Colo.: Westview Press, 1988.

Stein, Peter. "China Learns to Like Migrant Workers." *Wall Street Journal,* December 12, 1995.

Stuart, Robert C., and Paul R. Gregory. "A Model of Soviet Rural-Urban Migration." *Economic Development and Cultural Change* 26, no. 1 (1977): 81–92.

Summary of World Broadcasts (Calversham Park). Selected issues, 1996–97.

Sun, Changmin. "Floating Population in Shanghai: A Perspective of Social Transformation in China." Paper presented at International Conference on Migration and Floating in China, Cologne, May 2–4, 1996. Published in *Floating Population and Migration in China: The Impact of Economic Reforms,* edited by Thomas Scharping, 201–15. Hamburg: Institut für Asienkunde, 1997.

Sun, Lena H. "The Dragon Within: As Millions of Underclass Migrants March into the Cities, Will China's System Collapse?" *Washington Post,* October 9, 1994.

Suro, Roberto. "Boom in Fake Identification Cards for Aliens." *New York Times,* February 19, 1993.

Taeuber, Irene. "Migrants and Cities in Japan, Taiwan, and Northeast China." In *The Chinese City Between Two Worlds,* edited by Mark Elvin and G. William Skinner, 359–84. Stanford: Stanford University Press, 1974.

Tan, Zongtai, ed. *Zhongguo renkou: Hubei fence* [Chinese population: Hubei volume]. Beijing: Chinese Finance and Economics Publishing, 1988.

Tang, Xiaotian, and Chen Donghu. "Qiangxing jiju yu chengshi shehui fanzui" [Forced residence away from home and urban society's criminals]. *Shehui* [Society (Shanghai)] 9 (1989): 19–21, 41.

Tang, Xuemei. "Changzhu liudong renkou di tezheng ji yingxiang fenxi— beijingshi dongchengchu di xici renkou pucha ziliao fenxi" [An analysis of the permanent floating population's characteristics and influence—Analysis of the data from the 4th population census for Beijing's Dongcheng district]. *Zhongguo renkou kexue* [Chinese population science (Beijing)] 4 (1992): 36–43.

Tannen, Michael B. "Labor Markets in Northeast Brazil: Does the Dual Market Model Apply?" *Economic Development and Cultural Change* 39, no. 3 (1991): 567–83.

Taylor, Jeffrey R. "Rural Employment Trends and the Legacy of Surplus Labour, 1978–86." *China Quarterly* 116 (1988): 736–66.

Taylor Jeffrey R., and Judith Banister. "China: The Problem of Employing

Surplus Rural Labor." CIR Staff Paper no. 49. Washington, D.C.: Center for International Research, U.S. Bureau of the Census, 1989.

Telles, Edward E. "Urban Labor Market Segmentation and Income in Brazil." *Economic Development and Cultural Change* 42, no. 2 (January 1993): 231–50.

Thompson, Stephen. "Afloat in the Bitter Sea." *China Now* 143 (winter 1992–93): 26–27.

Tian, Fang, and Zhang Dongliang. "Renkou qianyi liudong di jingzhong he duice" [The alarm bell of population migration and mobility and policy measures]. *Qunyan* [Voice of the many (Beijing)] 9 (1989): 16–18.

Tian, Xueyuan. "Gaige he kaifang gei renkou chengshihua dailai xin di shengji" [Reform and liberalization brings new vitality to population urbanization]. *Zhongguo renkou kexue* [Chinese population science (Beijing)] 3 (1988): 12–17, 6.

Tianjin ribao [Tianjin daily]. Selected issues, 1988–90.

Todaro, Michael P. *Internal Migration in Developing Countries: A Review of Theory, Evidence, Methodology and Research Priorities.* Geneva: International Labour Office, 1976.

"Trouble at Zhejiang Village." *Fazhi wencui bao* [Legal culture news], March 31, 1994. Translated in *China Perspectives* 2 (1995): 15–16.

Tse, Olivia K. M. "A Study of Job-Related Attitudes of Workers in Foreign-Funded Enterprises in Shenzhen Special Economic Zone." Working Paper no. 91-2, 1991. Hong Kong: Department of Business and Management, City Polytechnic.

Turner, Bryan S. *Citizenship and Capitalism: The Debate Over Reformism.* London: Allen and Unwin, 1986.

———. "Contemporary Problems in the Theory of Citizenship." In *Citizenship and Social Theory*, edited by Bryan S. Turner, 1–18. London: Sage Publications, 1993.

———, ed. *Citizenship and Social Theory.* London: Sage Publications, 1993.

Tyler, Patrick E. "China Proposes Huge Aqueduct to Beijing Area." *New York Times*, July 19, 1994.

———. "China's Migrants: Economic Engine, Social Burden." *New York Times*, June 29, 1994.

———. "Crime (and Punishment) Rages Anew in China." *New York Times*, July 11, 1996.

United States Consulate General, Hong Kong. *Survey of China Mainland Press.* Selected issues, 1953.

"U.S. Arrests of Illegal Immigrants in '90 Continued an Upward Trend." *Los Angeles Times*, November 19, 1991.

Vargas, Zaragosa. *Proletarians of the North: A History of Mexican Industrial Workers in Detroit and the Midwest, 1917–1933.* Berkeley: University of California Press, 1993.

Verhovek, Sam Howe. "Stop Benefits for Aliens? It Wouldn't Be That Easy." *New York Times*, June 8, 1994.

Vogel, Ezra. *One Step Ahead in China: Guangdong Under Reform.* Cambridge, Mass.: Harvard University Press, 1989.

Wakabayashi, Keiko. "Migration from Rural to Urban Areas in China." *Developing Economies* (Tokyo) 28, no. 4 (1990): 503–23.

Wakeman, Frederic, Jr. *Shanghai Police, 1927–1929.* Berkeley: University of California Press, 1995.

Wakeman, Frederic, Jr., and Wen-hsin Yeh. Introduction to *Shanghai Sojourners,* edited by Frederic Wakeman Jr. and Wen-hsin Yeh, 1–14. China Research Monograph no. 40. Berkeley: Institute of East Asian Studies, University of California, 1992.

Walder, Andrew G. *Communist Neo-Traditionalism: Work and Authority in Chinese Industry.* Berkeley: University of California Press, 1986.

———. "The Remaking of the Chinese Working Class, 1949–1981." *Modern China* 10, no. 1 (1984): 3–48.

Wang, Chunguang. "Communities of 'Provincials' in the Large Cities: Conflicts and Integration." *China Perspectives* 2 (1995): 17–21.

Wang, Feng. "Invisible Walls Within Cities: Migration and the Emergence of a Dual Society in Urban China." Paper prepared for the Conference on Social Consequences of Chinese Economic Reform, Harvard University, May 23–24, 1997.

———. "The Breakdown of a Great Wall: Recent Changes in Household Registration System in China." Paper presented at International Conference on Migration and Floating, Cologne, May 2–4, 1996. Published in *Floating Population and Migration in China: The Impact of Economic Reforms,* edited by Thomas Scharping, 149–65. Hamburg: Institut für Asienkunde, 1997.

Wang, Feng, and Zuo Xuejin. "Rural Migrants in Shanghai: Current Success and Future Promise." Paper prepared for presentation at International Conference on Rural Labor Migration in China, Beijing, June 25–27, 1996.

Wang, Jianmin, and Hu Qi. "Zhongshi tiaojie wailai liudong renkou jiekou di duice yanjiu" [Research on policy measures to regulate the structure of the floating population from outside]. *Zhongguo renkou kexue* [Chinese population science (Beijing)] 6 (1988): 71–75.

Wang, Ju, Shi Chongxin, and Song Chunsheng. "Beijing's Mobile Population: Current Status, Policy." *Renkou yu jingji* [Population and economy (Beijing)] 4 (1993). Translated in Joint Publications Research Service-CAR-93-091, 44–47.

Wang, Mengkui. *Xuexi shi nian guihua he "ba wu" jihua gang yao bai ti wen da* [In studying the Ten-Year Plan and the draft of the eighth Five-Year Plan, we must answer 100 questions—Guidance materials for the government work report of Premier Li Peng to the fourth session of the seventh National People's Congress]. Beijing: Renmin ribao chubanshe [People's daily publishing], 1991.

Wang, Shaoguang. "The Rise of the Regions: Fiscal Reform and the Decline of Central State Capacity in China." In *The Waning of the Communist State: Economic Origins of Political Decline in China and Hungary,* edited by Andrew G. Walder, 87–113. Berkeley: University of California Press, 1995.

Wang, Shuxin, and Feng Litian. "Jingji tizhi gaigezhong di beijingshi liudong renkou" [Beijing's floating population in economic system reform]. *Renkou yu jingji* [Population and economy (Beijing)] 1(1986): 5–11.

Wang, Sijun, ed. *Zhongguo renkou: Zhejiang fence* [China's population: Zhejiang volume]. Beijing: Zhongguo caizheng jingji chubanshe, 1988.

Wang, Sijun, and Han Changxian. "The Speed of Recent Urbanization and the Distribution of Urban Population in China." *Jingji dili* [Economic geography] 6, no. 1 (1986): 3–9. Translated in *Chinese Sociology and Anthropology* 19, nos. 3–4 (1987): 73–91.

Wang, Xiamin. "The Public Order Situation in Pudong's Alien Worker Gathering Points Demands Immediate Attention." *Shehui* [Society (Shanghai)] 118 (1994): 27–29. Translated in Foreign Broadcast Information Service, January 26, 1995, 23–24.

Wang, Xiangming. "Renkou qianyi liudong dui renkou chengzhenhua jincheng di yingxiang" [The influence of population migration and mobility on the process of population urbanization]. In *Zhongguo renkou qianyi yu chengshihua yanjiu* [Research on Chinese population migration and urbanization], edited by Zhongguo shehui kexueyuan renkou yanjiusuo [Chinese Academy of Social Science, Population Research Institute], 42–57. Beijing: Beijing jingji xueyuan chubanshe [Beijing economics academy publishing], 1988.

Wang, Yanling, Wu Yekang, and Jiang Jianping. "Cong xue di jiaoxunzhong dedao qishi" [Get enlightenment from a bloody lesson]. *Shehui* [Society (Shanghai)] 8 (1990): 2–3.

Wang, Yuzhao. "Pros and Cons of Interregional Peasant Migration." *Nongmin ribao* [Peasants' daily (Beijing)], March 30, 1995, 4. Translated in Foreign Broadcast Information Service, May 26, 1995, 64–67.

Wang, Zhiwang, and Jiang Zuozhong. "Baiwan 'yimin' xia jujiang" [One million 'migrants' go down to the Pearl River]. *Nanfang chuang* [Southern window (Guangzhou)] 5 (1988): 27–31.

Wank, David L. "Bureaucratic Patronage and Private Business: Changing Networks of Power in Urban China." In *The Waning of the Communist State: Economic Origins of Political Decline in China and Hungary*, edited by Andrew G. Walder, 153–83. Berkeley: University of California Press, 1995.

Wei, Yehua. "Urban Policy, Economic Policy, and the Growth of Large Cities in China." *Habitat International* 18, no. 4 (1994): 53–65.

West, Loraine A. "The Changing Effects of Economic Reform on Rural and Urban Employment." Paper prepared for the conference Unintended Social Consequences of Chinese Economic Reform, Harvard School of Public Health and the Fairbank Center for East Asian Studies, Harvard University, May 23–24, 1997.

West, Martin, and Erin Moore. "Undocumented Workers in the United States and South Africa: A Comparative Study of Changing Control." *Human Organization* 48, no. 1 (1989): 1–10.

White, Gordon. *Riding the Tiger: The Politics of Economic Reform in Post-Mao China*. Stanford: Stanford University Press, 1993.

———. "The Politics of Economic Reform in Chinese Industry: The Introduction of the Labour Contract System." *China Quarterly* 111 (1987): 365–89.

White, Lynn T., III. *Careers in Shanghai.* Berkeley: University of California Press, 1978.

———. *Policies of Chaos.* Princeton: Princeton University Press, 1989.

———. "Workers' Politics in Shanghai." *Journal of Asian Studies,* 36, no. 1 (1976): 99–116.

White, Tyrene. *Against the Grain.* Berkeley: University of California Press, forthcoming.

Whyte, Martin King. "The Changing Role of Workers." Paper presented at the conference The Non-Economic Impact of China's Economic Reforms, Fairbank Center, Harvard University, September 20–22, 1996.

———. "The Rural-Urban Gap in China's Development." Paper prepared for the conference Rural China, Columbia University, East Asian Institute, March 31–April 2, 1995.

———. "The Social Roots of China's Economic Development." *China Quarterly* 144 (1995): 999–1019.

Wilson, Francis, and Mamphela Ramphele. *Uprooting Poverty: The South African Challenge.* Report for the Second Carnegie Inquiry into Poverty and Development in Southern Africa. New York: W. W. Norton, 1989.

Wong, Christine P. W. "Central-Local Relations in an Era of Fiscal Decline: The Paradox of Fiscal Decentralization in Post-Mao China." *China Quarterly* 128 (1991): 691–715.

———. "Economic Reform in the People's Republic of China." Manuscript. Santa Cruz, 1994. Published as *Economic Reform in the People's Republic of China: From Centrally Planned to Market Economies, the Asian Approach,* edited by Pradumna B. Rana and Naved Hamid, vol. 2 (Hong Kong: Oxford University Press, 1995).

———. "Financing Local Government: Feasts, Famines, and Growing Regional Disparities in Postmao China." Draft. Santa Cruz, November 1993.

Wong, Christine P. W., Christopher Heady, and Wing T. Woo. *Fiscal Management and Economic Reform in the People's Republic of China.* Hong Kong: Oxford University Press, 1995.

Wong, Linda. "China's Urban Migration—The Public Policy Change." *Pacific Affairs* 67, no. 3 (1994): 335–55.

Wong, R. Bin. *China Transformed: Historical Change and the Limits of European Experience.* Ithaca: Cornell University Press, 1997.

Wood, Charles H. "Equilibrium and Historical-Structural Perspectives on Migration." *International Migration Review* 16, no. 2 (1982): 298–319.

Woon, Yuen-fong. "Rural Migrants and Regional Development in the People's Republic of China: The Case of Kaiping County in the Pearl River Delta Region." Paper prepared for delivery at the 50th anniversary meeting of the Association for Asian Studies, New Orleans, April 22–23, 1991. Published in *International Migration Review* 27, no. 3 (1993): 578–604.

Wu, Cangping, and Xin Dupeng. "Dadishang di renkou hongliu" [The mighty torrent of population on the land]. *Dili Zhishi* [Geographic knowledge] 5 (1990): 2–3.

Wu, Huailian. "The Wave of Peasants Leaving the Land in the 1980s." *Renkou xuekan* [Population bulletin (Changchun)] 5 (1989): 41–49.

Wu, Li. "Houniao renkou di chengyin, xiaoying ji qi pingjia" [The facets and effects of the migratory bird population and an assessment]. *Renkou xuekan* [Population bulletin (Changchun)] 6 (1990): 37–43.

Wu, Ruijun. "Guanyu liudong renkou hanyi di tansuo" [Defining the floating population]. *Renkou yu jingji* [Population and economy (Beijing)] 3 (1990): 53–55, 27. Translated in Joint Publications Research Service-CAR-90-073 (September 28, 1990), 42–45.

Wu, Zhe. "Job Hot Line May be Answer." *China Daily Business Weekly*, January 16–22, 1994, 8. Reprinted in Foreign Broadcast Information Service, January 24, 1994, 60.

Wuhan shi laodongju bian [Wuhan City Labor Bureau, ed.]. *Chengshi wailai laodongli guanli* [The management of outside urban labor]. Wuhan: Wuhan chubanshe, 1990.

Xiang, Biao. "How to Create a Visible 'Non-State Space' Through Migration and Marketized Traditional Networks: An Account of a Migrant Community in China." Paper presented at European Science Foundation Workshop on European Chinese and Chinese Domestic Migrants, Oxford, July 3–5, 1996.

Xiang, Weimin. "Shanghai wailai liudong renkou di tedian he guanli." *Shehui kexue* [Social science (Shanghai)] 8 (1994): 59–62, 37.

Xie, Bailing. "Chengshi liudong renkou wenti tantao—Shanghai 'liudong renkou wenti yantaohui' zongshu" [An investigation into the question of the floating population in the cities—a summary of the Shanghai "Research forum on the problem of the floating population"]. *Shehui kexue* [Social science (Shanghai)] 2 (1990): 73–75.

Xu, Keren. "Nongcun shengyu laoli nilun xianxiang di si da chengyin" [The four elements in the countercurrent of rural surplus labor]. *Gaige yu Zhanlue* [Reform and strategy (Nanning)] 4–5 (1989): 102–4. Reprinted in *Zhongguo renmin daxue shubao ciliao zhongxin* [Chinese People's University Books and News—paper materials center (Beijing)] 1 (1990): 48–50.

Xu, Miaofa. "Cong renkou liudong kan huji guanli tizhi di gaige qushi" [From the situation of population mobility look at the trend of reform of the household management system]. *Shehui kexue* [Social science (Shanghai)] 2 (1989): 37–40, 36.

Xu, Tianqi, and Ye Zhendong. "Inevitable Trend and Major Course of China's Agricultural Labor Force Shift." *Renkou yanjiu* [Population research (Beijing)] 5 (1985): 16–20. Translated in Joint Publications Research Service-CPS-86-033 (April 25, 1986).

Xu, Xiaoyong. "Shanqu nongcun renkou xiao chengzhenhua shi shanqu jingji fazhan di biran qushi" [The urbanization of small towns is the necessary trend for the rural population in mountain districts]. *Renkou yanjiu* [Population research (Beijing)] 3 (1985): 26–29.

Xu, Xue-qiang, and Li Si-ming. "China's Open Door Policy and Urbanization in the Pearl River Delta Region." *International Journal of Urban and Regional Research* 1 (1990): 49–69.

Xu, Yingjian. "Da chengshi liudong renkou di yiban fenlei he jingji fenlei" [A general analysis of the floating population in large cities and their economic categories]. *Wuhan jingji yanjiu* [Wuhan economic research] 2 (1988): 56–59, 68.

Xue, Muqiao. "Guanyu chengzhen laodong jiuye wenti di jidian yijian" [Some opinions on urban labor and employment problems]. In *Zhongguo dangdai shehui kexue mingjia zixuan xueshu jinghua congshu, 8: Xue Muqiao xueshu jinghua lu* [A collection of selected scholarly works by China's modern social science masters, vol. 8: A collection of scholarly works by Xue Muqiao], edited by Bao Ji, 405–11. Beijing: Beijing shifan xueyuan chubanshe, 1988.

Yan, Shan-ping. "The Movement of Labor in Chinese Rural Areas: With a Focus on Developed Regions." *Developing Economies* (Tokyo) 28, no. 4 (1990): 524–43.

Yang, Dali. *Beyond Beijing: Liberalization and the Regions in China.* London: Routledge, 1997.

———. "Reforms, Resources, and Regional Cleavages: The Political Economy of Coast-Interior Relations in Mainland China." *Issues and Studies* (Taipei) 27, no. 9 (1991): 43–69.

Yang, De-hua. "The Nature of the Floating Population in China and Its Impact: A Case Study of the Floating Population in Some Major Chinese Cities." Paper prepared at the Institute of Development Studies, Brighton, England, 1992.

Yang, Xiaoyong. "Mingong liudong yu Zhongguo chengxiang jingji fazhan" [The flow of migrant labor and the development of China's urban and rural economy]. *Renkou yu jingji* [Population and economy (Beijing)] 5 (1995): 26–32.

Yang, Xiushi, and Sidney Goldstein. "Population Movement in Zhejiang Province, China: The Impact of Government Policies." *International Migration Review* 24, no. 3 (1990): 509–33.

Yang, Yunyan. " 'Temporary Residents' in China: Causes and Characteristics." *Chinese Environment and Development* 7, nos. 1–2 (spring–summer 1996): 103–17.

Yang, Zhonglan. "Come and Gone Overnight." *Shehui* [Society (Shanghai)] 3 (1996): 40–41. Translated in Foreign Broadcast Information Service, May 30, 1996, 32–33.

Ye, Shengyao. "Suzhoushi wailai zhanzhu renkou wenti tantao" [Inquiry into the issue of the temporary population in Suzhou City]. *Renkou xuekan* [Population bulletin (Changchun)] 2 (1989): 55–58.

Young, Susan. *Private Business and Economic Reform in China.* Armonk, N.Y.: M. E. Sharpe, 1995.

Yuan, Xin, and Tang Mingda. "Xinjiang liudong renkou di chubu yanjiu" [A preliminary investigation of Xinjiang's floating population]. *Renkou yu jingji* [Population and economy (Beijing)] 3 (1990): 46–52.

Yuan, Yue, et al. *Luoren—Beijing liumin di zuzhihua zhuangkuang yanjiu baogao* [The exposed—a research report on the condition of the organization of migrants in Beijing]. Beijing: Beijing Horizon Market Research and Analysis, 1995.

Yuan, Yue, Shouli Zhang, and Xin Wang. "Self-Organize: Finding Out the Way for Migrants to Protect Their Own Rights." June and July 1996, Beijing and Oxford.

Zeng, Jingwen. "Dadushi di 'shihuangzhe' " [Big cities' "trash collectors"]. *Nanfang chuang* [Southern window (Guangzhou)] 1 (1988): 24–25.

Zhai, Huisheng. "Adroitly Guide the 'Tide of Laborers' According to Circumstances." *Guangming ribao* [Bright daily (Beijing)], August 12, 1993, 4. Translated in Foreign Broadcast Information Service, August 24, 1993, 50.

Zhang, Kaimin, Zhang Henian, and Shen Annan. "Shanghai liudong renkou jiegou pouxi" [A dissection of the structure of Shanghai's floating population]. *Shehui kexue* [Social science (Shanghai)] 8 (1988): 56–60.

Zhang, Li. "Strangers in the City: Space, Identity, and the State Among China's 'Floating Population.' " Ph.D. dissertation, Department of Anthropology, Cornell University, 1998.

Zhang, Qingwu. "Basic Facts on the Household Registration System." *Chinese Economic Studies* 22, no. 1 (1988).

———. "Dui woguo liudong renkou di chubu tanxi" [A preliminary probe into China's floating population]. *Renkou yu jingji* [Population and economy (Beijing)] 3 (1986): 3–5.

———. "Guanyu chengshi liudong renkou wenti di sikao" [Thinking about relative problems of floating population in cities]. *Zhongguo renkou kexue* [Chinese population science (Beijing)] 3 (1989): 50–55.

———. "Luelun woguo di hukou qianyi zhengce" [A sketch of our national migration policy]. *Zhongguo renkou kexue* [Chinese population science (Beijing)] 2 (1988): 35–38, 15.

———. "Woguo liudong renkou fazhan di licheng yu duice" [The course of development of our country's mobile population and policy measures]. *Renkou yu jingji* [Population and economy (Beijing)] 6 (1991): 13–19, 12.

Zhang, Shanyu, and Yang Xiaoyong. " 'Mingongchao' jiang dailai 'huixiang chuangyechao'—yi Anhuisheng Fuyang diqu weili" [The tide of labor will give rise to a tide of returning to the countryside to create enterprises—using Anhui province, Fuyang prefecture as an example]. *Renkou yu jingji* [Population and economy (Beijing)] 1 (1996): 43–47.

Zhang, Wenyi. "The Mobile Population Should Not Have Free Reign of the Cities." *Minzhu yu Fazhi* [Democracy and the legal system (Shanghai)] 208 (1995): 16–18. Translated in Foreign Broadcast Information Service, March 21, 1996, 23–24.

Zhang, Xiaohui, Zhao Changbao, and Chen Liangbiao. "1994: Nongcun laodongli kuaquyu liudong di shizheng miaoda" [1994: A real description of rural labor's cross-regional flow]. *Zhanlue yu guanli* [Strategy and management (Beijing)] 6 (1995): 26–34.

Zhang, Ying. "Guanyu beijingshi Fengtaiqu 'Zhejiangcun' liudong getihu jihua shengyu wenti di diaocha" [An investigation of the problem of planned birth among the individual firms in "Zhejiang Village" in Beijing

City's Fengtai district]. *Renkou yu jingji* [Population and economy (Beijing)] 3 (1989): 23–25.

Zhang, Youren. "Zunzhong 'waidiren' yingdang chengwei shehui gongde" [Respecting "outsiders" should become social public morality]. *Shehui* [Society (Shanghai)] 6 (1987): 25–26.

Zhao, Geng. "Is It Good for the Peasants to Come to the Cities?" *China Focus* 3, no. 8 (1995): 5.

Zhao, Minghua, and Theo Nichols. "Management Control of Labour in State-Owned Enterprises: Cases from the Textile Industry." *China Journal* 36 (1996): 1–21.

Zhao, Yaqin. "Floating Population and Compulsory Education." *Renmin jiaoyu* [People's education] 380 (June 1996): 16–17. Translated in Foreign Broadcast Information Service, 159, 1996.

Zhao, Renwei. "Some Special Phenomena of Income Distribution During Transformation of Economic System in China." *Jingji yanjiu* 1(1992): 53–63. Translated in Joint Publications Research Service-CAR-92-043 (June 22, 1992), 13.

Zheng, Guizhen, Guo Shenyang, Zhang Yunfan, and Wang Jufen. "Shanghai shiqu liudong renkou wenti chutan" [A preliminary investigation of the problem of the floating population in Shanghai's urban district]. *Renkou yanjiu* [Population research (Beijing)] 3 (1985): 2–7.

Zhongguo 1986 nian 74 chengzhen renkou qianyi chouxiang diaocha ziliao [China migration 74 cities and towns sampling survey data (1986)]. Special issue of *Zhongguo renkou kexue zhuankan* [Chinese population science (Beijing)] 2 (1988).

"Zhongguo nongcun laodongli liudong yu renkou qianyi yanjiu zongshu" [Summary of research on Chinese rural labor forces mobility and population migration], April 1995. In Ba jia, ed., *Nongcun laodongli jingji yanjiu tongxun* [Bulletin of rural labor mobility studies], D-01, D-17. N.p., 1995.

Zhongguo nongcun laodongli liudong yu zhuanyi ketizu [Chinese rural labor forces' mobility and transfer study group]. "Zhongguo nongcun laodongli jiuye xiankuang ji fazhan qingjing yanjiu" [Investigation of China's rural labor forces' employment situation and development prospects]. *Nongye wenti* [Agricultural issues (Beijing)] 12, no. 7 (1989): 12–20.

"Zhongguo pinkun diqu renkou jiegou yu qianyi wenti yantaolun zongshu" [A summary of a research forum on the population structure and migration questions in Chinese poor districts]. *Renkou yu jingji* [Population and economy (Beijing)] 6 (1992): 57–60.

Zhongguo renmin daxue renkou xuexi xuesheng diaochazu [Chinese people's university population study student investigation group]. "Dui Miyunxian renkou liudong wenti di fenxi" [An analysis of Miyun county's population flow]. *Renkou yanjiu* [Population research (Beijing)] 5 (1985): 34–38.

Zhongguo shehui kexueyuan, Renkou yanjiusuo [Chinese Academy of Social Science, Population Research Institute, ed.]. *Zhongguo renkou nianjian 1987* [Chinese population yearbook 1987]. Beijing: 1988.

Zhongguo tongjiju bian [Chinese statistical bureau, ed.]. *Zhongguo tongji nianjian 1993* [Statistical Yearbook of China 1993]. Beijing: Zhongguo tongji chubanshe [Chinese statistical publishing], 1993.

Zhongguo tongjiju nongcun shehui jingji tongjisi bian [Chinese Statistical Bureau, Rural Social Economic Statistics Office, ed.]. *Zhongguo nongcun tongji nianjian 1992* [Chinese rural statistical yearbook 1992]. Beijing: Zhongguo tongji chubanshe [Chinese statistical publishing], 1992.

Zhonghua renmin gongheguo gongan falu chuanshu [Complete legal documents of the public security of the People's Republic of China]. Changchun: Jilin renmin chubanshe [Jilin people's publishing], 1995.

Zhonghua renmin gongheguo guowuyuan gongbao [Bulletin of the State Council of the People's Republic of China (Beijing)]. Selected issues, 1981–92.

Zhou, Daming. "Guangzhou 'wailai sangong' di diaocha yu fenxi" [An investigation and analysis of "outside casual labor" in Guangdong]. *Shehuixue yanjiu* [Sociological research (Beijing)] 4 (1994): 47–55.

———. "Zhujiang sanjiaozhou wailai liudong renkou fenbu tezheng ji yidong qushi fenxi" [On the outside labor in the Pearl River Delta]. Paper presented at the conference Reflections on the Pearl River Delta's Economic Development and its Prospects, Zhongshan, Guangdong, May 7–11, 1992.

Zhou, Kate Xiao. *How the Farmers Changed China: The Power of the People.* Boulder, Colo.: Westview, 1996.

Zhou, Weirong. "Children of Migrants Get Access to Education." *China Daily* (Beijing), June 22, 1996.

Zhou, Yixing. "Urbanization Problems in China." *Chinese Sociology and Anthropology* 19, nos. 3–4 (1987): 14–41.

Zhu, Baoshu. "Nongcun renkou chengshihua xin taishi he xin wenti" [New trends and new issues of urbanization—a survey of peasants who have moved into towns in the Shanghai suburbs]. *Zhongguo renkou kexue* [Chinese population science (Beijing)] 6 (1989): 59–61, 36.

Zhu, Baoshu, Shen Ying, Zhang Jingyue, and Yan Haihua. "Nongcun renkou xiang xiao chengzhen zhuanyi di xin taishi he xin wenti" [The new trend of rural population transferring to small towns and new questions]. *Zhongguo renkou kexue* [Chinese population science (Beijing)] 1 (1991): 49–55.

Zhu, Fengchun. "Cong zhua chuzuwu rushou, ba liudong renkou di jisheng guanli luodao shichu" [Keeping tabs on rented housing to curb excessive childbirths among the migrants]. *Nanfang renkou* [Southern population (Guangzhou)] 2 (1992): 12–13, 7.

Zhu, Hong. "The Sale of Women in China—Now." *China Focus* 2, no. 3 (1994): 4–5.

Zhu, Suhong. "Chengshizhong di nongmin: dui Beijingshi zhanzhu nongcun renkou di yanjiu" [Peasants in the city: An investigation of the peasant population temporarily living in Beijing]. Master's thesis, Department of Sociology, Beijing University, 1992.

Zhu, Xiaoyang. "Mangliu Zhongguo" [The blind wanderers of China]. *Zhongguo zuojia* [Chinese writer] 4 (1987): 349–86.

Zhu, Ze. " 'Mingongchao' wenti di xiankuang, chengyin he duice" [The present condition of the "labor tide," its elements and countermeasures]. *Zhongguo nongcun jingji* [Chinese rural economy (Beijing)] 12 (1993): 33–36.

Zweig, David. "The People, the Politicians, and Power." *China Journal* 38 (1997): 153–68.

Index

Africa: discrimination toward urbanizing peasants, 5; formal/informal sectors, 205; gender of migrants, 243. *See also* South Africa

age: criminal, 135; floater, 21

Agence France-Presse, 284

agency, 147, 149–50, 152, 281, 282, 286; bounded, 149, 150

agriculture: dynastic times, 29; gross output percentage, 169, 171table11, 334n88; income from, 154, 156, 157–62, 166–67, 168tables8&9, 190; labor, 53, 63, 154–58, 169, 170table10, 185, 334n90; market forces and, 128; migrants in, 174–75, 206, 207; person-to-arable land ratios, 29, 154–57, 164, 165table5, 171, 297n79; prices, 52, 128, 157, 158, 159; TVEs, 165, 166; unprofitability of, 157–62, 330n20. *See also* communes; grain; land; Ministry of Agriculture; peasants; produce markets

Anhui: beggar cliques from, 368n225; Beijing migrants from, 72, 252, 256, 265, 287, 352n207, 361n74, 367n201; children sent home to study, 367n201; crime, 136; "cyclical migration" from, 174–75; Feidong county, 156; Hefei city, 156, 188, 237; incomes of migrants from, 175; interprovincial "agreement plan" *(xieyi jihua)*, 95; labor

export, 163; Nanjing migrants from, 157, 182, 237, 345, 352n207; nursemaids from, 202, 223, 352n207; regional discrimination, 202; remittances to, 190–91; scrap collectors from, 156, 157, 202, 236, 237, 256, 287; shantytowns of migrants from, 260–61; Tianjin migrants from, 342n37. *See also* Fuyang; Guanting; Wuwei

Asian Games (1990), 72, 357n298

associations: entrepreneur, 63, 76, 92, 226, 269; neighborhood, 130, 251. *See also* informal sector; social organizations, migrant; trade unions

Banister, Judith, 17, 47

Bao'an: foreign-invested sector, 220; savings of migrants, 143

baojia system, 28, 31

beggars, 126, 203, 206, 225, 234–38; children, 235, 269; gangs, 203, 236–37, 238, 272, 368n225. *See also* scrap collectors

Beijing, 31, 60; Anhui migrants in, 72, 252, 256, 265, 287, 352n207, 361n74, 367n201; bureaucratic impotence, 81, 141; capital construction, 47; and central agency for floating population, 85; Chaoyang district, 252; commodifying *hukou*, 90, 91; commodifying migrants, 87,

313n133; business certificate *(jin-gying zhengming)*, 82; certificate identifying place of work, 82, 209; construction work, 209, 214; to enter cities, 82, 209; entrustment letter *(weituoshu)* for, 82; fees, 77, 82, 141, 142; home government certification/introduction letter, 39–40, 82–84, 95, 209; pregnancy certificate, 83; problems with, 81–84; quality specifications credential *(zizhi zhengshu)*, 209; temporary residence, 77, 82–83, 92–93; temporary work *(linshi gongzuo xukezheng)*, 83; workers lacking, 212. *See also* licenses; registration

Perry, Elizabeth, 335n113, 370n35

Peru: discrimination by income, 343n51; informal sector, 344n71, 369n243. *See also* Lima, schools

Philippines: dependency theory on, 184; and migrants' occupational mobility, 279; satisfaction of migrants, 247

Pieke, Frank, 100

Piore, Michael J., 200, 203–5

planned economy/socialist state, 35, 60–79, 102–3, 292n5; benefits excludable in, 4, 105; bureaucrats' networks emerging from, 181; bureaucrats' perspectives dominated by, 66, 72, 107–10, 129–30, 207, 289; compassionate, 2; employment system, 112; faltering, 7, 60–79, 101, 105–6, 197, 252; gaps in, 114–15, 199; horizontal/vertical, 84, 153; infrastructure planning, 108–9, 120; lingering, 8, 149–50, 277, 278; markets and migrants and failure of, 57, 79, 81, 91, 129–30, 138–41, 280; peasants exploited in, 27, 37–42, 45, 48; plan as key institution, 59; registration tied to planning, 16, 33–34, 42–43, 44, 108–9; rules, 1, 11, 57–58, 83, 86–88, 105–6, 141; Soviet, 33–34; urban bias of, 45, 101; urbanites' perspectives domi-

nated by, 117–19; urban labor limitations, 302n65; water pricing, 120; Western welfare state like, 278. *See also* bureaucrats; control, state; economic reform; institutions; transition from planned to market economy; welfare

planning commission (Wuhan), 62

Polanyi, Karl, 57

police: bribed, 237; vs. migrant influx, 74; vs. migrant protests, 284, 285, 286; and migrant victims, 135, 136; residence permits issued by, 313n133. *See also* public security

Politburo, 52, 53

political community: citizenship in relation to, 1, 6, 7; popular organization and, 269, 272, 284–85; transitions in power, 59

political economy, of state policies, 154–62, 176. *See also* capitalism; planned economy/socialist state

political movements, and economic policies, 8, 9–10, 38–52 *passim*, 114, 289. *See also* protests

poor. *See* peasants; poverty

population: Beijing recruitment percentages, 177–78; in construction, 206, 207, 208; floater, 17–23, 84–85, 137, 139, 142, 292n2, 296n65, 297n67, n79, n81, 343n56; floater numbers surging (after 1983), 16–17, 34, 50, 292n2, 297n79; floater occupations, 206–7; foreign-invested firms/workers (1996), 349n165; with household registration (1990s), 296n58; with individual identity cards, 95; industrial employment vs. urbanite, 37; labor exports, 166; *mangliu*, 137, 235, 260; peasant (1953–80), 154–55; peasant deportation (1961–62), 41; peasant employees in state-owned firms, 42, 113–14, 118, 307n174, 321n85; permanent worker (1996), 113; person-to-arable land ratios, 29, 154–57, 164,

Breinigsville, PA USA
09 September 2009
223793BV00001B/20/A